Basic Criminal Law

SECOND EDITION

Allen Z. Gammage, Ph.D.
Professor of Criminal Justice, Emeritus
California State University
Sacramento, California

Charles F. Hemphill, Jr., M.S.
Doctor of Jurisprudence
Member of the Texas Bar

GLENCOE

Macmillan/McGraw-Hill

Lake Forest, Illinois   Columbus, Ohio
Mission Hills, California   Peoria, Illinois

Library of Congress Cataloging in Publication Data

Gammage, Allen Z
    Basic criminal law.

    1.   Criminal law—United States—Compends.
2.   Police—United States—Handbooks, manuals, etc.
I. Hemphill, Charles F., joint author. II. Title
KF9219.8.P65G3 1979   345'.73   78-1778
ISBN 0-07-022756-X

Basic Criminal Law, second edition

Imprint 1991

Send all inquiries to:
Glencoe Division
Macmillan/McGraw-Hill
936 Eastwind Drive
Westerville, Ohio 43081

12 13 14 15 RRD-C 00 99 98 97 96 95 94 93 92 91

The editors for this book were Susan H. Munger and Susan L. Schwartz, the designer was
Eileen Thaxton, the cover designer was Tisa Schrenk, and the production supervisor was
Kathleen Morrissey.
It was set in Illumna by KBC/Rocappi, Inc.
Printed and bound by R. R. Donnelley & Sons Company.

Contents

. . . no person is secure in society
unless the laws are known and respected.
—Noah Webster (1785)

Preface

This second edition of *Basic Criminal Law* reflects recent changes in the law brought about by reported decisions of the U.S. Supreme Court and a number of state courts. It also includes changes, in terms of student needs, as suggested by instructors who have used the text. Additionally, some examples have been replaced with cases that provide greater day-to-day application for working criminal justice personnel.

Peace officers throughout the nation are receiving more on-the-job instruction than ever before. In the past thirty-five years we have witnessed an increased emphasis on education and training for both prospective and working police and corrections officers.

Law enforcement curricula and course offerings presented at colleges and universities have been growing steadily. This increased emphasis and added enrollments in both pre-service and in-service programs have pointed up a need for better instructional materials.

The necessity of study in the substantive criminal law field has been thoroughly recognized; any pre-service or in-service police program worthy of the name includes a course in criminal law. On the other hand, available textbook materials tend to be detailed, comprehensive works written for the legal student. In fact, dominant characteristics of these writings which contribute most to the student of law are those very characteristics which detract from their value as guides to the law enforcement student.

Basic Criminal Law is a handbook on the substantive criminal law written especially for the present or prospective police or corrections officer. First, it is a summary textbook, not a casebook. Only basic principles of law are presented. No effort is made to expound on principles nor to trace their development. Second, this work is a basic reference book. In developing its content, every effort has been made to keep the material practical so that peace officers and prospective peace officers may refer to it and apply it to their work.

The book is presented in two parts: (I) Criminal Law and How It Is Used and (II) The Law of Crimes. Part I is designed as orientation material and includes basic legal principles applicable to the whole of the criminal law field. It defines criminal law, points out its sources, classifies crimes, explains the meaning of the act, intent, and corpus delicti. It tells who may commit a crime and who may not, and under what circumstances people may be excused for acts which otherwise are classified as crimes. This is knowledge that any police officer needs, in advance, when assigned to investigate complaints, accidents, and crimes. Moreover, this is basic information essential to a thorough understanding of the criminal law as it relates to the specific crimes discussed in the second part of the book.

Part II, "The Law of Crimes," is a presentation of common law criminal acts. Incidental to the discussion and in an effort to clarify the common law, some statutory law is offered. Criminal offenses are classified in terms of social harm: offenses against the person, home, property, public health, safety, morality, and public peace; and offenses affecting the conduct of governmental functions. Each specific act, as it exists in the common law, is defined; special effort is made to explain the exact act and intent necessary to constitute the crime. This is basic knowledge any police officer can use to investigate an incident, report a case, and present testimony in court.

In summary, *Basic Criminal Law*, second edition, is designed to accomplish three principal objectives: (1) to fill a gap in police instructional literature; (2) to serve as a legal guide to police and corrections personnel and to present these people with an informal study of criminal law principles; and (3) to provide background knowledge necessary to a thorough understanding of statutory and codified law in state and local jurisdictions.

A student who has first read *Basic Criminal Law* and become familiar with the fundamental principles and concepts of criminal law in the United States is then well prepared to study his or her own state and local codes. This book will serve students of business or general students as well who want a basic understanding of our criminal law and how society is involved in the criminal justice process.

Allen Z. Gammage
Charles F. Hemphill, Jr.

PART ONE
Criminal Law and How It Is Used

CHAPTER 1
Introduction

The notion that every human being possesses certain inalienable rights, "the rights of man," is rooted far back in antiquity, and the idea that individuals are entitled to protection under an orderly system of criminal laws is almost as old as government itself.

NATURE OF THE CRIMINAL LAW

If people lived in isolation, no law would exist for them, nor would it be necessary. But as individuals come into frequent contact with their fellows, differences arise. Might is often substituted for right, and the will of the strong prevails.

The early history of criminal law is the story of society's struggle to control individuals who impose their wills on others. It is the account of how people have learned to work out rules for living together. At the risk of oversimplification, we can say that all crimes are violations of the basic controls observed by society. They are acts which tend to destroy those desirable conditions of safety, welfare, and integrity that work for the benefit of the community as a whole.

No one can say how or when some acts first came to be regarded as criminal ones. Law has no divine origin. It is not the establishment of infallible and eternal principles of justice. It developed to control human activity; human misconduct caused its establishment.

Most primitive societies have had some basic customs and taboos that were respected by everyone. Often these beliefs were based on the feeling that the gods would deal out horrible punishment to anyone who violated the custom. In the modern world we may be inclined to laugh at many of these early tribal taboos, labeling them as ignorant superstitions, but common acceptance in primitive society gave many of these beliefs the force of law.

In some of these early societies, the community as a whole was not always greatly concerned with persons whom we, today, treat as dangerous criminals. Even murder was sometimes recognized as nothing more than a private matter to be settled between the killer and the close kin of the victim. While at times the family of the victim might feel obligated to kill the murderer, on some occasions they even settled for the payment of a substantial quantity of goods or money. Regardless of how detestable the offense, the act was of little concern to the community as a whole; but as people became more civilized, new ideas developed regarding each individual's responsibility to all humanity. No longer was a crime an offense against one single individual. Rather, it was a revolt against all society, an attack against all people.

Essentially, then, criminal law is a stabilization of social policy, based on experiences of the past. Some laws may eventually be considered unsound in the light of experience, while others seem to survive the conditions that justified them. Changing slowly, the law usually lags behind social demands. Sometimes legislatures and courts (makers of law) also make mistakes; they err in their interpretation of human experience.

In the final analysis, however, criminal law is effective only to the extent that it represents the will of the majority of the people it serves. Criminal law is seldom a spontaneous development. It had its origins some time before in the customs and usages of the people.

Individuals Must Exchange a Small Part of Their Freedom to Gain the Protection of the Law

Some persons like to claim that an ideal government is one under which people are wholly free, but people seldom live in a condition of complete freedom. In a lawful society an individual is at liberty to do only those acts that ought to be done. Civilization has been sometimes described as a voluntary rearrangement of society, surrendering some rights for the benefit of society as a whole. To put it in other terms, individuals are held together by the invisible bonds of common regulation. Since people need society, they must pay society's price. That price is the criminal law and the punishment imposed for disobeying it.

The object of criminal law, then, is to guide and to regulate the conduct of individuals in relations with other people, in whole or in part. It is an instrument for social control.

BASIC APPROACHES TO THE STUDY OF CRIMINAL LAW

Two basic approaches to the study of criminal law are usually followed. One is to learn the law by memory or rote, as it applies to each specific situation in a particular location. The second approach is to seek out general principles and to obtain an understanding of how these principles are used. This approach also examines the ways in which judges, lawyers, and judicial and administrative officials apply the criminal laws, along with their reasoning and attitudes in doing so. This approach does not furnish the student much detail about the specific law in a particular state at a given time. In the end, however, it provides greater understanding of the law and how it operates. It also furnishes a better grasp of future changes that are likely to occur. The second approach is the one used in this book.

First, let us realize that some peculiarities and differences exist in the laws of every state. If we search for these peculiarities, they will become obvious, but we should not be overly concerned with unusual features until broad principles have been brought into focus.

To some extent the traditional examination of law has been closely linked with the study of legal history. A number of scholars think that current criminal law can be understood only in the light of legal development and background. From the viewpoint of the criminal lawyer, great value exists in this historical material; but for the working police officer, continuity with the past is not a duty—merely an unavoidable necessity. Therefore, the historical basis of law will be explored, but only as it appears helpful to an understanding of modern police problems.

Furthermore, law schools have traditionally used the so-called casebook method in teaching criminal law. Under this system, a case is read and analyzed to determine the legal principles (points of law) represented in the decision of the court. Other cases that exhibit similar facts are then compared and analyzed. Decisions that seem to present completely opposite views are examined, and factual differences between the cases are studied to reconcile or "explain away" the holdings of the courts.

Incidentally, different courts sometimes reach rather opposite decisions on facts that appear to be identical in every respect. When a preponderance of decisions appears on one side of a question, the lawyers speak of this as the *majority view*, or *majority rule*. Those courts that reach an opposite decision are said to represent the *minority view*, or *minority rule*.

When using this casebook method, future lawyers learn how to seek out legal principles that may be persuasive to a court on either side of a legal dispute. They learn to find decided cases with facts that are similar or identical to the position of their clients, later presenting these cases to the court as precedents for a decision favorable to their side of the question. If lawyers are unable to find decided cases that support their position, they learn how to distinguish logically these decisions from the actions attributed to their clients.

The problems of practicing police officers are clearly different. They need a working knowledge of the law that they can apply to everyday happenings. In most situations they have little practical use for the casebook approach or the historical development of a particular doctrine of law.

VALUES FOR POLICE OFFICERS IN THE STUDY OF CRIMINAL LAW

Thus, in pursuing the study of criminal law, police officers are not seeking training that will help them to act as attorneys or as prosecutors. They are engaged in developing skills involving principles and rules of law that will be useful in daily contact with the public. As a result of this study, police officers should be able to handle problems with confidence, efficiency, and fairness to all concerned, as they arise in all sorts of cases.

Only a relatively short time ago, newly recruited police officers did not enjoy this advantage. They were given an oath of office and immediately put out on the street. Handed badges, revolvers, and uniforms, they were expected to learn the problems of law enforcement as they went along. Of course, some matters can best be learned only through actual experience; but all too often seasoned officers who were expected to guide the new recruits had never, themselves, received adequate training in the legal aspects of their jobs. Eventually the new officers gained knowledge by trial and error, usually at considerable expense to the taxpayer.

The pattern of activity for today's patrol officer is quite similar in most areas of the United States. In many situations he or she is the first officer who is dispatched. The patrol officer is the "combat soldier" of law enforcement and usually will be the first to arrive at the scene of an accident, an explosion, a drowning, or a liquor store holdup. Of course, much of the work involves disposing of relatively minor complaints: a family cat to be rescued from the garage roof, a child who has caught a hand inside a section of old pipe, or juveniles who have taken blossoms from an elderly citizen's flowerbed.

On the other hand, the patrol officer is also the first to arrive at the scene of almost all major crimes; reaction must be almost automatic upon reaching the site. Regularly, day in and day out, prompt and correct decisions must be made, many of which require knowledge of the criminal law. Every car that passes in the night may carry a mugger, a burglar with loot, a murderer, or a person devoid of reason because of drink, insanity, or drugs. The patrol officer must know in advance the criminal restrictions and legal provisions that can be applied to each case.

Without this knowledge of the criminal law, police officers cannot protect society. In many instances they may not know how far they can go to protect themselves or their fellow officers. In still other cases, they may subject themselves or the government agency they serve to costly lawsuits because of incomplete knowledge or lack of understanding of legal processes and how they operate. Police officers must know, without hesitation, whether the acts committed are sufficient to constitute a crime. This is because the person responsible for the acts can often be arrested at the scene, or can be located nearby if pursuit is immediate. Given a delay of even a few minutes, this advantage is often lost.

Then, too, a person can be tried only once for a single crime. If the case as presented to the court by the prosecution does not fit the required facts, the prosecution will be "thrown out"; the accused will go free. This is why it is absolutely essential that the officer shall furnish correct facts to the prosecutor and that the prosecutor shall correctly draft the legal documents. Neither the prosecutor nor the law enforcement officer can do an effective job unless both are conversant with the criminal law.

Later, when the case is scheduled for trial, the officer is frequently the star witness for the state. Almost invariably this testimony carries great weight in court not only because of the personal integrity of the officer, but because the general public has confidence in a police officer's judgment as to what actually is in violation of the law.

At times the harried, overworked prosecutor may come into court without an opportunity to review evidence and interview police witnesses. In these cases it is especially important that the officer be well acquainted with the criminal law.

If furnished inadequate training in the law, officers may not even recognize a violation. Once on the scene of the crime, they may overlook some material that is a vital element of the offense or fail to understand how to get this evidence accepted in court.

In still other instances the untrained officer may persistently investigate a course of action that does not constitute a crime, even if proved.

SCOPE OF THIS STUDY   *or procedural*

Thus, this study is limited to the substantive aspects of criminal law. In this connection we should note the two large divisions into which all law is divided: *substantive* and *adjective* law. Substantive criminal law is that part of the whole which deals with the rights and duties of persons to each other and to society in general. Adjective criminal law is concerned with the legal machinery by which rights and duties are enforced. It regulates the rules for bringing defendants into court as well as the actual proceedings.

To consider an example, one Snyder was arrested for assaulting a plain-clothes police officer who just happened to be passing down the street. Following prosecution, he was convicted of assault and sentenced to jail. Six months later, he filed an appeal, claiming, "I didn't know the man I clobbered was a policeman! He didn't wear a uniform."

The appellate court declined the appeal for two reasons. (1) It didn't matter whether Snyder struck a policeman or just any citizen. He had been convicted of assaulting another person; the fact that the victim was a police officer was not important. An unprovoked assault on another person is all that is required. (2) The court further said that nothing could be done for Snyder because the law of that state said that all appeals must be filed, in writing, with a higher court, within thirty days after conviction.[1]

The first reason given by the court involved substantive law. Here the court was stating, in effect, that the accused (Snyder) had no right to make unprovoked attacks on others. The second reason involved the failure to file the appeal within the specified legal period. This was an adjective, or procedural, matter. This book deals primarily with problems like the first one; procedural law is discussed occasionally to make the substantive law clear.

---

[1] In explaining its ruling the court pointed out that when the law provides no time limit for filing appeals, a convicted person may appeal whenever he thinks the witnesses against him have become unavailable or scattered. Of course, we find some possibility that new evidence might suddenly be discovered, evidence of such importance that it could cast an entirely new light on the facts presented at the time of the trial. If these new facts are presented to the court, then a new trial may be granted, regardless of the time that has elapsed since the conviction.

CHAPTER 2

Sources of the Criminal Law

As law developed in the civilized world, it became increasingly complex. In general, new law has originated in response to prevailing social and economic forces. Sometimes the courts have been able to make adjustments in response to the requirements of industrialization, population growth, and other factors. At other times these changes have been made by the legislatures.

In summary, all criminal law in the United States comes from four basic sources:

1. The English common law
2. Federal and state constitutions
3. Laws passed by federal (Congress) and state legislatures
4. Decisions of the courts in criminal prosecutions

THE ENGLISH COMMON LAW SYSTEM

Practically all modern criminal law in Europe or in the American continents is an outgrowth of one of two sources: the early English common law or the ancient Roman legal system.

With some exceptions, the bulk of the criminal law in the United States and in all English-speaking countries traces its beginning to the English system. On the other hand, most of the European nations, along with

Latin American countries, base their criminal law on the old Roman law. Louisiana, because of its early French and Spanish heritage, drew from the background of the Roman system. However, the common law of England was adopted as the basis of the criminal law in that state by a statute passed in 1805.

Earliest Law in English-Speaking Countries

No one knows for certain when criminal violations were first recognized by the English tribes. Sketchy records go back as far as A.D. 600, but these explain very little. The early English kings indicated that they felt responsibility for maintaining law and order, but they took no action to set up criminal courts or to make a list of offenses known. These kings allowed local officials, usually the sheriff, to apply traditional tribal rules and procedures in each community. From what we know, these rules and procedures differed from place to place. In general, most of them were quite similar to the old barbaric ones that had evolved in Scandinavia, Germany, and northern France, apparently brought to England by bands of invaders from these countries.

In 1066 William the Conqueror, a local Norman ruler, invaded the British Isles. He quickly captured most of England and made himself king. Bringing very little law from France, William and his followers contributed instead a genius for organization. Practical enough to assess actual conditions in the country, William realized he needed to curb some powers of the local English officials, while cultivating a measure of their loyalty.

At this stage in England's development, individual county courts were dominated by the sheriff, an official who was quite powerful on the local level. William took steps to reduce the authority of the sheriff, but to preserve the best features of local institutions at the same time. To accomplish these dual aims, he issued writs commanding that the sheriff do justice in the king's name, while subjecting the courts to strict royal control. He then invited the common people all over England to come into his courts and seek justice.

Centralization of Royal Control

William's successors continued to centralize royal control over the courts. Within a hundred years after the conquest, criminal laws were of equal or "common" application in all English communities. To this extent, the criminal law in the king's courts was the countrywide law of England, but this was not the most frequently understood meaning of the term "common law."

English kings had the good sense not to interfere in the workings of their courts. They didn't insist on drawing up a list of activities that they recognized as crimes; but then, neither did the judges. As new cases came before the courts, the judges decided each on its own merits.

Crimes by Common Understanding or by Public Consent

The list of acts that the early courts recognized as crimes came from natural reason, from the experience of decent human beings over hundreds of years, and from the accumulated expressions of the people themselves as to what was right and what was wrong.

In deciding what acts should be criminal, the judges drew from "folk law," notions, and common experience traditions. Thus, some acts were regarded as criminal from time immemorial, both by the average person in the street and by the judge on the bench. These, then, were crimes by common understanding or by popular consent; they have been known ever since as common law crimes. Murder, battery, robbery, arson, burglary, rape, and larceny were the principal ones.

Parliamentary Additions to the Common Law

Over the years new situations arose where recognized crimes were not inclusive enough to constitute the current concept of justice. By this time the English Parliament had gained considerable power and proceeded to add some new crimes to the accepted list. Thus, parliamentary legislation became an additional source of English common law growth.

English Court Interpretations of Parliament's Laws

After these new criminal violations were created by Parliament, the English courts soon applied the words of the enactments to a great number of widely varying factual situations that had not previously been before the courts. Therefore, these judicial decisions and court interpretations also came to be regarded as a part of the common criminal law.

Common Law Comes to America

When the first English settlers came to America, they formed compacts among themselves, bringing as much of the English law to the new world as they were able to remember. Eventually, as more settlers came, they brought all the body of common law that had been reduced to writing. Colonial governments, as extensions of the government of England, thus continued to follow the common law.

As a practical matter, after independence, the states continued to use the basic English system. In some United States locations the new governments automatically retained the old common law. In some new states the governments felt compelled to adopt formally the English common law, confirming this continuance with a statement of ratification. In still others the legislatures did not adopt the common law as such, but passed criminal laws of their own, incorporating into writing practically all the basic principles of the common law as the new statutes of the state.

For example, in Ohio, the court held that it was necessary for the state legislature to pass specific statutes before conduct could be punished as criminal.[1] In some other states that had been settled by the French or Spanish, the original foreign law continued in force until modified by statute, as in Louisiana and New Mexico.

Because of these differences, we should note that the so-called common law of one state may not necessarily be the common law of another state. The fact is, however, that the entire body of criminal law available in all states is an inheritance from the old English common law. (See Table 2-1.)

[1] Mitchell v. State, 42 Ohio St. 383 (1844).

Table 2-1. Status of Common Law Offenses in the United States

State	Preserved by Case Law	Preserved by Statutory Retention	Abolished (Statutory Law Only)	Abolition Implied	Status Unsettled
Alabama	•				
Alaska		•			
Arizona			•		
Arkansas	•				
California			•		
Colorado				•	
Connecticut	•				
Delaware	•				
D.C.	•				
Florida		•			
Georgia			•		
Hawaii			•		
Idaho			•		
Illinois			•		
Indiana			•		
Iowa			•		
Kansas			•		

Table 2-1. Status of Common Law Offenses in the United States (cont.)

State	Preserved by Case Law	Preserved by Statutory Retention	Abolished (Statutory Law Only)	Abolition Implied	Status Unsettled
Kentucky	●				
Louisiana			●		
Maine	●				
Maryland	●				
Massachusetts	●				
Michigan	●				
Minnesota			●		
Mississippi		●			
Missouri	●				
Montana				●	
Nebraska			●		
Nevada		●			
New Hampshire	●				
New Jersey		●			
New Mexico		●			
New York			●		
North Carolina	●				
North Dakota					●
Ohio			●		
Oklahoma			●		
Oregon				●	
Pennsylvania			●		
Puerto Rico			●		
Rhode Island		●			
South Carolina	●				
South Dakota				●	
Tennessee	●				
Texas			●		
Utah					●
Vermont	●				
Virginia	●				
Washington	●				
West Virginia	●				
Wisconsin			●		
Wyoming					●
TOTAL	19	8	18	4	3

An excellent statement of the present-day meaning of the common law is expressed in an old Montana Case.

> The "common law" of England, which is the rule of decision in all courts of Montana, in so far as it is not repugnant to the Constitution of the United States or laws of that state, means that body of jurisprudence as applied and modified by the courts of this country up to the time it was adopted in Montana.[2]

Clearly, the common law is applicable in all states when it is not in violation of the Constitution of the United States or of the constitution of the state, or in conflict with the laws adopted by the state.

Looking to the Common Law for Definitions of Crimes

In some states today laws passed by the state legislatures list specific acts as punishable crimes. Nowhere in these state laws, however, do we find a definition or description of the specific act listed as a crime. On the other hand, the courts in some other states have taken the position that a person cannot be convicted of a crime unless the offense is first named and later clearly defined in the legislative enactment. In the first group, where the courts have not required a specific definition of the crime, the trial court will look to the common law for a definition or understanding of what acts are necessary to constitute a particular crime.

For example, in Texas a man was accused of rape. When brought to trial, he admitted that he had attempted to commit a sexual assault on the female victim, but contended that he was guilty of an attempt only. A conviction on a charge of attempt would have been to the defendant's advantage since the penalty was considerably less than that for a rape conviction. In the evidence presented to the court, the accused admitted that he had made a slight penetration of the unwilling female. The defendant's lawyer argued, however, that the accused had not made a complete penetration, that he had not completed the sexual act. Therefore, reasoned the attorney, the client was guilty of only an attempt.

The state statute in this jurisdiction enumerates rape as a criminal offense, but does not define exactly what is meant by rape. In the trial the court noted that early English cases, decided hundreds of years ago, had held that "any penetration of an unwilling female, even the slightest, is sufficient to constitute rape." In effect, the modern court looked to the old

[2] Herrin v. Sutherland, 241P 328, 74 Mont. 587.

common law for a definition of the crime. The defendant was therefore convicted.

FEDERAL AND STATE CONSTITUTIONS

The fundamental written law in this country is the Constitution of the United States and the constitutions of the individual states. This is a second source from which we obtain our criminal laws. These constitutions, both federal and state, define and limit the powers of the government; they also provide for the establishment and operation of courts to handle both criminal and civil matters. Thus, they are a source of criminal law in that they provide the skeletal framework for the entire criminal law system.

THE U.S. CONGRESS AND THE STATE LEGISLATURES

State constitutions further provide for the establishment of state legislatures, while the Constitution of the United States provides for the creation of Congress as the federal legislative body. Each one of these legislative units is given the power to enact legislation making certain acts crimes.

American courts have constantly held that Congress and the legislatures of the various states have the inherent power to prohibit and punish any act as criminal, provided they do not violate constitutional restrictions. When a state legislature passes a law, thus making an act a crime, we speak of it as a "state statute," or simply as a "statute." When Congress passes a similar kind of federal law, we call it a "federal statute," or United States statute"; but when a city council or other legislative body of a city or municipality passes a law, we refer to it as an "ordinance."

A compilation or collection of ordinances or statutes is a code. Therefore, if we were to assemble all the California criminal statutes, the collection might be called the California Criminal Code. The federal equivalent is known as the Federal Criminal Code, or the United States Criminal Code, usually abbreviated as USC.

The state criminal code is one of the most useful books or sets of books that a police officer may possess. In most instances, a sheriff's deputy or police officer will have little occasion to use the United States Code. However, both a good law dictionary and a copy of the state criminal code may be of considerable help in understanding the legal problems that arise on a day-to-day basis. Just keep in mind that law is subject to change at any time by legislative action or by court decisions. Legislative acts and decided cases may alter the material in the code book.

As a matter of interest, criminal codes are among the oldest specimens of legal writings that have been discovered. The Code of Hammurabi, king of Babylon, dates back to approximately 1900 B.C., six hunderd years before the time of the famous Hebrew lawgiver Moses. Cut in the face of a stone about 7 feet high, with 4000 lines of writing in 51 columns, Hammurabi's code set out penalties for specific crimes. For example, the code stated: "If anyone breaks a freeman's bone, his own bone shall be broken. If a freeman knocks out a tooth of a freeman of his own rank, his own tooth shall be knocked out."

Archaeologists have found even more ancient codes than that of Hammurabi; but its systematic order, state of preservation, and treatment of the subject matter have made Hammurabi's code noteworthy.

Another famous ancient code was Roman—the Twelve Tables. Based on an earlier, unwritten collection of laws, this criminal code was carved on twelve brass tablets about 450 B.C. To make the common people aware of the laws, the Twelve Tables were given a prominent place in the public forum. For hundreds of years they served as the basis for Roman criminal law, under both the Empire and the Republic.

Changing Statutory Law

The Book of Daniel in the Old Testament contains a well-known phrase which refers to the "law of the Medes and the Persians, that alters not." This saying attracted attention, even in the ancient world, because the laws of practically all nations are subject to change.

When a criminal statute is outdated by current social standards, it can be repealed by the legislature, and thus wiped out. Police officers, however cannot turn their backs and deliberately ignore an existing law. This is because they have sworn to uphold all existing laws of the state and the nation. So, it is of no consequence that a police officer may not be in sympathy with a particular law or would like to see it abandoned.

On the other hand, if outlived statutes could not be repealed, police officers in Massachusetts might still be saddled with an old law of 1648 which stated:

If any man have a stubborn or rebellious son, of sufficient years and understanding, to wit, sixteen years of age, which shall not obey the voice of his father, or the voice of his mother, and that when they have chastened him, will not harken unto them, then shall his father and mother, being his natural parents, lay hold on him and bring him to the magistrates assembled in court and testify unto them, that their son is stubborn and rebellious and will not obey their voices and chastisement, but lives in sundry notorious crimes, such a son shall be put to death.

Modern Statutes Are Generally Directed toward Promoting the Public Welfare

In contrast, many laws passed in the United States in recent years have involved efforts to anticipate criminality and to prevent it by eliminating causes of crime. A number of these statutes are far-reaching in application and involve social and industrial problems—such as favorable working conditions, minimum wages, education, sanitation, recreation, and vocational guidance.

Basic Approaches to Statutory Law by World's Legal Systems

Two basic approaches are generally used in legal systems throughout the world to determine what acts are crimes. Under one system all conduct recognized as crime is clearly spelled out and carefully defined in easily available statutes. Here little possibility exists that the average man may misjudge the consequences of wrongful acts. No conduct is regarded as criminal unless it falls squarely within one of the definitions in the statutes.

The advantage of this approach is that the criminal law can never be extended by politicians during some period of popular indignation or public excitement. First it is necessary for the legislature to alter existing laws or change the definitions of crimes. In this type of society, people are always free to engage in any conduct, except when the law specifically forbids it. This, of course, narrowly limits those activities that can be regarded as criminal.

An individual who succeeds in thinking up a new kind of crime, or figures out a different way of "pulling off" an old one, may escape conviction. Obviously, with a system of this kind, the law generally lags behind public demand for change. The remedy here is an alert legislature, passing laws as dictated by social developments. This is the kind of approach used in legal systems in the United States.

On the other hand, legal systems in some other countries refuse to grant immunity to "criminal-type" activity merely because it has not been precisely covered in the language of penal statutes. Under this approach, the courts are charged with the duty of deciding whether an unprecedented kind of activity is criminal. The advantage is that the real objectives of harmful conduct are kept firmly in view, and the courts are not sidetracked because of technicalities. This type of handling results in activity that lawyers call "judicial legislation," or judge-made law. This, of course, allows the courts to take over the functions of the legislatures and is prohibited in the United States.

However, in either of the two legal systems previously mentioned, the eventual results may not be far different, provided the courts function independently of other branches of the government. But totalitarian nations sometimes force their courts to regard as criminal any thinking that conflicts with the views of the state. It is, therefore, dangerous to human liberty to follow a system which allows a court, rather than a legislative body, to set standards of criminal conduct.

The Crimes Must Be Clearly Defined
Either in the Statutes or in Common Law Cases

In practically all instances the courts in the United States have taken the position that criminal statutes must be definite and clear. Also, criminal laws must be interpreted or construed in favor of the accused. Thus, almost all the decided cases in the United States have recognized the danger in convicting persons on criminal statutes that are vague or subject to more than one reasonable interpretation. In the words of some of the judges who have decided cases of this type:

> . . . A penal law should be sufficiently definite for those affected by it to know their duty thereunder.
> . . . It is the legislature, not the court, which is to define a crime and ordain its punishment.

Our courts have also consistently held that the words of a statute must be given their full meaning and that the courts will not strain to look for a meaning which will have the effect of declaring the statute void.

Furthermore, the Supreme Court of the United States has consistently held to the rule that "A criminal offense cannot be created by inference or implication, or extended by implication or intendment."

Courts May Inquire as to Just What
the Legislature Intended in a Statute

While the courts say that they will strike down a statute that is unclear, these same tribunals sometimes conduct an inquiry to determine the legislature's intent in a particular statute. In making this inquiry, they may study not only the wording of the statute proper, but the wording of the preamble to the law as well. In fact, some courts have carried this farther, inquiring into the wording of other state statutes on the same subject, particularly as to the type of conduct the legislature was seeking to correct.

In any event, if the language of the statute is too vague or the intent of the legislature cannot be clearly determined, the courts will free (acquit) any person previously convicted on the basis of that statute.

If the crime is one that did not develop out of the common law, obviously the courts can never look to the common law for a definition of that crime. Embezzlement, for instance, is a relatively modern crime. Business practices were such that early England had little need for this law. Minus a common law background, the definition of a crime like embezzlement, then, must be sufficiently clear in the statute which makes it a crime.

Also, the courts are in agreement that, when the legislature fails to include a provision for penalty, the forbidden acts do not constitute a crime. A penalty may not be presumed or added by the courts.

In summary, the laws of Congress and those of the state legislatures are a valid source of law when they satisfy two basic constitutional principles: (1) they are reasonably related to the health, safety, welfare, and morals of the people; and (2) they are not unduly vague.

DECISIONS OF THE COURTS

The discussion above suggests one fact: It is extremely difficult for a legislature to write a new law that is always clear to everyone. Unanticipated situations frequently present themselves. Often some question may arise as to just what was intended by the wording of the statute, and doubtful matters are for the courts to decide. Of course, a case cannot be taken to an appellate court merely because someone is doubtful as to what the legislature intended. The courts make decisions only after cases come to trial. If a defendant is found guilty in a trial court under the terms of a questionable statute, then, on appeal, the judges will decide whether the activities of the defendant are forbidden by a valid criminal statute.

Thus, it is logical to assume that recently decided court cases are merely an extension of the old English common law, filling in gaps that were not previously covered. Generally, however, we refer to these court decisions and interpretations as "case law," or "precedents."

The Principle of Stare Decisis

Once a decision has been reached by a court in an actual case, that decision thereafter becomes a precedent for that court and for all subordinate courts. This is the legal principle of stare decisis,[3] or following the decision of a prior case already decided on the same facts.

The great benefit of this principle is that it makes for legal stability. Once a matter is decided on the basis of mature deliberation by the courts,

[3] Even today many legal principles stated by the courts, in both criminal and civil cases, are expressed in Latin terms. It is not completely clear how this practice began. Many years ago educated persons took pride in their ability to read Latin and Greek. It seems likely that early English judges first used these old Latin legal expressions as proof of their scholarship.

the community can assume that the decision is a settled statement of law. People need to know that they can conduct their affairs, secure in the knowledge that the decision will represent the law for the future. This kind of stability is also needed by lawyers, who must give advice to clients with reasonable certainty in anticipation of events that may occur in the future.

Court decisions thus become precedents and will not be lightly regarded or disturbed. As the British judge Lord Eldon once remarked, "It is better that the law should be certain than that every judge should be speculating on improvements in it."

Still, the principle of stare decisis does not always mean blind adherence to a previously decided case. It prevents capricious change, but it does not forbid a review of a case in view of a clear showing of error or injustice at the time of a later case. Also, in some instances, conditions on which the earlier decision was based may have changed, so that the precedent is no longer desirable or just. Therefore, the doctrine of stare decisis provides for stability, but it is not so binding as to forbid change in the law when this is desirable to keep pace with changing social and economic forces that are an outgrowth of the times. It also gives future judges an "out" if the court reaches a decision that is obviously wrong.

So it is that established precedents, regardless of the idea of stare decisis, may be challenged, and the courts may be asked to review a former decision. As a result, our law is relatively stable, but not completely inflexible.

Since court decisions may reverse what appears to be well-settled law at any time, lawyers usually feel obligated to go into their libraries and consult up-to-date law books before advising a client. Attorneys sometimes say, "We never like to furnish a 'curbstone' opinion."

Parties to Criminal Litigation

Criminal trials in the United States are usually presided over by only one judge or magistrate, who regulates and directs the trial, has power to hold persons in contempt, and can enforce orderly proceedings. When lawyers speak of "the court," they generally mean the judge. When the judge tells someone to "address the court," what is meant is that the conversation should be addressed to the judge.

If the accused (the defendant) is convicted, the defense attorney will often appeal the case to a higher court; during the course of this appeal, the accused may be called the "defendant" or the "appellant."

Higher courts, appellate courts, may often consist of more than one judge, and almost always have several. An even number of judges seldom sit on one court, although a judge who feels a personal interest in the matter under consideration may disqualify himself or herself. The Supreme Court of the United States, the highest appellate court in the land, has nine judges, called "justices." If five justices agree, then the majority rules. If one justice disqualifies himself and only eight consider the case, then a split of four to four will uphold the decision of the lower court.

A single judge of an appellate court may consider some motions or take some actions independently, but an appeal from a conviction in a lower criminal court is heard by all judges on the appellate court or by a panel of an odd number of judges chosen from all the judges (for example, in the Federal District Courts of Appeals). The judges are often called justices, especially those on the higher courts.

A police officer or other witness will almost never appear before a higher (appellate) court, since prosecutive trials are held in so-called *trial courts*, or *courts of primary jurisdiction*. This is where the testimony of witnesses and other evidence is presented. Additional testimony or new evidence of any kind is not allowed before the appellate court. Also, no jury is provided to settle questions of fact or determine guilt. The appellate court decides as a matter of law whether the evidence furnished to the jury was proper, obtained by legal means, and sufficient for a jury to be entitled to find a verdict of guilty, along with other appealable matters. In short, all the appellate court ever considers is the record of the stenographic transcript of the trial court. The names by which the trial courts are known vary from state to state; but frequently they are called *county courts*, *district courts*, or *superior courts* (in some jurisdictions, or locations, the superior courts are an intermediate class of appellate courts). Minor criminal cases and other minor matters, such as traffic violations, are usually heard in justice-of-the-peace or municipal courts.

The verdict or judgment of the trial court is *affirmed* by the appellate court when it determines that the party who won in the lower court is again the winner. The decision of the lower court is *reversed* when the party who lost in the lower court has become the winner through appeal. If the higher court states that the case is *reversed and remanded*, then the case is sent back to the lower court for retrial, discharge of the accused, change in sentence, or other trial court action.

Lawyers' Books and Legal Citations

Almost any lawyer's office or law library will contain some code books, setting forth the statutes passed by the legislature. In addition, it will have some legal encyclopedias, digests, form books, dictionaries, citators, and miscellaneous legal periodicals. The encyclopedias set out legal principles and theories that an attorney may present to a court in support of arguments, along with decided cases based on each one of these principles. Digests are indexes to these decided cases.

On the other hand, the majority of the lawyer's books are usually bound volumes called *reported cases,* or simply *reporters.* These are the printed decisions of the appellate courts—the reported opinions on which the judicial system relies for precedents.

Figures and abbreviations follow the names of the parties to a case cited in these reporters. Each of them is called a *citation;* it includes the volume and the page of the reported case in which the opinion of the appellate court is set forth. Using this citation, a lawyer or researcher can locate a pertinent case.

Reported cases are printed in chronological order, state by state, including cases heard on appeal. In addition, a private publisher, the West Publishing Company of St. Paul, Minnesota, publishes the appellate decisions of an entire block of states by geographical area in the so-called National Reporter System.

For example, volumes covering the Western states in the National Reporter System are called the *Pacific Reporter.* They contain appellate decisions from the courts of Arizona, California, Colorado, Idaho, Montana, New Mexico, Oregon, Utah, Washington, and Wyoming. The Pacific Reporter is abbreviated as P. in legal citations. The Northeastern Reporter (abbreviated as N.E.) contains appellate decisions from the courts of Illinois, Indiana, Massachusetts, New York, and Ohio. Some volumes report only cases decided in the United States circuit courts of appeal; others include U.S. Supreme Court cases.

The citation for the case that follows is: *People v. Fioritto,* 441P.2d 625, 68 Cal. 817. This means that in Volume 441 of the Pacific Reporter, second series (the first series got so bulky that a second was published), at page 625 this case is set out. It is also set out in the California Reporter series in volume 68 at page 817. The material that follows shows a reported decision in the Pacific Reporter.

PEOPLE v. FIORITTO
Cite as 441 P.2d 625

This was originally a prosecution by the state of California ("the People") as plaintiff. The accused was convicted on trial, and the state is the respondent on appeal.

68 Cal. Reptr. 817
The PEOPLE, Plaintiff and Respondent,

v.

The "v." means "against" or "opposed to."

Peter Paul FIORITTO, Defendant and Appellant.

Peter Paul Fioritto was the defendant in the prosecution before the trial court. He was convicted and is called the "appellant."

Cr. 11948.

This is the case docket number, or file number, used by the clerk of the court. The "Cr." designates a criminal case, and "Cv." would designate a civil matter before the court.

Supreme Court of California,
in Bank.
June 20, 1968.

This was an appeal to the Supreme Court of California, sitting *in bank*, or as a full court. This was the date of the decision.

Defendant was convicted of second-degree burglary. The Superior Court, Riverside County, John G. Gabbert, J., entered judgment, and the defendant appealed. The Supreme Court, Mosk, J., held that defendant's initial refusal to waive his constitutional rights after being given the *Miranda* warnings invoked his Fifth Amendment privilege, and further police interrogation attempts should have ceased, and, therefore, confession obtained from defendant by police officers after they confronted defendant with his accomplices who had confessed and implicated him and after he had signed waiver of his constitutional rights was inadmissible, and that introduction of a confession obtained from defendant in violation of constitutional guarantees was prejudicial per se and required reversal regardless of other evidence of guilt.

This is a statement of the background of the facts of this case, up to the time it came up to the Supreme Court of California. This is a synopsis prepared by legal experts for West Publishing Co., who printed this opinion.

Reversed.

This means the decision of the lower court was reversed. The defendant Fioritto was therefore set free.

Burke and McComb, JJ., dissented.

Two judges of the court (Justices Burke and McComb) *dissented* (disagreed with the majority decision).

Opinion, 64 Cal. Rptr. 797, vacated.

This was not an appeal directly to the California Supreme Court. The matter had gone from the trial court to an intermediate appellate court, and from there to the California Supreme Court. The decision of the intermediate appellate court had been previously reported in Volume 64 of California Reporter, at page 797, and this decision of the intermediate appellate court was *vacated* (reversed), or set aside, by the opinion under examination here.

1. Criminal Law 412.2(3)

Principal objective of *Miranda* decision was to establish safeguards that would liberate courts insofar as possible from difficult and troublesome necessity of adjudicating in each case whether coercive influences, psychological or physical, had been employed to secure admissions or confessions.

2. Criminal Law 1134(1)

Supreme Court has constitutional responsibility to determine in every criminal case that the full panoply of *Miranda* "protective devices" is satisfied.

Ten points of law are represented by this decision. This is not an "official" part of the opinion. These numbered paragraphs express the opinion of legal experts from West Publishing Company as to the points of law that were considered and decided in the decision of the California Supreme Court.

3. Criminal Law 412.2(2)

Procedural safeguards in form of *Miranda* warnings come into play only where "custodial interrogation" is involved, and quoted phrase means questioning initiated by law enforcement officers after a person has been taken into custody or otherwise deprived of his freedom of action in any significant way.

4. Criminal Law 412.2(2)

Suspect must be fully apprised of his rights upon being ushered into a police station and detained for questioning.

5. Criminal Law 412.2(2)

Defendant was entitled to be given *Miranda* warnings at time he was brought into police station prior to questioning by police.

6. Criminal Law 412.1(4)

If suspect indicates in any manner, at any time prior to or during custodial interrogation, that he wishes to remain silent, interrogation must cease.

7. Criminal Law 412.1(1)

Any statement taken from suspect after he has invoked his Fifth Amendment privilege prior to or during custodial questioning cannot be other than the product of compulsion, subtle or otherwise.

8. Criminal Law 519(4)

Defendant's initial refusal to waive his constitutional rights after being given the *Miranda* warnings invoked his Fifth Amendment privilege, and further police interrogation attempts should have ceased, and, therefore, confession obtained from defendant by police officers after they confronted defendant with his accomplices who had confessed and implicated him and after he had signed waiver of his constitutional rights was inadmissible in subsequent burglary prosecution. West's Ann. Pen. Code. §459.

These are key numbers in the West Publishing Company's *Digest*. Lawyers use these numbers to find other cases decided on the same point of law.

Continuation of the ten points of law.

9. Criminal Law 406(1), 517.1(1), 519(9)

Continued questioning of suspect who has once asserted his constitutional rights is prohibited, but subsequent statements, whether admissions or confessions, voluntarily initiated by suspect may be used in subsequent criminal prosecution.

Continuation of the ten points of law.

10. Criminal Law 1169(12)

Introduction of a confession obtained from defendant in violation of constitutional guarantees was prejudicial per se and required reversal regardless of other evidence of guilt.

Donald F. Powell, Riverside, under appointment by Supreme Court, for defendant and appellant.

Thomas C. Lynch, Atty. Gen., William E. James, Asst. Atty. Gen., Elizabeth Miller and Mark W. Jordan, Deputy Attys. Gen., for plaintiff and respondent.

Donald F. Powell, Riverside, California, was the defense lawyer, appointed by the court to handle the appeal. California State Attorney General Thomas C. Lynch and assistants represented the state before the Supreme Court.

Mosk, Justice.

Justice Mosk of the court was assigned to write the opinion for the majority.

Defendant Peter Paul Fioritto appeals from a judgment convicting him of burglary in the second degree. (Pen. Code, §459.) At trial the People introduced into evidence a confession signed by defendant, and defendant contends that this confession was elicited under circumstances that were violative of the standards enunciated by the United States Supreme Court in *Miranda v. State of Arizona* (1966) 384 U.S. 436, 86 S.Ct. 1602, 16 L.Ed.2d 694. We conclude that under the explicit directives of *Miranda* defendant's confession was inadmissible, and accordingly the judgment must be reversed.

What the court actually decided is set out here. This is the majority opinion. Minority opinions are sometimes included in the reported decision, depending on the importance of the case and other factors. Sometimes no minority opinion is given. The dissenting justices write the minority opinion. Occasionally, when justices dissent for differing reasons, more than one minority opinion may be included.

Defendant and two companions burglarized a market in the early morning hours, stole a small amount of cash and three cardboard boxes packed with cartons of cigarettes, and proceeded to a bowling alley where they peddled the cigarettes at a dollar a carton.

Continuation of the court's decision.

(Note: The remainder of this decision is not included here.)

CITED CASES

Herrin v. Sutherland, 74 Mont. 587, 241 P. 328.
Mitchell v. State, 42 Ohio St. 383 (1884).
People v. Fioritto, 441 P.2d 625, 68 Cal. 817.

CHAPTER 3

Crime, Criminal Law, and Punishment Defined

In recent years we have heard a great deal about individual liberty. Considerable stress is frequently placed on the right of every person to "do his or her thing," but all of us must agree to some restraints on our individual liberties or other people may be seriously injured. For example, practically everyone agrees with the basic right of freedom of religion; but if worship involves the sacrifice of a human victim to appease one of a cult's gods, then most people say that individual freedom has gone too far.

While the majority of people agree that human sacrifice is a crime, other cases might not be so easy to decide. Most of our criminal law is a changeable, never a completely settled, body of rules. This is true because conduct that appears reasonable to one generation may be wholly unacceptable to another. Changing economic and social conditions work for different moral standards and eventually result in new or changed laws.

PURPOSE OF CRIMINAL LAW

The object of criminal law, then, is to guide and to regulate the conduct of individuals in their relations with society—in whole or in part. The law is an instrument for social control, used to protect people in general from the consequences of dangerous individual conduct.

"CRIME" DEFINED

Crime is social harm, defined and punished by law. This is stated another way in *Black's Law Dictionary:*

> A crime may be defined to be any act done in violation of those duties which an individual owes to the community, and for the breach of which the law has provided that the offender shall make satisfaction to the public.[1]

From these definitions we may note that a crime can be either a positive act, such as deliberately hitting your neighbor in the head with an ax, or a failure to act, such as failing to carry lifeboats on a passenger vessel, while failure to install lifeboats is the omission of an act required by law.

Mere Sin Is Not Sufficient Evidence of Crime

One authority has said that the test for crime should be whether it is an act which actually tends to prejudice the moral values of a community. Still another has said that crime is an act which threatens human life or safety, property, habitation, or the means of making a living.

A justice of the Supreme Court of the United States once stated, "We're not here to regulate sin." He was only saying that a serious threat to the values of the community must be involved. So, generally, a gap exists between the morals of the community and the penalties imposed by the criminal law.

The Claim That the Act Was Directed Only at the Victim

The claim is sometimes made by the accused that the wrongful act was a private matter—not intended to harm society in general. Legally it makes no difference that the act was aimed at only one person. Society simply

---

[1] Section 15 of the *California Penal Code* states: A crime or public offense is an act committed or omitted in violation of a law forbidding or commanding it, and to which is annexed, upon conviction, either of the following punishments: (1) death; (2) imprisonment; (3) fine; (4) removal from office; or (5) disqualification to hold and enjoy any office of honor, trust, or profit in this state.

cannot afford to have people running about who are not responsible to anyone for their conduct.

Most Crimes Involve Civil Wrongs (Torts), but the Reverse of This Is Not Necessarily True

In general, the courts say that if an act is merely a threat to private interest or offends it, then the act is only a *civil wrong*—not a crime. In fact, many wrongful acts are both criminal and civil wrongs. Lawyers speak of civil wrongs as "torts," or personal damage matters. In other words, the victim in a tort case can come into a court that handles civil lawsuits and request recovery of money damages from the person who committed the wrongful act.

Because of our ideas of *dual responsibility* (liability for both civil and criminal wrongs), the wrongdoer may be made to answer in both a *criminal prosecution* and a *civil lawsuit* for damages. These involve completely separate trials, in different courts; but some of the testimony or evidence in either trial may be used as evidence in the other.

To take an actual case, Charles Manson was brought to trial in a state criminal court in Los Angeles, California, for the murder of movie actress Sharon Tate and seven other persons. About this same time relatives of the alleged victims of Manson's so-called gang filed a civil suit to recover money damages.

Some Laws Give Special Protection to Children

A number of laws in most of the states are designed to furnish special protection to children. Of course, these laws also say that it is the special responsibility of a child's parents to be sure that their own child does not fall into delinquency or use liquor, or narcotics. These laws recognize the fact that it is natural for parents to want to protect their own children, but these same laws offer great concern for children as a class and for orphans as well.

The Seriousness of the Crime May Be Determined by the Consequences of the Act

Some experts argue that a crime should not be explained as a wrongful act, but as the consequences (result) of a wrongful act. To take an example, suppose a student activist threw a large rock at a police officer for the intended purpose of knocking out the officer's eye. At least four different situations could result:

Assault — 1. The police officer managed to dodge and felt only a momentary brush as the rock whizzed past.

Battery — 2. The officer moved her head just enough; the rock struck a glancing blow, causing a bad headache but no lasting injury.

Mayhem — 3. The victim tried to duck but was unsuccessful; she eventually lost the sight of her eye.

Murder — 4. The officer's skull was crushed and she died.

Under the four listed possibilities, the crime committed is: (1) an assault, (2) a battery, (3) mayhem, or an assault with intent to commit murder, and (4) murder. Let us also note that, under (3) or (4), whether the eyesight or the life of the officer was saved or lost might depend upon the urgency with which medical attention was obtained, or upon the skill with which the medical assistance was rendered.

So, some writers on criminal law have urged that the seriousness of a crime should depend entirely upon the intended harm on the part of the wrongdoer, not upon the consequences of the act.

WHY THE POLICE OFFICER MUST KNOW WHAT CRIMES MAY BE INVOLVED IN A GIVEN SITUATION

Now let us take a look at the job of the police officer as it relates to crime definition. The officer on the scene must have a working knowledge of existing crimes and be able to apply it to almost any given situation.

On the other hand, you might ask: Why not just allow the officer to bring in the wrongdoer and let the prosecuting attorney decide whether or not the arrestee has committed a crime?

In the first place, practically all courts like to discourage the making of an arrest without a warrant. In a situation of this kind, they almost invariably say that the police officer who brings in the citizen under these circumstances has actually made an arrest. Then, if it should turn out that the acts committed were not sufficient for a crime, the courts will also say that the officer's act constitutes a false arrest. In many of these cases, we can anticipate that the citizen will be awarded a sum of money in a lawsuit for false arrest. The police officer or the government agency represented by the officer is the loser.

Clearly, the legality of the officer's action depends upon sufficient probable cause to arrest. The police officer must know the elements of the offense and match them with the available evidence in arriving at a reasonable decision to arrest or not to arrest.

Also, it is clear that an invalid arrest will result in the exclusion of any evidence obtained at the time of arrest. The courts generally say that evidence collected under these circumstances it *tainted*. In fact, the Supreme Court of the United States has used even more colorful language in stating that illegally obtained evidence "is the fruit of the poisoned tree."

Let us note at this point, however, that an invalid arrest alone will not result in the release of an accused criminal, provided his guilt can be proved by other outside evidence; but invalid arrest places a heavier burden on the prosecution in almost all instances.

Then too, if the arresting officer doesn't know the elements that make up or serve to prove a specific crime, evidence may often be overlooked at the place of arrest or scene of the crime.

To complicate the problem further, remember the possibility of a successful federal civil rights prosecution against the police officer who arrests an individual without cause. This usually does not hold true when a warrant has been issued. Yet, some police officers have been sued even after a warrant was issued if, for example, they failed to investigate the case adequately and to determine the reliability of the *affiant*, or the one who makes the affidavit before the magistrate.

So, in any event, it is to the officer's best interest to recognize whether a crime has been committed and precisely what that crime is.

"CRIMINAL LAW" DEFINED

The average person probably thinks of the criminal law as that conglomeration of law, procedures, and machinery that is called "the administration of criminal justice." Generally, law students, lawyers, judges, and policemen see the criminal law as being much narrower in scope than this. They think of it as the *substantive* criminal law alone. To be more specific, they define this law as the *law of duties and rights*.[2] In other words, the criminal law "relates to rights and duties of people that cause criminal cases to be brought into court."[3] One authority has defined it as "that part of the law which the courts are established to administer, as opposed to the rules according to which the substantive law itself is administered."[4] Blackstone speaks of criminal law as "that branch of jurisprudence which teaches of the nature, extent and degrees of every crime and adjusts to it its adequate and necessary penalty."[5]

Substantive criminal law, then, includes the definition and classification of all crimes, the criminal act, criminal intent, capacity to commit crime,

[2] Jones v. Erie Railway Co., 106 Ohio St. 408.
[3] *Ibid.*
[4] See BLACK'S LAW DICTIONARY.
[5] United States v. Reisinger, 128 U.S. 398.

exemptions from criminal liability (responsibility), parties to crime, and all the important elements or characteristics of particular offenses (crimes). These are the broad topics discussed later in this book. Only occasionally do we get into the procedural (adjective) law, and then only to explain the criminal (substantive) law a little better.

Criminal laws depend for support on custom and approval of the general public. Enactments cannot be too far in advance of these factors without shriveling from lack of support.

The Criminal Law Is What the Legislatures Say It Is

Regardless of how we define criminal law, when we look at it from a practical point of view, we should add: the criminal law is what the legislatures say it is. This is, in simple terms, just a recognition that the law-making branch of each of our governments was established for the sole purpose of making the laws. No other branch of the government has been given this exclusive authority; the criminal law, then, is what these legislative bodies declare it to be. This law may, in fact, be just or unjust, fair or unfair, reasonable or unreasonable, adequate or inadequate; but, if it deals with the subject matters that we have previously described, it is the criminal law. This also means that the criminal law of today may not necessarily be the criminal law of tomorrow. To illustrate, let us say that the law in one of the states provides a criminal penalty for serving hard liquor to any person under twenty-one years of age. In the last session of the state legislature, this law was changed; the law now says that the penalty shall apply only to people under eighteen. Today the act of serving liquor to a nineteen-year-old (recently a criminal act) is now perfectly legal. The criminal law is clearly what the legislatures say it is.

The Criminal Law Is Also What the Courts Say It Is

Also, the average person possibly thinks that all law is made by legislative bodies, and we most likely gave that impression in the above discussion. This is not entirely true. Our courts have been handed the responsibility to interpret the law. In doing this, they actually say what the law is. Continually, through actual court cases, they are telling us what the legislatures meant in the criminal law that the lawmakers adopted. This point is dramatically illustrated in recent pornography cases where the courts have interpreted the word "obscene" in such manner as to cause the criminal law on the subject to be almost meaningless.

So, the courts change the criminal law, add to it, subtract from it, and abolish it. In the face of this kind of power, we must admit that the criminal law is also what the courts say it is.

DOUBLE JEOPARDY

It is also basic to all English and American law that an individual can be forced to stand trial only once for one crime. This is what we call "protection against double jeopardy"; it is set out in Amendment 5 of the U.S. Constitution, as follows:

> . . . Nor shall any person be subject for the same offense to be twice put in jeopardy of life or limb . . .

Following a valid indictment, the accused has been put in jeopardy as soon as the trial begins before a judge or a properly selected jury. It doesn't matter if the judge makes a mistake and orders the release of the accused. Jeopardy still has occurred.[6]

So, as the lawyers say, one trial is a bar to further prosecution. As a matter of fact, we find only a limited number of rare situations in which the prosecution may appeal to a higher court. On the other hand, the accused may appeal through the state courts and the U.S. Supreme Court, if the defense can convince the higher court of any possibility that the rights of the defendant have been violated. Of course, if the jury in a criminal case is unable to agree (hung jury), no double jeopardy exists and the case may be retried until a decision is reached. As a practical matter, however, a case is seldom tried more than twice, since the prosecuting attorney by the time of a second trial may have developed doubts as to the merits of the case. In other cases, the matter may be sent back by the appellate court for further proceedings in the trial court; this also is not double jeopardy.

What this all means is that the evidence presented at the time of the trial must fit the charge against the accused. A specific criminal charge or violation must always be named against the accused in the papers filed with the court by the prosecuting attorney. If the facts presented at the time of trial prove that an armed robbery was committed, the judge will throw out the case if the accused has been charged with arson. At this stage the prosecution cannot start over and file an armed robbery charge—the double jeopardy rule applies. That is why it is essential that the correct facts be developed and understood at the very outset by the arresting officer and each investigating officer. Then too, the prosecuting attorney also must understand the criminal law and file the proper charge before the trial is held. It is, therefore, obvious that a good grasp of the criminal law is essential to both the prosecutor and the police officer.

To examine an actual case, the local bully in a small Texas town, for no apparent reason, hit a neighbor over the head with a baseball bat, injuring

---

[6] Fong Foo v. United States, 369 U.S. 141; Downum v. United States, 372 U.S. 734.

him severely. This constituted the crime of battery, and the accused was brought to trial. Although the facts didn't indicate that the defendant meant to go that far, the investigating officer and the prosecutor jumped to the conclusion that the bully intended to rob the victim. Acting on this assumption, the prosecutor filed a charge of robbery against the defendant, ignoring the battery charge. Since the elements of the crime of robbery could not be proved, the judge said that the bully was a free man.

This was not the end of the matter, however. As the free man left the courtroom, he became enraged at the victim for having testified against him. Picking up the baseball bat that had been brought into the courtroom as evidence, he again clubbed the victim senseless. The prosecutor again filed charges against the bully; but this time he accused him of battery.

When facing the judge the second time, the accused admitted that he had hit the victim. Claiming that this was double jeopardy, the bully argued that he could not be prosecuted. The judge, however, did not allow this contention; he pointed out that two separate crimes were involved. Noting that the release on the first charge had nothing to do with the second crime, the judge found the defendant guilty of the charge of battery.

We also find other applications of the double jeopardy rule. For example, let us consider a case of murder where all the available evidence left considerable room for doubt as to the defendant's guilt. Since the judge instructs the jury that the evidence must be "beyond a reasonable doubt," the accused, after a short trial, was released. Later, evidence was turned up that convinced even the most skeptical that the accused was guilty. When confronted with the new evidence, the accused even blurted out his guilt before a large group of people. Regardless of this and because of the double jeopardy rule, the murderer was never brought to justice. On the other hand and in spite of isolated cases of this kind, we can easily defend the double jeopardy rule. It is contrary to our sense of fairness to bring a man into court time and again, requiring that person to spend all his or her energies and money on self-defense, when the prosecution has no provable case. The courts think that this rule of law controls a prosecutor who might be inclined to bring charges of a frivolous nature. It serves to make prosecution a serious matter; but remember this, it leaves no margin for error by the police officer or prosecutor.

Prosecution of Both a State Crime and a Federal Crime from One Set of Facts Is Not Double Jeopardy

For example, a person who knowingly brings a stolen car from one state to another may be prosecuted under criminal laws of the United States that are commonly known to law enforcement officers as the Dyer Act.[7]

---

[7] UNITED STATES CODE, title 18, sect. 2312.

An individual who is convicted for violation of the Dyer Act in federal court may also be prosecuted under the automobile theft law in the state where the car was stolen (this assumes, of course, that the thief was also the individual who transported the car). In addition, the culprit may be convicted of concealing stolen property in the state where the automobile was eventually transported.

Surprisingly enough, this is not regarded by the courts as double jeopardy, for the federal law makes the transportation from one state to another (interstate transportation) the basis of the federal violation. It is the transportation that is punished under the Dyer Act; the theft is punished in the state where the theft was committed. In most instances, of course, the thief and the transporter are one and the same. Regardless, the courts say there is no double jeopardy. The U.S. Attorney General does, however, have a policy of not prosecuting after a state prosecution has begun, unless a substantial federal interest is not properly served by failure to prosecute in federal court.

As a sidelight here, in most situations Congress does not have the power to make theft a crime. Federal lawmakers must find some basis in the U.S. Constitution for all federal criminal laws. Amendment 10 to the U.S. Constitution says:

> The powers not delegated to the United States by the Constitution, nor prohibited by it to the States, are reserved to the States respectively, or to the people.

In addition, Article I of the U.S. Constitution states that "The Congress shall have power . . . to regulate Commerce . . . among the several States, and with the Indian Tribes . . . ." The courts have said that the Dyer Act is a regulation of commerce (traffic in stolen cars) between the states.

Similarly, under the Federal Kidnapping Law, the *interstate transportation* of a kidnapped victim is the heart of a federal crime. When no interstate transportation occurs, no violation of the law takes place. Of course, when the kidnapper sends an extortion letter through interstate mails, demanding ransom money, the Federal Extortion Statute as well as the state kidnapping law has been violated. We may add that when the victim is murdered, the suspect may also face a state murder charge.

The robbery of a bank chartered under federal laws may involve the federal crime of bank robbery,[8] as well as the state crime of robbery. Here also we find no double jeopardy, even when the accused is convicted in state court after being acquitted on the federal charge.[9]

[8] UNITED STATES CODE, title 18, sect. 2113.
[9] Bartkus v. Illinois, 359 U.S. 422 (1956).

Multiple Charges against a Criminal

It is also possible for a criminal to commit several separate crimes in one series of acts on the same occasion. For example, a holdup man may rob a female clerk in a liquor store at gunpoint (an armed robbery). The bandit may then take her as a hostage against her will (a kidnapping); steal her car to make a getaway (car theft); take the victim into the woods and sexually attack her (rape); and kill her to get rid of the witness (murder).

In the prosecution separate charges may be brought against this criminal, seeking to convict him of armed robbery, kidnapping, car theft, rape, and murder. He may be found guilty of any or all of these charges. Because of recent decisions of the U.S. Supreme Court, the prosecutor must bring all the charges based on the "same transaction" (*Asch v. Swenson*, 397 U.S. 436, 90 S. Ct. 1189) or the "same acts" (*Waller v. Florida*, 397 U.S. 387, 90 S. Ct. 1148) at the same time. Later charges and trial constitute double jeopardy.

Dropping or Reducing Charges at the Time of Prosecution

As an alternative, the prosecution may work out a deal with the accused, dropping some charges in exchange for a guilty plea on some of the others. The accused may be convicted of each charge; this is not double jeopardy. The claim can be made, of course, that the crime was one continuous action, but the courts do not view it in this manner.

From the police officer's point of view, it is sometimes difficult to determine whether or not more than one crime was committed in a course of conduct or in one single act. Just remember the test: different evidence is needed to prove more than one crime; adequate evidence must be uncovered to prove each crime of which the suspect is accused.

EX POST FACTO LAWS

As with double jeopardy, the practicing police officer should also know something about *ex post facto laws*. An ex post facto law is one passed after the occurrence of an act, which retrospectively changes the legal consequences or relations of the individual who committed the act. Prosecution in such an instance is illegal; it is unconstitutional. The legislature can't decide today to punish some act that was legal when done yesterday. Section 9 of Article I of the U.S. Constitution provides that "No Bill of Attainder or ex post facto Law shall be passed."

For example, suppose the state of Arizona passed a law in 1970, stating that it had been a criminal violation to ride an unshod horse since 1965.

Regardless of the statute, a cowboy could not be prosecuted for riding an unshod horse in 1968. This is because the conduct declared illegal was innocent at the time it was committed. No one should be required to anticipate what may later be declared criminal.

To take another situation, in recent years a number of small childern have been asphyxiated by climbing into abandoned refrigerators left around residences, shops, and other places. Children of tender years do not realize that a refrigerator has no inside door handle, and that they will be unable to get out. Incidents of this kind have happened with such frequency that many states have passed laws spelling out the criminal violation in abandoning a refrigerator or icebox without removing the handle. Suppose such a law was passed by one of the states in 1970. A child lost his life in a refrigerator in 1971; however, the appliance in question had been abandoned at this location in 1968. Under the ex post facto rule, no criminal violation occurred. The law cannot be made retroactive.

Of course, it might be possible to word the law in such manner that the act of abandonment would be a continuing violation; but this raises a number of other legal problems that will not be considered here.

Still other laws may carry this ex post facto defect. One court has stated:

> To render a statute "ex post facto," it must be one which imposes punishment for an act which was not punishable when it was committed or imposes additional punishment or alters the situation of the accused to his disadvantage.[10]

If a new law is passed, increasing the penalty for a criminal offense already on the books, the new penalty will apply only to violations after the change was made.[11] A statute reducing the amount of evidence necessary to convict for an existing crime would also be an ex post facto law.[12] But a law decreasing the penalty of a crime is not an ex post facto law, with respect to violations committed before the reduction of penalty. The courts also say that trial procedures may be changed by the legislature and made applicable to trials for offenses previously committed, provided the accused is in as favorable a position as previously.[13]

BILL OF ATTAINDER

Also, as previously noted in another connection, Section 9 of Article I of the U.S. Constitution provides that "No Bill of Attainder or ex post facto law shall be passed." A bill of attainder is a legislative act directed against

[10] Andrus v. McCauley, D.C. Wash., 21 F. Supp. 70.
[11] Southern Kraft Corp. v. Hardin, 205 Ark. 512, 169 S.W.2d 637.
[12] Hill v. State, 146 Tex. Cr. R. 333, 171 S.W.2d 880.
[13] Pincus v. Adams, 274 N.Y. 447, 9 N.E.2d 46.

a particular person, pronouncing him guilty of a crime without allowing or providing a court trial. The idea started in England, when the early rulers had considerable fear of plots or plans to overthrow the king. Terrible penalties were imposed on everyone who might be even remotely connected with one of these plots. Persons believed guilty by the king were said to have suffered "corruption of blood." What was meant was that all the blood relatives of the guilty individual also were punished, even though these people had no knowledge of the plot. Generally, those who suffered "corruption of blood" lost all their property and civil rights. Even those who were powerful lords and barons had their properties seized by the king; this included real estate and castles, personal property, money, and goods.

Later, when Parliament became powerful and was less under the influence of the king, it passed so-called bills of attainder. Each of these was a legislative act directed against a specific person, pronouncing him guilty of the crime of treason—without trial or conviction—and forfeiting his rights and property to the king.

Even during the Revolutionary War, bills of attainder were passed in many of the colonial legislatures, taking away the rights of persons who worked against the American patriots in favor of the British king; but the U.S. Constitution was drawn up after more calm reflection, and it provides that no state may pass any bill of attainder.

What this means is that no person can be found guilty of a crime by a legislature. Every person must be tried by a court, with the protections and safeguards set up by the court system. The legislature cannot simply pass a law saying that someone is guilty of crime, regardless of how terrible the acts committed. Neither can the legislature take away a person's property just because that person has violated the law. The property will revert to the lawful heirs, even when the criminal is found guilty and executed.

Under the American system of government, the Congress or state legislatures can pass laws and provide penalties, but in all cases the actual trial must be held by a legally established court, with safeguards and rules of evidence to guarantee the rights of the accused.

Two specific cases may be of interest in this regard. In the first a provision in a congressional appropriation bill named three federal employees who should not receive any pay from the federal treasury, other than for military or jury services, unless reappointed by the President with the advice and consent of the U.S. Senate.[14] In the second case Congress had passed a law stating that no person who is or who has been during the preceding five years a member of the Communist Party should serve as an officer of a labor union.[15] In both of these cases the Supreme Court of the

[14] United States v. Lovett, 328 U.S.303.
[15] United States v. Brown, 381 U.S. 437.

United States held that to deprive people of employment is punishment and that punishments can be passed out only by the courts.

CONFLICT OF LAWS

Another matter that is often confusing is that the laws in some states are sometimes completely opposite to those in other states. State law may also be contrary to the federal law. How these conflicts may be resolved is a complicated field—not within the scope of this study. However, we should say this: If federal and state laws are in conflict, the federal law prevails over the laws of the states.

EXTRADITION

Also, some of the relations of one state to another are set out in the U.S. Constitution. For example, Article IV provides:

> A person charged in any State with Treason, Felony, or other crime, who shall flee from justice, and be found in another State, shall on Demand of the executive Authority of the State from which he fled, be delivered up, to be removed to the State having Jurisdiction of the Crime.

This describes the process called "extradition." Yet, in spite of the positive wording of this article, the Constitution and federal law provide no method for compelling one state to take action in favor of another. The statement above is well proved in a case that received considerable publicity a number of years ago. The governor of New Jersey declined to extradite a fugitive who had escaped from a Georgia chain gang. Georgia was not able to obtain the escapee through the extradition process.

ENTRAPMENT

Entrapment is the act of officers or agents of the government, leading or inducing a person to commit a crime not contemplated by the accused. If the crime has previously been planned by the accused, then entrapment cannot be claimed. To use entrapment as a defense, the accused must first admit committing the violation. The basis of the defense is then that it is unconscionable for the government to punish, since the same government induced the accused to commit the wrongful act in the first place. The attitude of the courts is that it is socially desirable for criminals to be apprehended and brought to justice. Nothing whatsoever is wrong when traps are set to catch those seriously involved in crime. But the courts consistently say that they cannot allow the government's police officers, those clearly responsible for the enforcement of law, to create crime by planting illegal schemes in innocent minds, thereby originating some violation that otherwise would never have occurred.

The above attitude is precisely expressed in the historic federal case *Sherman v. United States.*[16] The court emphasized that "The function of law enforcement is the prevention of crime and the apprehension of criminals and does not include the manufacture of crime." Along this same line, another federal court said: "Prevention, not incitation, of crime is the duty of the officer."[17] In a 1953 case in California the court explained, "It is not the entrapment of a criminal upon which the law frowns, but the seduction of innocent people into a criminal career by its officers is what is condemned and will not be tolerated."[18] As a practical matter, however, many people argue that an individual who has been sent off on a career of crime by a slight suggestion is not completely innocent.

The test of entrapment laid down by the U.S. Supreme Court is this: If the police officer or government agent originates the scheme for a crime, then a claim of entrapment will be sustained. But if the accused already had the plan in mind, there is nothing legally wrong with action by a governmental officer in supplying the accused with the conditions needed to carry out the original plan. If the criminal has laid plans for the crime and if the officer discovers the plan and becomes involved in details, then the officer may continue for the purpose of trapping the wrongdoer.

In some states entrapment is not recognized as a defense for the criminal; but in most jurisdictions the wrongdoer actually is allowed to go free if entrapment can be proved.

Now, since we have examined the basic ideas involved in entrapment, let us examine several leading cases on this subject.

The Baymouth case, decided in the Oklahoma state courts in 1956,[19] disclosed that time after time one Baymouth made telephone calls to a female victim making indecent proposals and suggestions to the woman. The victim reported the calls to a police officer. She was instructed that, when a future call was made, she should agree to meet the caller and point him out to the police. This was done; Baymouth was arrested when he appeared for the agreed meeting. A prosecution was then undertaken; Baymouth was convicted—enticing a woman to commit an act of lewdness. On appeal, Baymouth's attorney argued that the action of the police offi-

[16] Sherman v. United States, 356 U.S. 369.
[17] Newman v. United States, 382 F.2d 479.
[18] People v. Braddock, 41 Cal. 2d 794, 264 P.2d 521, 525.
[19] Baymouth v. State, 249 P.2d 856.

cer was entrapment and that his conviction should be nullified. The court did not accept this argument; Baymouth's conviction was allowed to stand. The reasoning was that the criminal idea had actually not originated in the mind of the police officer, the officer had merely set a trap to catch Baymouth, after the defendant had entered into the criminal scheme.

In the *Sorrells* case[20] a federal prohibition agent went to the home of the defendant, claiming to be a tourist who was eager to purchase a bottle of liquor. At first the defendant (Sorrells) completely refused to grant this request. After some talk, however, he learned that he had served in World War I in the same division as that of the caller. The prohibition agent and the defendant reminisced at some length on their war experiences. Continuing to plead for some liquor, the agent eventually received the promise of half a gallon of whiskey. Sorrells then left his house and returned with a jar of whiskey, which he delivered for the price of five dollars. He was arrested by the prohibition agent and charged with an illegal sale of liquor.

The Supreme Court of the United States reversed his conviction, declaring Sorrells a free man. In this case the idea for the unlawful sale of whiskey originated with the prohibition agent, not with the defendant. Whether the preliminary refusal to sell arose out of a sense of caution made no difference, according to the court. Without doubt, the solicitation or idea for the criminal sale was planted in the defendant's mind by the government agent.

In an Alabama case, *Browning v. State,*[21] local officers attempted to arrest the defendant (Browning) without evidence of any kind. This arrest attempt was, of course, illegal. The defendant fled, and the officers fired their guns at his car. In the effort to avoid his pursuers, the defendant drove at a high rate of speed and in a reckless manner. He was subsequently arrested and convicted of reckless driving. Upon appeal the defendant's attorney claimed that his client was forced to flee in order to escape the gunfire of the pursuing officers. The attorney's argument continued to stress the fact that the illegal acts of the officers had forced the defendant to resort to reckless driving, that the defendant had entertained no thought of reckless driving until forced to do so in the act of saving his life, and that the action of the officer was therefore entrapment. The court agreed with this argument; Browning was released.

A Kentucky case decided in 1946, *Scott v. Commonwealth,*[22] originated out of a state law that made possession of alcohol a state crime. The chief of police seized a quantity of liquor in the possession of the defendant (Scott), but later learned that it could not be used as evidence. The liquor

[20] Sorrells v. United States, 287 U.S. 435.
[21] Browning v. State, 31 Ala. App. 137, 13 So. 2d 54.
[22] Scott v. Commonwealth, 303 Ky. 353, 197 S.W. 774.

had been seized without a proper search warrant. On the advice of the prosecuting attorney, the liquor was returned; but the chief of police was not so easily turned aside. He obtained a search warrant based on his knowledge of the location of the whiskey, and seized the liquor a second time.

The court reasoned that, insofar as the original possession of the liquor was concerned, the defendant intended to possess the contraband before the chief even knew of its existence, but the second illegal possession by the defendant was first thought of by the chief of police, who returned the liquor for the purpose of obtaining a conviction. This last act of the chief's was entrapment.

This case *(Scott v. Commonwealth)* and the previous one *(Browning v. State)* seem to add another rule to the law of entrapment. That is, if the action of the police officer forces a defendant into a position where the accused violates the law, the prosecution will not be allowed to take advantage of it.

In the Colorado case *DeBell v. People,*[23] the defendant was under prosecution on a charge of statutory rape. With his attorney and two other individuals charged with the same crime, defendant DeBell went to the home of the mother of the victim. After some conversation DeBell paid the mother $3000 to sign certain affidavits (which the mother said later were untrue) to cause her daughter to drop the prosecution.

Through a prearrangement the sheriff and a deputy district attorney watched these proceedings, listening from a nearby hiding place in the home of the victim. After the money was paid and immediately before the affidavits were signed, the authorities entered the room; the sheriff arrested DeBell and the others who were attempting to pay off the victim's mother.

In addition to the original rape charge, this attempt to bribe the mother of the victim resulted in prosecution for compounding a felony. On appeal the defendant claimed that the action of the sheriff and deputy district attorney in concealing themselves was entrapment. Since the scheme to bribe the victim's mother had originated with DeBell and the other defendants, the court held otherwise.

In *Hampton v. United States,* decided in 1976, the U.S. Supreme Court upheld the conviction of Hampton on a claim of entrapment. In this case the accused was supplied contraband drugs by a government agent or informer, and Hampton was convicted for the prohibited sale of these articles under Title 21, U.S. Code, Section 841(a)(1). The facts indicated that it was Hampton, not the government agent, who originated the criminal scheme. The Court held that "it is only when the Government's deception

---

[23] DeBell v. People, 244 P. 600, 79 Colo. 137.

actually implants the criminal design in the mind of the defendant that the defense of entrapment comes into play."[24]

It should also be pointed out that the entrapment defense applies only to officers of the law or to prosecutors. Suppose that the inducement or persuasion under which the defendant became involved in the crime was supplied by a third party in no way connected with police officials or agents of the government. That was the situation in *Polski v. United States*.[25] In upholding the Polski conviction, the federal court said that when the person supplying the inducement to crime is not an officer of the law, or someone acting for him, the defendant cannot claim entrapment.

JURISDICTION

The fact that a judge and administrative assistants have been assigned to a court does not mean that the court automatically has authority to try a case. A court can act only within the power given by a constitution or by statutes. Guidelines, called "rules of procedure," control the conduct of officials and all the parties involved in a criminal trial. All authorities agree that all criminal courts have a right to everyone's evidence.

Jurisdiction also carries limitations. For example, a state court in Texas cannot try an individual for murder when the crime was committed in Illinois. This right to take legal action is called "jurisdiction." Generally, the jurisdiction of a court is limited by territorial boundaries and by subject matter. For example, a civil court cannot usually conduct a trial in a criminal matter. In some states, however, certain of the courts are empowered to handle both civil and criminal cases.

Generally, federal enforcement officers have jurisdiction anywhere in the United States. On the other hand, local and state officers only have jurisdiction to investigate or to arrest for crimes committed within certain territorial limits.

In view of this limited arrest and investigative jurisdiction, Congress passed the Federal Fugitive Act, or Unlawful Flight to Avoid Prosecution Statute, as it is sometimes called. This national legislative body has said that it is a federal crime to travel from one state to another to avoid prosecution, at least for certain serious crimes. This law also covers interstate flight to avoid confinement in a jail or penitentiary. Under the Federal Fugitive Act, violators are extradited or brought back to the same

[24] Hampton v. United States, Cause 74-5822, decided by the Supreme Court of the United States Apr. 27, 1976, not yet officially reported.
[25] Polski v. United States, 356 U.S. 369.

federal judicial district where the state crime was committed. The FBI can locate a state fugitive in one state and cause the person to be returned by United States marshals to the state where he or she is charged with a more serious crime. In most instances the federal charge is then dismissed, and the individual is released to state authorities for trial.

DEFINITION AND PURPOSES OF PUNISHMENT

We have previously seen that criminal law defines the kind of conduct that cannot be tolerated by society. Punishment is the restraint imposed by the courts when someone has overstepped established boundaries. As defined by *Black's Law Dictionary*, it is:

> Any pain, penalty, suffering, or confinement inflicted upon a person by the authority of the law and the judgment and sentence of a court for some crime or offense committed by him, or for his omission of a duty enjoined by law.

As previously stated, the courts will not regard an act as a crime unless the statute prohibiting this action includes a penalty or punishment of some sort. Of course, we find exceptions, since some states have general statutes that fix the penalty for any law that fails to include a specific punishment.

As the famous English judge and legal commentator Blackstone explained in 1769, "Punishments are therefore only inflicted for the abuse of that free will which God has given to man."[26]

It is obvious that the ultimate object of the criminal law is to protect society and the individuals in it, but opinions differ widely as to how this object is to be accomplished. Most penologists are agreed that punishment should be neither cruel nor excessive. Ideally, penalties should never be greater than those needed to keep an individual "in line." On the other hand, punishment should not in any case be less than enough to balance out, in the offender's mind, the benefits that might come to him by committing the crime.

Furthermore, laws are not the private property of judges, lawyers, or penologists. Theoretically, we may say that all laws should constitute a flexible answer to the social needs of the times. They should be neither impractical explorations of sociological theories nor detached rules that have no practical implications. Yet, penalties or punishments as set out in the statutes and the ways in which these punishments are applied are among the most disputed areas in the study of criminal law. Ever since

[26] W. BLACKSTONE, COMMENTARIES ON THE LAWS OF ENGLAND, sec. 4, para. 5, 1769.

civilization began, men have debated what should be done to keep criminals in check. In fact, we find any number of theories to justify certain penalties against the lawbreaker. Most criminologists and judges have definite opinions of their own as to what punishments should properly be imposed. The result is that we scarcely find a state penal code that can be said to have a single basic principle running through it.

The four most common ideas on this subject are: (1) retribution, (2) correction, or rehabilitation, (3) deterrence, and (4) incapacitation. To describe these types of punishment, we might say that retribution is "settling the score, getting even" with the criminal. Correction, or rehabilitation, is trying to get criminals to realize that they have infringed on some of the rights of others and to persuade them to reform. The idea in deterrence is to make the criminal think the penalty so unpleasant that being involved in crime in the future is not worthwhile. Also, deterrence causes the penalty to serve as an example to others who might be tempted. Incapacitation is simply taking the criminals out of circulation, where thay can no longer strike out at society. For criminals who are habitually dangerous or violent and are not capable of self-restraint, incapacitation may be the only method by which protection for society can be provided.

Retribution

Retribution actually may be the oldest of all theories of punishment. The notion that the score should be settled goes far back into history. It was ancient even when Moses mentioned an eye for an eye in the Old Testament. The Code of Hammurabi, and other codes that predated Moses, handled offenders according to this kind of justice. When a criminal cut off a man's hand in a fit of anger, the ancient law courts ordered him held down while his own hand was chopped off at about the same location.

The discovery of a revolting or disgusting crime gives rise automatically to feelings of outrage, indignation, and fear. Some of these emotions may be deeply rooted in human nature.

Today, however, the retribution idea is seldom advocated in any country. Undoubtedly, this type of punishment has had some deterring effect, but on the whole, it harms society. In the first place, any show of cruelty on the part of those in power seems to discredit the authority of the entire government. It has a demoralizing effect on people in all walks of life. Then too, cutting off a person's hand is a destructive act. Punishment of this type is final. We find no way that the criminal can be physically rehabilitated, even in the event of a later mental and moral change. In a case of this kind, the punished person can seldom become completely productive, and may always be a burden on society or the welfare system.

Besides all this, the Eighth Amendment to the U.S. Constitution provides that cruel or unusual punishments may not be used. In a decision handed down on appeal from the state of Louisiana in 1947, the federal court ruled that this restriction applies to punishments imposed by state and local governments, as well as by the federal government. Therefore, cruel or unusual punishments cannot be sanctioned by the courts or used in state or local jails or prisons. This automatically eliminates many of the ideas of retribution as a deliberate method for the control of crime. Pure vengeance is no longer a recognized punishment. Nevertheless, we find a natural resentment in any society against those who have attacked it. Thus, it is reasonable to predict that vengeance will never completely be eliminated as an element of punishment.

Correction, or Rehabilitation

Some modern penologists state that punishment should be measured solely in terms of the possibility of rehabilitating the individual lawbreaker. Their hope is to "straighten out" or to "adjust" the criminal, at least to the point of learning to live under the rules by which other people get along, whether or not the offender is actually in sympathy with society's rules. The idea is neither to hold criminals' mistakes against them nor to be vengeful. The objective is to bring out the good side of prisoners and to encourage them to live normal, useful lives.

To some extent, this theory of punishment rests on the idea that the environment in which criminals lived has conditioned them to do things that society regards as abnormal or criminal. If criminals are made to understand what influenced their thinking, they may be able to adjust their attitudes so as to live normally with their fellows; but considerable argument is possible about this idea. Identical twins living in the same neighborhood may turn out completely different. One may be a criminal repeater, while the other may become a member of the clergy.

Some of the ideas of rehabilitation may also be based on the idealistic notion that all people are basically good; that it is society which has sinned against the individual, rather than the individual who has wronged society. Judge Benjamin N. Cardozo stated in the *Gitlow* decision, "Although the defendant may be the worst of men, the rights of the best of men are secure only as the rights of the vilest are protected."[27]

Amplifying this theme, Winston Churchill said:

> A calm, dispassionate recognition of the rights of the accused, and even of the convicted criminal against the state—a constant heartsearching by all charged with the duty of punishment—a desire and

[27] Gitlow v. New York, 268 U.S. 652, 45 S. Ct. 625.

eagerness to rehabilitate in the world of industry those who have paid their due in the hard coinage of punishment—tireless efforts toward the discovery of curative and regenerative process—unfailing faith that there is a treasure, if you can only find it, in the heart of every man—these are the symbols which, in the treatment of crime and criminal, mark and measure the stored-up strength of a nation, and are sign and proof of the living virtue within it.[28]

On the other side of the picture, M. R. Cohen wrote in the *Yale Law Journal*:

The most popular theory today is that the proper aim of criminal procedure is to reform the criminal so that he may become adjusted to the social order. A mixture of sentiment and utilitarian motives gives this view its greatest vogue . . . . A growing belief in education and in the healing powers of medicine encourages people to suppose that the delinquent may be reeducated to become a useful member of society . . . .

There are, however, a number of highly questionable assumptions back of this theory which need to be critically examined . . . . Benevolent social reformers are apt to ignore the amount of cold calculating business shrewdness among criminals. Some hotblood ones may respond to emotional appeal; but they are also likely to backslide when opportunity or temptation comes along. Human beings are not putty that can be remolded at will by benevolent intentions . . . .

Let us abandon the light-hearted pretension that any of us know how all cases of criminality can be readily cured.

If the causes of crime are determined by the life of certain groups, it is foolish to deal with the individual as if he were a self-sufficient and self-determining system. We must deal with the whole group to which he naturally belongs or gravitates and which determines his morale. Otherwise, we have to adapt him completely to some other social group or social condition, which is indeed a very difficult problem in social engineering.

And here we must not neglect the question of cost . . . . Suppose that fiendish perpetrators of crimes on children could be reformed by being sent first for several years to a special hospital. Will people vote large sums for such purposes when honest law-abiding citizens so often cannot get hospital facilities? Suppose that we find that a certain social environment or that an elaborate college course will reform a burglar or gunman, would our community stand for the expense when so many worthy young people cannont afford to go to college because they have to go to work? We certainly should not give even the appearance of reward for criminality . . . . Will people be satisfied to see one who is guilty of horrible crimes simply reformed, and not give

---

[28] H. Sol Clark, *Today's Advocate*, Case and Comment, 27, March–April 1971.

vent to the social horror and resentment against the miscreant? It is difficult to believe that any such course would not result in a return to personal vengeance on the part of the relatives or friends of the victim?[29]

Another aspect of rehabilitation that may be noted here is in the indeterminate sentence. The law in some states allows the judge to sentence a convicted person to a maximum sentence, subject to termination by a parole board or other agency at any time after service of the minimum period. As a practical matter, observers sometimes point out that the confrontation between the offender and the parole board often has more to do with the length of sentence than the facts surrounding the crime itself. If the offender can convince the board that he or she has reformed, the sentence may be relatively light. Some argue that, under these circumstances, the merits of the case are ignored.

Current opinion in the fields of criminal law and criminal procedure appears to favor definite sentencing laws. The trend is away from indeterminate sentencing.

Deterrence

As for deterrence, fear of punishment may keep some people from repeated violations of the law, while serving as an example to discourage others who may be tempted to engage in crime for the first time. Punishment may have little deterring effect on some others, however. In the past some professional burglars have been frank to admit that they expect to serve prison time as one of the regular features of their criminal occupation. They are not pleased by this, of course, but accept it as an occupational hazard. Still another criminal may say, "I don't hesitate to pull a bank job, but I can't stand to serve twenty years in the joint." Thus, part of the theory of deterrence is that loss of freedom is so distasteful that a convicted person will not be tempted to repeat. "Separation from society is believed to be punishment enough."

The second idea of deterrence, of course, is to discourage others from a life of crime. Almost 200 years ago, in sentencing a thief, an English judge said, "You are to be hanged, not because you have stolen a sheep, but in order that others may not steal sheep."

On the other hand, criminologists frequently argue that fear of punishment is not a deterrent. While open to debate, this may be true in some types of cases. The death sentence was imposed in England for all felony convictions about 200 to 300 years ago. The available records show that during one period of ten years 167 people were hanged as convicted pick-

[29] M. R. COHEN, *Moral Aspects of the Criminal Law*, 49 YALE LAW JOURNAL, 987, 1012–14 (1940).

pockets and thieves. Of this number all but three admitted that they had witnessed one or more public hangings.

Thus, some observers believe that the certainty of immediate apprehension and punishment is more convincing to a criminal as a deterrent than is the actual severity of the sentence. But then too, fear of punishment, even a death sentence, may not be an effective deterrent against a murderer who kills in the heat of passion. Conversely, fear of a death sentence may act as a strong deterrent against murder of the kind that is carefully planned in advance.

Incapacitation

An element of the incapacitation theory may be found in almost every prison sentence. This is because the criminal who is behind bars is out of circulation and therefore has no opportunity to commit more crimes against society. Thus, one may have good reason to argue that incapacitation should be the main object of the law in some cases. An armed bandit who regularly shoots the victim of the crime may be a definite threat to every person who walks down the street, even though no one yet has died from the bandit's bullets. If certain criminals cannot learn from past experiences, the argument goes, it may be in the best interests of society to lock them up for life.

Some criminologists and medical authorities also point out that certain types of criminal activity may be caused or influenced by correctable disease or abnormalities. Examples of this kind may call for incapacitation and treatment, rather than retribution or incapacitation alone. Under this idea, treatment is provided during incarceration. If, following treatment, offenders still are dangerous to society, they may have to remain in prison not as punishment for crime but because of the need for incapacitation.

The real problem here is to be able to judge precisely when the particular criminals are no longer dangerous to society. In many instances they may be able to convince authorities they are now willing to live within the rules. They may honestly believe this, but may be unable to stand up to the pressures of life outside a prison.

The high rate of criminal repeaters, "recidivists," as they are called points to the fact that nobody knows with certainty whether the criminal has responded to treatment during the period of incapacitation.

Whom is Punishment Designed to Benefit?

In summary, the criminal law in the United States has long leaned toward protecting individual rights, especially those of the accused. As it is frequently expressed in legal circles, "Better that a hundred guilty people should go free than that one innocent person should be convicted."

The Supreme Court of the United States said in 1894, and has in effect said frequently since:

> The law of our country takes care, or should take care, that not the weight of a judge's finger shall fall upon anyone except as specifically authorized by the criminal law.

Because of this philosophy, criminals sometimes may be freed even though the judges are satisfied as to their real guilt. When the rights of the defendant are disregarded to the slightest degree in obtaining evidence, the courts do not allow the conviction to stand.

Without deliberately seeking to justify or to criticize this position, we may note that a substantial number of individuals question whether or not this philosophy of the courts has been pursued to excess. Clearly, criminal law should be geared to the protection of three classes of interests: (1) the interests of society as a whole, (2) the interests of the victim that the law seeks to protect, and (3) the interests of the accused wrongdoer. Striking a balance between all these interests is often extremely difficult because they sometimes seem to be directly opposed.

In examining the development of criminal rights as extended to the accused person by the courts, let us remember that the men who framed our early governments were only slightly removed from the governments of Europe. For thousands of years the rulers of the Old World had used criminal prosecution as a means to stamp out political opposition. Our founding fathers had seen, at first hand, how the tyrants of Europe used criminal prosecutions to beat down opposition and the criminal law to accomplish their individual ends. With this background in mind, American courts have gone to great lengths to make certain that the rights of the accused individual are preserved.

CITED CASES

Andrus v. McCauley, D.C. Wash., 21 F. Supp. 70.
Asch v. Swenson, 397 U.S. 436, 90 S. Ct. 1189.
Bartkus v. Illinois, 359 U.S. 442.
Baymouth v. State, 245 P.2d 856.
Browning v. State, 31 Ala. App. 137, 13. So 2d 54.
DeBell v. People, 244 P. 600, 79 Cal. 137.
Downum v. United States, 372 U.S. 734.
Fong Foo v. United States, 369 U.S. 141.
Furman v. Georgia, 92 S. Ct. 19.
Gitlow v. New York, 268 U.S. 652, 45 S. Ct. 625.

Hampton v. United States, Cause 74-5822, decided by U.S. Supreme
    Court, April 27, 1976; not yet officially reported.
Hill v. State, 146 Tex. Cr. R. 333, 171 S.W.2d 880.
Jones v. Erie Railway Co., 106 Ohio St. 408.
Newman v. United States, 382 F. 2d 479.
People v. Braddock, 41 Cal. 2d 794, 264 P.2d 521, 525.
Pincus v. Adams, 274 N.Y. 447, 9 N.E.2d 46.
Polski v. United States, 356 U.S. 369.
Scott v. Commonwealth, 303 Ky. 353, 197 S.W. 774.
Sherman v. United States, 356 U.S. 369.
Sorrells v. United States, 287 U.S. 435.
Southern Kraft Corp. v. Hardin, 205 Ark. 512, 169 S.W.2d 637.
United States v. Brown, 381 U.S. 437.
United States v. Lovett, 328 U.S. 303.
United States v. Reisinger, 128 U.S. 398.
Waller v. Florida, 397 U.S. 387, 90 S. Ct. 1148.

CHAPTER 4

Classification of Crimes

Crimes may be classified in a number of ways: (1) as to the moral turpitude involved, (2) according to applicable procedures, and (3) in terms of the social harm imposed by the act involved.

Since it is obvious that society regards some violations as more serious than others, crimes are, in turn, grouped according to their seriousness. For several important reasons each police officer needs to understand these classifications as they apply in his or her jurisdiction.

For example, the officer's right to apprehend a criminal without being sued for false arrest, the right to use force in making the arrest, and a number of other actions may hinge on whether the officer is able immediately to classify the type of crime involved. Other duties and responsibilities that depend on the ability to classify crimes will become apparent as we continue.

CLASSIFICATION OF CRIMES BY GRADE OF SERIOUSNESS

Analyzed from the standpoint of seriousness, crimes at commom law are broken down into three classifications. Listed in order of seriousness, these are: (1) treason, (2) felonies, and (3) misdemeanors.

Most states in this country commonly divide offenses into only two classes: (1) felonies and (2) misdemeanors. Very few list *treason* in a separate classification.[1] In addition, some jurisdictions list *infractions* as a third

[1] ROLLIN M. PERKINS, CRIMINAL LAW AND PROCEDURE, The Foundation Press, Mineola, N.Y., 1972 p. 5.

category of crime.[2] Still others classify offenses in this last grouping as *less than misdemeanors.*

Felonies

Under early English law a felony was any crime below the grade of treason, upon conviction carrying a penalty of forfeiture of all lands and goods to the king. This same forfeiture also applied to treason. In fact, some legal writers have made the statement that treason was but a special kind of felony, so serious that it was placed in its own class.

Today the average person thinks of a felony as any crime of a serious nature. This, of course, is a generality. Crimes most commonly spoken of as felonies are murder, manslaughter, mayhem, arson, robbery, rape, burglary, and kidnapping. Most crimes that are not as serious as felonies are misdemeanors. However, we find a lack of uniformity; some jurisdictions completely fail to divide crimes into felonies and misdemeanors.

Under the federal law a felony is an offense punishable by death[3] or by imprisonment for a term exceeding one year.[4] The test under the federal law, then, is the *length of the sentence* that may be imposed. If the penalty set by the judge is a year or less, the crime is a misdemeanor.

A number of states conveniently follow the federal definition. In terms of the federal rule, the courts of these states have generally said: "The offense is measured by the penalty that might be imposed, and not by the leniency of the sentencing tribunal."[5] Stated in other words, this means that if it is possible under the state law to sentence a convicted person to ten years in prison, that person is guilty of a felony, even though the actual sentence was only six months in jail. Thus, a felony under federal law may or may not be a felony under the definition in some states.[6]

The definition of a felony in other states provides that "A felony is a crime . . . punishable with death or by imprisonment in the state prison."

[2] See CALIFORNIA PENAL CODE, sec. 16.

[3] On June 29, 1972, the U.S. Supreme Court held in Furman v. Georgia, 92. S. Ct. 19, in a 5 to 4 decision, that the death penalty, as it was imposed under the then-current laws in the United States, was unconstitutional. The court simply said: ". . . The imposition and carrying out of the death penalty . . . constitutes cruel and unusual punishment in violation of the 8th and 14th Amendments." Yet, the mass of sharply divergent opinions by which the court decided the case left some crucial questions unanswered. The door seemed to be open for Congress or the states to write new laws that might be valid. In fact, in 1976, in the case of Gregg v. Georgia, 428 U.S. 153, the Supreme Court upheld the rewritten Georgia death-penalty law.

[4] UNITED STATES CODE, title 18, sec. 335.

[5] People ex rel. Seagrist v. Mederer, 33 N.Y.S. 2d 114.

[6] Caminetti v. Imperial Mutual Life Insurance Co., 59 Cal. App. 2d 476, 139 P.2d 681.

The federal test, as we have seen, is based on the length of the sentence, whereas this second definition turns on the *place*—the penitentiary where the confinement is to be served.

In general, the courts state that they "will not presume that the legislature intended to make a transaction a misdemeanor under one statute and to make it a felony under another."[7]

To complicate the picture further, however, some states treat certain criminal acts as either a felony or a misdemeanor. This seems to be a modern trend in the criminal law, motivated by the belief that an individual should not be branded for life as a felon because of one mistake, if the judge pronounces a jail sentence rather than a prison sentence.

For example, California is one of those states that classify a crime as a felony if "punishable with death or by imprisonment in the state prison."[8] However, the penalty clauses, a part of some statutes, have qualifying provisions, such as the penalty clause for grand theft, providing that this crime is "punishable by imprisonment in the county jail for not more than one year or in the state prison for not more than 10 years."[9]

This, of course, is confusing except for the provision that "When a crime, punishable by imprisonment in the state prison, is also punishable by fine or imprisonment in a county jail, in the discretion of the court, it shall be deemed a misdemeanor for all purposes after a judgment imposing a punishment other than imprisonment in the state prison."[10]

Thus, if an individual in California is convicted of a lesser offense than that originally charged, whether it is a felony or a misdemeanor depends upon the penalty of the offense for which the actual sentence was pronounced.[11]

In those states where a crime is punishable either as a felony or as a misdemeanor, the police officer must know what the legal situation is at the time of arrest. Under the common law and in perhaps the majority of states, a peace officer may

> **without a warrant, arrest a person . . . whenever he has reasonable cause to believe that the person to be arrested has committed a felony whether or not a felony has been committed.**[12]

[7] Clark v. State, 53 Ariz. 416, 89 P.2d 1077.

[8] CALIFORNIA PENAL CODE, sec. 16. See footnote 3 of this chapter. Prior to the U.S. Supreme Court decision outlawing the death penalty, the Supreme Court of California in People v. Anderson, 6 Cal. 3d 628, declared the death penalty unconstitutional under art. 1, sec. 6, of the state constitution. Without doubt and regardless of the decision of the Supreme Court of the United States, the death penalty has been abolished in California, in the absence of constitutional and statutory revisions.

[9] CALIFORNIA PENAL CODE, sec. 489.

[10] CALIFORNIA PENAL CODE, sec 16.

[11] People v. Apgar, 35 Cal. 389; People v. Ambrey, 35 Cal. 427.

[12] CALIFORNIA PENAL CODE, sec. 836.

While intending to make a felony arrest without a warrant shortly after a crime is committed, a police officer can run the risk of suit for false arrest if the criminal is later sentenced for a misdemeanor under one of the options available to the judge. The courts, however, have given protection to the police officer in this situation. For purposes of the original arrest or for other legal purposes prior to trial, the crime can only be regarded as a felony.[13] In other words, the legality of the arrest is judged by the facts and circumstances known to a reasonable, prudent, and cautious officer at the time of the arrest.

Misdemeanors

Under the common law, crimes of less serious nature than felonies were originally called "trespasses," but later came to be known as "misdemeanors."[14] The courts have frequently said that misdemeanors include all indictable offenses inferior to felonies.[15] Misdemeanors also have been defined as those crimes to which the law has not given particular names.[16] Neither of these definitions is adequate, however, because many minor or petty offenses may be prosecuted without indictment, either upon informations or on complaints filed before magistrates, and some misdemeanors have particular names while some felonies, newly created by statute, have not. Under statutes that define felonies, misdemeanors are frequently defined as being any crimes not punishable by death or imprisonment in the state prisons.[17] Often a new law itself will define the offense as a felony or misdemeanor. In any event:

> When an offense, not known to the common law, is created by statute, in the absence of a contrary definition in the statute, it will be classified as a misdemeanor rather than a felony.[18]

Offenses Less Than Misdemeanors

Some jurisdictions insist upon and have actually created a third classification of offenses, less serious than misdemeanors. As previously stated, some jurisdictions list these as "infractions." These offenses are sometimes further described as those of which magistrates have exclusive jurisdiction, or

---

[13] State v. Amey, 7 Ariz. App. 59, 436 P.2d 153; People v. Cowan, 38 Cal. App. 2d 231; People v. Boggess, 75 Cal. App. 499.

[14] STEPHEN, COMMENTARIES ON THE LAWS OF ENGLAND, 19th ed., p. 6.

[15] State v. Hunter, 67 Ala. 81; Walsh v. People, 65 Ill. 58.

[16] *Ex parte* Garrison, 36 W. Va. 686, 15 N.E. 417.

[17] People v. Stravrakas, 335 Ill. 570, 167 N.E. 852; Bopp v. Clark, 165 Iowa 697, 147 N.W. 172.

[18] JUSTIN MILLER, HANDBOOK OF CRIMINAL LAW, West Publishing Co., St. Paul, Minn., 1934, p. 46; Cosidine v. United States, 112 F. 342.

as "police regulations."[19] Most violations of city and county ordinances are in this classification, assuming of course that these offenses are recognized by the jurisdiction as distinct from misdemeanors. Examples might be the burning of trash inside the city limits without a permit; a common traffic violation, such as overtime parking; or wading in a watershed that drains into the city water system. These offenses are variously termed *infractions, violations* or merely *status offenses.* Some are punished by only a fine or forfeiture.

Are Violations of Municipal and County Ordinances Crimes?

When state law defines crime in terms of only two classifications (felonies and misdemeanors), obviously all municipal and county ordinances may be classified as misdemeanors. If state law defines crimes as felonies, misdemeanors, and offenses less than misdemeanors (infractions), violations of municipal and county ordinances are usually classified as less than misdemeanor offenses.

On the other hand, great difference of opinion exists about whether acts in violation of municipal and county ordinances actually are crimes at all. Many courts have held that these are not crimes, since they are not violations of public law.[20] A few have held that they are crimes, being breaches of law established for the protection of the public as distinguished from infringements of private rights.[21] Justice Miller in *State v. West* offers a most convincing argument in this respect:

> A municipal ordinance is as much a law for the protection of the public as a criminal statute of the state, the only differences being that the one is designed for the protection of the municipality and the other for the protection of the whole state; and in both cases alike, the punishment is imposed for the violation of the public law. If the state itself directly should make the act an offense, and prescribes the punishment, there could be criminal prosecution; . . . how can it make any difference, either in the intrinsic nature of the thing or in the consequences to the accused, whether the state does this itself or delegates the power to the municipalities?[22]

The question most frequently arises in cases involving the right of the accused to a trial by jury. No trial by jury was guaranteed under the common law in petty offenses, and the courts generally have held that the constitutional guarantee is no broader than the common law right.[23]

[19] United States v. Balint, 258 U.S. 250, 42 S. Ct. 301; People v. Roby, 52 Mich. 577, 18 N.W. 365.
[20] City of Greeley v. Hamman, 12 Colo. 94, 20 P. 1; State v. Heuchert, 42 La. Ann. 270.
[21] Castle Dale City v. Woolley, 61 Utah 291, 212 P. 1111; State v. Vail, 57 Iowa 103.
[22] State v. West, 42 Minn. 147, 43 N.W. 845.
[23] Inwood v. State, 42 Ohio St. 186; Wong v. Astoria, 13 Ore. 538.

Also, the question has often been considered in cases involving the determination of the defendant's right (against double jeopardy) to prevent prosecution for the same act which is a violation of both city ordinance and state law. If the offense against the city ordinance is a criminal offense, it logically follows that the same act may not be punished under both ordinance and state statute.[24] The opposite conclusion, however, has been most frequently reached, the two offenses being recognized as distinct.[25] Clearly, then, the basis and contingent questions most often must be answered in terms of the peculiar language of the Constitution, state statutes, court cases, and municipal and county ordinances of the jurisdictions involved.

WHY THE CLASSIFICATION OF THE CRIME MAY MAKE A DIFFERENCE AT THE TIME OF ARREST

A police officer who makes an arrest that is not legally justified may be sued for false arrest. In addition, the city, county, state, or federal agency represented by the officer may be sued. The outgrowth of such an incident may be that the arrested person is awarded a large sum of money in damages. No police officer wants to be sued for false arrest, both because of the possible financial cost and because of the risk of embarrassment to the police department.

Now, we clearly understand that the laws of arrest are an important part of the law of criminal procedure. This, of course, is technically outside the substantive field of criminal law. However, we must pursue some examination of the laws of arrest because of the relationship between the classification of crimes and these important laws.

If it is reasonable to do so, the courts will almost invariably insist that the arresting peace officer obtain a warrant prior to making an arrest. Since warrants are issued only by magistrates, commissioners, judges, justices, or other officials of the court, this precaution serves as a reasonable guarantee that persons will not be arrested at the whim of one person or without reasonable likelihood of guilt.

Of course, if it is possible to obtain an arrest warrant, police authorities should obtain one in every case. Once a warrant has been issued, the officer should be concerned about whether the person arrested is in fact identical with the individual named in the warrant. After the question of identity has been settled, an arrest made on the warrant relieves the police officer from suit for false arrest.

[24] State v. Thornton, 37 Mo. 360; Barry v. People, 36 Ill. 423.
[25] Ex parte Hang Shen, 98 Cal. 681; State v. Gustin, 152 Mo. 108.

The problem here, however, is that the officer seldom has the time to get a warrant. In many cases, the criminal may be fleeing from the scene of the crime. Frequently, too, vital evidence of guilt may come to the attention of the investigating police officer in such manner that it is simply not practical to leave the unprotected evidence or to lose knowledge of the whereabouts of a nearby criminal. In cases of this kind, the police officer may have little choice but to make an arrest without a warrant.

In view of these circumstances, it is settled law in most jurisdictions that a peace officer may make an arrest without a warrant for any violation of the law committed or attempted in the presence, or sometimes even not in the presence of the officer. The class of the crime does not matter here; the violation may be a felony or a misdemeanor.

On the other hand, if the crime is a misdemeanor not committed in the presence of the officer, the arresting officer usually must obtain a warrant. This is because a person who commits a misdemeanor is not likely to flee. Therefore, the accused is not brought to trial until the legal protection of the machinery afforded through the warrant process has been brought into play.

A felon, however, most likely will flee. So, the law allows the arrest of a felon without a warrant, even though the felony was not committed in the presence of the arresting officer. From state to state this authority is generally controlled by statute. The California statute, as we have seen, is typical, providing that a peace officer

> may, without a warrant, arrest a person . . . when a person arrested has committed a felony, although not in his presence [or] (3) whenever he has reasonable cause to believe that the person to be arrested has committed a felony, whether a felony has in fact been committed.[26]

Under a statute of this kind, proof that the arrested individual was in fact guilty of felony is all that is necessary. Also, if there is probable cause, the police officer may arrest without a warrant, even though it later is proved that a felony was not committed.

In defining probable cause, the courts say:

> Probable cause is a reasonable ground of suspicion, supported by circumstances sufficiently strong to warrant a cautious man to believe that an offense has been or is being committed by the person arrested.[27]

---

[26] CALIFORNIA PENAL CODE, sec. 836.
[27] Scott v. People, 444 P.2d 388.

The Classification of the Crime Affects the Amount of Force that May be Used to Make the Arrest

In addition to circumstances of arrest, the classification of the offense has some positive effect upon the amount of force that may be used in making an arrest; this varies with the classification of the crime. Generally, the arresting officer may use deadly force for the purpose of stopping one who is fleeing from arrest on a felony charge, or to protect the life of an innocent bystander.

Pointing out the allowable differences in force for a felony and a misdemeanor arrest, one court said: "It is considered better to allow one guilty of only a misdemeanor to escape altogether than to take his life."[28]

Once again the need for the police officer to distinguish between a felony and a minor violation is emphasized by this difference in the amount of force that may be used.

Furthermore, depending on whether a crime is classified as a felony or a misdemeanor, some other legal differences arise in the handling of criminal prosecutions. For example, many states do not impose as severe a penalty on those who harbor or aid and abet a criminal as is imposed against the actual perpetrator of a felony; but all persons involved in any way in a misdemeanor are treated the same as the principal (the actual perpetrator). Differences of this kind are not usually so important to the police officers; however, they must, without doubt, be cognizant of them.

DISTINGUISHING BETWEEN SINGLE AND MULTIPLE CRIMES

The matter of distinguishing between single and multiple crimes is an important adjunct to the classificatiaon of crimes. If the accused does one single forbidden act which results in injury to more than one person, has there been a single crime or a series of them? If the prosecution fails in one instance, can the accused be brought to trial for the harm done to another victim? Situations of this kind sometimes present some thorny problems for the courts, and the law has not always been uniform in this regard. In general, however, the courts have said that the question of single or multiple crimes is not dependent on the number of unlawful motives in the mind of the accused, but whether separate and distinct prohibited acts have been committed.

An unprovoked assault on a seventeen-year-old theater ticket taker, followed by an assault on the theater manager who came to her assistance, was ruled to be two separate crimes.[29] Even though a continuous course of

[28] Reneau v. State, 70 Tenn. 720.
[29] Broestler v. State, 186 Tenn. 523, 212 S.W.2d 366.

action was involved, the courts have indicated that an indiscriminate assault is an assault on each one of the victims involved.[30] The fact that the accused, when apprehended, possessed narcotic drugs, as well as a concealed weapon, did not prevent prosecution for two offenses. Somewhat similarly, a forcible rape, followed by an armed robbery, is an example of multiple violations. Multiple rapes, committed on three women on the same day, have also been held to be three distinct crimes.

In a situation where one man fired a rifle repeatedly into a crowd, the courts seem to be in agreement that a number of crimes have been committed. If the accused, however, wounds or kills two victims with one single shot, the courts differ in their opinions. Of course, we find few situations of this kind that are the result of a single act, and the courts generally say that the defendant should not suffer multiple punishment for a single act.

In *Neal v. California*,[31] the accused threw gasoline into the bedroom of a man and his wife and ignited the fluid. As a result the victims were both severely burned. In the trial court the accused (Neal) was convicted of attempting to murder the man and his wife, as well as of arson. Upon appeal, the California Supreme Court held that Neal had been properly convicted of attempted murder, but that the arson conviction should not be allowed. In its ruling the court conceded that all the requirements for an arson conviction had been satisfied, but that the act of arson was identical with the act of attempted murder.

Cases like the above also remind us of the common law *doctrine of merger*. Often a person while engaged in the commission of a single act commits more than one crime, some of them misdemeanors and some felonies. The rule of the common law was that the doctrine of merger operated to wipe out the lesser crime and make the accused liable only for the greater one. In other words, if by the same act the defendant committed both a felony and a misdemeanor, the misdemeanor was merged into the felony and the defendant was liable for the felony only. When the crimes were of the same degree, both misdemeanors or both felonies, no merger occurred.[32] Consequently, it followed that at common law, on indictment for a felony, the courts could not prosecute for a misdemeanor although the offense charged necessarily included the lesser offense.[33]

The doctrine of merger rested on the reason that persons indicted for misdemeanors had certain advantages at the trial that were not enjoyed by those indicted for felonies. Today in the United States, the defendant has the same privileges in a felony trial as in a misdemeanor trial. So, most courts have refused to recognize the doctrine. In many states the rule has

[30] Church v. State, 231 N.C. 39, 55 S.E.2d 792.
[31] Neal v. California, 55 Cal. 2d 11, 357 P.2d 839.
[32] Graff v. People, 208 Ill. 312, 320, 70 N.E. 299.
[33] Commonwealth v. Cooper, 15 Mass. 187; Commonwealth v. Newell, 7 Mass. 245, 249.

been changed by statutes which provide that, on an indictment, if the proof falls short of the offense charged, the defendant may be convicted of a lesser offense included in the offense charged.[34] In turn, the courts have generally held that, when the act charged is an integral part of some higher offense, the defense cannot object, upon conviction, that the evidence shows that the defendant is guilty of the higher offense.[35] In a few states the common law doctrine of merger has been preserved.[36]

As a practical matter, the prosecuting attorney determines whether multiple violations have been committed by the accused. The police officer must, however, make certain that each possible criminal violation is recognized and that all evidence regarding each separate crime is brought to the attention of the prosecutor.

CLASSIFICATION OF CRIMES WITH REGARD TO MORAL TURPITUDE

Also of some importance to the police officer is another classification plan that is sometimes used to separate all crimes into two groups on the basis of moral turpitude. Used in this sense, "turpitude" means something that is evil by its very nature, morally base or vile. The two classifications here are those that are bad in themselves and those that are bad only in the sense that they are forbidden by law.

Crimes that involve moral turpitude are mala in se (bad in themselves). Others that do not involve moral turpitude are mala prohibita (bad because they are prohibited). Incidentally, we would like to get away from the use of Latin legal phrases, but sometimes they have become so deeply embedded in the language of modern law that they can't be ignored. As one court said:

> An offense malum in se is properly defined as one which is naturally evil as adjudged by the sense of a civilized community, whereas an act malum prohibitum is wrong only because it is made so by statute.

Under the above classification system—murder, armed robbery, arson, kidnapping, burglary, and rape are all essentially evil and involve moral turpitude. It follows, then, that each one of these crimes is malum in se (the plural is mala in se). Since the common law punished no act that was not wrong in itself, it is apparent that all common law crimes are malum in se.

An act that is malum prohibitum is not the kind that outrages the community; it is not inherently immoral or evil. The act is a crime because it is expressly prohibited by law. No moral turpitude is involved in walking

---

[34] People v. McNutt, 98 Cal. 658, 29 P. 243; People v. Abbott, 97 Mich. 484, 56 N.W. 862.
[35] People v. Tugwell, 32 Cal. App. 520; Commonwealth v. Walker, 108 Mass. 309.
[36] State v. Durham, 72 N.C. 447; Reed v. State, 141 Ind. 116, 40 N.E. 525.

across the street against a red traffic light; it is usually forbidden by law, for the pedestrian's well-being.

Accidental Killing Resulting from an Unlawful Act Is Manslaughter, If the Unlawful Act Is Malum in Se

An accidental killing (homocide) resulting from an unlawful act less than a dangerous felony constitutes the crime of manslaughter if the unlawful act is malum in se. When the accidental death results from an unlawful act that is malum prohibitum, it is not a crime, merely an unfortunate accident (unless criminal negligence is involved, as we shall see later). We can say, then, that whether an accidental death is a crime (manslaughter) may turn on whether the illegal act that resulted in death was malum in se or malum prohibitum.

For example, in *State v. Horton*[37] the appellate court released the accused who had been wrongfully convicted of manslaughter by a trial court. This case involved the accidental killing of a man by his hunting partner (Horton), who had committed a misdemeanor by hunting without obtaining the landowner's permission as required by law. In reversing the conviction of Horton and allowing him to go free, the court pointed out that the unlawful act committed in connection with the killing must be one that is malum in se. Horton's failure to obtain the landowner's permission to hunt was not inherently evil; it was merely malum prohibitum.

Criminal Negligence Nullifies the Excuse of Malum Prohibitum

Now, the result in the Horton case might have been different if criminal negligence had been involved. The kind of negligence we are talking about here is that which falls below the standard established by law for the protection of others against unreasonable risk of harm.

Let us assume that in the situation presented in the Horton case the accused and the deceased were drinking while en route to the hunting location. Suppose the accused, as the driver of the automobile, lost control of the car while under the influence of alcohol, and the hunting companion was killed in the resulting accident. In this kind of a situation, the courts say that the accused is guilty of criminal negligence in driving while under the influence of alcohol and, consequently, guilty of manslaughter.

To take another example, let us also assume that a hunter killed his companion who was inside an old outhouse near a field where they were hunting. The latter's death occurred because the accused repeatedly discharged his rifle into the outhouse, not realizing that the man was inside.

[37] State v. Horton, 139 N.C. 588, 51 S.E. 945.

The act of firing the gun was not intended to harm anyone, therefore not malum in se. However, firing into the outhouse was criminal negligence, far below the standards expected of a responsible person under similar circumstances.

Please note, in turn, that we have examined only a small part of the criminal law of manslaughter—that which relates to malum in se and malum prohibitum. A more detailed examination of this crime will be found in a later section of the book.

CLASSIFICATION OF CRIMES WITH REGARD TO PROCEDURE

Another classification of crimes, done strictly for *procedural* (prosecutive) purposes, is: (1) major and (2) petty crimes.

Accusations in major federal cases are brought against the accused through indictment by grand jury only; this is also true in accusations for the same category of cases in a majority of the state courts. A few jurisdictions (California, for example) provide an optional procedure for accusations in major crimes. An information, filed by the prosecuting attorney (without grand jury indictment), is allowed after a preliminary hearing, and the accused, charged with a felony, is *bound over* for trial.[38]

On the other hand, authorities have recognized that considerable time and expense is involved in obtaining grand jury indictments and in conducting preliminary hearings and jury trials. To avoid this waste in petty cases, the prosecutor may initiate a prosecution by use of a *complaint*, filed before a magistrate or justice (a procedure not possible in major crimes). This procedure is limited almost everywhere to minor offenses, such petty crimes as traffic violations, and the less serious types of misdemeanors.

CLASSIFICATION OF CRIMES IN TERMS OF SOCIAL HARM

A fourth and last classification is one based on the social harm that results from the criminal act. Under this breakdown, crimes may be grouped as offenses: (1) against the person, (2) against the home, (3) against the property, (4) against public health, safety, and morality, (5) against public peace, (6) affecting the administration of justice, and (7) affecting the conduct of governmental functions.

The classification itself and the groupings within it are largely academic ones, set up principally for systematic treatment and discussion. Various

[38] PERKINS, *op. cit.*, p. 826.

groups within the broad classification are established in terms of the aspect of society most directly affected. These groupings are used in our later examination of specific crimes, such as murder, arson, robber, bigamy, embezzlement, official bribery.

CITED CASES

Barry v. People, 36 Ill. 423.
Bopp v. Clark, 165 Iowa 697, 147 N.W. 172.
Broestler v. State, 186 Tenn. 523, 212 S.W.2d 366.
Caminetti v. Imperial Mutual Life Insurance Co., 59 Cal. App. 2d 476, 139 P.2d 681.
Castle Dale City v. Woolley, 61 Utah 291, 212 P. 1111.
Church v. State, 231 N.C. 39, 55 S.E.2d 792.
City of Greeley v. Hamman, 12 Colo. 94, 20 P. 1.
Clark v. State, 53 Ariz. 416, 89 P.2d 1077.
Commonwealth v. Cooper, 15 Mass. 187.
Commonwealth v. Newell, 7 Mass. 245, 249.
Commonwealth v. Walker, 108 Mass. 309.
Cosidine v. United States, 112 F. 342.
Furman v. Georgia, 92, S. Ct. 19.
Ex parte Garrison, 36 W.Va. 686, 15 N.E. 417.
Graff v. People, 208 Ill. 312, 320, 70 N.E. 299.
Ex parte Hang Shen, 98 Cal. 681.
Inwood v. State, 42 Ohio St. 186.
Neal v. California, 55 Cal. 2d 11, 357 P.2d 839.
People v. Abbott, 97 Mich. 484, 56 N.W. 862.
People v. Ambrey, 35 Cal. 427.
People v. Anderson, 6 Cal. 3d 628.
People v. Apgar, 35 Cal. 389.
People v. Boggess, 75 Cal. App. 499.
People v. Cowan, 38 Cal. App. 2d 231.
People v. McNutt, 98 Cal. 658, 29 P. 243.
People v. Roby, 52 Mich. 577, 18 N.W. 365.
People *ex rel.* Seagrist v. Mederer, 33 N.Y.S. 2d 114.
People v. Stravrakas, 335 Ill. 570, 167 N.E. 852.
People v. Tugwell, 32 Cal. App. 520.
Reed v. State, 141 Ind. 116, 40 N.E. 525.
Reneau v. State, 70 Tenn. 720.
Scott v. People, 444 P. 2d 388.
State v. Amey, 7 Ariz. App. 59, 436 P. 2d 153.
State v. Durham, 72 N.C. 447.

State v. Gustin, 152 Mo. 108.
State v. Heuchert, 42 La. Ann. 270.
State v. Horton, 139 N.C. 588, 51 S.E. 945.
State v. Hunter, 67 Ala. 81.
State v. Thornton, 37 Mo. 360.
State v. Vail, 57 Iowa 103.
State v. West, 42 Minn. 147, 43 N.W. 845.
United States v. Balint, 258 U.S. 250, 42 S. Ct. 301.
Walsh v. People, 65 Ill. 58.
Wong v. Astoria, 13 Ore. 538.

CHAPTER 5

Parties to Crimes

When two or more persons take part in a single crime, some may be involved to a greater extent than others, and so, responsibility under the law may not be limited simply to the one individual who actually commits the forbidden act. Thus, in this chapter we are concerned with individual responsibility in group criminality. Who is guilty in the eyes of the law, and to what extent?

Further, and from the viewpoint of fairness, some participants almost always appear to be more deeply involved and more blameworthy than others. Most people will agree that justice requires different punishments, varying from defendant to defendant.

To illustrate this difference in criminal participation, consider the case of the Kentucky moonshiner who shot a federal revenue agent (U.S. Treasury officer). Ma got involved when she saw the federal officer approaching, loaded the shotgun, and handed it to her husband. Pa actually committed the criminal act when he fired the shots at the government agent. Shortly thereafter, the oldest son became involved when he drove Pa over to Grandpa's after the shooting. For his part, Grandpa got into the act when he hid Pa in the cellar.

It is quite apparent that each member of this mountain family should be held responsible to some extent, if the acts of each member were coupled with a guilty state of mind (criminal intent). It is doubtful, however, whether any court would attach equal weight to the responsibility of each member of the group.

Of course, Ma might be expected to come into court and argue that she did not know that Pa intended to commit murder, since no verbal communication passed between them. The courts say that Ma's intent in handing the loaded gun to Pa must be decided by the jury, in accordance with the attendant circumstances. The law is well settled that it is not necessary for the person perpetrating the forbidden act to communicate verbally with those working in concert with him. From all the surrounding facts, when it appears that Ma knew the crime was to be committed, she cannot escape responsibility.[1]

It would have been a different matter if Ma had not given assistance. As a general proposition, one who merely stands by watching a crime, and even approving of it, is not in violation of the law.[2]

At the time of trial, one might also argue that Pa was reaching for the gun himself when Ma handed it to him. Continuing this argument, we could also say that he could have accomplished the same result without Ma's act. Since this was true, Ma had not actually assisted him in any practical way and should not be responsible. To this argument the courts say that any help given, however slight, makes Ma a participant.

The oldest son and Grandpa could both point out that they had no knowledge of the crime until after it was an accomplished fact. From the earliest times in the English law, however, those who helped a criminal to escape, or concealed or harbored him, shared in the responsibility. As a practical matter, perhaps the oldest son and Grandpa might expect to receive no more than a year or two in the penitentiary, whereas Pa might expect to get the maximum sentence for murder, if the victim died.

Ma might be able to show that she was under the domination of Pa, but that fact would not excuse her from criminal responsibility for a felony. In the usual situation of this kind, Ma would be more blameworthy than the oldest son or Grandpa, but perhaps meriting more consideration than the person who actually pulled the trigger.

BASIC APPROACHES

Two basic approaches have been taken by the law in examining these relationships between criminal participants and in assessing individual punishments.

The Common Law Approach

Different grades of criminal involvement were set up under the common law, holding some to answer as *principals*, or main actors, and others to answer as *accessories*, or secondary parties. Liability depended upon the

---

[1] People v. Carlson, 177 Cal. App. 2d 201.
[2] People v. Wooten, 162 Cal. App. 2d 804; People v. Volla, 156 Cal. App. 2d 128.

individual's role in the commission of the crime and presence at the time of commission.

Apparently, the reason why these classes or grades of guilt were set up under the common law system was that the penalties for all serious crimes were very harsh, even under the standards in those times. A person who participated in a felony (even in a minor way), might be executed or sentenced to a long term in prison. In setting up less severe penalties for secondary parties, the common law courts softened some of the penalties.

This common law approach, with grades of involvement, is still followed in a number of states and is the system used under federal criminal law.

The Statutory Approach

Common law classification of parties has been changed by statute in a number of states. The basic approach in these statutes is to treat all persons who become involved, up to and at the time of the commission of the crime, as a single class. To prevent injustices, a wide range of punishments is available to each convicted defendant. In other words, the law does not attempt to classify according to grades of involvement during the trial process. After the trial has been completed and defendants are convicted, this system relies on the good sense of the sentencing judge or on the discretion of a parole board 'eventually to impose a punishment that the individual defendant seems to deserve. Stated another way, the principle is that, while all participants are treated as members of a single class, wide latitude is left to the legally specified authorities as to the amount of prison time that must be served by each.

Furthermore, we find a great deal of variance from state to state in the statutes that regulate this approach. Yet, the modern trend seems to be toward the statutory idea, that is, doing away with distinctions between principals and accessories.

COMMON LAW CLASSIFICATIONS OF PARTIES TO CRIME

As previously noted, the common law separated the guilty parties into two classes: principals and accessories. According to the thinking of the early English courts, only the actual perpetrator of the criminal deed was the principal. All the other guilty individuals were accessories; and these in turn were divided into three groups, according to the time and the place where they assisted the principal: (1) accessories before the fact, (2) accessories at the fact, and (3) accessories after the fact.

All who helped the perpetrator before the crime was committed were called accessories before the fact. Those who helped at the time of the commission of the crime were accessories at the fact; those who assisted after the perpetration were accessories after the fact.

After a time the common law courts came to think that the accessory at the fact was involved in most crimes about as deeply as the actual perpetrator. So, the courts dropped this classification and called this criminal a principal in the second degree.

The outgrowth of this is that, under the common law and in most locations where the common law approach is now followed, we find the following classifications:

1. The perpetrator is a principal in the first degree.
2. Those who aid and abet the principal at the crime scene are principals in the second degree.
3. Aiders and abettors who were not present at the scene of the crime are accessories before the fact.
4. Criminal protectors after the crime are accessories after the fact.

In recent years the distinction between principals in the first degree and principals in the second degree has been abolished in most jurisdictions that follow the common law. Here, all principals are considered in the same class, unless special statutes apply.

The Principals

Under the common law approach, a principal is the perpetrator of the forbidden act. The principal commits the act that creates the crime. In the language of one court, a principal "is the perpetrator, the man that struck the actual blow." Under the explanation of another, "Principals . . . are those who commit the deed as perpetrating actors."

Multiple Principals. It is also worth noting here that a single case may involve two or more joint principals, as where all the members of a gang simultaneously attack the victim with knives. A somewhat similar situation is that of a gang of organized check forgers. In this type of case the facts may indicate that one of the conspirators is a master printer and prepares all the printed check blanks for the gang. Another member of the group supplies false signatures; a third actually passes the fraudulent checks. The courts say that there are three principals, all equally chargeable.

In those jurisdictions where a difference is recognized between a principal in the first degree and a principal in the second degree, a principal in the second degree is one who did not perpetrate the forbidden act but was at the scene of the crime aiding or abetting the perpetrator.

In a case illustrative of this situation, a man and a woman were both prosecuted for rape. The female defendant was the madam and owner of a house of prostitution. The victim, a comparatively naive farm girl, had been brought to the house of prostitution while drunk and had been forced to remain there after she became sober. When the victim declined to engage in an act of prostitution with a customer, the madam and another prostitute held the unwilling girl while the paying customer had sexual intercourse with her. The male customer was convicted as a principal in the first degree. The madam of the house of prostitution was convicted as a principal in the second degree. The prostitute who assisted the madam in holding the unwilling victim might also have been convicted as a principal in the second degree had she been available for trial.

Constructive Presence. Earlier we also said that a principal is the party who is present at the time the crime is committed and who actually perpetrates it. This seems to be somewhat inconsistent with the fact that the principal may be guilty of murdering the victim by planting a bomb, sending poisoned candy through the mail, or loosing a caged beast. In all these examples, the killer may not be physically there when the victim is killed. The killer's instrumentality for destruction is, however, present at the scene.

On the one hand, we say that the principal is present *constructively*, while in other cases we may say that the principal has taken action at long distance. Perhaps we could explain this better by saying that the forces set in motion by the principal are present at the scene of the crime. At times the courts and the lawyers say that they get involved in some legal "fictions." This is one of those fictions. The courts consistently agree that the principal must always be present at the crime scene, but that "he need not be an eye and ear witness to the deed." The principal must be actually or constructively present by setting in motion the chain of circumstances that cause the killing.[3]

The Innocent Agent. Let us also note that in any number of situations a guilty perpetrator may use an innocent agent or outside person in the perpetration of the criminal act.

For example, in a kidnapping case, one of the criminals seized a banker's son while the boy was en route home from school. Later the kidnapper called a taxi and instructed the driver to go to the banker's home and pick up a package for delivery. The taxi driver was told nothing regarding the contents of the package, which in fact contained the ransom money demanded by him. Since the cab driver had no knowledge of the kidnap plot, he was not guilty of a crime.

A similar example was exhibited in the case of a school stage play. Some of the action in the plot included a stage murder. As a part of the script the stage villain pulled a pistol, fired three shots at pointblank range; the victim

[3] Smith v. State, 21 Tex. App. 107, 17 S.W. 552.

fell gasping to the floor as the act ended. Unknown to anyone in the cast of the play, the actor who took the part of the victim had an enemy who was looking for an opportunity to murder him. The gun used in the play was normally loaded with blank ammunition. Confiding in no one, the man, bent on murder, managed to substitute live ammunition for the blank bullets.

Here again, we have an example of the principal using an innocent man to perpetrate the forbidden deed. The actor who pulled the trigger was not guilty of a crime since he had no mens rea, or criminal intent, as we shall see in a subsequent chapter.

Principals in the Second Degree. Where this classification is now used, we say that principals in the second degree are those who counsel, incite, command, or aid and abet the commission of a felony, and who are present at the scene when the crime occurs. A typical example of a principal in the second degree is the person who remains outside to keep guard or who drives the getaway car in a robbery.[4]

A guard who deliberately deserts the guard post while an associate burglarizes an unattended building also is regarded as a principal in the second degree, although the guard did nothing affirmative to further the crime. In a situation of this kind, the courts say that the guard was constructively present at the time of the burglary.

Accessories before the Fact

Those persons who command, counsel, incite, or aid and abet another to commit a crime, but who are not present at the time of the crime, are accessories before the crime. The term "incitement" includes any encouragement to the principal to commit the crime. It makes no difference whether the encouragement or urging is by words, by gestures, or by any other type of conduct.

The term "abetting" covers any type of assistance given the principal in committing the crime. It is not necessary for the principal even to realize that assistance was given. For example, without the principal's knowledge the bullets may have been removed in advance from the gun of a victim killed by the principal in a gunfight. Also, it is not necessary for the principal to know the identity of the accessory before the fact or to plan any illegal activity with that person. We must continue to keep in mind, however, that a person who helps a principal must have a criminal intent in order to be held liable as an accessory.

[4] Pierce v. State, 130 Tenn. 24, 168 S.W. 851.

Some of the borderline cases in this part of the law involve persons who sell merchandise to be used for criminal purposes. An example might be a hardware dealer who sells dynamite to a burglar who intends to crack a business safe. The fact that a sale has taken place does not necessarily cause the seller to be a party to the crime. This is true even when the seller suspects the intended unlawful use of the merchandise or has actual knowledge of it.

The principle generally followed by the courts here is: A seller who gives any kind of special assistance to the criminal plan must be held liable as an accessory before the fact. Concealing the facts of sale from authorities has been held to be the type of special assistance that establishes the seller's liability as an accessory.

Although they seem to be in the minority, a few verdicts have held a seller guilty as an accessory before the fact, when it was clear that the seller knew at the time of the sale that the customers intended to make use of the merchandise to commit a murder or other serious crime.

Another angle that should be considered involves *misprision of a felony*. As we shall see from the section on misprision, unlawful concealment or nondisclosure of a crime may be a crime in itself, under some circumstances. But, generally, mere observation of a crime places no obligation on the observer.

Withdrawal of an Accessory. An inciter, or one who urges another to crime, may escape responsibility for the crime of the principal, but only by completely withdrawing the urgings and by communicating that fact to the incited individual before the commission of the crime. If the inciter is not able to communicate with the principal before the perpetration of the crime, the inciter remains responsible, despite any repentance that took place before the crime was committed.

Withdrawal of an Abettor. It is also possible for an abettor to escape responsibility for abetting a crime. This is allowed, however, only when the abettor makes a clear renunciation of the intended crime and exerts a substantial effort to undo the harm, prior to the commission of the crime. Exactly what constitutes a substantial effort to withdraw by the abettor may vary from court to court. For example, the abettor who furnishes a machine gun to the principal as a murder weapon, but then wishes to withdraw, must warn the victim of the approaching danger, immediately alert police authorities, or try to wrest the weapon away from the principal. Merely asking the principal to drop the murderous plan is not enough to escape responsibility.

Accessories after the Fact

Anyone who comforts, assists, or receives another, knowing that that person has committed a felony, is an accessory after the fact. To be guilty, this accessory must have actual knowledge of the crime committed by the principal.

For example, under federal law, one who harbors a military deserter is guilty as an accessory after the fact (technically, the federal crime is called "harboring"). In cases of this kind, the FBI contacts all known relatives of the deserter, thus placing them on notice that they may be prosecuted for aiding the wanted individual.

Assistance provided by the accessory after the fact must be given personally to the felon, helping an escape from the law. Money to purchase food, shelter, or an airplane ticket is the kind of aid that is sufficient to charge the person who supplies the money as an accessory after the fact. If, however, the felon is given money to pass on to his nephew who wishes to enroll in an art class, this is not regarded as sufficient assistance by the courts.

In addition, a person who withholds information from investigating officers as to the felon's whereabouts is guilty as an accessory after the fact. This withholding of information must be coupled with the intent to aid the felon, however.

THE MODERN STATUTORY APPROACH

As previously pointed out, statutes in a number of states have replaced the old common law classification of parties to crimes. The trend is to lump principals, principals in the second degree, accessories before the fact, and accessories at the fact into one class, regarding all as principals.[5]

For example, the California Penal Code, section 31, provides:

> All persons concerned in the commission of a crime, whether it be a felony or misdemeanor, and whether they directly commit the act constituting the offense, or aid and abet in its commission, or, not being present, have advised and encouraged its commission and all per-

---

[5] In discussions regarding parties involved in crime, lawyers, newspapermen, and police officers sometimes use the word "accomplice." This is a broad lay term which generally describes anyone who knowingly and voluntarily unites with another in the commission of a crime. As commonly understood, it includes accessories of all kinds and may also refer to principals. In short, an accomplice refers to anyone involved with others in a crime. Conspirators in the crime of conspiracy are parties to that crime; in a number of states they are principals; in common terminology they are often called accomplices in the conspiracy (see Chapter 7 for details on conspirators and conspiracy).

sons counseling, advising, or encouraging children under the age of fourteen years, lunatics or idiots, to commit any crime, or who, by fraud, contrivance, or force, occasion the drunkenness of another for the purpose of causing him to commit any crime, or who, by threats, menaces, command, or coercion, compel another to commit any crime, are principals in any crime so committed.

Statutes similar to the California enactment have been the law in a number of states for many years. The public sometimes appears surprised, however, to discover that aiders and abettors are regarded as principals in these states. Considerable hue and cry was presented in the national press when citizens discovered that Angela Davis was regarded as a principal in her prosecution in California in 1971. The prosecution made no claim that Davis was present at a shootout at the Marin courthouse in which the trial judge was killed. Instead, the prosecution alleged that she had previously supplied one of the murder weapons to a principal for use at the murder scene.

Accessories after the Fact Are in a Separate Class, under Either the Common Law or the Modern Statutory Approach

Accessories after the fact, as we have seen, were placed in a separate class under the common law approach. This same distinction has continued intact in practically all jurisdictions, including California.

Under the California statute every person who, with knowledge that the principal has committed a felony, gives aid or comfort to that individual with the intent that the felon may avoid arrest, trial, conviction, or punishment is an accessory after the fact. An accessory after the fact is still in a separate category from that of the principal.[6]

In Misdemeanor and Treason Cases There Are Only Principals

We must emphasize, however, that classifications as to principals and accessories apply only in felony cases.

The common law rule has always been that all parties to treason are principals. Apparently, treason was judged so serious that individuals involved in only a minor way expected to receive the full fury of the king's wrath. The early courts, dominated by the king, backed this policy. Courts have rendered very few treason decisions in modern times, but this probably is still the law in all jurisdictions.

Under the common law all participants in misdemeanor cases are princi-

[6] CALIFORNIA PENAL CODE, sec. 32.

pals.[7] No criminal penalty of any kind is provided for aiding, comforting, or assisting one who has committed a misdemeanor.

PROSECUTIVE AND POLICE PROBLEMS IN DISTINGUISHING BETWEEN PRINCIPALS AND ACCESSORIES

Also, under the ancient common law idea it was not possible to convict anyone as an aider, abettor, or accessory after the fact until a principal had first been convicted. The reasoning was: no principal, no crime. In other words, how is it possible to convict an individual for something that did not happen in the first place?

The old common law approach, of course, often works a hardship on the prosecution in those jurisdictions where it is followed. If the principal should die before the time of the trial, then an accessory cannot be prosecuted, regardless of the certainty of his guilt.

This old idea may yet be followed at times; but under modern practice the trend is toward conviction of a principal in the second degree, even before the trial of the principal in the first degree, or even when the principal has been acquitted.

This procedure has been aided by statute in some states, as in California where the penal code provides:

> **An accessory to the commission of a felony may be prosecuted, tried and punished, though the principal may be neither prosecuted nor tried, and though the principal may have been acquitted.[8]**

Under the California statute each person involved may be prosecuted as if he or she were the individual who actually did the unlawful act and may be convicted upon proof either of having done the act or of having aided and abetted or advised and encouraged its commission.

In practically all states it is also clear that not all coprincipals (two or more people charged as principals) need be prosecuted.[9]

In states that follow the common law idea of principals and accessories, the investigating officer and the prosecuting attorney must also understand that the accused is either a principal or an accessory. The prosecution must charge each defendant as one or the other. In fact, the case may be lost on trial when the facts show that the defendant who is charged as a principal is really only an accessory. On the other hand, when the evidence satisfies the court that an accused who is charged as an accessory is in fact a principal, the case may be thrown out for this reason.

[7] Boggs v. Commonwealth, 218 Ky. 782, 292 S.W. 324.
[8] CALIFORNIA PENAL CODE, sec. 972.
[9] People v. Latona, 2 Cal. 2d 714.

In order to convict, the prosecution must show that the accused is guilty as charged. While a defendant may be charged as both a principal and an accessory on separate counts of the same prosecutive indictment, is is a rule of law that the prosecution may be required to specify upon which count it will rely, prior to the time the case is finally submitted to the jury.

This, of course, is being very technical, but it is the way the courts require the prosecution to proceed. So, the entire case against one defendant may be dismissed because of carelessness in the way the papers are drawn up by the prosecuting attorney or because of a police mistake in the facts as to whether the available evidence makes the defendant a principal or an accessory.

CITED CASES

Boggs v. Commonwealth, 218 Ky. 782, 292 S.W. 324.
People v. Carlson, 177 Cal. App. 2d 201.
People v. Latona, 2 Cal. 2d 714.
People v. Volla, 156 Cal. App. 2d 128.
People v. Wooten, 162 Cal. App. 2d 804.
Pierce v. State, 130 Tenn. 24, 168 S.W. 851.
Smith v. State, 21 Tex. App. 107, 17 S.W. 552.

CHAPTER 6
The Basic Elements (Requirements) of Crime

Those basic elements necessary to a crime are found within the corpus delicti of that crime. The Latin legal term "corpus delicti" may be roughly translated to mean "the body of the crime." Thus, incomplete knowledge of the criminal law sometimes leads to confusion regarding this term. It is the word "body" that causes the problem. Quite frequently individuals believe and say that an accused cannot be convicted of murder unless the body of the victim is found. According to these people, the body of the deceased is the corpus delicti, or body, of the crime. This interpretation is a misconception, at best.

The corpus delicti of a crime means the total of the individual essentials that together spell out a violation of the criminal law. It is the essence of the criminal wrong. Sometimes the corpus delicti is defined as the substance of a crime, the material proof of the commission of a crime, or the prima facie evidence of a crime.

EVERY CRIME MUST CONTAIN A CORPUS DELICTI

We should also note that the term "corpus delicti" refers to every type of crime, not simply to murder or to other crimes that somehow involve a human body. For instance, the corpus delicti in an arson case might well be: (1) a dwelling house, (2) evidence that the house was burned, and (3) evidence that this burning was the result of someone's criminal act.

In every case where a conviction is expected, the prosecution must prove:

1. That a specific kind of legally forbidden harm or injury has occurred.
2. That the criminal act of some individual caused this harm—no accident being involved.
3. That the accused person was the particular individual who caused this criminality (in other words, identity must be established).

In practically all instances a crime consists of a group of elements or requirements (corpus delicti) laid down by common law understanding or by the statute that made it a crime. Every one of these elements must be proved, or the statute has not been violated—no corpus delicti exists.

Recovery of the Victim's Body May Not Be Essential to Prove the Corpus Delicti in a Murder Prosecution

Of course, if the victim's body is never recovered in a murder case, the police officer and the prosecutor may experience difficulty in proving that a murder actually took place.

One very unusual Texas statute goes so far as to require the recovery of the body of the deceased, or an identifiable portion of it, prior to conviction for murder. This statute however, is unique.[1]

Disregarding the Texas situation, the courts in almost all other jurisdictions do not seem to require the recovery of the body in a murder case. This was decided very early in the English cases and has been consistently followed in the United States. In explanation, one famous American judge, Justice Storey, explained that requiring the prosecution to produce the victim's body in a murder case merely serves to protect some murderers, especially those on the high seas where the victim's body may be thrown into the sea. Recent American cases have continued this same idea.[2]

Let us emphasize, however, that proof of the mysterious disappearance of the supposed murder victim is never sufficient in itself to prove the

[1] VERNON'S ANNUAL (Tex.) P. C., art. 1204. See Puryear v. State, 28 Tex. Crim. 73, 11 S.W. 929.
[2] State v. Lung, 70 Wash. 2d 365, 423 P. 2d 72; People v. Scott, 176 Cal. App. 2d 458, appeal dismissed in 364 U.S. 471, 81 S. Ct. 245 (1960).

corpus delicti. Some other evidence must exist, coupled with the unexplained disappearance.

Some of the early English and American cases prove how dangerous it is to assume that an individual has been murdered when no body has been found; the victim has merely dropped out of sight.

In an early English case, a servant, John Perry, was sent to look for one Harrison, who had not returned from an assignment to collect some rent money. Perry himself also failed to return when expected, and an extensive search was undertaken for both of the missing men. Perry was subsequently located, wandering aimlessly about; but Harrison was not to be found. Later a hat, a comb, and some other personal belongings of Harrison's were located, along with what appeared to be particles of blood on the hatband.

Because of his peculiar behavior, suspicion soon centered on Perry. The latter at first maintained that he was not involved in wrongdoing, but he later advised authorities that Harrison had been killed in a robbery by Perry's brother Richard. After disclosing this information, John Perry then made statements implicating his mother and himself in the robbery.

Richard Perry and the mother of the Perry boys consistently denied all guilt, insisting that John Perry's confession was a complete fabrication. Although Harrison's body was never found and no additional evidence of any kind was forthcoming, John Perry continued to repeat his version of murder during a robbery. After a trial, all three members of the Perry family were executed (1661).

Two or three years later, Harrison reappeared, claiming that he had been kidnapped by unknown persons and transported to Turkey. He maintained that he had been held as a slave until he was able to escape and return to his home. The real facts surrounding Harrison's disappearance were never completely resolved, but some observers believed that he had faked the kidnapping to cover his embezzlement of the collected rent money. At any rate, three persons obviously were hanged for a crime that never occurred.

A somewhat similar case involving two brothers who were convicted for the supposed murder of Russell Colvin was reported to authorities in colonial America. The accused brothers, Stephen and Jesse Boorn, were both found guilty after Stephen Boorn had made a detailed confession to authorities that implicated both himself and his brother. Fortunately, however, this case had a different outcome from the Perry affair because the supposed victim reappeared in the community in time to prevent the scheduled execution of the Boorn brothers.[3]

---

[3] The trial of Stephen and Jesse Boorn, 6 Am. St. Tr. 73 (1819).

Confessions Out of Court; the Corpus Delicti Rule

As a result of trials like the Perry and Boorn cases, the courts in England and the United States developed a legal principle that has become widely known in criminal law as the "corpus delicti rule." What this means is that out-of-court confessions or admissions of an accused will not be admitted in court as evidence until the corpus delicti of the crime has been established, or at least a prima facie showing of it has been made through other evidence. The result of this, of course, is that the prosecution must present more evidence than the bare confession of the accused; otherwise, no conviction is possible.

A few states, like Hawaii and Massachusetts, have taken an opposite view, allowing introduction in court of the defendant's out-of-court admissions even before all the elements of the corpus delicti have been proved. Even in these states, however, the admission is permitted only after it appears to the court that the confession was freely and voluntarily given.

On the basis of past cases, one might expect that practically all courts outside of Hawaii and Massachusetts will continue to insist on following the corpus delicti rule. A distinction that should be made here, however, is that the corpus delicti rule does not apply to confessions made by the accused while on the witness stand or while in open court.[4] Or, when the accused makes partial admissions in the courtroom, these admissions will be accepted only as proof of that part of the corpus delicti. If the accused pleads guilty in the courtroom, this statement is taken as proof of guilt. Of course, this can come only after the accused has been advised of the right to the services of an attorney.

Apparently, the reasoning of the courts is that an out-of-court confession might have been obtained by force or by trick. Conditions that may result in this type of tainted confession do not ordinarily exist when the accused makes an admission in open court. Therefore, the courts think that such a confession is trustworthy. Following this same reasoning, some courts have gone so far as to state that a confession made in open court is the most reliable type of available evidence. While this may be true in many cases, we find no certainty that the confession may not be the imaginings of a deranged individual like John Perry, whether the admissions are made in court or outside it.

[4] Manning v. United States, 215 F. 2d 945.

Making Sure the Accused Is Advised of His Rights Prior to Confession

For hundreds of years criminal law in both England and the United States has declared that an involuntary confession may not be introduced into evidence against the accused in any criminal case. By tests of the courts, a confession is not voluntary if the accused is convinced to sign it or to verbally confess because of any form of physical or mental force, coercion, threat or duress.[5] Also, a confession is not allowed if it is obtained under the assurance that leniency will be extended by the sentencing judge.

While always excluding confessions that appear to be given under conditions of mental or physical force, the Supreme Court of the United States in recent years has also excluded a number of confessions that seemed to have substantial guarantees of both voluntariness and trustworthiness. This action, developed under the so-called NcNabb-Mallory rule, is based not on involunatry confessions but on the court's supervisory authority over the lower federal courts and court officers.[6] The idea of the McNabb-Mallory rule is that a confession may not be used in evidence against an accused in a federal case if the accused was not first taken promptly before a committing magistrate.

The Supreme Court of the United States has followed the McNabb and Mallory decisions in other cases of far-reaching police significance: *Escobedo*[7] and *Miranda*.[8] The effect of the Supreme Court decisions in these opinions has been that a confession may not be used in a trial against the accused unless police authorities take certain steps prior to interviewing a suspect. These steps include the following advice to the suspect:

1. You have an absolute right to remain silent and to say nothing.
2. If you do talk, anything you say may be used in court against you.
3. You have the right to an attorney, including the right to have the attorney present during questioning.
4. If you are unable to hire an attorney, a lawyer will be appointed for you.

[5] Brown v. Mississippi, 297 U.S. 278, 56 S. Ct. 461. This point of law, along with others presented here, is highly abbreviated. The matter of admissibility of confessions should be explored more extensively in the cases and texts dealing with the constitutional criminal law.
[6] McNabb v. United States, 318 U.S. 322, 63 S. Ct. 608; and Mallory v. United States, 354 U.S. 449, 77 S. Ct. 1356.
[7] Escobedo v. Illinois, 378 U.S. 478, 84 S. Ct. 1758.
[8] Miranda v. Arizona, 384 U.S. 436, 86 S. Ct. 1602.

Corroborating the Confession; Proving Corpus Delicti by Circumstantial Evidence

The courts in this country also consistently follow the rule that a conviction will not be allowed on the uncorroborated out-of-court confession of the accused, as noted earlier. We find, however, a lack of uniformity in the court decisions as to just what is needed to supply this corroboration. Some jurisdictions tend to accept as adequate corroboration any *side evidence* that reflects the trustworthiness of the confession. Perhaps the majority of the courts, however, take the approach that the prosecution must present independent evidence of the corpus delicti of the crime.

   In practically all states the courts allow the corpus delicti to be proved by any kind of relevant evidence. While we find some exceptions, generally, the corpus delicti of any criminal violation also may be proved solely by circumstantial evidence.[9]

The Three Basic Parts to Every Crime

The corpus delicti of every true crime is made up of three basic parts or elements. If any one of these requirements is absent, no crime exists. These elements are:

1. Some type of mens rea (criminal state of mind, or criminal intent).
2. Some kind of actus rea (the forbidden or prohibited act).
3. Coming together of the criminal intent and the criminal act in point of time, the criminal act resulting from the criminal intent.

THE CRIMINAL STATE OF MIND OR CRIMINAL INTENT (MENS REA)

The first requirement for a crime is a criminal state of mind. The Latin term most frequently used by the courts and lawyers is "mens rea." In essence, mens rea is a universal principle of modern American criminal law that "a crime has not been committed when the mind of the person doing the act is innocent."

   To take an actual case, a worker in a factory was not liked by her coworkers. Without the knowledge of this worker, another employee at the plant deliberately stuck a tool into this worker's lunch pail to get her in trouble with management. When the tool was found in the lunch pail by the company guard at the plant exit, the worker was held for theft. Eventually all the facts came to light, and the pending prosecution was dismissed by the court. The judge stated that the worker had no intent to

[9] People v. Moore, 48 Cal. 2d 541.

steal the tool. In fact, she had no knowledge of its presence in her lunch pail. In other words, the judge pointed out that the accused had no guilty state of mind, thus no corpus delicti was present.

In situations of this type, investigating police officers should be able to recognize the difference between an accident and a crime. Of course, in some situations it is not possible to distinguish, certainly not before outside investigation is undertaken. In any event, the decision as to prosecution rests upon the prosecution attorney.

A case that illustrates this difference is one in which a farmer accidentally injured another man in a farming accident. At the time the harm was done, visibility was very poor because of a heavy cloud of swirling dust that surrounded the farm machinery. Later the farmer who had caused the harm learned that the injured man was his sworn enemy. That night at a local bar, he expressed considerable pleasure that he had done his enemy in. Since the farmer who had caused the injury had no guilty state of mind at the time of the accident, no crime occurred.

In another case, a goat jumped into the back of a pickup truck driven by a woman who was visiting a neighbor. The driver of the truck did not realize that the goat had gotten into her vehicle. She discovered the animal when she arrived home. Here again, the court found no theft, since no criminal intent was present at the time the goat was carried away.

The situation would have been completely different, however, if the driver of the pickup had formed an intent to keep the goat after she had discovered the animal in her vehicle; the necessary criminal intent would have clearly been present at that time.

It may be worth pointing out, also, that questions of fact, such as whether the accused had a criminal intent in the goat case, is a matter for the jury to decide at the time of trial. The judge gives instructions and decides whether the law is being properly applied to the facts. If the jury decides that the accused had no criminal intent, then the judge must declare that, as a matter of law, no criminal violation has occurred.

The Kind of Mens Rea Differs with the Type of Crime; General Intent

In describing criminal intent, the courts have said that this intent is "the act or fact of proposing," "a design, resolve, or determination of the mind," and that "it is the necessary thinking to accomplish the criminal result."

For most crimes, the courts also say that a general criminal intent is all that is required. In this thay mean that the accused need not necessarily intend to violate the law, to harm the person or property of another, or even to do anything wrongful. All that is required is that the accused shall

not necessarily True

have the intent to do the prohibited act. In other words, the criminal intent requirement is satisfied if the accused actually meant to do what he or she did. This is general intent.

jury question

The Requirement of Specific Criminal Intent, as Distinguished from General Criminal Intent

An old case, decided in 1889, said that the term "criminal intent" was impossible of definition in such a manner as to make it apply to all crimes, because of the wide variation in mental elements of different crimes. What the court meant was that some crimes require more than a general criminal intent in order to satisfy the mental requirement.

For example, some crimes consist not merely of performing a specific act but of performing it with a specific intent in mind. An excellent example of this is burglary. The average person thinks of burglary as the unlawful breaking into a house or business establishment. From a technical standpoint, burglary involves more than this. Mere breaking and entering is not enough. Burglary is the breaking into a building or dwelling house with the intent (beforehand) of committing a felony (in some states a misdemeanor) inside the building. The intended crime to be committed inside the building may be any sort of felony (or misdemeanor). A typical situation involves an intention to break in to steal property inside the building. The intention might just as well be to break in with the preconceived idea of killing the owner of the premises or placing a bomb inside a bank.

Apart from the idea of general intent, to be guilty of burglary the accused must have done something more in mental planning than forming a general criminal intent. The act of breaking in is sufficient to show that the accused intended to enter, but additional evidence is needed to indicate that a specific crime inside was planned. A cold homeless woman might break in to get out of a storm, but it takes a more specific intent to convict her on a burglary charge.

On the other hand, our homeless woman, after breaking and entering to obtain shelter, might form the intent to steal something she found inside the building. Clearly, the necessary criminal intent for theft does exist, but the required criminal intent for breaking and entering is absent.

In cases of specific intent, for crimes such as burglary many jurisdictions hold that intoxication, though it is voluntary, eliminates the capacity to form the specific intent. Thus, the accused cannot be found guilty of burglary, but of a lesser general-intent crime. So, for example, the defendant might be charged with breaking and entering with the intent to commit a felony or misdemeanor but plead that he was highly intoxicated at the time and was, therefore, unable to form the specific intent. In this case, in some states he might be found guilty of the lesser general-intent crime of trespass.

As a practical matter, of course, every person who breaks and enters a building may claim that he or she did not have the necessary specific criminal intent for burglary. In situations like this the jury must decide the intruder's actual mens rea. This decision will be based on all the attendant circumstances, on any conversation that might have occurred, and on whether a crime was actually committed after the breaking and entering occurred.

In addition to burglary, some other crimes require more than a general criminal intent to satisfy the courts. For example, in robbery the accused must specifically intend to take property or money from the person or from the presence of the owner or the owner's representative. At the time of trial, the jury is entitled to conclude that the specific mental intent did exist, taking account of all known circumstances.

Illegal abortion and larceny also require a specific criminal intent. These will be explored in more detail in our later study of specific crimes.

With respect to the crime of battery, however, some courts require only a general mens rea, holding that a voluntary blow struck against the victim is sufficient. Other courts require that the injury necessary to convict must be committed by an individual in an "angry, revengeful, or rude" mental state.

Still, in some situations the courts look to the working of the statutes to decide whether a general criminal intent is sufficient or whether something more specific is required. Generally, if the statute describes the criminal act as "voluntary," "willfull," "intentional," or "deliberate," the courts rather uniformly hold that the general type of criminal intent is all that is necessary.

Moreover, some statutes define the prohibited act in terms of a *malicious* one, rather than by use of words such as voluntary, willful, intentional, or deliberate. When this is done, the courts are not uniform in their decisions. Some say that a narrow, specific mental intent must be present, with a deep-seated animosity on the part of the accused. Others say that only a general criminal intent is adequate.

Knowledge of Certain Pertinent Facts May Also Be Required, in Addition to General Intent

We also find some types of crimes that require the accused to have some mental knowledge of certain pertinent facts, along with his general criminal intent. The legal expression for this is "scienter." — *guilty knowledge*

For example, a general type of criminal intent is sufficient to convict a person who passes a bad check, but the accused must also have knowledge that the check was not good. Most courts say that in the type of situation where scienter (notice) is required, it is not necessary that the accused shall have absolute knowledge. The test generally is whether a reasonable person should have known from all the circumstances in the case; a general mens rea is sufficient.

If an accused, prosecuted for selling fraudulent stock certificates, knows that an accomplice printed them on a home printing press, then a general criminal intent is sufficient to satisfy the courts.

Presuming the Natural and Probable Consequences of the Accused's Acts

We all know that the investigating officer or trial jury cannot look into the mind of the accused. All that can be done is to draw conclusions about the mental intent of the accused from what was said, the acts committed, and the attendant circumstances or evidence from which reasonable conclusions may be drawn.

The courts also consistently agree that since we cannot look into a person's mind, we must be bound by the outward manifestations of mind—by acts. Except when mentally unbalanced or acting under duress, an individual must be responsible for his or her own acts. Therefore, an important legal principle is that a person "is presumed to have intended the natural and probable consequences of his acts." Thus, in many cases the courts say that the mental intent is presumed from the act itself. The accused, whose intent was otherwise, must convince the jury of the true mental state behind the act.

A case in point is one in which the accused saw a neighbor, whom he disliked, passing down the street. Upon observing this individual, he went into his garage, selected a section of two-inch steel pipe, and used it to strike his neighbor on the head. The neighbor died as a result of the blows from the heavy pipe; a murder prosecution resulted. When brought to trial, the accused admitted that he had a mental intent to commit an assault and battery on the victim. He denied, however, that he had the necessary criminal intent required for murder. He further maintained that he never intended to kill the victim. The accused testified that he "just wanted to rough the deceased up a bit, not to seriously hurt him with the pipe."

In this case the courts said that the accused intended the "natural and probable consequences of his act." If the blow was a little too hard and killed the victim, it made no difference in terms of mens rea, since the accused meant to do that which he actually did. The only difference then would be in whether a charge of assault and battery or a charge of murder was brought against the accused.

In another situation, a bar owner found a customer "playing around" with his girl friend. He then tied up the customer at gunpoint, intending to shoot holes through the victim's ear lobes "to teach him not to fool around with someone else's girl." The bar owner slipped a little bit when he fired the second shot, and one bullet went through the victim's neck, causing death. When the matter came to trial, the court said that death was a reasonable consequence of shooting at another with a gun and that the bar owner had the intent necessary both to assault and to murder.

In a similar case, a man placed poison in his companion's glass when she was not looking. Claiming that he put only half a lethal dose in the glass, the accused argued that his intent had been to cure her of "running around by giving her one hell of a stomach ache."

Arguing that the accused had no real intent to kill, the attorney for the defense pointed out that his client had carefully measured out only half of the poison recognized as a lethal dose. Another argument presented by the defense attorney was that the victim was pregnant, out of wedlock. He claimed that, had she not been pregnant, the victim would have had the physical stamina to survive the poison; and, had the accused known that she was pregnant, he would not have placed the poison in the victim's glass.

Brushing aside all these arguments, the court pointed out that the accused was responsible for the results he achieved, even though he miscalculated. The legal test seems to be: A defendant who intends harm is criminally responsible for whatever harm results, even though it exceeds the original expectations.

In some situations, considerable force may be required to kill the victim of the crime. In other instances, comparatively little force may be needed. For example, a small cut might result in death if the victim's blood does not clot properly. The courts consistently say that the accused individual takes the victim in whatever condition the victim happens to be.

In still another case of this type, a student activist planted a bomb in a college building one night, under the impression that no one would be in the building. His claimed purpose was not murder, but to "shake up the establishment." In an effort to avoid harm to the occupants of the building, he called the police station and warned that a bomb was to go off in the building in a short time. The police were not able to warn the janitor in the building in sufficient time. The bomber had miscalculated, and the timing device set off the blast while the call was being received at the police switchboard. Here again, the court said that the accused intended the natural and probable consequences of his act.

In a hypothetical case, we can suppose that an activist planted a bomb in a bank. To continue the facts, we may further suppose that she then called the institution and warned all the occupants. The president of the bank, who was something of an individualist, reacted by saying: "To hell with the

activists and the hippies! It's my bank and no one is going to run me out."
The argument can be made, of course, that the banker was asking to be
killed; but we can safely predict that the courts would recognize sufficient
criminal intent on the part of the accused, who would be responsible for
the natural and probable consequences of her act.

Has to be similar outcomes

The Legal Principle of Transferred Intent

In addition, when an individual intends one criminal wrong but accom-
plishes another, the law says that the necessary criminal intent for the
second act is present. In other words, if the accused had the necessary
criminal intent to club one person but missed and struck an innocent
bystander, then the law says that the criminal intent transfers to the innocent bystander.

This is the so-called legal idea or doctrine of *transferred intent*. The
idea does seem to reach a correct result, affording some protection to
innocent persons in that it holds individuals responsible for uncontrolled
physical violence.

However, this idea is not applied by the courts to all types of cases.
Certain serious crimes such as murder, arson, robbery, rape, and burglary
involve a strong element of human danger. Thus, the courts say that when
the original intent is to commit one of these dangerous felonies, the original intent will be transferred to an innocent victim. If, for example, the
accused discharged a gun, intending to kill an enemy, the law declares that
he had the necessary criminal intent if his aim proved bad and he killed his
best friend instead.[10] As said by one court, "The crime is exactly what it
would have been if the person against whom the intent to kill was directed
had been in fact killed."[11]

Besides the restriction that the original intent must be to commit a
dangerous felony, we find still another. The idea can be applied only if the
act that was actually committed requires the same kind of mens rea that
was present in the first place. For example, in one case the accused fired a
gun at an enemy; however, the bullet missed the mark and set a nearby
haystack on fire. The haystack was adjacent to a dwelling house; the house
caught fire and burned. A specific mental intent is required for arson, while
a general criminal intent to shoot an enemy was not transferred to the
burning. A conviction for attempted murder was sustained, but the court
did not find the proper intent for an arson conviction.

In deciding cases of this kind, the courts look to the original intent on
the part of the individual who performed the act in question. If, for exam-

---

[10] People v. Fruci, 67 N.Y.S. 2d 512.
[11] People v. Siplinger, 252 Cal. App. 2d 817, 60 Cal. Rptr. 914.

ple, a parent is moderately punishing a wayward son, no transferred intent occurs when she accidentally strikes a stranger who is passing by at the time. The parent, here, has not committed an illegal act in administering punishment and has no unlawful purpose insofar as the wayward son is concerned. Since no criminal intent exists at the onset, no guilty intent is transferred.

The Criminal's Motive Is Immaterial from the Standpoint of Criminal Intent

Something that should be considered, however, is the criminal's motive. In many instances we find that the criminal intent, or mens rea, and the criminal's motive are not one and the same thing. Putting it quite bluntly, one prosecuting attorney pointed out, "The law doesn't care what your motive is—the law looks only to the criminal intent."

Motive, Generally. In this regard, the courts consistently say that the prosecution is only required to prove by clear evidence that the accused committed the necessary act. Then it is presumed that the accused intended the natural and probable consequences of the act. Failure of the prosecution to turn up a motive is not a defect in its case; this is immaterial.

In an armed robbery, for example, if two witnesses testify that John Smith was the man who held up a service station and another witness presents evidence that Smith was in possession of marked bills obtained in the robbery, then the case against Smith is very strong. The prosecutor need not be concerned with Smith's reason for "pulling the job," even though he may learn that Smith's girl friend was putting considerable pressure on him for money; but, if a motive can be proved or even implied by the evidence presented at the time of the trial, it may be helpful to the prosecution. When the investigating police officer can discover a motive, this fact may be considered by the jury as a motivating factor that induced the accused to perform the criminal act.

Commendable Motive It is also immaterial that the motive, in and of itself, may be very commendable. For example, you might steal from a grocery store where you work and take some of the food to the neighbor's starving children. The motive is admirable. Nevertheless, the action in taking the food constitutes a crime. One legal scholar who wrote on this subject said: "No motive, regardless of how it appears to be justified to the defendant, can serve as a defense to a crime. A person may decide to overthrow the government, believing that his act is not treasonous because his desire is to set up a better one. Regardless, this activity is treason."

In a recent case, one that received considerable newspaper publicity, two elderly sisters worked as tellers in a Midwestern bank. Together they embezzled more than two million dollars in bank deposits and used this money to keep an orphanage in operation when it seemed that the institution would be forced to close its doors. The defense offered by the attorney for the two women was that they received nothing for themselves. This, of course, was a motive and not a defense; both were found guilty. The use made of the embezzled money was, however, a matter to be considered by the judge in determining the severity of the sentences of the two.

In one case, a husband who was waving a gun chased his wife into the street. Concentrating on the husband's gun, the unfortunate wife was struck and killed by an oncoming car. The driver of the car was not held, but the husband was convicted of murder. The courts usually say that the accused is criminally responsible, if the accused's acts place the victim in a position where the risk of harm is substantially increased.

Multiple Motives. Sometimes cases occur in which the accused appears to have had more than one motive and may, likewise have more than one criminal intent. In one case, a prisoner was in jail, awaiting trial on a serious charge. He was unable to make bond. The jail in question was a small antiquated building, located in a semirural area. Walls of the cells were made of wood; the prisoner set fire to the building, intending to escape by burning one of the walls or by escaping when the jailer opened the cell door. The fire was eventually put out by the jailor, but the prisoner was not able to make his escape. Thereafter he was prosecuted for arson. At the time of trial, he admitted his action in setting the fire but claimed that his criminal intent was merely to escape from jail. Apparently, the accused made this claim because the penalty for escape was not as serious as that for arson. The court said that the prisoner had the necessary criminal intent for jailbreaking (escape), but that setting fire to the building was merely incidental to his plan and the accused did not have the necessary intent to commit arson.

The court in this case was apparently confused. The decision reached is in conflict with the legal principle we have previously considered: The accused is presumed to have intended the natural and probable consequences of his or her acts. Exactly this same situation has occurred in a number of cases; other courts have consistently said that the prisoner had the intent to set the jail on fire, and therefore had the necessary specific criminal intent. The accused's motive in setting the fire was to escape from jail, and maybe in the above case the court failed to distinguish between the prisoner's motive and his intent. In most such cases, the courts agree that the prisoner had the necessary mental intent for both escape and arson.

The decision in this case does not represent the law. Quite frankly, it was described to show that our courts reach different results on the same set of fact, and that we must recognize that the human element can never be completely eliminated from the criminal law.

Absolute Liability, or Strict Liability, Crimes

— vicarious liability
intent not needed

Earlier the statement was made that no true crime can exist without a criminal state of mind or criminal intent. However, legislatures have the power to do away with the required criminal state of mind and to punish individuals for their acts alone, without regard to mental intent. This power is restricted to matters within the *police powers,* or the so-called *public welfare offenses.* In general, this means laws that regulate health, education, safety, sanitation, and use of the streets, with other regulatory statutes that promote the general welfare of society.

On the other hand, legislatures do not have the power to eliminate the mens rea requirement from *true crimes,* those violations not based on the regulatory powers of the government. Statutes passed by legislatures, purporting to do away with the required criminal intent in these crimes, have been held unconstitutional.

Violations for which the legislatures have eliminated the mens rea requirement are called *absolute liability,* or *strict liability,* crimes. In other words, someone must be held responsible for every violation of this type. An act committed in good faith, or as an innocent mistake, cannot be used to avoid guilt.

Additionally, legislative bodies have had good reasons to pass laws that impose strict liability in some types of situations. Recent development of automobiles, airplanes, and mechanical devices has greatly increased the physical dangers of everyday life. Taking into account these dangers, many states have adopted statutory regulations that involve negligent handling of machinery or automobiles. "The purpose of such laws is," according to one court, "to require a degree of diligence for the protection of the public which shall render the violation almost impossible." This, of course, may be an overstatement.

Common situations of this type include prosecutions for manslaughter following a death in a drunk driving accident, excessive speed by the driver who hits and kills a pedestrian in a crosswalk, or the motorist who unintentionally runs a red light. In each of these cases, the accused has no real intent to commit manslaughter. The legislature is well aware, however, that if we do not have some type of regulation for situations of this kind, death rates, as a result of such activity, will soon get out of hand.

In the kinds of cases above, we find criminal negligence. In still another class of cases, the courts declare absolute criminal liability regardless of negligence. Often the legislature thinks that laws should be passed to protect the young, defenseless, and inexperienced people in our society. For instance, some young females may not have the judgment of older more mature women. Therefore, most states have their so-called statutory rape laws providing that a female under the age of consent (usually eighteen) cannot give her permission to sexual intercourse. While the statutory rape laws may be included in that part of the criminal code that prohibits the old common law crime of rape, we do observe a difference. From a legal standpoint, the prohibition against statutory rape is within the police powers of the state, including the power to regulate houses of prostitution and similar establishments.

Of course, other differences are obvious in the two kinds of rape. The type prohibited by the common law is an inherently dangerous crime, frequently resulting in death or great bodily harm to the victim. This danger is not so likely in statutory rape cases.

Statutory rape and bigamy have both been traditionally regarded as absolute liability offenses. For instance, an individual's second marriage, when the first mate was alive, was regarded as bigamy, regardless of the sincerity of the accused in the belief that the first mate was dead.

Similarly, the man was held to strict liability in a statutory rape case by most courts, notwithstanding the fact that he had made careful inquiry and mistakenly believed that the girl was over the age of consent.

Today, however, many courts think that they should not cause widespread imposition of strict criminal liability. If large numbers of respectable individuals without criminal intent are convicted, a loss of public support for the criminal laws may be the result. Accordingly, a growing number of courts are requiring the acquittal of defendants in bigamy and statutory rape cases when criminal intent is clearly absent.

Crimes of Possession

Other violations are classified as crimes of possession. For example, many states have statutes that declare the possession of a specific substance a violation of law. Prohibiting marijuana, whiskey, guns, dynamite, and dangerous drugs, practically all these statutes were passed to control or limit the use of potentially dangerous substances. Under these statutes possession is not usually an act but a state of mind or condition. The possessor must knowingly have such possession and control that a choice to return or terminate possession is possible. The intention of control is definitely involved to the extent that the possessor can exercise power over the prohibited substance.

In some states the criminal law has been violated when a person possessed dynamite without a permit for commercial use. Suppose an activist allows other members of his group to bring this explosive into his home. If he puts the forbidden sticks into a locker and retains the key, he has the type of possession which makes for guilt. In other words, he retains the ability to keep the dynamite or get rid of it.

Similarly, the police found a marijuana plant growing in a field behind an accused's home. This was in a lawful search of the property and in a state where possession of marijuana was forbidden by law. The plant in question was the only marijuana plant in the entire field; no evidence indicated that it has ever been cultivated or that anyone had recently been in that part of the field. Unless the owner of the field admitted that she knew of the existence of the plant, she could not be found guilty of possession. It is difficult to argue that she had possession when she did not even know of its existence.

Yet, along the same lines, suppose the marijuana plant had been in a flowerpot on the back porch and the soil was so damp that it was evident someone had been watering it. In addition, the flowerpot was inside a locked fence, inaccessible to anyone except the accused. Since evidence indicated that someone was tending the plant and since the area was under the exclusive control of the accused, the court might be expected to instruct the jury to make a finding as to whether the accused had legal possession of the forbidden plant. The key idea here seems to be control. In fact, exercising control over the forbidden article appears to be the legal requirement for the possession that is forbidden by the statutes.

The matter of proving control is most difficult in cases where the forbidden article or substance is actually in the custody of several people at the same time. This is typically true when two or more people are found in an automobile or room with marijuana or other illegal drugs. If two or more people are charged with possession, those who charge the defendants must be able to prove that two or more people controlled it.

THE CRIMINAL ACT

Actus Reus —the criminal act
Actus Rea

Previous discussion has noted that few people are so high-minded as to be able to exclude all criminal thoughts from entering their minds, under any and all circumstances. Since an act must be coupled with criminal intent, it is important to know specifically what constitutes the act.

The courts consistently say that an involuntary contraction of the muscles in the nature of a spasm is not an act. In legal terms, an act is an exertion of the human will manifested in the external world.

If an epileptic who is carrying a gun should suffer a seizure and pull the trigger, most courts hold that no act has occurred within the meaning of the criminal law. This is a muscular movement or spasm over which the actor has no mental control. Some crimes occur upon the happening of very simple, muscular acts, such as the hitting of another over the head in an assault with a baseball bat. On the other hand, some crimes require a series of two or more acts for their commission. Any movements committed by a person who is asleep, under anesthetic, or otherwise not in control are insufficient to meet the requirements of a criminal act.

Generally, however, the courts hold alcoholics and drug addicts responsible for acts committed under the influence of liquor or drugs. Although the courts do not regard such acts as specific-intent crimes, they do think that such persons have sufficient choice and control over their actions to prevent intoxication or addiction.

The courts also say that acts may be sufficient to constitute a crime, even though they are committed under fear or threats. The fact is that the actor's body moves as he or she intends it to move. We should point out, however, that at least some acts committed under duress or threats may be excused by the courts.

Criminal Responsibility for Passive Participation

In some types of cases, criminal responsibility may also result from mere passive participation in a criminal scheme. A typical case was one in which a woman desired an illegal abortion. The accused hired a moonlighting doctor, who anesthetized the pregnant woman and induced an abortion. The woman was found guilty on an abortion charge.

In a similar type of case, one of the parties allowed himself to be used in an illegal sex act. The court said, as in the abortion situation, that passive participation is sufficient to satisfy the requirement for the criminal act.

A third case in this category involved a violation of the federal draft laws. Under a federal statute persons registered for the draft were forbidden to cripple themselves to avoid service in the armed forces. In the case in question, a surgeon was hired to cut off the draft registrant's toes. When the draft evader was brought to trial, his attorney pointed out that the accused had been unconscious from the anesthetic. Because of this unconsciousness, he argued that the defendant could not have committed a criminal act. The federal court held that the draft registrant was guilty of setting up the scheme and that he engaged in a continuous course of conduct when he hired the doctor, got on the operating table, and allowed the operation.

Action May Be Required If a Duty Exists

For hundreds of years the law also has recognized that parents owe certain legal duties to children and that other duties exist between partners to a marriage. Some states require the parents to fulfil their duties because of statutory requirements, while others look to common law obligations. For example, in a state where medical aid was the obligation of the parents by statute, a child died because of medical inattention. The father had refused to obtain medical assistance because he was a member of a religious sect that did not believe in using the services of doctors. When prosecuted, the father made several claims. He urged that the criminal act was lacking. Claiming that his right to religious freedom was threatened, he also urged his religious feelings as a defense. A conviction resulted, the court pointing out that a criminal act is not a requirement for a crime where the duty to act is imposed by law.

In a hypothetical case, let us assume that the child died during the night, even before the parent realized that the youth was seriously ill. In a situation of this kind, the courts find no obligation on the part of the parent until such time as a reasonable parent should have realized the seriousness of the child's condition.

The husband, in most jurisdictions, also has a legal obligation to furnish support to his wife and minor children,[12] and may be criminally prosecuted for failure to do so.

Cases under the Police Powers
Where No Criminal Act Is Required

Interestingly enough, we find some cases in which no act of any kind is required. These are generally situations in which a duty is imposed by statute under the police powers of the state.

For example, the Supreme Court of the United States has repeatedly affirmed the right of state and municipal governments to enact laws protecting the general public by requiring sanitary conditions for the preparation and distribution of food, regulating the usage of dangerous chemicals and drugs, requiring safe working conditions, and regulating and controlling the operation of automobile traffic that endangers human life. These are, of course, only a few of the matters that may be regulated under the police powers.

In one case, a city health department found a dangerous amount of bacteria in bottled milk in the area. As soon as this was brought to the attention of the city council, a municipal ordinance was passed, requiring all bottled milk sold in that city to be capped twice. Under the procedure to be used, the milk was to be capped with an inner cardboard cap, then with an outer covering of foil. A mere failure to apply the double capping was all that was required for a criminal violation, provided the milk was sold. A positive act was not required. So here we have an example in which

[12] CALIFORNIA PENAL CODE, sec. 270.

the accused may neither have had a criminal intent nor have committed a positive criminal act. The simple failure to act constitutes the crime.

In an Illinois case, a city ordinance placed a regulatory duty on all railroads, stating that railroad crossings could not be blocked by trains for more than fifteen minutes. Challenged in the courts, this ordinance required neither criminal intent nor a criminal act. The railroad was not, however, successful in the appeal, since the court said that this was a situation that could be regulated under the state's police powers and that the regulation appeared reasonable.

When Is the Criminal Act Committed?

Sometimes a legal question arises as to just when the criminal act was committed. In the case of a drunken driver, for example, one might argue that the criminal act was committed: (1) when the accused took the first drink, (2) when the drinker became drunk, (3) when the drunk first drove, or (4) when the drinker hit and killed a pedestrian.

In this case, the violation is driving while drunk; therefore, the courts agree that the action occurred when the defendant caused the vehicle to move after drinking enough to be under the influence of liquor.

very question

CONCURRENCE OF THE ACT WITH THE CRIMINAL INTENT

must occur concurrently (mens rea + actus reus)

Let us also not forget the necessary causal connection or interlocking relationship between the criminal intent and the criminal act. Some writers say that the prohibited act must be the result of the criminal intent or that the criminal activity must be attributable to the criminal desire.

In one case, the accused set out to kill his enemy. Knowing her husband's bad temper, his wife cut across a field and headed him off. After considerable pleading she convinced the defendant to give up his criminal idea and make peace. About that time, however, the enemy appeared on the scene; and the accused agreed to show the enemy his new rifle. Through carelessness the rifle discharged and killed the victim.

Because of the trouble that had previously existed between the two men, the prosecutor filed a murder charge. If the facts were as stated, a murder charge could not be sustained. In most situations of this kind, the case boils down to a question of fact: The jury decides whether the accused actually gave up his intention to kill at the time the act happened. If we assume that the jury finds the accused had given up his criminal intent, the necessary elements of murder are lacking, since we find no concurrence of guilty intent and the prohibited act.

It might well be that a conviction for negligent homicide (manslaughter) could be sustained in this situation, depending on the state law (this possibility will be considered in our later study of manslaughter). At least, we find no concurrence of the criminal intent and the criminal act as required for murder, if the accused is to be believed.

Distance in time or geographical space between the accused's acts and the accomplished result may be of little consequence in such cases. This is illustrated by a murder case in which the defendant in California mailed a box of poisoned candy to an individual in Delaware. The candy arrived several days after it was mailed. Eventually the victim ate it and died. A conviction for murder resulted.

Cases in which the prosecution encounters difficulty are usually those where remoteness exists between the causal act and the eventual result. A causal relationship generally exists when the forbidden act is the logical cause of the injury. Usually the courts hold that the injury must result from the defendant's act or omission, or as a natural and foreseeable consequence of that act. The accused is not responsible for remote or indirect consequences that a reasonable person would not have foreseen as likely.

In one case, the accused chased the victim into a public street, intending to cut him with a knife. In running to make his escape, the victim was struck by a car and killed. The court held that the risk of harm must have been foreseeable to the knife wielder and that he was responsible for the murder.

In a similar situation, the victim was struck by lightning while running down the street to escape an individual who threatened him with a knife. In that case, the victim's death was not a foreseeable result of the assault. While the accused could not be convicted for murder, he could be convicted for assault.

Where the cause of death is due to surgical or medical complications resulting from the original injury, the courts generally hold that these complications are the natural and probable consequences of the accused's acts.

If the victim contracts a completely unrelated ailment, resulting from exposure to infections in the hospital while being treated, a more difficult legal problem arises. Some courts hold that any disease or condition contracted by the victim is foreseeable and is a probable consequence of the defendant's wrongful act. These cases usually say that when the accused set in motion the developments that eventually caused death, a murder violation was committed. We must, however, recognize a difference of opinion on the part of courts in situations of this kind.

Multiple Causes of Injury

The courts do agree that the defendant's act need not be the only cause of the injury, provided that cause is reasonable, logical, and actually contributory to the harm.

In an old Kentucky case, the victim was shot by two enemies, one after the other. A short interval occurred between the two shootings, and the medical testimony indicated that the victim was bleeding to death from the first wound at the time his brains were blown out by the defendant, Hopkins. Eventually Hopkins was brought to trial for murder. Introducing the testimony of a doctor to the effect that the victim was bleeding to death, Hopkins' attorney argued that his client merely hastened a death which was certain to happen. The court said that either of the men who inflicted a mortal wound should be held for murder.

The courts in more recent cases exhibit no difficulty in finding that the acts of each contributed to the death and that both assailants are guilty of murder, even though they did not act in concert. Of course, if the first wound was superficial and death was due to the independent, intervening act, the first wrongdoer is not guilty of murder.

CITED CASES

Brown v. Mississippi, 297 U.S. 278, 56 S. Ct. 461.
Escobedo v. Illinois, 378 U.S. 478, 84 S. Ct. 1758.
McNabb v. United States, 318 U.S. 322, 63 S. Ct. 608.
Mallory v. United States, 354 U.S. 449, 77 S. Ct. 1356.
Manning v. United States, 215 F.2d 945.
Miranda v. Arizona, 384 U.S. 436, 86 S. Ct. 1602.
People v. Fruci, 67 N.Y.S.2d 512.
People v. Moore, 48 Cal.2d 541.
People v. Scott, 176 Cal. App.2d 458.
People v. Siplinger, 252 Cal. App.2d 817, 60 Cal. Rptr. 914.
Puryear v. State, 28 Tex. Crim. 73, 11 S.W. 929.
State v. Lung, 70 Wash.2d 365, 423 P.2d 72.

CHAPTER 7

Incomplete or Partly Perpetrated Crimes

This chapter deals *incomplete or partial* with incomplete, partly perpetrated, or preliminary violations—inchoate crimes, as they are sometimes called by lawyers. The basic problem in these cases is whether the acts in question are sufficient for the courts to say they should be subject to criminal punishment. In these situations the criminal courts have moved the line of responsibility backward from the intended crime to the preliminary acts that signal guilt.

 Three separate violations may result from this incomplete criminal activity: (1) attempt, (2) solicitation, and (3) conspiracy.

ATTEMPT

To be guilty of a crime, it is not always necessary that the doer shall perform acts which equal the intended, completed violation. Once the basic elements have been satisfied, an attempt is a distinct crime in itself. Prosecutable, whether the criminal effort is a partial success or a complete failure, an attempt merits punishment on the theory that it constitutes a large segment of the completed crime.

Why Attempts Should Be Punished

As previously emphasized, the criminal law does not punish people for their guilty intentions or criminal schemes. But it does punish at some point between the formation of the evil intent and the actual completion of the crime, when the accused has become so involved that it is obvious a public wrong is being attempted. The reasoning is that the accused should not be allowed to escape punishment because of lack of skill in criminal endeavors, nor because, through chance or intervening circumstances, the intended crime never came into being.

Preventing Crime before the Safety and Welfare of the Public Can Be Menaced

The public interest is definitely served if the police are given every encouragement to intervene early when a suspect is clearly intent on a specific crime. Police action may prevent serious bodily harm or even a loss of life when it occurs before the crime proceeds to the dangerous stage. On the other hand, when the police come on the scene before any sort of criminal act has occurred, little can be done except to warn the potential victim and admonish the intending lawbreaker.

Also, preventive action in breaking up a crime has minimal deterring effect on hardened criminals. Society benefits most when they are arrested, taken into court, and made to answer for their conduct. This is especially true when they know that the authorities have learned of their schemes while they are in the process of unfolding. Unless an arrest is made, criminals often are openly contemptuous of police efforts to suppress crime.

In past efforts to interpret attempts, some courts have taken the approach that the wrongdoer must be left alone until the last act has been completed that sets the criminal plan in motion; but, if the requirements of the law are so strict that the criminal must be irreversibly committed before authorities may intervene, we have every reason to believe that crimes will multiply.

Under modern jurisprudence, however, the courts generally have wide authority for supervision and probation. Thus, we can argue that any substantial act done toward the perpetration of a violation should be treated as criminal. Public good is served when intending offenders are caught at the earliest possible time, with the prospect of court authorities and supervision to cure them of their criminal inclinations. This appears definitely preferable to leaving wrongdoers alone on the idea that their acts are mere preparation, even when it is obvious that they were initiated crimes.

Then too, let us recognize the possibility that the potential wrongdoers may change their minds before they become seriously entangled in a forbidden scheme. To brand them as criminals at this stage may work a lasting hardship; or, in some instances at least, their acts may be misinterpreted by the authorities. One judge said: "The suspect's acts in purchasing kerosene and matches may appear to the prosecutor as part of a plot to burn down his neighbor's house, when in fact the suspect has done nothing more harmful than purchase fuel for the lamp in his modest home."

The basic problem, then, in the law of attempts is to allow each individual as much freedom as possible, but at the same time to hold everyone accountable for his or her criminal attempts.

Definition

An attempt to commit a crime, in terms of the definition most often used by the courts, is an endeavor carried beyond mere preparation, but falling short of execution of the ultimate criminal design.

The Law of Attempt Applies to True Crimes Only

One fact should be understood, however: The law of attempts applies to so-called *true crimes*, only. These include violations such as murder, robbery, arson, burglary, kidnapping, and rape. It does not apply to crime under police powers or to public welfare offenses—burning garbage in an unauthorized area, selling adulterated food to the public, or speeding on a public highway.

The Common Law and Modern Attempt Statutes

Interestingly enough, the early English common law seldom gave much attention to attempted crimes. By about 1800, however, attempt violations had become a recognized part of the common law. In addition, modern penal statutes have continued and extended the law on criminal attempts. Most states now have a general attempt statute, similar to that of California, forbidding "an attempt to commit any offense prohibited by law."[1]

In addition to this general attempt statute, a number of jurisdictions have separate and additional statutes prohibiting certain kinds of specific attempts. For example, California provides individual enactments prohibiting attempts to commit arson, to escape from criminal detention, and to extort.[2]

[1] CALIFORNIA PENAL CODE, sec. 664.
[2] CALIFORNIA PENAL CODE, secs. 451a, 107, 4531, 4532, 524.

Penalties for Attempt Violations

Penalties imposed for attempt violations vary from state to state. Commonly, attempt statutes provide penalties of one-half the prison sentence required for the completed crime, with twenty years as the maximum for crimes that carry a sentence of life imprisonment or death.[3]

Elements of the Corpus Delicti of an Attempt Violation

In order to establish the corpus delicti of attempt, four basic facts must be proved:

1. The accused must have had a specific intent to commit the major crime in question.
2. The accused must have committed some act in furtherance of this wrongful intent: one that fell short of actual completion of the intended wrong.
3. The accused must have had apparent ability, or at least thought he or she had the ability, to perpetrate the crime in question.
4. The attempted crime must have been legally possible of commission.

The law recognizes a clear distinction between an intention to commit a crime and an attempt to commit it. In fact, practically all the decided cases state that mere preparation, before or unaccompanied by an overt act toward the actual commission of the intended crime, does not amount to an attempt;[4] but they disagree as to when the accused's acts change from preparation to perpetration.

The Last Act Theory

— old common law theory

The earlier cases (common law view) were decided on the grounds that the accused must have committed all the acts which, if not prevented, would have resulted in the full consummation of the crime. This is the *last act theory*. In other words, the person who was accused of arson must have actually set the "kindling" on fire and the house would have burned, except for a neighbor's quick action in putting out the blaze. The courts that follow this idea say that when any of the physical acts needed to complete the violation have not taken place, an attempt has not been committed. This approach is followed today by some courts.

Under this line of reasoning, a bomber might not be guilty of an attempt, even after placing a fuse in an explosive device, not having struck

[3] CALIFORNIA PENAL CODE, sec. 664.
[4] People v. Lombard, 131 Cal. App. 525.

the match when stopped by authorities. The reasoning of the common law courts is that the wrongdoer may yet abandon the evil plan, and should have a way to back out until the last necessary act has been committed.

Still another argument has been made to justify the last act theory. It says that an individual's intent must be irrevocably clear; to punish under other circumstances has the effect of punishing a person for a mental state, rather than for criminal acts. For example, in deciding a case a number of years ago, Justice Oliver Wendell Holmes of the United States Supreme Court expressed this basic philosophy when he said, "The act done must come pretty near to accomplishing the result before the law will take notice of it."

In determining what set of facts might be sufficient under the last act theory, we might examine the case of the frustrated bank burglar. Tunneling under the vault of the bank, this criminal was stopped only when the roof on the tunnel caved in, exposing the interior of the bank vault and knocking the burglar unconscious. Later found by the sheriff, this defendant was convicted.

Another example is that of a man who intended to kill his ex-wife by blowing up her apartment. He lit a fuse leading to the dynamite; the fuse cord was defective; the fire went out—no explosion. The janitor of the building discovered the accused and called the police before he could set another fuse to the explosive charge. A conviction resulted.

In another case, several bank robbers drove to the scene during a violent windstorm. After parking in front of the bank and obtaining their guns and equipment, the gang got out of their car and headed for the front door of the financial institution. Arriving at the bank entryway, these hoodlums were startled to see a large tree snap off in the wind and fall on top of the getaway car. Deprived of a means of transportation, the bank robbers hurriedly left on foot and were later captured and convicted.

The Material Factor Cases

On the other hand, many modern courts believe that the old last act theory requires too much of the prosecution, allowing many to escape conviction when no real question exists as to the accused's intentions. Consequently, numerous present-day courts are using a different test to decide just when criminal preparation has ended and perpetration has begun. This is called the *material factor test*, or *material factor approach*. Perhaps the majority of modern courts will uphold a conviction when this test can be satisfied.

Material Factor Standard. The requirement is that the acts performed by the accused must be a material factor in bringing about the harm intended. If the acts of the accused are subject to more than one interpretation, then they may or may not prove a criminal intent. If, however, the defendant does something that tends to bring about the crime, this is a material factor; the defendant must be held responsible.

Buying a high-powered rifle, for example, may or may not reflect an intent to commit a serious crime. The suspect may have bought it because of a need for self-defense or with the intention of going hunting.

On the other hand, when an investigation showed a plot to kidnap for ransom, the obtaining of a cabin in a remote area, purchase of materials to tie and gag the victim, and preparation of a ransom note, coupled with travel to a place where the note was to be delivered, the court held that an attempted kidnapping had been committed. In an explanation it said that a number of these acts seemed to be material factors to support the necessary mental intent. Clearly, however, the last necessary act had not been completed in this case.

In another case, the defendant's acts were held sufficient for a conviction of attempted murder when she placed a bomb in the victim's automobile. Here again, the accused had not committed the last act, since she had made no attempt to attach a detonating device to the bomb.[5]

What Are the Material Factors in These Cases?   In material factor cases, the courts usually analyze the defendant's acts from two diverse viewpoints:

1.   Did the accused's conduct seem clearly to indicate the intent to commit the crime, or might the conduct be subject to another reasonable interpretation?
2.   Did the accused's scheme come close to actual completion of the crime? This analysis usually considers the number of acts yet to be performed prior to completion, as well as how near the accused came to the criminal goal from the standpoint of time.

So, we find no hard and fast rules as to just what material factor really is. In the final analysis, some cases seem to have been decided on whether the court believed that the total conduct of the defendant deserved punishment.

Some Activity That Is Only Preparatory
Is Nevertheless Punishable under Special Statutes

Then too, when the accused's acts are not sufficient to prosecute for an attempt violation, this does not necessarily mean that there cannot be a prosecution under some special statutes. Legislatures in a number of states

[5] See Chapter 10, "Homicide," for greater details on this and related points of law.

have passed laws prohibiting the placing of combustible materials in or against the exterior of a building with the intent to eventually burn it. In most instances, prosecutors find it easier to prove a violation of this special statute than to prove an attempt to commit arson.

In a somewhat similar kind of situation, a suspect may be carrying a handgun with intent to use it in an armed robbery when a suitable victim is located. Unless the suspect has a license to carry the gun, a statute against carrying a concealed weapon has been violated. It is unlikely, however, that a conviction for attempt to rob could be sustained on this fact alone.[6]

Physical Impossibility as a Defense for Attempt

The courts generally assume that an attempt violation will not be recognized if success is obviously impossible. For example, in a prosecution in Indiana a number of years ago, the accused struck the victim with an object described as a "slight switch." The court said, as a matter of law, the defendant could not be found guilty of attempted murder, even if he admitted that this was his plan. The point was that he was not in possession of the physical means designed to accomplish his objective. A similar result was reached in a Texas case involving a defendant who pointed a child's popgun at the victim.[7]

Conversely, the courts generally hold to the idea that the accused "cannot protect himself from responsibility by showing that, by reason of some fact unknown to him at the time of his criminal attempt, it could not be fully carried into effect in that particular instance."[8] The test used by the courts is whether a reasonable person in the accused's position would have thought that the act performed could bring about the harm intended. In other words, to be an attempt violation, the deed committed by the defendant must have appeared to be capable of being done.

For example, a police officer bored a peephole in the ceiling of a room where he believed illegal gambling was taking place. One of the gamblers discovered the peephole and fired a pistol shot at the spot, on the supposition that the police officer was there. The police officer was not in fact in position to be struck by the bullet. When brought to trial, the accused,

---

[6] Statutes covering handguns are in use in a number of states. See sec. 695.2, I.C.A. (Iowa). A number of states also have statutes that prohibit the possession of unregistered weapons of certain kinds, such as sawed-off shotguns or machine guns. See CALIFORNIA PENAL CODE, sec. 12220.

Some jurisdictions have special statutes prohibiting the placing of poison in food or drink, with the intent that it shall be consumed by a human being. See I.C. (Idaho), sec. 18-5501.

[7] Smith v. State, 32 Texas 593, 594.

[8] Hamilton v. State, 36 Ind. 280; People v. Cummings, 141 Cal. App. 2d 610.

through his attorney, pointed out the fact that made murder a physical impossibility. The court said, however, that the accused was guilty of an attempt to commit murder.[9]

The cases quite consistently say that when one person points a pistol at another and pulls the trigger with the intention of murder, believing the gun to be loaded, the accused may be convicted of an attempt to commit murder. When no harm occurs because the weapon is unloaded, this fortunate circumstance does not relieve the accused from criminal responsibility.

In addition, we find in some states specific statutes that declare a criminal violation when a loaded or unloaded gun is pointed at another in a threatening manner.[10] Some states, on the other hand, require a *loaded* gun, and a conviction cannot be obtained when the evidence shows the gun is empty. The specific wording of the enactment will generally be determining. Assuming that a statute requires the gun to be loaded, the prosecution may ignore this law and proceed on the idea that an attempt has been committed.

Today the courts consistently hold that an attempt to steal money from the pocket of another is prosecutable, even though the victim is carrying nothing of value. The very early English cases did not agree with this result, possibly because judges were hesitant to apply the required death penalty in a case of this kind. Later English judges admitted that this reasoning was faulty and that an attempt to commit a theft was prosecutable in each instance.[11]

No Attempt Violation When the Act Is Legally Impossible

We have seen that physical impossibility does not excuse from criminal responsibility, if the act appears possible. This does not hold true, however, if the commission of the attempted crime is legally impossible. When the crime attempted is one which, as a matter of law, cannot be committed, the defendant must be excused.

It is legally impossible, for instance, to be guilty of statutory rape on a willing female who is over the age of consent. Therefore, if a husband should try to rape a woman passing down a darkened alley and later discover that the woman is his wife, the husband cannot be held for attempted rape. Prosecution can be had on a charge of assault and battery,

[9] People v. Lee King, 95 Cal. 666.
[10] CALIFORNIA PENAL CODE, sec. 417.
[11] People v. Fiegleman, 33 Cal. App. 2d 100.

however, since it is legally possible for a husband to be guilty of assault and battery against his wife.

In a New York case, the defendant attempted to buy cloth, believing it to have been stolen. Proof offered by the prosecution at the time of trial clearly showed that the merchandise had lost its stolen character at the time it was sold to the defendant; however, no one corrected the defendant's impression that the cloth was stolen. The court said, "If all which an accused person intends to do would, if done, constitute no crime, it cannot be a crime to do with the same purpose a part of the thing intended." The tribunal here took note of the language of a prior New York court decision that said, "The question whether an attempt to commit a crime has been made is determinable solely by the condition of the actor's mind and his conduct in the attempted consummation of his design." Distinguishing the cloth case as one of legal impossibility, which was different from a mistake of fact, the court continued:

> If what a man contemplated doing would not be in law a crime, he could not be said, in point of law, to intend to commit the crime. If he thinks his act will be a crime, this is a mere mistake of his understanding . . . . If the thing is not a crime, he does not intend to commit one, whatever he may erroneously suppose.[12]

Abandonment of an Attempt

Also, practically all courts are in agreement that, once the necessary perpetrating act has taken place, the attempt has been completed. The accused cannot, by abandoning the scheme or by having a change of heart, erase the criminal violation of attempt. As said by the court in one case, "It is no less a crime, though the aggressor should abandon his intentions before the consummation of the act, by reason of the pains of a stricken conscience alone."[13]

A few states, such as New York, allow a clear showing of abandonment to be used as a defense to criminal prosecution. However, these jurisdictions are definately in the minority.[14]

[12] People v. Jaffe, 185 N.Y. 497, 78 N.E. 169.
[13] People v. Stewart, 97 Cal. 238.
[14] NEW YORK PENAL LAW, sec. 35.45 (1967):
  3. In any prosecution pursuant to Section 110.00 for an attempt to commit a crime, it is an affirmative defense that, under circumstances manifesting a voluntary and complete renunciation of his criminal purpose, the defendant avoided the commission of the crime attempted by abandoning his criminal effort, and, if mere abandonment was insufficient to accomplish such avoidance, by taking further affirmative steps which prevented the commission thereof.

Prosecutive Problems

The federal courts and most of the courts of the states allow an individual to be convicted for an attempt, even though the facts at the time of trial prove that the major crime was actually completed. This results from court decisions in some states. Statutes, however, authorize this procedure in a number of other jurisdictions.[15]

Conversely, some state courts consider failure to complete the crime as a part of the corpus delicti of an attempt. Consequently, they reason that no conviction for an attempt can be accomplished when the violation was eventually completed.

SOLICITATION — *has To be for a felony*

A crime has been solicited when a person requests, commands, or encourages another to commit it, with the intent that the crime in question be perpetrated. Solicitation covers any use of words or other devices through which an individual is enticed, incited, instructed, requested, advised, counseled, or tempted to commit a crime.

Effects of Solicitation

We note a sharp difference of opinion, however, as to how much danger the crime of solicitation may be to society. On the one side, we may argue that one who solicits a crime is afraid to commit the actual violation and is only an indirect party to the offense. Under this reasoning, the solicitor may be a small-time punk as criminals are classified.

On the other hand, we may recognize that the criminal solicitor is a person who uses a sophisticated approach in which others may take the blame for the wrongful act. Under this approach, it is difficult for the law to actually get at the person behind the crime, and others may be taking the rap for the real culprit. In this sense, the solicitor may be more dangerous to society than the criminal because the solicitor is shielded from the law.

Differences between Solicitation and Other Incomplete Crimes

Also, we have seen that a criminal attempt requires an act directed toward the commission of some substantive crime. Solicitation is different in that no act of any kind is required, other than the request by the accused to commit a crime.

[15] FEDERAL RULES OF CRIMINAL PROCEDURE, 31; CALIFORNIA PENAL CODE, sec. 663.

Solicitation must, in turn, be distinguished from conspiracy, which is basically a criminal agreement or scheme between two or more persons. In a solicitation violation the person solicited need not agree to do anything. On the contrary, the person who is solicited may immediately report the matter to the police, having no inclination whatever to get involved in the proposed criminal plan.

We should point out, however, that the person who makes the solicitation must intend that the crime be committed. Therefore, if the crime is intended by both parties, an attempt may result. If the crime is completed, then the individual who solicited may be prosecuted, both for solicitation and for the completed offense (substantive crime). Generally, however, the courts will allow a prosecution for only one or the other.

Solicitation as a Common Law Violation

The idea that one who had unsuccessfully solicited another had committed a crime was recognized late by the courts. However, since 1801 the common law has recognized that solicitation of any felony is punishable as a misdemeanor.[16] Lack of agreement exists among the cases as to whether solicitation to commit a misdemeanor is also punishable, but this makes little difference in most states because of the statutes covering the law of solicitation.

Solicitation under Statutory Law

Most courts in the United States have limited solicitation prosecutions to those crimes specifically set out in the written laws. A typical law provides:

> Every person who solicits another to offer or accept or join in the offer or acceptance of a bribe, or to commit or join in the commission of murder, robbery, burglary, grand theft, receiving stolen property, extortion, rape by force, perjury, subordination of perjury, forgery, or kidnapping is punishable by imprisonment in the county jail not longer than one year, or in the state prison not longer than five years, or by a fine of not more than five thousand dollars. Such offense must be proved by the testimony of two witnesses or of one witness and corroborating circumtances.[17]

In interpreting this law, the California courts have said that the corroborating evidence is satisfactory if it tends to connect the accused with the commission of the crime, so that the jury is reasonably satisfied that the witness, who must be corroborated, is telling the truth.[18]

[16] The King v. Higgins, 102 Eng. Rep. 269.
[17] CALIFORNIA PENAL CODE, sec. 653f.
[18] People v. Rissman, 154 Cal. App. 2d 265.

The crime requested by the solicitor need not necessarily be committed within the state. Where the criminal acts are to be performed is also of no consequence; the prosecution need not prove that these acts constitute a crime in the state where they are to take place.[19]

Some statutes require the combined action of two individuals, but impose a penalty on only one. In these cases the courts say that this is clear indication that the legislature intends that only one of the parties should be punished. They refuse to hold the second party guilty on the idea that he or she aided and abetted the individual against whom the penalty was imposed. The decision is to the effect that penalties cannot be applied in such manner as to defeat the obvious intent of the statute.

We find another example of this kind in federal prohibition laws which prohibited the sale of liquor but imposed a penalty against the seller only, not against the buyer.[20]

CONSPIRACY

"It has been long and consistently recognized . . . that the commission of the substantive offense and a conspiracy to commit it are separate and distinct offenses."[21]

The courts also universally recognize that, when the substantive crime is committed by one conspirator in furtherance of the unlawful plan, all members are guilty of the substantive offense. In other words, all coconspirators are guilty as principals or accessories, defending on the laws of the state.

Definition of a Conspiracy

Black's Law Dictionary defines a conspiracy as follows:

> A consultation or agreement between two or more persons, either falsely to accuse another of a crime punishable by law; or wrongfully to injure or prejudice a third person, or any body of men, in any manner; or to commit any offense punishable by law; or to do any act with the intent to prevent the course of justice; or to effect a legal purpose with a corrupt intent, or by improper means.[22]

In terms of this definition, obviously, a conspiracy may cover many kinds of situations. This very problem caused U.S. Supreme Court Justice Jack-

[19] People v. Burt, 45 Cal. App. 2d 311.
[20] United States v. Farrar, 281 U.S. 624, 50 S. Ct. 425.
[21] Pinkerton v. United States, 328 U.S. 640.
[22] BLACK's LAW DICTIONARY, 4th ed. (1968), p. 383.

son to remark, "A conspiracy almost defies definition."[23] Another judge pointed out, "The comprehensiveness and indefiniteness of the offense of conspiracy has made an exact definition a very difficult one."[24]

On the other hand, some other definitions have been less involved. For example, U.S. Supreme Court Justice Holmes referred to a conspiracy as a "partnership in criminal purposes."[25] The legal writer Rollin Perkins quotes the often repeated statement that "an agreement for a lawful purpose is a contract; an agreement for an unlawful purposes is a conspiracy." Perkins hastens to add, however, that this is a broad generalization which does not represent the end of the search, but is "merely a convenient starting point for the consideration of the problems involved."[26]

Why Conspiracies Are Punished

All courts agree on the need for a strong public policy to break up criminal conspiracies. They concede that an organized society must have legal weapons for combating organized criminality. As said by Justice Jackson of the U.S. Supreme Court, " . . . The basic conspiracy principle has some place in modern criminal law, because to unite, back of a criminal purpose, the strength, opportunities, and resources of many is obviously more dangerous and more difficult to police than the efforts of a lone wrongdoer."[27]

Then too, the chances for abandonment of a criminal plan before completion are considerably reduced when it is group-planned, rather than an individual effort. Possibilities for success may also be increased when it is backed by many; the extent of social harm may be expanded.[28]

Unity of Agreement in a Conspiracy: Two or More Parties Are Necessary

The courts have never required a formal or written agreement of any kind, but they do demand an understanding between the parties, involving a meeting of intent and purpose. An unexpressed or undeclared understanding is sufficient with respect to the unlawful purpose, provided it is believed by the jury from all surrounding circumstances and happenings.

A conspiracy is not only a meeting of the minds, but a meeting resulting from agreement. For example, two burglars who saw the same possibility

---

[23] Krulewitch v. United States, 336 U.S. 440, 69 S. Ct. 716.
[24] Commonwealth v. Donohue, 250 Ky. 343, 63 S.W. 2d 3.
[25] Marino v. United States, 91 F. 2d 691; United States v. Kissel, 218 U.S. 601, 31 S. Ct. 124.
[26] ROLLIN M. PERKINS, PERKINS ON CRIMINAL LAW, 2d ed., The Foundation Press, Mineola, N.Y., 1969, pp. 612, 613.
[27] Krulewitch v. United States, 336 U.S. 440, 69 S. Ct. 716.
[28] People v. Comstock, 147 Cal. App. 2d 228.

for criminal profit may have been caught inside a jewelry store when the police answered a burglar alarm. Based on appearances, the supposition might be that the two were engaged in a joint criminal venture, but keep in mind that this is evidence of a conspiracy, not the equivalent to it.

Also, it is not absolutely essential to the meeting of minds that each party in the conspiracy shall know the name or identity of each of the other parties involved.

Any number of conspirators may be involved, but "Two or more persons must participate to create the crime."[29] Under the old common law rules, a husband and wife were recognized as one person in the eyes of the law; neither could be convicted for a conspiracy unless a third party was also involved in the scheme. This still represents the law in some jurisdictions. Since the law requires at least two persons with a common understanding, the courts have said, when only two persons conspire together and one is acquitted, the second cannot be guilty. A dismissal of charges against one party, however, in return for testimony against the other parties, does not prevent conviction of others involved.[30]

When one conspirator dies, the charge or charges are dismissed because of the inadvertent immunization; yet, the other coconspirator may be successfully prosecuted.

In explaining what may happen in a conspiracy, one federal court said:

A conspiracy may be a continuing one; actors may drop out, and others drop in; the details of operation may change from time to time; the members need not know each other or the parts played by the others; a member need not know all the details of the plan or the operations; he must, however, know the purpose fo the conspiracy and agree to become a party to a plan to effectuate the purpose.[31]

Types of Partnerships Involved in a Criminal Conspiracy

Unless regulated by statute, the rule of most courts is that the object of the conspiracy need not be an offense against the criminal law for which an individual could be prosecuted or convicted. Generally, the intent is sufficient when the purpose of the agreement is unlawful. By "unlawful" we mean those acts that injure the general public, such as placing adulterants or fillers in food for sale or in injuring the public generally.

In some cases civil courts have held the conspirators criminally liable on the same set of facts.[32]

[29] United States v. Weinberg, 129 F. Supp. 514.
[30] Sherman v. State, 113 Neb. 173, 202 N.W. 413; United States v. Fox, 130 F.2d 56; State v. Goldman, 95 N.J. Super. 50, 229 A.2d 818.
[31] Craig v. United States, 81 F.2d 816.
[32] Cole v. Associated Construction Company, 141 Conn. 49, 103 A.2d 529.

Some types of conspiracies that have been held criminally punishable include: (1) conspiracy to ruin the reputation of an individual by falsely accusing him of fathering an illegitimate child,[33] (2) conspiracy to force the dismissal of police officers through improper harassment,[34] (3)conspiracy to wrongfully wreck the business of another.[35]

no overt act was needed under the common law

The Overt Act in a Conspiracy

Under the common law, criminal conspiracies were regarded as so danger- ous to the government and to the general public that, for conviction, no overt act of any kind was required. Only clear proof of the conspiratorial plan was demanded by the courts. Unless changed by statute, this is now the situation, at least where the common law is followed; but in the great majority of the states the view of the courts is that some act must be committed in furtherance of the conspiracy.

The overt act that brings the conspiracy into being may be committed by any one of the conspirators; this single act renders all of them individ- ually punishable for the violation.

From the practical viewpoint of the police officer and the prosecutor, we must also note an important difference between an attempt and a conspir- acy. We know from our study of attempts that many courts require com- pletion of all the physical acts needed to set the criminal act in motion (the last act theory). Other courts, being not quite so strict, nevertheless insist on completion of acts that are a material factor in bringing about the criminal harm intended.

In contrast, the courts uniformly require only a minimum of physical activity to satisfy the physical (act) requirement of conspiracy. All that is necessary in a conspiracy is one overt (observable) act committed by any one of the parties in furtherance of the plan. Furthermore, the act may be merely preparatory in nature. It need not be so material that it is an important factor in bringing about the crime. This is why the courts say, "The minimum of proof in a conspiracy is very low."

Since the courts seem to feel that the heart of a conspiracy is the crimi- nal agreement, the federal courts have said that, when the conspiracy is entered into within the United States, the necessary act may be committed outside the country.[36]

---

[33] The King v. Armstrong, 86 Eng. Rep. 196.
[34] State v. McFeely, 25 N.J. Misc. 303, 52 A.2d 823.
[35] State v. Huegin, 110 Wis. 189, 85 N.W. 1046.
[36] Dealy v. United States, 152 U.S. 539, 14 S. Ct. 680.

Withdrawal of a Conspirator from the Criminal Scheme

Any of the conspirators may withdraw from the criminal plot prior to the commission of that one overt act that converts the plan into a criminal conspiracy, and be free from the charge. The test used by almost all courts is whether the accused brought home to the coconspirators with sufficient clarity the fact of the withdrawal.

is a specific intent crime

Changes in Law of Conspiracy Made through Modern Statutes

Two most significant changes have been made in the law of conspiracy through modern criminal statutes. In the first place, some state legislative enactments have limited or eliminated some of the unlawful purposes necessary to spell out a criminal conspiracy. Second, the federal statute limits conspiracies to plans to "commit any offense against the United States, or to defraud the United States or any agency thereof . . . ."[37]

While not so restrictive, statutes in a large number of states limit the types of criminal conspiracies to the following:

1. Conspiracies to commit a crime.
2. Conspiracies to falsely and maliciously prosecute another for crime.
3. Conspiracies to falsely initiate or maintain a lawsuit, criminal action, or proceeding.
4. Conspiracies to cheat and defraud anyone of property by criminal means, or to obtain money by false pretenses.
5. Conspiracies to commit acts injurious to the public health, to public morals, or to obstruct justice or the due administration of the laws.

Punishments for Conspiracy

Punishments for conspiracy violations vary widely from state to state. In summary, four approaches are used:

1. In some states a conspiracy is a misdemeanor, regardless of the scheme's original objective.
2. Some fix a maximum sentence for conspiracy, regardless of the type of crime intended.
3. Other jurisdictions set up three categories of maximum sentences, depending on the seriousness of the crime attempted.
4. A few directly relate the general conspiracy sentence to the substantive crime intended. Wisconsin, for example, fixes the maximum at the same sentence provided for the completed crime, except for crimes

---

[37] UNITED STATES CODE, title 18, sec. 371.

that may be punished by life imprisonment—for which the maximum sentence for conspiracy is thirty years.

CITED CASES

Craig v. United States, 81 F.2d 816.
Cole v. Associated Construction Co., 141 Conn. 49, 103 A.2d 529.
Commonwealth v. Donohue, 250 Ky. 343, 63 S.W.2d 3.
Dealy v. United States, 152 U.S. 539, 14 S. Ct. 680.
Hamilton v. State, 36 Ind. 280.
The King v. Armstrong, 86 Eng. Rep. 196.
The King v. Higgins, 102 Eng. Rep. 269.
Krulewitch v. United States, 336 U.S. 440, 69 S. Ct. 716.
Marino v. United States, 91 F.2d 691.
People v. Burt, 45 Cal. 2d 311.
People v. Comstock, 147 Cal. App. 2d 228.
People v. Cummings, 141 Cal. App. 2d 610.
People v. Fiegelman, 33 Cal. App. 2d 100.
People v. Jaffe, 185 N.Y. 497, 78 N.E. 169.
People v. Lee King, 95 Cal. 666.
People v. Lombard, 131 Cal. App. 525.
People v. Rissman, 154 Cal. App. 2d 265.
People v. Stewart, 97 Cal. 238.
Pinkerton v. United States, 328 U.S. 640.
Sherman v. State, 113 Neb. 173, 202 N.W. 413.
Smith v. State, 32 Texas 593, 594.
State v. Goldman, 95 N.J. Super. 50, 229 A.2d 818.
State v. Huegin, 110 Wis. 189, 85 N.W. 1046.
State v. McFeely, 25 N.J. Misc. 303, 52 A.2d 823.
United States v. Farrar, 281 U.S. 624, 50 S. Ct. 425.
United States v. Fox, 130 F.2d 56.
United States v. Kissel, 218 U.S. 601, 31 S. Ct. 124.
United States v. Weinberg, 129 F. Supp. 514.

CHAPTER 8

Who Can Commit a Crime: Crimes under Threat or Duress

It may come as a suprise to some people to learn that not everyone can commit a crime, or some may be confused as to the conditions that excuse a person from the criminal responsibility attached. Police personnel in particular must maintain a continued interest in these matters and use the law on the subject as guides in investigations, arrests, searches, and seizures.

JUVENILES

For example, early English cases said that a child was not criminally responsible for his acts if he was of such tender years as to be incapable of distinguishing between right and wrong, or not able to understand the real nature and consequences of his act. The common law recognized a conclusive (absolute) presumption of incapacity for all children under seven years of age to commit crime.

In the age group seven to fourteen, the English common law took notice of a rebuttable (questionable) presumption of criminal incapacity. In other words, it was the job of the prosecutor to prove that the accused understood the difference between right and wrong and had an appreciation of the facts. So, in the language of the law, the burden of proof was on the prosecution to show mental capacity on the part of a defendant age seven to fourteen. Lacking that proof, the law recognized the fact that no crime had been committed.

On the other hand, when a child became fourteen years of age, the common law regarded him or her as having the same criminal capacity as an adult. Anyone fourteen or older was held fully responsible for violations of criminal law unless incapacity was proved on some other basis, such as insanity.

In prosecuting children between the ages of seven and fourteen, the English courts did allow proof of threats to a witness as bearing on the mental ability (capacity) of the accused. Proof that the accused had attempted to buy off another young person who had witnessed the crime was also allowed, as was evidence that the accused had hidden from the authorities and had concealed a weapon.

In fact, until very modern times in England, some of the violators in the seven- to fourteen-year-old age group were roughly handled by the English courts. Execution was the penalty for the more serious crimes; the law provided no probation or leniency. The records show that a child of eight years was executed for maliciously burning some barns (arson). Other records reflect that a thirteen-year-old girl was executed for murder, as were several boys in the ten-to-twelve-year-old bracket.

The courts in the United States have also consistently held that a very young child cannot commit a crime. In an old Georgia case, for example, "A three-and-one-half-year-old boy pulled the trigger on his daddy's pistol and killed his little brother." The court said, "A person three and one-half years old is not accountable for any act he commits."

In writing laws in this regard, a number of states have used the Canadian code as a model. This code says:

> No person shall be convicted of an offense in respect of an act or omission on his part while he was under the age of seven years.
>
> No person shall be convicted of an offense in respect of an act or omission on his part while he was seven years of age or more, but under the age of fourteen years, unless he was competent to know the nature and consequences of his conduct and to appreciate that it was wrong.

Several states have raised the age limit for criminal capacity. In Texas the age has been set by statute at nine years; in Georgia ten; and in Arkansas twelve.

The age here refers to actual calendar years of age. For instance, in a

New York case the defendant's attorney admitted that his client was more than eighteen years of age. After seeing a robbery on TV, the accused had robbed a grocery store with a pistol. The attorney pointed out, however, that the accused had been tested and actually had the mental age of a child of five years. Claiming that the mental age should excuse, the attorney argued that no crime had been committed. This claim was not allowed by the court.

On the other hand, a few courts have held that, when the youthful defendant's mentality is so low that it meets the test of insanity, the sub-normal mentality will be an excuse.

In a California case, *People v. Day,* the court likewise ruled that the calendar age, not the mental or moral age of the accused, is the controlling factor.[1]

Section 26 of the California Penal Code provides:

> Persons capable of committing crime; exceptions.
> All persons are capable of committing crimes except those belong-ing to the following classes:
> One—Children under the age of fourteen, in the absence of clear proof at the time of committing the act charged against them, they knew its wrongfulness.
> Two— . . .

In interpreting this section of the code, the California courts noted that the law takes into consideration the inexperience and probable extent of understanding of children of tender years. A 1948 case, *People v. Nichols,* involved an alleged murder by a thirteen-year-old girl. In its opinion the court said:

> While the age and condition of this appellant accused are not, in themselves, controlling here, they are a part of the general circum-stances which must be considered with other facts in determining whether the evidence is sufficient to show beyond a reasonable doubt that this killing was deliberate and premeditated, within the meaning of the statute.[2]

Keep in mind, however, that in many instances the practical effect of state and federal juvenile delinquency control statutes had been to raise the age limits for juvenile crime above the minimum set by the written law. As will be observed when we later examine in detail the subject of juvenile delinquency, practically all persons below the age of adulthood are han-dled by juvenile courts. The process in these courts in a *hearing,* not a trial; thus, the act or omission is not treated as a crime.

[1] People v. Day, 248 P. 250, 199 Cal. 78.
[2] People v. Nichols, 88 Cal. App. 2d 221, 198 P.2d 538.

CAPACITY OF MARRIED WOMEN

Blackstone, the famous eighteenth-century English legal writer, also said that it had been settled for at least a thousand years that a woman could not commit a crime if she acted under the coercion of her husband. In a later English case (1826) *Rex v. Archer,* the court said that if the husband and wife were both charged with a crime, "the wife cannot properly be convicted if the husband is."[3]

This failure to hold the wife responsible apparently grew out of ideas frequently expressed in the English courts. They often said that "The wife is only the servant of the husband," and "The husband and wife are one in the eyes of the law." Running all through the English and American law, both criminal and civil, is the basic idea that the courts should lessen friction between parties to a marriage.

Do not forget the fact, however, that even in Blackstone's time a married woman was held responsible for criminal acts that she committed of her own free will. This, of course, is the law in the United States today.

Yet, the lack of capacity of the wife to commit a crime while in the presence of her husband was recognized in early law in our country. A Massachusetts case in 1857 actually described the wife as "incapable of committing an offense,"[4] and a Tennessee case as late as 1919 spoke of "the disability of the wife by virtue of marriage."[5]

Recent social changes and the advancement of women's liberation have, nevertheless, made the married woman totally responsible for her crimes in most of the states, even though she was influenced or coerced by her husband. Leading the way, Arkansas eliminated this excuse by statute in 1872. Colorado, Georgia, Illinois, Iowa, Kansas, Kentucky, Michigan, Virginia, and other states have followed.[6]

In a few states the courts continue to say that the whole matter is a rebuttable presumption of coercion if the wife commits an offense in the presence of her husband. This presumption can, of course, be disproved in court by showing that she acted on her own free will.

The California Penal Code, revised in 1978, dropped the inclusion of married women acting under threats of the husband.[7]

[3] Rex v. Archer, 168 Eng. Rep. 1218.
[4] Commonwealth v. Burk, 77 Mass. 437, 438.
[5] Morton v. State, 141 Tenn. 357, 209 S.W. 644.
[6] For example, the Michigan statute (sec. 789.401) reads: "In the prosecution . . . no presumption shall be indulged that a married woman committing an offense does so under coercion because she commits it in the presence of her husband."
[7] CALIFORNIA PENAL CODE, sec. 26: "Persons capable of committing crime . . . exceptions: All persons are capable of committing crimes except those belonging to the following classes: . . . Seven—Married women (except for felonies) acting under the threats, command, or coercion of their husbands."

Currently, however, perhaps most of the states that have no specific statute on the subject agree with the holding of the court in a 1956 federal case that "It is clear that the common-law fiction of unity of husband and wife has no place in modern criminal law."[8] The wife may, on the other hand, be excused under the general rule of compulsion or duress, as where the husband holds a gun on her, forcing the wife to commit a crime on a third person.

CAPACITY OF CORPORATIONS

Now, regarding corporations, Chief Justice John Marshall of the U.S. Supreme Court said in an early case that a corporation is an "artificial being, invisible, intangible, and existing only in contemplation of law." This, however, represents little more than an echo from a bygone day.

Nevertheless, corporate criminal responsibility has been a very controversial subject. The argument can and has been made that a fine against a corporation is eventually paid by the stockholders, most of whom had nothing to do with the criminal violation and had no legal power to prevent it. So, the result is that the penalty can't touch the real violator.

This is not completely true. Most present-day courts agree that the agents of a corporation can have the intent necessary for a crime and can commit a criminal act. While a corporation cannot be found guilty of a true crime in the sense that it can be sent to jail, the officers of the corporation may be convicted.

In an Iowa case the court held that the president of a corporation was not criminally responsible for the acts of his employee unless he authorized or consented to these acts,[9] and in *Nye & Nissen v. United States*, the court held that an officer of the corperation can be convicted for aiding and abetting subordinates in their criminal activities.[10]

In addition, the Supreme Court of the United States has held that a corporation itself may be found liable in damages for harm caused with a "wanton, malicious, or oppressive intent by its controlling officers."[11]

CRIMES COMMITTED UNDER ORDERS OR COMMANDS FROM OTHERS

Now, what about crimes committed under orders from the boss or commands of a police superior or commander in the military?

[8] Kivette v. United States, 230 F.2d 749.
[9] State v. Carmean, 126 Iowa 291, 102 N.W. 97.
[10] Nye & Nissen v. United States, 336 U.S. 613, 69 S. Ct. 766.
[11] Denver, etc., Ry. v. Harris, 122 U.S. 597, 7 S. Ct. 1286.

Orders from the Boss

If an employee takes some merchandise owned by another from the dock of a neighboring warehouse on instructions of the boss, then the boss has also committed a crime (larceny or theft). In addition, if the employee is under the impression that the firm owns the merchandise, then the employee has not committed a crime; the necessary intent to steal is not there. On the other hand, if the employee takes the merchandise from the dock, knowing that the goods belong to another person, then having acted on the boss's orders is no excuse.

In *Susnjar v. United States,* the court said:

> An employee is not immune from punishment for his participation in criminal conspiracy upon any such idea as that his employment required him to engage therein.[12]

Also, in a somewhat similar situation, another federal court said, in *United States v. Decker:*

> Loyalty to a superior does not provide a license for crime.[13]

As to the liability of the boss, in a 1965 California case the court held that a principal (boss) is not criminally liable for a criminal act of an agent (employee) unless the boss consented to, advised, aided, or encouraged the specific act of the employee.[14]

Orders of the Police or Military

In general, an individual will not be excused for a crime committed while under the discipline or orders of another, as in a police department or military unit.

In a Florida case the accused was a police officer who maintained that he entered a store and committed a larceny, but only on the orders of his superior officer. The court said this was no excuse for his crime.[15]

The position of the soldier in the military is different. Under military regulations, the soldier has no right to question any order that is received from a superior. Thus, the soldier is not held responsible if the order appears to be lawful on its face and there is no reason to believe it is not.

[12] Susnjar v. United States, 27 F.2d 223.
[13] United States v. Decker, 304 F.2d 702.
[14] Nuffer v. Insurance Company of North America, 45 Cal. Rptr, 918, 236 Cal. App. 2d 349. See also *Ex parte* Marley 175 P.2d 832.
[15] Hall v. State, 144 Fla. 333, 198 So. 60.

However, if it is obvious to the soldier that the order violates the criminal law, then the soldier too will be held resposnsible. For example, a soldier who kills enemy troops in time of war definitely is not guilty of murder, but he is guilty if he kills unarmed women and children on instructions of his superior. Likewise, a command to a soldier to aid his superior officer in the commission of rape is not sufficient to excuse him from criminal responsibility.

CONTRACTS INVOLVING CRIMINAL ACTS

It is also well established that civil courts try to encourage both parties to a contract to live up to their obligations; but, as a matter of criminal law, no person can expect to escape criminal responsibility on the excuse that a contract calls for the performance of a criminal act.

CRIMES COMMITTED UNDER DURESS (THREATS)

Then too, the criminal law has always exhibited an unwillingness to place a stamp of approval on the taking of an innocent life under any circumstances. In general, a person who is threatened with death has no excuse for killing an innocent victim to save his or her own life; but the victim may justifiably kill the threatening person.

Court cases seem to say uniformly that the threat against the victim "must have arisen without the negligence or fault of the person who insists upon it as a defense."[16]

Consider the case in which an individual willingly joined a hardened criminal in an armed robbery attempt. During the commission of this crime, the hardened criminal forced the other participant at gunpoint to kill one of the victims. In this example, the participant who was forced to kill the victim could not claim duress as an excuse. As stated in one early English case, "One conspirator is frequently in fear of the other to a certain extent." The law takes the attitude that people who deliberately enter into a criminal undertaking must expect to be held accountable for all their actions and cannot lightly drop the whole matter when unexpected developments occur.

In fact, the type of duress or compulsion which will excuse a person who commits a crime must be the kind of threat that will "induce a well-grounded apprehension of death or great bodily harm if the act is not done." In other words, an immediate threat (not one of future harm) of death must exist with no reasonable opportunity to escape.[17] The courts

[16] People v. Merhige, 212 Michigan 601, 180 N.W. 418.
[17] People v. Sanders, 82 Cal. App. 778.

usually emphasize that fact that the threat also must be substantial. Additionally, the excuse is not available to someone who obviously has a safe avenue of escape before committing the prohibited act.

A few courts have held that the threat need not be so great that death or serious bodily harm seems immediate. These courts are exceptional, however, and most courts completely refuse to compromise on this. All courts seem to agree that the threat must be one of physical harm and that a threat to "burn his house and destroy all his cattle and stock of corn and to lay waste all that belonged to him" is not allowed as the kind of threat that would excuse.

The test used in some locations is that the crime committed under duress will be excused if it was done to avoid greater harm than was actually inflicted.[18]

While the legislatures of some states recognize extreme bodily threats as an excuse in any kind of criminal case, five states do not allow this excuse under any set of circumstances (Georgia, North Dakota, Oklahoma, South Dakota, and Texas).

Interestingly enough, statutes in nine states allow duress to excuse some types of crimes but do not allow it for others. In these states duress will not excuse if the crime is so serious that it carries a possible penalty of death (Arazona, Arkansas, California, Colorado, Idaho, Illinois, Montana, Nevada, and Utah). The practical effect here is to allow a claim of duress in less serious types of crime. If the crime is punishable by the death penalty, no kinds of threats, duress, or coercion will excuse someone who participates in its commission.[19]

NECESSITY AS A DEFENSE AGAINST CRIME

The claim is sometimes made that a crime is justified if done under necessity. What we are talking about here is a set of circumstances so forceful that, in the mind of the violator, there is no choice of conduct—the defendant does something against his or her judgment, but thinks there is no option.

To take an actual case, a ship was crippled on the high seas, and the crew was in danger of starving. Neither the captain nor the crewman debated the moral or criminal issues here. Without hesitation they broke into food cartons in the hold and survived until rescued. The court said this would be theft under normal circumstances. However, it held that the accused peo-

[18] REVISED LAWS OF HAWAII, sec. 10624 (1945), provides, "No one shall be able to justify himself against a charge of his doing an injury to another by showing the threat of imminent danger of an equal or less injury to himself."
[19] People v. Petro, 13 Cal. App. 2d 245.

ple had committed no crime. Undoubtedly, the owners of the merchandise could have sued the owner of the ship for the value of the goods consumed, but this was a civil court matter.

In another similar kind of case, consider bank tellers who give bank money to bank robbers. In effect, the tellers embezzle bank money for the purpose of saving their own lives. Yet, the courts have always said this kind of action is excused by necessity. As a practical matter, of course, prosecution of cases of this kind is never even considered by the prosecuting attorney.

In another modern type of case, the state or local law may require children to attend school on a daily basis. If the parent thinks the child is too sick to attend, the absence is excused by necessity; but when parental judgment is abused in this situation, a criminal violation has occurred.

In 1841 the English ship *William Brown*, en route from Liverpool, England, to Philadelphia, Pennsylvania, struck an iceberg and sank. The crew was able to put two lifeboats into the sea, but both boats were badly overcrowded. In one the passengers were barely able to move, and the boat sprung a leak. A squall came up; it was obvious to everyone that the boat could not stay afloat much longer. The mate then gave an order to the sailors to throw some of the passengers overboard. After fourteen men were thrown into the ocean, the boat was manageable. A rescue ship arrived the following day, and the suvivors were taken to America. One of the two sailors who carried out the mate's orders was eventually convicted of manslaughter in a federal court in Philadelphia. Considering the seriousness of the charge, the accused received a light sentence—imprisonment for six months.

In speaking of this case many years later, Justice Benjamin Cardozo (U.S. Supreme Court) set out the law in this kind of situation:

> **Where two or more are overtaken by a common disaster, there is no right on the part of one to save the lives of some by the killing of another. . . . Who shall choose in such an hour between the victims and the saved? Who shall know when masts and sails or rescue may emerge out of the fog?**

The courts of a number of states, such as California, have said that a crime of this nature is never excused even if committed under the compulsion of necessity.[20]

While we cannot predict with complete certainty, perhaps most courts would never excuse the taking of a life by necessity, but the same court might excuse the taking of property under this same excuse.

[20] People v. Young, 70 Cal. App. 2d 28.

CONSENT OF THE VICTIM

As a general proposition, the consent of the victim also does not excuse one who commits a crime. We do find, however, a number of situations in which no crime is involved when the victim consents. The difference here seems to be in the relationship between the parties at the time. For example, players tackle and block with great force in a football game and no crime is committed. After the game, however, if they exchange blows likely or intended to cause considerable bodily harm either or both may be guilty of criminal assault and battery. The difference is that players involved in an activity such as football have implied consent to these physical blows which can be anticipated in the normal course of the physical contest.

As pointed out before, the relationship between the parties definitely makes a legal difference. The law looks to this relationship in making a decision. A man who is dating a woman may kiss her without committing a crime. If the same man forced a kiss on a woman who happened to be passing down the street, he might be guilty of assault and battery.

In a Massachusetts case, the accused was prosecuted for feeding a fig containing a dangerous drug to an unsuspecting woman. The defense claimed at the time of the trial that the victim had given her consent. The court held against the accused, pointing out that the woman had merely consented to eat what she presumed was a normal piece of fruit—not one to which a drug secretly had been added.[21]

In an early English case, the accused was prosecuted for cutting off the hand of a beggar. The evidence revealed that the vagabond actually had asked the accused to amputate his hand, with the idea that the victim might receive more generous contributions. This was not allowed as an excuse, and the accused was found guilty of mayhem. In effect, the court said here that a victim has no legal right to consent to activity which can reasonably be expected to harm him or her. This is still the law in the so-called mercy killing situation in which the victim may wish to die.

Of course, there is the possibility that a patient may die during the course of any sort of medical surgery, but the surgeon is not normally guilty of any crime, since the purpose of the operation is to restore health or to prolong life.

GUILT OF THE OTHER PARTY

It is also an established rule of criminal law that a separate crime committed by the victim cannot be used to justify or excuse a crime against that victim. In other words, it is larceny to steal from a thief.

[21] Commonwealth v. Stratton, 114 Mass. 303.

To illustrate further, the payment of a prostitute with a counterfeit bill is a violation of counterfeit laws, although the prostitute might well be guilty of a morals charge. As said in one case, "One crime cannot be permitted to become a shield against the punishment of another crime." This principle is followed quite uniformly in all our courts.

FAILURE TO PROSECUTE ONE CRIMINAL

In turn, a criminal may not be excused for a crime because he or she is the only individual who has been singled out for prosecution when others were equally guilty. The responsibility to make criminals answer to the courts rests with the prosecuting attorney and/or the grand jury.[22]

NEGLIGENT CONDUCT OF THE INJURED PARTY

Some basic differences also appear between legal ideas in the criminal and civil law. For instance, a negligent driver in a civil lawsuit may cause great damage to another individual but suffer no personal harm. If the injured person was also negligent, even in the smallest way, the victim cannot recover damages against the first party. This is a principle in negligence law (tort law) that is followed in most states; they commonly call it *contributory negligence.* Even though the negligence of one party seems to be far greater than the other's, they are offsetting in the eyes of the courts.

Clearly, this legal principle of contributory negligence is never followed in the criminal law. For example, in a Kentucky case in 1930, the defendant deliberately threw some blasting powder into an open fireplace. A number of people were in the room, and a woman and her son were burned to death in the resulting fire. Several people actually escaped from the room, although they seemed to be physically less able to care for themselves than the two victims. At the trial the accused claimed that the victims were negligent in not getting out of the building in time to save themselves. The court rejected this claim, stating that negligence on the part of the victims was of no consequence. The accused was held criminally responsible.

In another case, the victim received a malicious blow by the defendant and death eventually resulted from this blow. Medical experts were of the opinion that emergency surgery would have saved the life of the deceased, but the victim reufsed to undergo the operation. This did not excuse the defendant on the charge of murder.

[22] People v. Darcy, 59 Cal. App. 2d 342; People v. Oreck, 74 Cal. App. 2d 215; People v. Hess, 104 Cal. App. 2d 642.

Also, the negligence of a third party who intervenes between the accused and the victim may not be used as an excuse. In a case in point, the victim was seriously injured in a traffic accident because of the criminal negligence of the accused. Contrary to the permission of the doctor who handled the case, the victim was removed from the hospital by his mother; he died. Evidence was not presented to show whether death might have been avoided had the victim remained in the hospital. The court said that this was immaterial. The only question was whether death had resulted from the action originating with the accused.

Numerous California cases have followed this same idea: contributory negligence is no defense to a criminal charge. This is true because a criminal prosecution is not a civil action on behalf of the injured party; it is an offense against the state.[23]

LEGAL JUSTIFICATION OR LEGAL EXCUSE

On the other hand, some acts, otherwise crimes, are excused by the law. For example, the execution of a convicted criminal for a capital offense (gas chamber, electrocution, hanging, shooting) by a public officer is justifiable if handled in obedience to the judgment of a competent court.

In a somewhat less serious case, authority from a state fish commissioner to take fish for the purpose of obtaining spawn was held to be a defense to a prosecution on a charge of illegally taking fish.[24]

 To prevent the spread of an epidemic disease, public health officials are justified in taking action that might otherwise be regarded as a criminal public nuisance (spreading smoke and vapors by burning infected bedding, clothing and debris). Public authority, then, is a justification, provided it is not excessive and is directed toward a public purpose.

DOMESTIC AUTHORITY

Domestic authority is also a justification to activity that could be otherwise criminal, provided the authority is not exceeded.

Parent and Teacher

For example, a parent, teacher, or master is not guilty of the crime of assault and battery in subjecting a child, pupil, or apprentice to moderate corrective action, but this action can never be cruel or excessive.

[23] People v. Collins, 195 Cal. 325; People v. Barnett, 77 Cal. App. 2d 299; People v. Rodgers, 94 Cal. App. 2d 166.
[24] State v. McDonald, 109 Wis. 506, 85 N.W. 502.

It is no crime for a parent, or one who "stands in" for the parent (teacher, guardian, etc.), to correct a child. Even killing the child will be excused if it is an unintended accident and the force used was not excessive.[25] The corrective action may be immoderate, however, because of the nature of the instrument used or the amount of punishment. If excessive, the corrective action becomes an assault and battery; and if death results, it is manslaughter. Of course, an actual intention to kill the child is murder. In ascertaining whether the corrective action is excessive, the age and physical condition of the child are taken into consideration.

The parent or school teacher, if acting in good faith, is the sole judge as to when punishment is required and, within reasonable limits, what punishment may be inflicted.[26]

> A parent has a right to punish a child within the bounds of moderation and reason, so long as he does it for the welfare of the child; but, if he exceeds due moderation, he becomes criminally liable.[27]

CORRECTIVE ACTION BY HUSBAND AGAINST WIFE

There was a time when a husband in England was allowed to chastise his wife with a whip or rattan "no bigger than his thumb," in order to enforce domestic discipline. Today in the United States, the husband who hits his wife, even to enforce compliance with his just commands, is guilty of a battery.[28]

CITED CASES

Carpenter v. Commonwealth, 186 Va. 851, 44 S.E.2d 419.
Commonwealth v. Burk, 77 Mass. 437, 438.
Commonwealth v. McAfee, 108 Mass. 458.
Commonwealth v. Stratton, 114 Mass. 303.
Denver, etc. Ry. v. Harris, 122 U.S. 597, 7 S. Ct. 1286.
Hall v. State, 144 Fla. 333, 198 So. 60.
Kivette v. United States, 230 F.2d 749.
Ex parte Marley, 175. P.2d 832.

[25] Court decisions to this effect have been backed up by statutes. For example, sec. 195 of the *California Penal Code* states: "Homicide is excusable in the following cases: 1. when committed by accident and misfortune in lawfully correcting a child or servant, or in. . . ."
[26] State v. Thornton, 136 N.C. 610, 48 S.E. 602; State v. Koonse, 123 Mo. App. 655, 101 S.W. 139.
[27] Carpenter v. Commonwealth, 186 Va. 851, 44. S.E.2d 419.
[28] State v. Oliver, 70 N.C. 60; Commonwealth v. McAfee, 108 Mass. 458.

Morton v. State, 141 Tenn. 357, 209 S.W. 664.

Nuffer v. Insurance Co. of North America, 45 Cal. Rptr. 918, 236 Cal. App. 2d 349.

Nye & Nissen v. United States, 336 U.S. 613, 69 S. Ct. 766.

People v. Barnett, 77 Cal. App. 2d 299.

People v. Collins, 195 Cal. 325.

People v. Creck, 74 Cal. App. 2d 215.

People v. Darcy, 59 Cal. App. 2d 342.

People v. Day, 248 P. 250, 199 Cal. 78.

People v. Hess, 104 Cal. App. 2d 642.

People v. Merhige, 212 Mich. 601, 180 N.W. 418.

People v. Nichols, 88 Cal. App. 2d 221, 198 P.2d 538.

People v. Oreck, 74 Cal. App. 2d 215.

People v. Petro, 13 Cal. App. 2d 245.

People v. Rodgers, 94 Cal. App. 2d 166.

People v. Sanders, 82 Cal. App. 778.

People v. Young, 70 Cal. App. 2d 28.

Rex v. Archer, 168 Eng. Rep. 1218.

State v. Carmean, 126 Iowa 291, 102 N.W. 97.

State v. Koonse, 123 Mo. App. 655, 101 S.W. 139.

State v. McDonald, 109 Wis. 506, 85 N.W. 502.

State v. Oliver, 70 N.C. 60.

State v. Thornton, 136 N.C. 610, 48 S.E. 602.

Susnjar v. United States, 27 F.2d 223.

United States v. Decker, 304 F.2d 702.

CHAPTER 9

Defenses That Often Excuse Criminal Responsibility

Certain conditions exist that excuse individual responsibility for acts which the courts otherwise regard as criminal acts. In legal terminology this set of conditions is called a "defense." A person, for example, who kills another to save his or her own life is excused on proof of the claim of self-defense (this particular defense will be considered in more detail in the section on homicide). Obviously, this same defense cannot be claimed in all kinds of criminal cases, since self-defense does not logically apply to all prosecutions. We do find, however, other defenses that relieve from criminal responsibility in all kinds of criminal prosecutions. One of these is insanity.

INSANITY AS A DEFENSE

legal term not a psychiatric term

Perhaps no other problem in the field of criminal law has stirred as much attention as criminal insanity. Broadly speaking and as a general principle, a person who suffers from the legally required kind and degree of insanity cannot be held responsible by the courts.

The American system of justice is based on the theory that an individual acts with free will. A person who is insane can no longer exercise this free choice.

However horrible the crime, the accused will not be convicted as a criminal when the evidence shows legal insanity at the time of commission of the prohibited act. This does not mean, however, that the accused will not be confined for treatment of mental illness.

Let us also note that, at the time of trial, the claim of insanity is a matter of fact for the jury to decide. This finding, of course, is based on the accused's behavior, involvement, statements, physical condition, and mannerisms, as well as on the opinions of expert witnesses.

In summary, the principle that an insane person shall not be held criminally responsible was followed under the common law and has been continued or adopted in statutes throughout the United States.[1]

Often the courts justify this principle by stating that an insane individual cannot entertain a criminal intent and that one of the necessary elements or any crime is, therefore, missing. As said in one case, "Our collective conscience does not allow punishment where it cannot impose blame."[2] Some other courts have explained that the defense of insanity is, in effect an admission of the crime charged, but that it is in the nature of an avoidance, based on the fact that the accused did not have the necessary criminal intent because of mental incapacity. Regardless of these and other explanations, the courts have consistently said that the excuse of insanity is not a type of legal leniency; it serves as a complete defense. We must emphasize, however, that the insanity from which the accused suffers must be of the required kind and degree that is recognized by the courts as legal insanity.

It Makes No Difference What Causes Brought About the Insanity

In the eyes of the law, it makes no difference what caused the insanity suffered by the accused. Even though the diseased condition of mind might have been brought-about by personal excesses or private vices, the accused is excused from criminal responsibility.[3] The mental condition of

---

[1] Barrett v. Commonwealth, 259 S.W. 25, 202 Ky. 153; Commonwealth v. Tompkins, 108 A. 350, 265 Pa. 97; McGee v. State, 238 S.W.2d 707, 155 Tex. Crim. 639; Foster v. State, 52 N.E.2d 358, 222 Ind. 133; State v. Mendzlewski, 299 P.2d 598, 180 Kan. 11; State v. Stern, 123 A.2d 43, 40 N.J. Super. 291.

[2] United States v. Fielding (reversed on other grounds), 251 F.2d 878.

[3] Korsack v. State, 154 S.W.2d 348, 202 Ark. 921.

the insane accused may have resulted from accidental injury, from syphilis, from excessive use of alcohol or drugs, or from any other cause.

Mere Anger, Emotional Instability, or Moral Depravity Will Not Excuse from Criminal Responsibility.

Excessive, uncontrolled temper, "hot blood," or passion will not excuse a person who has committed a crime. Conduct resulting from some defective or perverted moral weakness will also not relieve from responsibility; neither will a moral depravity that completely ignores normal dictates of conscience.[5] Hatred, intense jealousy, or a compulsion for revenge, within themselves, are not sufficient to acquit the accused.[6]

What Happens in the Trial Process When Insanity Is Involved?

From an investigative and prosecutive standpoint, the question as to when the accused became insane may be very important. If mentally sound when the offense was committed, the accused cannot be relieved of responsibility. However, if the accused became insane after committing the offense but before charges were filed or trial undertaken, then he or she may not be competent to understand the nature of the accusation. Also, in this situation, it is possible that the defendant may not be able properly to assist a lawyer in the defense. One federal court said, "One who has been convicted while he was incompetent to stand trial has been deprived of due process."[7]

On the other hand, an individual who becomes insane after the commission of the crime is not automatically excused. In practically all situations of this kind, the trial is postponed until the defendant's reason is restored. Then the individual is returned to court for prosecution.[8]

If the accused is acquitted by reason of insanity, the laws in twelve states provide for mandatory confinement in a state mental hospital. Most other states make at least some provision for commitment or for a hearing on the fitness of the accused for liberty.[9]

Still another difficult situation arises when the convicted person becomes insane after being given the death penalty for a capital offense. Insanity at this stage does not, of course, affect the question of guilt or innocence.

[4] Garner v. State, 73 So. 50, 112 Miss. 317.
[5] State v. Moore, 76 P.2d 19, 42 N. Mex. 135.
[6] Bryant v. State, 115 A.2d 502, 207 Md. 565; State v. Gardner, 64 S.E.2d 130, 219 S.C. 97; Korsak v. State, 154 S.W.2d. 348, 202 Ark. 921; State v. Butchek, 253 P. 367, 121 Ore. 141.
[7] United States v. Knohl, 379 F.2d 427.
[8] Miller v. Spring Grove State Hospital, 198 Md. 659, 80 A.2d 898.
[9] State v. Kolocotronis, 436 P.2d 774.

The problem is whether it is contrary to the sense of public morals to execute an individual who does not know what is happening, or why. In this connection, the Supreme Court of the United States clearly has upheld the constitutionality of a state statute that gives discretionary power to the governor, counseled by physicians, to determine whether the sentenced convict should be executed or committed to a state mental institution.[10]

What Kind of Insanity Will Excuse?

As pointed out previously, legal insanity must be of the requisite kind and degree. A basic problem, then, is just what kind of mental condition will excuse. The courts have no problem with an individual of sound mind, with a person who is so deranged that he is raving and wild, or with one who seems to be a "human vegetable"; but what about the countless shades of mental disorder that fall between these three extremes? As one judge put it, ". . . At what precise moment twilight becomes darkness is hard to determine." Those tests for insanity that are recognized by the courts must be included in the instructions given by the judge to the jury; the jury makes the actual decision.

From the standpoint of this discussion, then, insanity is purely a legal term. Let us not be confused by the medical or psychiatric meanings of the word. "Legal insanity" simply represents certain legal situations that excuse the accused person from criminal responsibility. Tests for legal mental capacity vary from state to state. Thus, a person mught be insane in the eyes of the courts in New York, but be regarded as sane a few miles away in New Jersey.

Either Mental Deterioration or Deficiency from Birth May Give Rise to the Legal Status of Insanity

Some medical authorities state that they find no such thing as a disease called insanity. A person may be mentally deficient due to syphilis, paranoia, thyroid poisoning, meningitis, or a hundred other causes; but, according to the legal tests used by the courts, this person may be legally insane. This does not mean that the legally insane person has contracted a disease called insanity. Let us just say that such an individual has contracted one of the many diseases which convey the status of legal insanity.

Please note also that the tests for insanity in the civil courts are not necessarily identical with tests for criminal insanity, even in the same state.

[10] Solesbee v. Balkom, 339 U.S. 9, 70 S. Ct. 457. The problem presented by this situation is no longer an issue in jurisdictions where the death penalty has been outlawed by the courts.

Commitment of an individual to a state mental hospital is not determinative of the question of that person's responsibility for criminal acts.[11] In one case, an adjudged lunatic shot and killed a sheriff a few minutes after that official had obtained a judgment committing the accused to an asylum. The court decided not to relieve the lunatic from criminal responsibility.[12]

Although a few of the early courts attempted to distinguish between one whose brain had deteriorated and an individual who was born mentally deficient, modern courts consistently say that the reason for the lack of mental capacity is unimportant, excusing those who have damage from injury or deterioration as well as those who are deficient from birth. In the eyes of the law, "Deficiency of intellect is a species of insanity. . . ."[13]

The Right-and-Wrong Test (M'Naghten's Case)

In attempting to furnish the jury some definite guidelines on legal insanity, both the English and American courts have followed four principal ideas. The most commonly used one (and the most strict from the standpoint of the defendant) is the so-called M'Naghten test, or the *right-and-wrong rule*. This test arose out of the prosecution in 1843 of one Daniel M'Naghten, who shot and killed a bystander while attempting to assassinate Sir Robert Peel, the prime minister of England.

Instructions were given by the court to the jury in the M'Naghten trial were to convict M'Naghten if the jury found him sound of mind, but to acquit him if M'Naghten "had not the use of his understanding, so as to know he was doing a wrong or wicked act."[14]

Under this right-and-wrong test, a person is excused for a criminal act only if, by reason of a diseased condition of the mind:

1. The individual was unable to understand the nature of the act—in other words, did not understand what he or she was doing, or
2. The individual understood the nature of the act, but still lacked the capacity to decide whether this act was right or wrong.

M'Naghten was acquitted by the jury; the test set up by the English judges has been followed by most American courts since that time. Under this standard the defendant's capacity to distinguish right from wrong is determined by mental ability rather than by emotional state or development. If the defendant knew that the act is regarded as wrong by society

[11] People v. Jackson, 234 P.2d 261, 105 Cal. App. 2d 811.
[12] People v. Willard, 89 P. 124, 150 Cal. 543.
[13] State v. Schilling, 95 N.J.L. 145, 112 A. 400.
[14] M'Naghten's Case, 8 Eng. Rep. 718.

but was not personally troubled by it from a moral standpoint, the defendant is nevertheless responsible. Also, the concept of right and wrong is used here in the moral sense, rather than in the legal sense. Accordingly, it is not necessary for the prosecution to be able to show that the accused knew the act was legally wrong. This follows the established principle that ignorance of the law is no excuse. To the contrary, a failure to realize that the act was morally wrong reflects that lack of mental capacity needed to convict.

Many courts today believe that the M'Naghten rule is too strict. A number of the states and the federal courts of appeals have rejected it. As a practical matter, our mental institutions are full of individuals who are regarded as insane by practically everyone in society, yet many of these patients have retained some touch with reality and are able to distinguish between right and wrong. As a result, in recent years the courts in a number of states have looked for other, less extreme tests. Because of the difficulty as to where to draw the line, most courts have continued to follow the M'Naghten rule where not otherwise directed by statute.

The Irresistable Impulse Test

In the effort to find a test for insanity that is not as restrictive as the M'Naghten rule, a minority of the state courts have adopted the so-called *irresistable impulse* test for insanity. Although some legal authorities think that this test is misnamed, what the courts seem to be saying is that the accused had the ability to distinguish between right and wrong, but was nevertheless so mentally diseased as to lack the mental ability to adjust his or her conduct to the requirements of the law. Expressing it in other terms, a New Mexico court said, "The jury must be satisfied that, at the time of the commission of the act, the accused as a result of disease of the mind . . . was incapable of preventing himself from doing it."[15]

Considerable support for the new test was expressed when the irresistible impulse standard was first used by a Pennsylvania court in 1846.[16] An Iowa court said, "The law must modify its ancient doctrines, recognize that truth, and give to this condition, when it is satisfactorily shown to exist, its . . . effect."[17] After a time, however, both Pennsylvania and Iowa rejected the doctrine. Many courts believed that uncontrolled vagueness and uncertainty resulted and that great numbers of offenders were allowed to go free, even though the public expected these people to be held responsible for their acts. One court commented that the irresistible impulse idea "may serve . . . to interest the speculative philosopher, but it must be discarded by the jurist and the lawgiver in the practical affairs of life."[18]

[15] State v. White, 58 N.M. 324, 270 P.2d 727.
[16] Commonwealth v. Mosler, 4 Pa. 264.
[17] State v. Filter, 25 Iowa 67.
[18] Cunningham v. State, 56 Miss. 269.

By 1955 the irresistable impulse test was in use by the courts in only fourteen states: Alabama, Arkansas, Colorado, Connecticut, Delaware, Indiana, Kentucky, Massachusetts, Michigan, New Mexico, Utah, Vermont, Virginia, and Wyoming. The federal courts and the state of Georgia also have used a somewhat similar delusional impulse standard. Since about 1955 other courts have generally shown little interest in changing to the irresistible impulse test.

The New Hampshire, or Durham, Test for Insanity *subject to acquittal if*

Another test for criminal insanity used by a small number of the courts has been called the New Hampshire, or Durham, rule. In enunciating this rule the courts have said that the proper approach is to ignore conventional tests for insanity and leave the question completely to the judgment of the jury. The approach is based on the belief that no single test should apply to all cases. Since members of the jury are experienced in the ways of the world and in human behavior, they should be able to decide the issue. In order to convict under this test, it is also necessary for the jury to find that the harmful conduct in question was the product of the accused's insanity.

First applied in New Hampshire in 1870,[19] this standard gained some backing when it was revived by a federal district court in the District of Columbia in the Durham case in 1954.[20] The Durham, or New Hampshire, rule has provoked considerable debate in criminal law circles, but has received very little following by the criminal courts. Only the Virgin Islands (1964) and the state of Maine (1965) have passed statutes adopting this test.

Criticism usually directed toward the Durham rule is that, in actuality, it furnishes the jury no guidelines or help of any kind. Thrown on their own resources, many jurors, especially those without great experience in practical affairs, have little to rely on except intuition. A number of legal scholars actually have contended that this test is so vague that it is useless.[21]

The Substantial Capacity Test *subject to acquittal if*

Still a fourth criminal insanity test has been laid down by the courts—the *substantial capacity test*. In summary, this rule says that a defendant is not responsible for criminal conduct if, at the time of such activity, the individual lacked substantial mental capacity, either (1) to appreciate the wrongfulness of the act, or (2) to conform to the requirements of the law. Clearly, the test goes beyond the right-and-wrong requirements of the

[19] State v. Pike, 49 N.H. 399.
[20] Durham v. United States, 214 F.2d 862.
[21] United States v. Freeman, 357 F.2d 606.

M'Naghten rule. It leaves to the jury the issue whether the accused's mental condition substantially precluded the ability to appreciate the wrong involved in the conduct. In short, the defendant may be said to have realized that the conduct was regarded as wrong by society, but to have suffered from a mental condition that precluded an understanding of the undesirable consequences that were bound to follow the criminal act.

Less rigid than the requirements of the right-and-wrong test, the substantial capacity approach also offers some standards for the jury to follow. It is not as liberal as the irresistable impulse test or the no-standards approach of the Durham rule.

Encouragingly enough, the substantial capacity test seems to be gaining headway, in both the state legislatures and the courts. In fact, it has been adopted in a number of jurisdictions since 1965.[22]

Partial Insanity

On the other hand, what do the courts do with some people who appear to be perfectly sane in most respects, but who have completely irrational delusions regarding certain subjects? This is sometimes called partial insanity. Unless this insane delusion interferes with the defendant's ability to differentiate between right and wrong, most courts refuse to allow partial insanity as a defense. Some courts, however, do allow it.[23] In any event, the defendant must, of course, present evidence of a causal relationship between the insane delusion and the criminal act.

Diminished Capacity

Defense attorneys frequently point out that it is quite difficult to convince a jury that the defendant is really insane. In recent years some courts have allowed the defense to plead that the defendant had *diminished capacity*. Under this idea, proof of mental problems short of insanity may be submitted as evidence by the defense. If this evidence is believed by the trial jury and the jury finds that the defendant had a mental derangement of a serious nature, the accused is entitled to have this finding considered as evidence of a lack of deliberate or premeditated design. Generally, this claim of diminished capacity has been allowed only in murder prosecutions. The result has been, in some cases, that the accused has been convicted of manslaughter, rather than murder. How far the courts will eventually go with this doctrine is a matter of conjecture.

[22] State v. Shoffner, 31 Wis. 2d 412, 143 N.W.2d 458; Commonwealth v. McHoul, 352 Mass. 544, 226 N.E.2d 556; ILLINOIS CRIMINAL CODE, para. 62.
[23] People v. Hubert, 119 Cal. 223.

The Burden of Proof

In most criminal courts the accused is presumed to be sane. It is therefore the burden of the accused to present evidence that will convince the jury of insanity. This must be proved by a clear "preponderance of the evidence."[24]

Notwithstanding the general rule, some states and the federal courts place the burden on the prosecution to prove the defendant is sane, prior to conviction, when the issue is raised.

AMNESIA, OR UNCONSCIOUSNESS, AS A DEFENSE

In contrast to the situation on insanity, the courts are in general agreement that a person who is unconscious does not have the mens rea, or guilty intent, necessary to commit a crime.[25] Thus, a mother who smothered her baby while she turned in her sleep was excused.

 Amnesia alone, however, will not serve as a defense to a criminal charge unless the jury is convinced that the defendant did not know the nature and quality of the action and that it was wrong.[26]

Sleepwalking, or the habit of the individual afflicted with exercising the power of locomotion during sleep, serves as a valid defense to a crime, when the accused was so unconscious that he or she did not comprehend the nature of the act committed. Sleepwalking, or somnambulism, is not a defense to a crime, however, when it is brought about by the accused who willfully drank intoxicating liquor to excess.[27]

INTOXICATION AS A DEFENSE

Intoxication is the condition which results when a poisonous substance is induced into the human body. In popular usage this generally means alcoholic intoxication.

The general rule of law has long been: "If a drunken man commits a felony, he shall not be excused because the imperfection came by his own fault."[28] In the eyes of the law, it makes no difference what type of substance caused intoxication—drinking too much alcohol, indulging in drugs, or contact with any other intoxicating substance.

[24] This is the rule in California (see People v. Hickman, 204 Cal. 470).
[25] Corder v. Commonwealth, 278 S.W.2d 77.
[26] Thomas v. State, 201 Tenn. 645, 301 S.W.2d 358.
[27] Lewis v. State, 196 Ga. 755, 27 S.E.2d 659.
[28] State v. Yarbrough, 39 Kan. 581.

However, the accused who became intoxicated by mistakenly drinking something under the impression it was not intoxicating will be excused. Likewise, duress will excuse. An individual who is forced to take drugs or drink liquor at gunpoint, who thereafter commits a crime while deranged by the intoxicating substance, is not held to answer.[29]

The argument is sometimes made that a drunken defendant does not have that guilty state of mind that is necessarily a part of any crime. Yet the courts generally agree that drunkenesss is not an excuse if the accused previously formed a specific intent to commit a crime, even though when the crime was committed the accused was too drunk to know what he or she was doing. Voluntary drunkenness may be used to negate the required element of intent only when the intent was not previously formed and the intoxication was so extreme as to suspend entirely the power of reason.[30]

In fact, the courts are usually inclined to require the accused to prove that the intoxication occurred without voluntary intent. Even a person who became drunk while consuming whiskey voluntarily for the purpose of relieving a toothache was not allowed to claim this condition as an excuse for a subsequent crime.[31]

Conversely, in the Penman case, cocaine tablets were given to the victim by a friend, with the explanation that they were "breath perfumers." Apparently, this was the friend's idea of some sort of prank. While completely out of his mind as a result of consuming the drug, Penman committed homicide. The court ruled that these facts were sufficient to acquit on a claim of intoxication by mistake.[32]

It is no excuse, however, for the defendant that the intoxication continued for many days.[33] If the original intoxication was voluntary, the courts do not look to the amount of time that the accused was in this condition.

RELIGIOUS BELIEF AS A DEFENSE

Laws are made for the regulation of actions. While they cannot interfere with mere religious beliefs and opinions, they may prevent and punish religious practices. Even one who believes that human sacrifices are a necessary part of religious worship cannot seriously argue that the government has no power to prevent this sacrifice.

To put it in other words, while freedom of religious belief is a constitutional right, freedom to express that belief in particular ways is not a constitutional right. The method of expressing religious convictions shall

[29] Pearson's Case, 168 Eng. Rep. 1108.
[30] State v. Heinz, 275 N.W. 10, 223 Iowa 1241.
[31] Johnson v. Commonwealth, 115 S.E. 673, 135 Va. 524.
[32] People v. Penman, 271 Ill. 82, 110 N.E. 894.
[33] People v. Lion, 139 N.E.2d 757, 10 Ill. 2d 208.

not be through acts that are contrary to established standards of peace and good order, as determined by the legislatures and the courts.

In many cases, people have claimed religious belief as a defense in doing what otherwise was criminal. The courts have consistently said that anyone has the right to engage in any religious observance, public or private, so long as the observance is not inconsistent with the peace and good order of society and the general welfare of the public.[34]

Clearly, conducting a religious service on the sidewalk in a location that prevents a firetruck from getting through to the location of a reported fire constitutes a violation of law. Conducting religious services at 3:00 a.m. on a private parking lot, without the consent of the owner, probably is a violation of the law on two counts.

In some past cases, religious fanatics have forced their way into private homes, refusing to leave when asked to do so. In others, they have insisted on playing to complete strangers phonograph records attacking other religious beliefs, when listeners repeatedly said they did not want to hear them. Still others have persisted in ringing doorbells after being refused an audience, five or six times within the space of a few minutes. When criminal charges were filed in these cases, the court consistently stated that such action cannot be excused on the grounds of religious belief, even though the accused claims that he "obeyed no law but that of Jehovah."

MISTAKE OF FACT AS A DEFENSE

While we find some exceptions, ignorance or mistake of fact is usually another excuse for what might otherwise be a crime. For example, a woman who takes an umbrella at a restaurant, believing it to be her own, has not committed an offense. In this case, she carried the article away without intent to steal. Her only intent was to take her own property, which negated a necessary element of the corpus delicti of theft.

Where mistake of fact is claimed as a defense, however, it must be based on reasonable belief and must be "honest and real." In requiring the belief to be reasonable, the courts say that a defendant cannot kill another under the mistaken notion that his or her own life is threatened when there is no reasonable basis for this delusion.[35]

On the other hand, the courts sometimes experience difficulty in deciding just what is a reasonable belief. The cases usually use language such as "might reasonably have been expected to induce such a belief in a man of ordinary firmness and intelligence."[36]

When a mistake of fact does exist and the circumstances constitute a

[34] State v. White, 64 N.H. 48, 5 A. 528.
[35] State v. Towne, 180 Iowa 339, 160 N.W. 10; Loy v. State, 26 Wyo. 381, 185 P. 796.
[36] State v. Cook, 78 S.C. 253, 59 S.E. 862.

crime regardless of this fact, then mistake of fact cannot be claimed as a defense.

Then too, we should also point out that mistake of fact is not allowed as a defense in cases where no criminal intent is required by law. For example, driving in excess of the speed limit may involve a mistake of fact, but may not be used to excuse the defendant. In practically all matters that come under the so-called police powers, or public welfare laws, mistake of fact is not allowed as a defense.

In particular, some serious problems often arise in bigamy cases, when one spouse remarries on the belief that the other is dead. For many years the courts held the surviving spouse responsible in determining whether the other partner was actually deceased. Sometimes this may work a hardship on the accused, who has no real way to gain knowledge that the former mate is dead or alive. In recent years, however, a number of courts have overturned prior decisions, allowing an honest mistake of fact to be used as a valid defense to bigamy.

IGNORANCE OR MISTAKE OF LAW AS A DEFENSE

On the subject of mistake of law, the courts sometimes repeat a number of ancient legal maxims such as: "Ignorance of the law is no excuse," or "Every person is presumed to know the law." They mean that the law makes a specific act a violation and does not go beyond this to require proof that by doing the prohibited act the accused intended to violate the law. As one court said, the intent to perpetrate a crime "is not the intent to violate the law, but the intentional doing of the act which is a violation of law."[37] So it is the accused's intent to do what the law labels a crime which counts, regardless of what the accused may call it.

The strength of this rule rests on the idea behind it. An opposite approach would allow an individual deliberately to choose ignorance as an excuse for breaking the law. It would serve to cultivate complete public disregard for order and actually relieve the individual of all responsibility. If the currently used approach were not followed by the courts, it would be almost impossible to convict anyone, regardless of the seriousness of the crime.

CITED CASES

Barrett v. Commonwealth, 259 S.W. 25, 202 Ky. 153.
Bryant v. State, 115 A.2d 502, 207 Md. 565.
Commonwealth v. McHoul, 352 Mass. 544, 266 N.E.2d 556.

[37] State v. Downs, 116 N.C. 1064, 21 S.E. 689.

Commonwealth v. Mosler, 4 Pa. 264.
Commonwealth v. Tompkins, 108 A. 350, 265 Pa. 97.
Corder v. Commonwealth , 278, S.W.2d 77.
Cunningham v. State, 56 Miss. 269.
Durham v. United States, 214 F.2d 862.
Foster v. State, 52 N.E.2d 358, 222 Ind. 133.
Garner v. State, 73 So. 50, 112 Miss. 317.
Johnson v. Commonwealth, 115 S.E. 673, 135 Va. 524.
Korsak v. State, 154, 202 Ark. 921. S.W.2d 348.
Lewis v. State, 196 Ga. 755, 27 S.E.2d 659.
Loy v. State, 26 Wyo. 381, 185 P. 796.
Mc Gee v. State, 238 S.W.2d 707, 155 Tex. Crim. 639.
Miller v. Spring Grove State Hospital, 198 Md. 659, 80 A.2d 898.
M'Naghten's Case, 8 Eng. Rep. 718.
Pearson's Case, 168 Eng. Rep. 1108.
People v. Hubert, 119 Cal. 223.
People v. Jackson, 234 P.2d 261, 105 Cal. App. 2d 811.
People v. Lion, 139 N.E. 2d 757, 10 Ill. 2d 208.
People v. Penman, 271 Ill. 82, 110 N.E. 894.
People v. Willard, 89 P. 124, 150 Cal. 543.
Solesbee v. Balkom, 339 U.S. 9, 70 S. Ct. 457.
State v. Butchek, 253 P. 367, 121 Ore. 141.
State v. Cook, 78 S.C. 253, 59 S.E. 862
State v. Downs, 116 N.C. 1064, 21 S.E. 689.
State v. Filter, 25 Iowa 67.
State v. Gardner, 64 S.E.2d 130, 219 S.C. 97.
State v. Heinz, 275 N.W. 10, 223 Iowa 1241.
State v. Kolocotronis, 436 P.2d 774.
State v. Mendzlewski, 299 P.2d 598, 180 Kan. 11.
State v. Moore, 76 P.2d 19, 42 N. Mex. 135.
State v. Pike, 49 N.H. 399.
State v. Schilling, 95 N.J.L. 145, 112 A. 400.
State v. Shoffner, 31 Wis. 2d 412, 143 N.W.2d 458.
State v. Stern, 123 A.2d 43, 40 N.J. Super. 291.
State v. Towne, 180 Iowa 339, 160 N.W. 10.
State v. White, 64 N.H. 48, 5 A. 528.
State v. White, 58 N.M. 324, 270 P.2d 727.
State v. Yarbrough, 39 Kans. 581.
Thomas v. State, 201 Tenn. 645, 301 S.W.2d 358.
United States v. Fielding, 251 F.2d 878.
United States v. Freeman, 357 F.2d 606.
United States v. Knohl, 379 F.2d 427.

PART TWO
The Law of Crimes

CHAPTER 10

Homicide

In Chapter 4, "Classification of Crimes," we noted one broad classification based upon the social harm that results from the criminal act. Under this breakdown crimes were grouped as offenses against the person; the home; property; public health, safety, and morality; public peace; and as those affecting the administration of justice and the conduct of governmental functions. Of the crimes against the person, certain types of homicide are most serious.

"Homicide" is sometimes defined as the killing of a human being by another human being. At times suicide is included in this class of offenses; thus, homicide may be defined as *any* killing of a human being by a human being. Homicides such as murder and manslaughter are punishable as extremely serious crimes, whereas other killings are unfortunate accidents, regarded as not deserving of prosecution. It is obvious, then, that the police officer who is assigned to work homicide may expect to investigate all kinds of unexplained or violent deaths.

HOMICIDE IS NOT PROSECUTABLE UNLESS VICTIM DIED WITHIN LEGALLY PRESCRIBED TIME

Some features of the criminal law apply to all homicides. One ancient rule of the common law said that homicide could not be prosecuted unless the victim died within a year and a day after the wrongful injury occurred. Otherwise, the causal connection between this wrongful act and the death

151

was insufficient; and death was regarded as resulting from natural causes. Some specific words of the law were:

> . . . It is requisite that the party die within a year and a day after the stroke received, or cause of death administered; in the computation of which the whole day upon which the hurt was done shall be reckoned the first.

Several of our states have abandoned this common law principle through statutes. For example, this time limit has been abolished in New York State; there death need not result within a year and a day from the time of the injury.[1] The California Penal Code has extended the limit to three years and a day.[2]

In one case dealing with the death time element, a holdup man shot the clerk in a liquor store during the perpetration of an armed robbery. The victim lingered in the hospital for six months, then died. When the robber was prosecuted for murder, his attorney argued that this charge could not be sustained because of lack of concurrence of the act and the intent. He maintained that the criminal intent stopped at the time of the holdup. In fact, he argued that the defendant was very sorry for what had happened and had a change of heart immediately after the robbery. The attorney conceded that his client was guilty of armed robbery or assault with intent to kill, but claimed he could not be convicted for murder. The court recognized the ingenious nature of the argument, but pointed to a concurrence of intent and act at the time the injury was inflicted and said that this was controlling. A conviction for murder was sustained.

EVIDENCE MUST SHOW A LIVE HUMAN BEING WHO DIED AS A RESULT OF THE INJURY

Moreover, before a homicide can be proved, the prosecution must convince the jury that a living human was killed. Evidence must show that the victim was not actually dead when the injury occurred and that the death was attributable to the act of the person who stands accused of the homicide. While the courts seldom require production of the victim's body, the prosecution must usually establish the fact that the victim expired within the legal time period.

Because of these requirements the courts have held it was no homicide

[1] People v. Brengard, 191 N.E. 850, 265 N.Y. 100.
[2] CALIFORNIA PENAL CODE, sec. 194; State v. Moore, 196 La. 617, 199 So. 661, sets out the year and a day requirement.

for the accused who threw a dead body into the sea, believing that the victim was still alive. Likewise, the shooting and mutilation of a body that was already a corpse was not homicide, even though this was done in the belief on the part of the accused that he was committing murder.[3]

In this connection, we should note that some jurisdictions have statutes that prohibit the molestation or mutilation of a corpse; prosecution can be undertaken under a statute of this kind, even though the facts do not constitute a homicide.

GENERALLY, THE VICTIM CANNOT BE YET UNBORN

In the case of an expectant mother, the general rule of law is that no homicide exists when the wrongful injury is to a stillborn infant. Ordinarily, a baby is fully born, so as to be the victim of a homicide, when the body of the child has been completely delivered and independent circulation has been established. Thus, according to some cases, the umbilical cord must have been severed, but this is not necessarily the opinion of all the courts.[4]

Another generally accepted view is that when a pregnant woman is subjected to an injurious act and thereafter delivers a stillborn baby, no homicide exists, since no human was killed. Of course, the accused may still be prosecuted for an assault on the mother; but when the baby is born alive, subsequently dying as a result of an injury to the mother inflicted before birth, the courts have held that this is homicide.[5]

A situation encountered with some regularity is that of the unwed mother who conceals her unwanted child by throwing the newborn infant into the nearest garbage can. In some of these cases, the mother may not have known, for certain, whether the infant was actually alive or dead at the time of delivery. When the child is born alive, the mother is guilty of homicide. No penalty, or at least less penalty, may be imposed when the baby is stillborn.

The legislatures in some states have approached this complex problem by providing a penalty for "concealing a child's death, concealing birth, concealing the death of a bastard, or attempting to conceal the death of a child."[6]

[3] United States v. Hewson, 26 F. Cas. 303, no. 15360 (C.C.D. Mass. 1844); 100 Ky. 239.
[4] Morgan v. State, 256 S.W. 433, 148 Tenn. 417.
[5] Id.
[6] See NDCC (N.D.), para. 12-25-05.

HASTENING THE DEATH OF ONE ABOUT TO DIE

Death, of course, is inevitable. Obviously, every homicide accelerates the time when this occurs; but the fact that the victim was about to die is no defense. The fact that the victim had an incurable disease or was at the point of death is immaterial. In an unusual incident of this kind, a convict, awaiting execution on the following day, was murdered during the night; his murderer was prosecuted.[7]

Responsibility for homicide attaches to one who hastens the death of another who is in poor physical condition, although the injury inflicted would not have killed a healthy person. The defendant's ignorance of the victim's poor physical condition is immaterial.

WHO IS RESPONSIBLE FOR THE HOMICIDE?

When people join in a common design to kill, whether in a sudden emergency or in a planned conspiracy, all are liable for the acts of each of their accomplices in furtherance of the scheme. Responsibility attaches to each individual who participates in this venture. As we have seen previously, it is immaterial which of the conspirators struck the fatal blow. From the standpoint of guilt, it makes no difference that the conspirator who actually committed the homicide cannot be identified.[8]

When the common plan is to kill a specific individual, a conspirator is answerable for the act of his coconspirator in killing another person who appears to be a menace to the safety of the conspirators or an obstacle to the execution of their original purpose. The same holds true when killing is necessary to overcome resistance to the conspirators' objectives.[10]

Let us note, however, that when the common design is merely to commit a misdemeanor or a trespass, the accomplices are not criminally liable for a homicide perpetrated by the principal, unless it was an obvious and direct consequence of the plan.[11]

Sometimes two individuals, acting quite independently, may be involved in almost simultaneous attacks against a lone victim. In cases of this kind, each of the attackers may be charged with assault; but when death results, we have a problem in deciding whether one or both are responsible for the homicide. In cases of this kind, the courts usually look to the medical cause

[7] Commonwealth v. Bowen, 13 Mass. 356.
[8] People v. Looney, 155 N.E. 363, 324 .375.
[9] People v. Sobieskoda, 139 N.E. 559, 235 N.Y. 411.
[10] Rowan v. State, 260 S.W. 591, 97 Tex. Crim. 130.
[11] State v. Shelledy, 8 Iowa 477.

of death in charging only one of the assailants with murder or manslaughter.

The facts in one case, for example, disclosed that the first attacker stabbed the victim, while a second knife-wielder slashed the victim almost immediately thereafter. Medical evidence showed that the victim was bleeding freely from both wounds and that he died from loss of blood. The court held that each of the attackers, although acting independently, should be convicted of the murder.[12]

Some courts say that the outcome should be different, however, when death results immediately from an intervening act. In a case decided a number of years ago, the victim was bleeding profusely from a seemingly fatal wound. A second attacker, acting independently of the first, killed the victim with a gunshot, causing immediate death. The court said that the intervening gunshot wound was the cause of death and that the first attacker should not be held for murder. It explained its reasoning as follows:

> If one man inflicts a mortal wound, of which the victim is languishing, and then a second kills the deceased by an independent act, we cannot imagine how the first can be said to have killed him, without involving the absurdity of saying that the deceased was killed twice.[13]

Most of the recent cases hold to the contrary, saying that they find no absurdity involved in finding that the acts of both contributed to the death and that both are guilty of murder, even though they were not acting in concert.

IMPORTANCE OF THE PLACE WHERE THE HOMICIDE OCCURRED

The fatal blow in a homicide may be delivered at a great distance from the place of death. For instance, the accused may stand in Kansas and shoot a victim across the state line in Oklahoma. As a procedural matter, most states will today assume jurisdiction in a case of this kind, even though the site of the completion of the crime is in another state. In doing this, they take a practical approach, treating the homicide as having been committed at the time of the accused's act.

NONCRIMINAL HOMICIDE

All homicides fall into two broad classifications: (1) noncriminal, or innocent, homicides, and (2) criminal homicides.

[12] Pitts v. State, 53 Okla. Crim. 165, 8 P.2d 78.
[13] State v. Scates, 50 N.C. 420.

Noncriminal, or innocent, homicides involve human death to which no criminal guilt is applied. This category, in turn, may be broken down into two major divisions: (1) justifiable and (2) excusable homicides.

Justifiable Homicide

Justifiable homicides are killings commanded or authorized by law. The perpetrator of the killings is without fault or responsibility. These include:

1. Execution of a death sentence in a jurisdiction where the death penalty is used.
2. Killing of enemy troops by soldiers acting under the rules of war.
3. Killing, by necessity, while effecting an arrest for a felony or in preventing the escape of a felon.
4. Killing by a peace officer or a private citizen in an effort to suppress a riot or a revolt.

Excusable Homicide

This classification includes killings which occur:

1. As a result of an unfortunate accident, caused by a person who was not involved in a serious crime and who was not criminally negligent at the time.
2. As a result of an act by one who is too young for blame (an example is that of the three-and-one-half-year-old child who killed his baby brother with the family pistol).
3. As the result of a reasonable mistake of fact.
4. As a result of the act of defending against an attempt to commit a violent felony such as murder, armed robbery, or forcible rape.
5. When an individual is engaged in reasonable self-defense (under some circumstances death of this kind may be manslaughter).

MURDER

Criminal homicide includes both murder and manslaughter. Degrees of murder were unknown at common law; they have been introduced into many of our states by statutes, the terms of which vary considerably. These statutes particularly express important differences between a cold-blooded murder and an unintended killing. In turn, these differences present some serious grading problems for both the legislatures and the courts.

Murder is defined as the unlawful killing of a human being by another with malice aforethought. Murder is a composite crime. It includes an assault committed with intent to kill the victim and the resulting death from that assault, but neither the attack nor the death of the victim alone constitutes the crime.

It does not matter how the attacker intends to accomplish the killing, so long as he or she has the required malice aforethought and puts the intentions into action. Murder may be committed by means of an attack with fists or feet[14] or with nothing more than one's bare hands. The unlawful killing may be by any of the various means by which death may be accomplished.[15] This killing need not necessarily involve brutality, great physical force, or atrocious conduct of any kind.

Application of Direct Physical Force Is Not Necessary

The application of direct physical force to achieve the killing is not necessary. A conviction may be upheld for a death caused by terror, fear, or fright alone; and when death results from the combined effect of a physical injury and fright caused by the accused's acts, a case also has been made for murder.[16]

Death from an Act of the Victim, Caused by the Accused's Conduct

The defendant is responsible for murder when the direct cause of the fatal injury involves the victim's own act, reasonably thought to be due to the defendant's unlawful action. To illustrate, the defendant's acts caused the victim to believe that his life was in danger unless he fled. Acting on this well-grounded belief, he tried to escape by jumping from a nearby window. Instead of escaping, he was killed in the fall. The court ruled that these facts constituted intentional killing (murder).[17]

In a somewhat similar situation, the victim ran into the street to escape an attacker armed with a knife. Unable to properly observe oncoming cars, he was struck and killed. The victim took action that a reasonably prudent person would have taken to avoid a serious attack, and the attacker was held responsible for the results of the act of avoidance.[18]

[14] State v. Lloyd, 87 S.W.2d 418, 337 Mo. 990.
[15] Commonwealth v. Kluska, 3 A.2d 398, 333 Pa. 65.
[16] Cox v. People, 80 N.Y. 500. See also 18 Idaho 566.
[17] Whiteside v. State, 29 S.W.2d 121.
[18] Patterson v. State, 184 S.E. 309, 181 Ga. 698.

When, however, the assault is not of a serious nature and the victim's act of avoidance is one which, in its consequences, does not naturally tend to destroy human life, the offense is manslaughter rather than murder.[19]

The fact that the victim was somewhat slow or negligent in leaving a place of danger is immaterial. Nor does it matter that the victim was negligent under the standards set for civil lawsuits. In a Connecticut case, the defendant was accused of murder after deliberately burning a building. He claimed that lives would not have been lost except for the negligence of the occupants. The court said that this negligence was immaterial.[20]

Improper Treatment of the Injury Does Not Excuse

In general, it is not a defense to an accused whose act contributed to death that improper treatment on the part of nurses or doctors may have played a part in the loss of life.[21]

When an injury has caused death indirectly, through the subsequent development of blood poisoning, or septicemia, the person who inflicted the wound or injury also is criminally responsible. Nor is it a defense that the injured person died as a consequence of surgery that was recognized as necessary to the treatment of the wound.[22]

In one stabbing case, a knife wound was not of itself fatal. The victim died, however, from loss of blood which might have been prevented if medical aid had been promptly obtained. The court held that this fact did not affect the defendant's guilt.[23] In another case, the victim probably would not have died had he remained in the hospital under his doctor's instructions. Yet, these facts also did not prevent a conviction.[24]

The Meaning of Malice Aforethought

When one person intentionally inflicts a wound on another with a deadly weapon and death results, without intervening cause, he or she is guilty of some type of criminal homicide. Whether this conduct constitutes murder or manslaughter depends on the intent of the accused. Manslaughter is distinguished from murder by the absence of malice aforethought.[25] In a

---

[19] Hendrickson v. Commonwealth, 3 S.W. 166, 85 Ky. 281.
[20] State v. Leopold, 147 A. 118, 110 Conn. 55.
[21] Ingram v. State, 194 So. 694, 29 Ala. App. 144.
[22] Hall v. State, 159 N.E. 420, 199 Ind. 592.
[23] Embrey v. State, 251 S.W. 1062, 94 Tex. Crim. 591.
[24] State v. Myers, 125 P.2d 441, 59 Ariz. 200.
[25] Quick v. State, 62 P.2d 1279, 60 Okla. Crim. 229.

prosecution for murder, this malice aforethought (intent) may be shown by the previous actions of the parties that lead to the final act.[26]

We have already noted that malice aforethought is an essential part of murder, but the courts sometimes point out how difficult it is to explain clearly what the law means by malice. Most of this confusion seems to arise from the fact that the usually accepted meaning of the word brings to mind the idea of bad feelings—ill will, hatred, or spite. While some murders are undoubtedly motivated by bad feelings toward the victim, this is not a requirement under the legal definition of malice. On the one hand, a mother who murders her illegitimate baby to protect her own reputation may have no ill will of any kind toward her innocent offspring. On the other hand, she may find herself "loving its life somewhat less that her own reputation."[28] Nevertheless, the law recognizes malice aforethought on the part of the mother.

The words "malice aforethought" long ago acquired a settled meaning in law entirely different from our common understanding of this term. The courts uniformly say that the legal meaning is a predetermination to commit the act of killing, without legal excuse.[29] Malice aforethought shows a condition of mind heedless of social duty and fatally bent on harm. It is that state of mind manifested in the intentional doing of a wrongful act, without just cause or excuse. It means any willful or corrupt intention of the mind.[30] Malice aforethought includes not only hatred, anger, or revenge, but every other unlawful and unjustifiable motive.

Expressed or Implied Malice

In fact, the courts often speak of two types of malice: expressed and implied. At common law and under state statutes, that malice necessary to constitute murder may be either expressed or implied. Malice is expressed when the accused has demonstrated a deliberate intention to take the life of a fellow human. The intention is made evident by explicit and direct words. Implied malice may be demonstrated by deduction from the circumstances, the general conditions existing, or the conduct of the involved parties. Distinction between expressed and implied malice rests in the character of proof by which it is established, not in the particular condition involved.

[26] Jones v. Commonwealth, 60 S.W.2d 991, 249 Ky. 502.
[27] State v. Galvano, 154 A. 461, 4 W. W. Harr. 409.
[28] Jones v. State, 29 Ga. 594.
[29] Rose v. Commonwealth, 149 S.W.2d 772, 286 Ky. 53.
[30] Pembroke v. State, 222 N.W. 956, 117 Neb. 759.

Five Kinds of Malice Aforethought

The cases uniformly say that malice aforethought exists in five types of situations. These are those involving:

1. *An intent to kill.* If the court finds no circumstances that excuse or justify the act, malice is implied in every intentional killing. Accordingly, one who kills another in a duel has the necessary criminal intent (malice aforethought).

2. *An intent to cause great bodily injury.* If the accused shoots with the intention of breaking the victim's leg but not of committing murder the act is sufficient for malice aforethought when the victim dies as a result of the injury.[31]

3. *Felony-murder.* This will be discussed in more detail in another section in this chapter; but basically, malice is automatically implied when the accused kills someone while in the commission of a dangerous felony such as arson, robbery, burglary, or forcible rape.

4. *Intent to resist by force, a lawful arrest.* An individual who resists a lawful arrest by intentionally killing the arresting officer is guilty of murder. The cases say that this resistance supplies the essential malice aforethought.[32]

5. *Action of the accused that obviously threatens death or great bodily injury.* If an individual throws a heavy rock from the walkway onto the windshield of a car on the freeway below, malice aforethought is presumed by the courts. Firing a rifle at a passing airplane or train or attempting to derail a speeding passenger train involves the same type of conduct, although the accused may have no real intent to kill.[33] The courts say that incidents of this type involve a wanton and willful disregard for people. One court spoke of this as "cruel and wicked indifference to human life."[34] We note at least two requirements in this kind of case: (1) that the danger shall be foreseeable; and (2) that the conduct of the accused must show a wanton disregard of human life.

The Intent to Kill One Person That Results in Killing Another (Transferred Intent)

That kind of legal malice which is a necessary part of murder does not require actual ill will toward the intended victim, however. The crime is

[31] State v. Calabrese, 151 A. 781, 107 N.J.L. 115.
[32] Davis v. State, 12 P.2d 555, 53 Okla. Crim. 411.
[33] Banks v. State, 211 S.W. 217, 85 Tex. Crim. 165.
[34] Jenkins v. State, 230 A.2d 262.

murder even though the deceased person is not the same one whom the defendant intended to kill. This is a legal principle that the courts call "transferred intent." For example, the defendant is a bad shot and kills someone standing alongside the intended victim; he is guilty of murder; his intent to kill is transferred to the person injured.[35] This, of course, is a legal fiction; but it tends to discourage those individuals who might kill indiscriminately. One court put it this way: "The intention follows the bullet."[36]

The Felony-Murder Rule   *Know this*

Any homicide committed while perpetrating or attempting to commit a felony is also murder with malice aforethought. The element of legal malice is supplied from the commission of the other felony itself.[37] In fact, the killing becomes a second crime, distinct and apart from the originally intended felony. This is the *felony-murder rule*; originating in the common law, it has been continued in almost all jurisdictions in the United States. Most states today, however, say that the felony-murder rule applies only to human life. This rule of law actually developed to discourage felons from death causes them to be less likely to use dangerous means.

A typical case of this kind was an armed robbery in which the victim was killed. The holdup man clearly had no desire to kill anyone, but he was "shaking and nervous and pulled the trigger" accidentally. He was successfully prosecuted for murder.[38]

Some states have adopted the felony-murder rule from the common law; others have incorporated this idea into their homicide statutes. For example, a Pennsylvania statute (1963) reads:

> **All murder which shall be perpetrated by means of poison or by lying in wait, or by any other kind of willful, deliberate, and premeditated killing, or which shall be committed in the perpetration of, or attempting to perpetrate any arson, rape, robbery, burglary, or kidnapping, shall be murder in the first degree. . . .[39]**

A minority of courts in the United States allow the felony-murder rule to be used when a killing occurs in the perpetration of any type of felony. As we have noted, however, most states hold that it applies only when the intended felony is one that is inherently dangerous to human life. Human experience indicates that a substantial possibility of danger may be con-

---

[35] Noelke v. State, 15 N.E.2d 950, 214 Ind. 427.
[36] State v. Batson, 96 S.W.2d 384, 339 Mo. 298.
[37] Commonwealth v. Cater, 152 A.2d 259, 396 Pa. 172.
[38] McCutcheon v. State, 155 N.E. 544, 199 Ind. 247.
[39] PENNSYLVANIA STATUTES, title 18, sec. 4701 (1963).

nected with any arson, rape, robbery, or burglary. Practically all courts apply the rule to these four felonies. In addition, some states have classified train-wrecking, kidnapping, attempted suicide, and furnishing narcotics to a minor among the inherently dangerous crimes to which the felony-murder rule is applied.

A few courts have applied the felony-murder rule quite strictly, holding that the killing must take place during the perpetration of the intended felony. Under this interpretation, the felon is not responsible for an accidental death that occurs while he or she is fleeing from the scene. Most courts, however, have applied the rule when the killing took place while the criminal was arriving on the scene, committing the crime, or making an escape.

Although we note some conflict of opinion, perhaps the majority of the courts hold that all the accomplices under the felony-murder rule are responsible for a killing committed by any one of the participants in an inherently dangerous felony.

The courts are divided, however, on whether the felon should be held under the felony-murder rule when the killing actually resulted from the act of a third party who was acting in self-defense or trying to prevent the felony. When the rule is strictly applied, the felon may be held to answer for both murder and the original felony. Some courts say that when the killing flows from the fact that the felon intentionally committed an act likely to cause death, the felon must be held responsible.

Withdrawal from Murder

An individual who joins others in a common plan to commit murder may withdraw before the crime is committed. Halfway measures are not adequate, however. The withdrawal must be under such circumstances that the change of mind is perfectly clear to the accomplices. One court has said that the withdrawal must be under such circumstances as to permit the accomplices to take the same action.[40]

In one murder prosecution, for example, the accused obtained an iron bar to be used by another participant in killing the victim. At the time of trial, he claimed that he made a motion or signal to the other conspirator to the effect that it was "no go." The evidence presented indicated that the meaning of the accused's signal was a matter of conjecture. Nothing indicated that the signaling was intended to stop the accomplice from using the bar, and the accused did not retrieve the weapon or remove it from the location where it was originally placed. In addition, he took no action to

[40] State v. Taylor, 139 So. 463, 173 La. 1010.

warn the victim. Under these circumstances the court said that the accused had not withdrawn; the conviction was upheld.[41]

Degrees of Murder   *no degree of murder in 6A.*

Under the common law we find no degrees of murder. Unless facts were presented that reduced the crime to manslaughter, all killings were treated alike. We have good reason to believe, however, that circumstances surrounding a killing, as well as the offender's state of mind, are indications that some convicted persons are less blameworthy than others. In taking these differences into acccount, the legislatures in many states have passed laws providing for several degrees of murder.

Most states divide the crime into murder in the first degree and murder in the second degree, though some provide three degrees.

The general intent of these statutes is to confine murder in the first degree to homicide committed by lying in wait and by poison, and to other killings done in pursuance of a deliberate and premeditated scheme, as well as those that may be classified under the felony-murder rule.

Murder in the second degree includes killings not deliberately designed to take life or to perpetrate one of the felonies required for the first degree; but with, nevertheless, a purpose to kill or inflict injury without concern as to whether it causes death, and without that excuse or provocation that reduces the crime to manslaughter.

A few states define murder in the third degree; this generally includes killings under the felony-murder rule, and so this kind of criminal homicide is removed from the first degree classification used by the majority of states.[42]

Murder Statutes

California statutes on murder are representative of those of many states that divide murder into only two degrees.

S. 187. *Murder Defined.* Murder is the unlawful killing of a human being, with malice aforethought.

S. 188. *Malice Defined.* Express and implied malice. Such malice may be express or implied. It is express when there is manifested a deliberate intention unlawfully to take away the life of a fellow-creature. It is implied when no considerable provocation appears, or when

---

[41] State v. Lee, 34 N.E.2d 985.
[42] Tillman v. State, 88 So. 377, 81 Fla. 558.

the circumstances attending the killing show an abandoned and malignant heart.

S. 189 *Degrees of Murder.* All murder which is perpetrated by means of poison, or lying in wait, torture, or by any other kind of willful, deliberate, and premeditated killing, or which is committed in the perpetration or attempt to perpetrate arson, rape, robbery, burglary, mayhem, or any act punishable under Section 288 (sexual perversion), is murder of the first degree; and all other kinds of murder are of the second degree.[43]

Sections of the New York Penal Law are interesting because of the defenses set out in the statutes. These include:

S. 125.25 *Murder.* A person is guilty of murder when:
1. With intent to cause the death of another person, he causes the death of such person or a third person; except that in any prosecution under this subdivision, it is an affirmative defense that:
   (a) The defendant acted under the influence of extreme emotional disturbance for which there was a reasonable explanation or excuse, the reasonableness of which is to be determined from the viewpoint of a person in the defendant's situation under the circumstances as the defendant believed them to be. Nothing contained in this paragraph shall constitute a defense to a prosecution for, or preclude a conviction of, manslaughter in the first degree or any other crime; or
   (b) The defendant's conduct consisted of causing or aiding, without the use of duress or deception, another person to commit suicide. Nothing contained in this paragraph shall constitute a defense to a prosecution for, or preclude a conviction of, manslaughter in the second degree or any other crime; or
2. Under circumstances evidencing a depraved indifference to human life, he recklessly engages in conduct which creates a grave risk of death to another person, and thereby causes the death of another person; or
3. Acting either alone or with one or more persons, he commits or attempts to commit robbery, burglary, kidnapping, arson, rape in the first degree, sodomy in the first degree, or escape in the second degree, and, in the course of and in furtherance of such crime or of immediate flight therefrom, he, or another participant, if there be any, causes the death of a person other than one of the participants; except that any prosecution under this subdivision, in which the defendant was not the only participant in the underlying crime, it is an affirmative defense that the defendant:

[43] CALIFORNIA PENAL CODE, secs. 187–189.

    (a) Did not commit the homicidal act or in any way solicit, request, command, importune, cause or aid the commission thereof; and

    (b) Was not armed with a deadly weapon, or any instrument, article or substance readily capable of causing death or serious physical injury and of a sort nor ordinarily carried in public places by law-abiding persons; and

    (c) Had no reasonable ground to believe that any other participant was armed with such a weapon, instrument, article or substance; and

    (d) Had no reasonable ground to believe that any other participant intended to engage in conduct likely to result in death or serious physical injury.[44]

The Death Penalty for Murder

The question whether capital punishment is an appropriate penalty for murder has caused considerable controversy, as a matter of both criminal law and criminal procedure. The arguments for and against the imposition of this penalty are extensive, and are outside the scope of this book.

In the case of *Furman v. Georgia,* 408 U.S. 238, decided in 1972, the U.S. Supreme Court struck down the death penalty for a murder sentence of a Georgia court. (This had the effect of reducing the sentence to life.) For a time, authorities on constitutional law were in dispute as to how this decision should be interpreted.

Actually, most opponents of capital punishment took this to mean that the death penalty was no longer acceptable.

Later, The decision in *Gregg v. Georgia,*[45] decided in July 1976 (and other cases considered at the same time) by the U.S. Supreme Court, cast new light on this area of the criminal law. In the *Gregg* decision, the court said that, while a state legislature may not impose excessive punishment, it is also not obliged to select the least severe penalty possible, and that a heavy burden rests on those courts attacking the judgment of the legislature.

The court concluded in the *Gregg* decision that the existence of capital punishment was approved by the framers of the Constitution and had been accepted by the Supreme Court for 200 years. It further noted that approximately thirty-five states had enacted new laws providing for the death penalty after the *Furman* decision, and that imposed under proper conditions, capital punishment would not be invalid per se.

[44] New York Penal Law, sec. 125.25 (1967).
[45] Gregg v. Georgia, 428 U.S. 153.

In explaining the prior *Furman* decision, the court said that the death penalty had been imposed on Furman under a Georgia state statute that left the jury with untrammeled discretion to impose or withhold the death penalty. After the *Furman* decision, the Georgia legislature passed a new law, giving the sentencing jury some definite guidelines that must be followed in arriving at the penalty to be imposed. *Gregg v. Georgia* upheld the constitutionality of this new Georgia law.

In distinguishing the *Gregg* and *Furman* cases, the Supreme Court pointed out that the jury could impose the death sentence in the *Furman* case arbitrarily or capriciously; but the new Georgia law gave the sentencing jury some guidelines and standards to be considered in deciding on the sentence. The new statute required the jury to inquire into the aggravating or mitigating circumstances of that particular crime, the known facts about the accused and the accused's character, the extent of premeditation, and the cruelty or atrocious nature of the crime.

In *Woodson v. North Carolina*,[46] decided at the time of the *Gregg* case in 1976, the U.S. Supreme Court held that a mandatory death sentence for specific offenses was excessive punishment. The court said that the sentencing process must consider individual aspects of the character of the individual offender, as well as the circumstances of the specific crime, and that an arbitrary death sentence did not allow appropriate leeway.

VOLUNTARY MANSLAUGHTER *Heat of passion fatal blow*

> Manslaughter is the unlawful killing of another without malice, either express or implied; which may be either voluntary, upon a sudden heat, or involuntary, but in the commission of some unlawful act.[47]

Manslaughter is a distinct crime, not a degree of murder. It came into the English law through the passage of ancient statutes. The concept eventually was brought to America as part of the common law; it is a modern felony in the United States, either under the common law or under state statutes.

Murder and Manslaughter Compared

In both murder and voluntary manslaughter, the defendant actually kills the victim. Yet, in contrast to murder, manslaughter is killing without malice aforethought. In cases of murder, except where malice is legally implied by the courts, a choice must have been available to the accused.

---

[46] Woodson v. North Carolina, 428 U.S. 280. In Roberts v. Louisiana, 428 U.S. 325, the Supreme Court also held mandatory death penalty provision was unconstitutional.
[47] BLACK'S LAW DICTIONARY.

Thus, malice aforethought makes use of the reasoning process of the accused in a deliberate and planned decision to kill. In some instances, this thought process may have been weeks or months in its development. Yet, the courts agree that this decision to kill can be reached by the murderer in a matter of seconds. Neither the statutes nor the courts ever undertake to measure the length of time needed to complete this mental process.

In an intentional killing, classified as voluntary manslaughter, the illegal act takes place when the defendant's reason is clouded by passion. When the killing is done after the defendant's reasoning processes are again under control, the crime is murder.

In practically all English-speaking countries, the criminal penalty for manslaughter is less than that for premeditated murder. This is why some of the most sensational criminal defenses in American history have been directed toward convincing the jury that the killing was done in a heat of passion, rather than in a deliberate, planned way.

The Nature of Voluntary Manslaughter

In essence, voluntary manslaughter is a killing in which the accused acted in a heat of passion or in a blind rage. The jury is always faced with the question whether the killing was committed under these circumstances or whether the act was one of cool calculation. In either case, the victim of the killing is just as dead; usually little doubt exists that the crime was committed by the defendant. The question, then, is not whether the accused should be exempt from the consequences, but whether the degree of guilt in such a case is equal to that in a deliberate scheme to take a human life.

The assumption is that even-tempered, moral people do not kill their fellows on even the gravest provocation. Relying on the courts to bring about justice, these people do not take the law into their own hands. So, in the manslaughter situation, the law distinguishes between law-abiding individuals and their hot-tempered counterparts to the advantage of the latter.

It is, however, the unusual nature of the situation into which the defendant is plunged, rather than extraordinary deficiency in the defendant's character, that reduces the degree of the crime. The concept of voluntary manslaughter is a concession to the frailty of human nature in those cases where the mere prohibition of the law is not enough. The idea of provocation is a compromise, neither conceding the excusability of the act nor exacting the full penalty for murder.

The whole concept of voluntary manslaughter was summed up in the opinion of a Michigan court more than a hundred years ago (1862).

> . . . If the act of killing, though intentional, be committed under the influence of passion or in heat of blood, produced by an adequate or

reasonable provocation, and before a reasonable time has elapsed for the blood to cool and reason to resume its habitual control, and is the result of the temporary excitement, by which the control of reason was disturbed, rather than any wickedness of heart or cruelty or reck-lessness of disposition; then the law, out of indulgence to the frailty of human nature, or rather, in recognition of the laws upon which human nature is constituted, very properly regards the offense as of a less heinous character than murder, and gives it the designation of man-slaughter.[48]

The Elements (Corpus Delicti) of Voluntary Manslaughter

When sufficient provocation exists, an unlawful killing may even be inten-tional and still be of a lower degree than murder; but provocation alone is not enough. It must be the kind that is recognized by the courts as ade-quate for this purpose.[49]

Actually, four requirements must be satisfied to reduce the crime from murder to voluntary manslaughter:

1. Sufficient provocation must exist on the part of the victim.
2. The accused must have experienced a sudden heat of passion, without reasonable time for it to abate.
3. A fatal blow must have been struck, while the accused was still in this heat of passion.
4. The causal connection must have been such that the provocation aroused passion, which was the cause of the killing.

Legal Sufficiency of Provocation

Not only must sufficient provocation exist, it must be of the kind that is legally adequate. This provocation must be enough to produce the re-quired degree of passion in a reasonable, ordinary, or average person. If the accused went into a blind rage for slight cause or for an imagined reason, the courts say that the provocation is not adequate; the killing is murder. When the accused provokes a fight to obtain an opportunity to kill, this is also murder.

Mere words alone are not enough provocation to reduce a killing to manslaughter. Apparently, this was the law in England as early as 1666 when one court said, "If one calls another the son of a whore. . . notwith-standing those words [the crime] is murder."[50] On the other hand, a few

---

[48] Maher v. People, 10 Mich. 212.
[49] McHargue v. Commonwealth, 21 S.W.2d 115, 231 Ky. 82.
[50] Huggett's Case, 84 Eng. Rep. 1082.

courts have recognized mere words as provocation when they were insulting to close female relatives. For a time, this was allowed by a Texas statute (since repealed).[51] Likewise, gestures, however insulting and abusive, will not reduce the crime from murder to manslaughter, according to practically all of the courts. If coupled with some action, however, words or gestures may add up to sufficient provocation.[52]

When the incident becomes one in which blows are struck, the courts test the adequacy of the provocation by looking at the entire transaction, considering the words as well as the ensuing acts.

A Battery Is Usually Sufficient Provocation

While words alone will not usually suffice, most courts say that an assault and battery is generally the kind of provocation that will satisfy the law. As a general proposition, the courts also hold that a reasonable relationship must exist between the provocative force and the force used to kill. A slight blow never justifies a reduction from murder to manslaughter.

In *Mullaney v. Wilbur*,[53] decided in 1974, the U.S. Supreme Court reversed the murder conviction of defendant Wilbur in a Maine state court in 1966. The murder prosecution was based on a pretrial statement by Wilbur and on circumstantial evidence showing that he fatally assaulted one Claude Herbert in the latter's hotel room. Wilbur's statement, introduced by the prosecution, showed that Wilbur claimed he had attacked Herbert in a frenzy provoked by Herbert's homosexual advance. A Maine statute required an individual charged with murder to prove he acted "in the heat of passion on sudden provocation" in order to reduce the charge from murder to manslaughter. On appeal, the U.S. Supreme Court said that the burden is always on the prosecution to prove every element of the crime charged, beyond a reasonable doubt. The court said manslaughter had been proved, but not murder, and that the state of Maine had not carried out the prosecution's burden to sustain a murder conviction, rather than manslaughter.

The Sudden Affray

A sudden affray is "a difficulty or fight suddenly resulting from the mutual agreement of two or more parties."[54] When both the defendant and the victim are spoiling for a fight and one is killed, both the English and

[51] TEXAS REVISED CRIMINAL STATUTES, sec. 1248 (1925), repealed in 1927.
[52] State v. Hardisty, 253 P. 615, 122 Kan. 527.
[53] Mullaney v. Wilbur, 421 U.S. 684 (1974).
[54] Gibbons v. Commonwealth, 68 S.W.2d 753, 253 Ky. 72.

American courts have traditionally classified the death of either combatant as manslaughter.[55]

The idea is that, in some fights, both parties enter willingly. Consequently, these differ from situations where one party is deliberately attacking and one is exercising self-defense. When the defendant has no intent to kill beforehand and the desire to kill or cause great bodily injury occurs during the heat of the affray, the courts have traditionally recognized *mutual provocation*. This mutual provocation is sufficient to reduce murder to manslaughter, unless the slayer was previously armed with a secret weapon. In a mutual combat situation, when both are attempting to do harm to the other, it is immaterial who struck the first blow.

On the other hand, when one party is obviously striving to inflict serious bodily harm or death and the other is merely exercising self-defense, we have a completely different situation. These facts do not spell out a sudden affray or mutual combat situation. They do indicate that the attacker already had that criminal intent required for malice aforethought.

In California, when parties reach a mutual understanding, become involved in a conflict with deadly weapons, and death results, the slayer is guilty of murder.[56] Apparently, the courts cannot condone a fight between persons armed with deadly weapons. The typical sudden affray, without weapons, is not so likely to cause such serious results.

When two parties enter into a duel, even though it is fairly conducted and both parties consent, a killing is not justified; this too is premeditated murder.[57]

Self-defense is also an aspect of the criminal law here. The California courts, for example, say that two persons engaged in mutual combat are, in effect, assailants. Neither party can justify killing the opponent, regardless of the danger, without having first, in good faith, attempted to decline further struggle, brought home to the other the intention to stop fighting, and given the other a chance to break off the fight. After this opportunity clearly has been given and the adversary continues the fight, the courts regard this as a new assault and battery, and thus recognize the right of self-defense. A killing under a righful claim of self-defense may then be regarded as excusable homicide.

In some states, when the accused starts the fight but does not intend to commit a felony (great bodily harm or death), some courts permit the charge to be reduced to manslaughter when the accused kills in defending against the victim's counterattack; this is sometimes described as *imperfect*

[55] Wiley v. State, 170 P. 869, 19 Ariz. 346.
[56] West's ANNUAL CALIFORNIA CODE, sec. 195, does not bring this under exceptions to murder; People v. Sanchez, 24 Cal. 17.
[57] State v. Hill, 20 N.C. 629.

self-defense.[58] Actually, it is almost impossible to decide whether or not the attacker intended to commit a felony.

Adultery with the Accused's Wife as Provocation

When an attacker is in the act of committing a forcible rape against a wife, it is justifiable homicide if the husband kills the attacker.

Early English cases recognized manslaughter for the husband who killed his wife's paramour in cases of adultery.[59] Our courts in the United States consistently adopted this same principle. Some states even extended the idea, holding to manslaughter when the husband killed both the wife and the paramour.[60] Perhaps most courts today continue to hold the husband for murder if he kills his wife in this situation. To the contrary, some states by statute and by occasional court decision have excused the death of either the wife or the paramour. In most of these situations, the courts impose a requirement that the husband and wife shall be living together as man and wife at the time of the homicides.

A few other outrages against the family also have been held sufficient for provocation. Murder or serious hurt to an immediate member of the family and rape of a female member of the family are good examples.[61]

Resisting Unlawful Arrest as Provocation

Resisting a lawful arrest by a police officer is murder when the officer is killed. Some courts have long followed an ancient rule, however, that recognized an unlawful arrest as a type of assault that can be rightfully resisted. Following this doctrine, a person who kills an officer during an unlawful arrest is guilty of manslaughter, assuming no malice aforethought.

Statutes in some states (California is one of these) require an individual to submit to *any* arrest by a police officer. In these jurisdictions killing a police officer while resisting arrest, even if unlawful, is usually murder.[62]

The Requirement of Sudden Heat

That kind of passion usually required to reduce a killing to manslaughter is not necessarily anger. The cases say that fright, terror, rage, or anger will suffice. The flare-up of intense emotion must temporarily blot out reason

---

[58] State v. Dollarhide, 63 S.W.2d 998, 333 Mo. 1087.
[59] Manning's Case, 83 Eng. Rep. 112.
[60] Dabney v. State, 21 So. 211, 113 Ala. 38.
[61] People v. Rice, 184 N.E. 894, 351 Ill. 604.
[62] CALIFORNIA PENAL CODE, sec. 834a.

and must be of such a degree to cause an ordinary man to act on impulse and without reflection[63] "for the time, being deaf to the voice of reason,"[64] or to ". . . render the ordinary man, of fair average disposition, liable to act rashly . . ."[65]

What Is the Cooling Time for Voluntary Manslaughter?

While the taking of a life in the heat of passion will reduce murder to manslaughter, the killing must occur before that passion cools.[66]

The question of "cooling time" has not been set by law. Like provocation itself, it depends

> . . . upon the nature of man and the laws of the human mind, as well as upon the nature and circumstances of the provocation, the extent to which passions have been aroused, and the fact, that the injury inflicted by the provocation is more or less permanent or irreparable. . . . The court should . . . define to the jury the principles upon which the question is to be decided, and leave them to determine whether the time was reasonable under all the circumstances of the particular case.[67]

When considerable time has elapsed, in fact sufficient time for passion to have subsided, the court may see, as a matter of law, no question to submit to the jury.

Undoubtedly, the passion that might be generated from a blow in a sudden quarrel might subside sooner than the kind aroused by rape commtted upon a man's wife. In *People v. Ashland*, decided in 1912, the accused had sought out his wife's defiler for approximately seventeen hours before eventually locating and killing him. The trial court refused to allow the jury to consider a verdict of manslaughter; the decision was upheld on appeal. If the evidence had shown that the husband was in emotional shock during this time, we have reason to believe that a modern court would instruct the jury to consider whether the accused was still in a state of passion at the time of the killing.[68]

The courts generally say, however, that "The law will not permit a de-

---

[63] State v. Plummer, 107 P.2d 319, 44 N.M. 614.
[64] State v. Primrose, 77 A. 717, 25 Del. 164.
[65] McHargue v. Commonwealth, 21 S.W.2d 115, 231 Ky. 82.
[66] Holcomb v. State, 281 S.W. 204, 103 Tex. Crim. 348.
[67] Maher v. People, 10 Mich. 212.
[68] People v. Ashland, 128 P. 798, 20 Cal. App. 168.

fendant to deliberate upon his wrong and, avenging it by killing the wrong-doer, set up the plea that his act was committed in the heat of passion."[69]

Voluntary Manslaughter and the Right to Protect Property

As a general rule, an offense against property is not sufficient to reduce a murder to manslaughter. This principle applies when the killing is intentionally committed with a deadly weapon, even though the larceny of personal property of a trespass on real estate in no other way could have been prevented.

It is clear that, when a burglar is attempting to break into a dwelling to commit a felony inside, the occupant or owner of the dwelling is justified in killing to prevent the felony. The courts seem to be divided as to whether a killing will be reduced to manslaughter in a situation where the accused has no reasonable cause to believe that the person breaking in intends a felony.

The Necessity of Causal Connection between Provocation and Passion

In any event, the courts consistently say that, before a killing in passion may be reduced to voluntary manslaughter, a causal connection between provocation and passion must be established. In one case, the claimed provocation was not even known to the accused until after the time of the killing. The court clearly pointed out that subsequently learning of the provocation did not reduce the degree of the crime.[70]

The Diminished Capacity, or Diminished Responsibility, Doctrine

A minority of the states follow court decisions that allow proof of mental derangement, short of insanity, as evidence of lack of deliberate or premeditated design. The effect of this is that the malice aforethought required to prove murder is not present, and an intentional homicide, under such circumstances, is reduced to voluntary manslaughter. The opinions of the judges in this line of cases is not always clear, but some legal scholars have concluded that the judges think that the right-and-wrong test for insanity is too severe. What the courts seem to be saying is that the accused need not have a mental problem that is so severe as to satisfy the legal tests, nor the kind of mens rea that justifies a prosecution for pre-

[69] See In re Fraley, 109 P. 295, 3 Okla. Crim. 719.
[70] Lacy v. State, 140 S.W. 461, 63 Tex. Crim. 189.

meditated murder. In other words, the accused may have a *diminished capacity* for murder and therefore should be held for manslaughter only.[71]

INVOLUNTARY MANSLAUGHTER

We have also observed previously that a homicide in the commission of a dangerous felony causes the killing to be a murder (under the felony murder rule). Similarly, an unintended killing during the commission of an unlawful act that is less than a felony but inherently dangerous (malum in se) makes the killing involuntary manslaughter. For example, drunken driving is wrong in itself, malum in se as opposed to being merely prohibited. A driver who is under the influence of liquor might be charged with involuntary manslaughter if he or she strikes and kills a pedestrian.

In the eyes of most people, killing game out of season is malum prohibitum, not malum in se. So, in a jurisdiction where this concept is followed, an accidental killing of a person while that hunter is pursuing out-of-season game is not manslaughter, that is, unless the hunter was negligent in the killing.

Manslaughter by Negligence

There is a second type of involuntary manslaughter which involves an unintentional killing during the commission of any act done in a criminally negligent manner. The amount or degree of negligence necessary to establish this criminal liability has troubled the courts of England and America for hundreds of years. A number of the decided cases recognize that an act of negligence occasionally is committed by even the most moral and wisest of men. Thus, generally more than simple negligence is demanded by the courts. They sometimes say that the defendant's conduct must show such reckless or gross disregard for the safety of others that it reflects indifference to the consequences. Carelessly pointing a loaded firearm at someone is that type of conduct that the courts have in mind.

For negligent homicide (manslaughter), the courts further say that the negligence must be gross or flagrant and reckless disregard for the safety of others, or willful indifference to the injury that will likely follow an act, otherwise lawful, that is converted into a crime when it results in death.[72]

[71] State v. Franco, 347 P.2d 312, 66 N.M. 289; People v. Conley, 411 P.2d 911, 64 Cal. 2d 310. California, one of the minority states that follow this idea, has been criticized for doing so. All criminal law in the state is statutory, and the courts seem to be making their own law to avoid upholding a conviction for murder where the accused is clearly able to distinguish between right and wrong.
[72] State v. Coulter, 204 S.W. 5.

Manslaughter by Motor Vehicle

We find a few instances in the criminal law where guilt is established without the commission of a willful, deliberate act that the accused knew was wrong. However, the simplest kind of negligence connected with the operation of an automobile often results in death. To minimize this, many states have passed laws that provide penalties for homicide in the negligent or reckless operation of a motor vehicle. Some jurisdictions divide the crime into two degrees, specifying that the violation is a felony when the vehicle operator is grossly negligent, and providing for a misdemeanor when the vehicle is used in an unlawful manner without gross negligence. In this connection, the courts do not seem clearly to have established the difference between gross negligence and simple negligence. Specific provisions of these statutes vary from state to state; they usually provide lesser penalties than for other classes of manslaughter.

SUICIDE

Where does suicide fit into the total homicide picture? Is it self-murder, self-manslaughter, or no crime at all?

Suicide is self-destruction—the deliberate termination of one's own life. When a person died of his own hand in early England, all his property and goods were forfeited to the king, and the body was not allowed a standard burial. Some early English legal authorities spoke of suicide as a form of homicide—"self-murder." Yet, we find a difference of opinion as to whether the common law courts actually regarded this kind of death as a form of murder or as a separate and distinct kind of offense. In any event, most of the early English courts did regard suicide as a felony; and an unsucessful attempt to commit suicide was a misdemeanor. All this would provide little or no interest to us today, except for the fact that it does have some effect on our current criminal law.

In those states where the common law crimes have been retained, suicide is still generally recognized as a criminal act. Of course, no forfeiture of property is provided, and no criminal penalty can be applied to a person who is dead. When the person who commits suicide does not harm another, what difference does it make whether the act is a crime or not?

If, however, suicide is a crime in a particular state and the accused kills another person in an unsuccessful attempt to kill himself, he is often held guilty of involuntary manslaughter. This, of course, is on the assumption that an attempt is a misdemeanor, as well as an act that is malum in se. A killing under either of these circumstances is manslaughter.

The approach taken by the South Carolina courts is that the killing of another in an unsuccessful suicide attempt is murder. This is on the theory that suicide is a felony and that any killing of another while attempting a dangerous felony must be interpreted under the felony-murder rule.[73]

In a state like California, where a penal code has replaced the common law crimes, suicide is not generally mentioned in the criminal code. Therefore, when no malice aforethought or criminal negligence exists, the accidental killing of another in a suicide attempt is no crime at all.

Encouraging or Aiding Another to Commit Suicide

We also find considerable difference of opinion in court decisions involving encouragement or aid to one who commits suicide. Some state courts say that, since suicide is not a crime, it is not a crime to encourage or aid and abet someone who ends his own life. Many judges follow the philosophy of the Massachusetts courts. In summary this is:

> The life of every human being is under the protection of the law, and cannot be lawfully taken by himself, or by another with his consent, except by legal authority.[74]

The Texas courts have held similarly. When the accused actually placed poison in the victim's mouth upon request, he was held guilty of murder, following the victim's death.[75]

Perhaps a majority of our courts take the view that one who aids or abets a suicide is actually guilty of murder. This seems to be the result of society's interest in protecting all life and discouraging any kind of killing.

While failing to treat suicide as a crime, some modern statutes definitely attempt to discourage it. Typical is the California statute that punishes for aiding, advising, or encouraging another to commit suicide.[76]

CITED CASES

Aven v. State, 277 S.W. 1080, 102 Tex. Crim. 478.
Banks v. State, 211 S.W. 217, 85 Tex. Crim. 165.
Commonwealth v. Bowen, 13 Mass. 356.
Commonwealth v. Cater, 152 A.2d 259, 396 Pa. 172.
Commonwealth v. Kluska, 3 A.2d 398, 333 Pa. 65.
Commonwealth v. Mink, 125 Mass. 422.

[73] State v. Levelle, 13 S.E. 319, 34 S.C. 120.
[74] Commonwealth v. Mink, 123 Mass. 422.
[75] Aven v. State, 277 S.W. 1080, 102 Tex. Crim. 478.
[76] CALIFORNIA PENAL CODE, sec. 401.

Cox v. People, 80 N.Y. 500.
Dabney v. State, 21 So. 211, 113 Ala. 38.
Davis v. State, 12 P.2d 555, 53 Okla. Crim. 411.
Embrey v. State, 251 S.W. 1062, 94 Tex. Crim. 591.
In re Fraley, 109 P. 295, 3 Okla. Crim. 719.
Gibbons v. Commonwealth, 68 S.W.2d 753, 253 Ky. 72.
Gregg v. Georgia, 428 U.S. 153.
Hall v. State, 159 N.E. 420, 199 Ind. 592.
Hendrickson v. Commonwealth, 3 S.W. 166, 85 Ky. 281.
Holcomb v. State, 281 S.W. 204, 103 Tex. Crim. 348.
Huggett's Case, 84 Eng. Rep. 1082.
Ingram v. State, 194 So. 694, 29 Ala. App. 144.
Jenkins v. State, 230 A.2d 262.
Jones v. Commonwealth, 60 S.W.2d 991, 249 Ky. 502.
Jones v. State, 29 Ga. 594.
Lacy v. State, 140 S.W. 461, 63 Tex. Crim. 189.
McCutcheon v. State, 155 N.E. 544, 199 Ind. 247.
McHargue v. Commonwealth, 21 S.W.2d 115, 231 Ky. 82.
Maher v. People, 10 Mich. 212.
Manning's Case, 83 Eng. Rep. 112.
Morgan v. State, 256 S.W. 433, 148 Tenn. 417.
Mullaney v. Wilbur, 421 U.S. 684.
Noelke v. State, 15 N.E.2d 950, 214 Ind. 427.
Patterson v. State, 184 S.E. 309, 181 Ga. 698.
Pembroke v. State, 222 N.W. 956, 117 Neb. 759.
People v. Ashland, 128 P. 798, 20 Cal. App. 168.
People v. Brengard, 191 N.E. 850, 265 N.Y. 100.
People v. Conley, 411 P.2d 911, 64 Cal. 2d 310.
People v. Looney, 155 N.E. 894, 351 Ill. 604.
People v. Sanchez, 24 Cal. 17.
People v. Sobieskoda, 139 N.E. 559, 235 N.Y. 411.
Pitts v. State, 53 Okla. Crim. 165, 8 P.2d 78.
Quick v. State, 62 P.2d 1279, 60 Okla. Crim. 229.
Roberts v. Louisiana, 428 U.S. 325.
Rose v. Commonwealth, 149 S.W.2d 772, 289 Ky. 53.
Rowan v. State, 260 S.W. 591, 97 Tex. Crim. 130.
State v. Batson, 96 S.W.2d 384, 339 Mo. 298.
State v. Calabrese, 151 A. 781, 107 N.J.L. 115.
State v. Coulter, 204 S.W. 5.
State v. Dollarhide, 63 S.W.2d 998, 333 Mo. 1087.
State v. Franco, 347 P.2d 312, 66 N.M. 289.
State v. Galvano, 154 A. 461, 4 W.W. Harr. 409.
State v. Hardisty, 253 P. 615, 122 Kan. 527.

State v. Hayden, 107 N.W. 929, 131 Iowa 1.
State v. Hill, 20 N.C. 629.
State v. Lee, 34 N.E.2d 985.
State v. Leopold, 147 A. 118, 110 Conn. 55.
State v. Levelle, 13 S.E. 319, 34 S.C. 120.
State v. Lloyd, 87 S.W.2d 418, 337 Mo. 990.
State v. Moore, 196 La. 617, 199 So. 661.
State v. Myers, 125 P.2d 441, 59 Ariz. 200.
State v. Plummer, 107 P.2d 319, 44 N.M. 614.
State v. Primrose, 77 A. 717, 25 Del. 164.
State v. Scates, 50 N.C. 420.
State v. Shelledy, 8 Iowa 477.
State v. Taylor, 139 So. 463, 173 La. 1010.
Tillman v. State, 88 So. 377, 81 Fla. 558.
United States v. Hewson, 26 F. Cas. 303, No. 15360 (C.C.D. Mass. 1844); 100 Ky. 239.
Whiteside v. State, 29 S.W.2d 121.
Wiley v. State, 170 P. 869, 19 Ariz. 346.
Woodson v. North Carolina, 428 U.S. 153.

CHAPTER 11

Mayhem, Kidnapping, Abduction, and Rape

Among the additional crimes against the person, mayhem (maiming), kidnapping, abduction, and forcible and statutory rape occur quite frequently and are most serious.

MAYHEM (MAIMING)

Under the early common law a person who injured another, so that the victim was deprived of the use of a limb or a member of the body which made self-defense in physical combat more difficult, was guilty of mayhem.[1] This, of course, was at a time when men depended on their abilities as swordsmen or knights-at-arms to maintain their wealth and social standing. The early law had nothing to do with disfigurement of the facial

[1] Hiller v. State, 218 N.W. 386, 116 Neb. 582.

179

features, punishing only for the loss or permanent injury of a part of the body that was useful in fighting.

At this stage in the development of the law of mayhem, an assault was made on Sir John Coventry, an important figure in the English government. Political opponents of Coventry waylaid him on the street and slit his nose, disfiguring him markedly, in revenge for a speech he had delivered in Parliament. The cowardly act emphasized the weakness of the law of mayhem; obviously, it did not cover this type of activity. This led to the passage of the so-called Coventry Act, imposing a penalty on anyone who should

> . . . with malice aforethought, cut out or disable the tongue, put out the eye, slit the nose, cut off a nose or lip, or cut off or disable any limb or member of any subject, with the intention in so doing to maim or disfigure him.

In essence, the Coventry Act has been included in the law of substantially all jurisdictions in the United States, aimed at stopping the ruffian who is intent on "carving a mark" on an enemy. In addition, mayhem now includes practically all malicious injuries that disfigure or destroy the victim's person.[2]

Many of these present-day statutes do not use the term "mayhem," simply describing the crime as maiming. Nevertheless, in the states where the common law is followed, the courts generally construe modern statutes in the light of common law principles.[3]

The Criminal Intent for Mayhem or Maiming

Like other true crimes, mayhem is a prohibited act if it is accompanied by the necessary guilty intent. Under both the common law and modern statutes, malice is generally required; but no special type of hate need be directed toward the victim. The courts say that the act must be done with the specific intent to injure or disfigure, and it must be voluntarily done. Premeditation is not required, unless by statute. Therefore, when the maiming is the outgrowth of a sudden affray, no conviction for mayhem is possible unless premeditation is proved.[4]

The Extent of the Injury

In general, the cases say that the type of wound required for a maiming conviction involves the complete severance of a part of the body, or at

---

[2] High v. State, 10 S.W. 238, 26 Tex. App. 545.
[3] Pierce v. State, 41 N.E.2d 797, 220 Ind. 225.
[4] Key v. State, 161 S.W. 121, 71 Tex. Crim. 642.

least that which amounts to a wound breaking the skin. The courts say that a mere bruise or scratch, alone, is not sufficient.[5]

The law establishes no particular requirement as to how the maiming shall be accomplished, whether by shooting, cutting with a knife, striking, or using any other instrument. The type of weapon used may be significant, however, since it must be one that is capable of causing maiming.[6] Even corrosive acid or some kinds of poisons may disfigure facial features and may be the instrument in this violation.

The Type of Injury

Under the early understanding of the common law, when an assailant merely cut off the ear of an enemy, no maiming occurred. The reasoning was that the loss of an ear did not seriously weaken the fighting ability of the victim. After early changes were made in the English law, however, all the facial features (Plus arms, legs, and private organs)were included. Ability to defend oneself from attack is no longer material. Modern statutes are generally written to protect the natural facial features and appearance and to preserve all the natural functions of the human organs. When the statutes speak of disfigurement or maiming of an arm of a leg, they generally intend a permanent crippling of that limb.

Many courts today hold that loss of a tooth during the course of a brawl does not constitute maiming. However, when the accused deliberately sets out to knock out the victim's tooth, this fact will constitute mayhem.

Crippling of an arm, a leg, or an eye is sufficent when the injury is permanent. Testicles are parts of the body, within the meaning of a statute providing punishment for depriving a person of a member of his body.[7]

Castration constitutes mayhem under the common law and under most modern state statutes. The mere biting off of the thumb, however, may not be sufficient to spell out mayhem.[8] When mayhem is not present, the facts will often be sufficient to constitute assault and battery or some other crime.

The language of the Ohio statute on maiming seems to be typical:

Whoever, with malicious intent to maim or disfigure, cuts or maims the tongue, puts out or destroys an eye, cuts or tears off an ear, cuts, slits

[5] Harris v. Commonwealth, 142 S.E. 354, 150 Va. 580.
[6] Brown v. State, 45 S.W.2d 586, 119 Tex. Crim. 12.
[7] 89 Tex. Crim. 264.
[8] Bowers v. State, 7 S.W. 247, 24 Tex. App. 542.

or mutilates the nose or lip, cuts off or disables a limb or other member of another person. . . [is guilty of maiming].[9]

KIDNAPPING

criminal Law
Georgia Law
Federal Law – interstate

Kidnapping was an ancient crime, described as a capital offense by the Hebrew lawgiver Moses.[10] This act was prohibited by the laws of the Greeks, the Romans, and other early peoples. Yet, it is not clear whether the early meaning of the English word "kidnapping" referred to the theft of children only. At any rate, common law kidnapping was the unlawful confinement of any person, child or adult, plus the removal of the victim from his or her own country and transporting the victim to a foreign land. It was a common law misdemeanor, not a felony.

A typical case under the common law involved selling the victim to the captain of a foreign ship, in port and in need of hands for a voyage of several years. The modern version of this activity is sometimes described as "shanghaiing." It has been continually recognized as kidnapping in the United States. Getting a sailor intoxicated for the purpose of leading him onto a vessel without his consent and taking him on board was held as kidnapping in an early New York case.[11]

A majority of our states provide statutes defining kidnapping as a felony. Most of these no longer require foreign transportation. Generally, removal from one place to another is sufficient. Most of the cases have pointed out that it is the removal or transportation, that is controlling.[12]

Invariably, a certain amount of forced movement may occur during the commission of a forcible rape. For example, the victim may be dragged into the undergrowth. Ordinarily, the crime is rape, not kidnapping. The separate and distinct crime of kidnapping is committed, however, when the woman is forced into a car at gunpoint, driven to an isolated area, and raped.[13] In one case, the forced removal, at the point of a pistol, was only 22 feet.[14]

In all of these cases, the transportation must be unlawful, or at least it must be done with an unlawful purpose. Thus, an adult who transports children from a camp in the country, upon hearing that a cyclone is approaching, has committed no kidnapping violation if the purpose is to protect the children.

[9] OHIO REVISED STATUTES, sec. 2901-19 (1953).
[10] Exodus 21:16.
[11] Hadden v. People, 25 N.Y. 373 (1862).
[12] People v. Chessman, 238 P.2d 1001, 38 Cal. 2d 166.
[13] People v. Florio, 92 N.E.2d 881, 301 N.Y. 46.
[14] See People v. Chessman, cited above, and State v. Ayres, 426 P.2d 21, 198 Kan. 467.

Secret Confinement May Be Enough under Some Statutes

Under most statutes, kidnapping is false imprisonment, plus forced transportation of the victim to another location. The wording of the statutes in some states defines kidnapping as forcibly or unlawfully confining another, secretly or against the victim's will. In these states actual transportation or asportation (removal) of the victim is not necessary. In some cases, under the latter type of statute, we find no real difference between false imprisonment and kidnapping.

In one case of this type, the defendant accosted two teenage couples in an isolated area at night, obtaining the driver's car keys at gunpoint. He then stated that the confinement of all four would continue until he had sexual intercourse with the girls. The girls resisted so vigorously that the defendant eventually gave up and left the scene. Subsequently identified, he was convicted of kidnapping, although he never removed or transported his victims.[15]

Taking of a Child

In any event, the seizing in a kidnapping must be against the victim's will. A young child is ordinarily regarded as incapable of giving consent.

As a general proposition, either parent of a child has a legal right to possession of the child. When a divorce has been granted, however, the court order may award custody to only one of the parents. Thus, the other parent has no right to the offspring even though the child may desire to be with this parent. So, under the law in some states, it is kidnapping for one spouse to carry away a child that has been awarded to the other.

There seems to be a trend toward the passage of statutes that impose less severe penalties than kidnapping in this situation. Some states call this taking by one parent *custodial interference,* making the punishment greater if the child is transported across a state line or is exposed to serious risk of harm in connection with this unauthorized taking.

Most courts hold that, when the mother and father are equally entitled to possession of the child, kidnapping is not committed when one takes exclusive possession of the offspring.[16]

Kidnapping for Ransom

Kidnapping for ransom is commonly separately defined and prohibited by statutes in all states. It involves the unlawful taking of an individual, for

[15] Cowan v. State, 347 S.W.2d 37, 208 Tenn. 512.
[16] State v. Dewey, 136 N.W. 533, 155 Iowa 469.

ransom or reward. When the victim is killed, rather than released, the defendant may additionally be charged with murder.

The Federal Kidnapping Law

Following the kidnapping and murder of the infant son of the celebrated flyer, Charles A. Lindbergh in 1932, Congress passed a law prohibiting the interstate transportation of a kidnapped person. This federal felony has been commonly called the Lindbergh Law since that time. Unless the kidnapped victim is released unharmed, the death penalty may be assessed.

The heart of the federal violation is the transportation of the kidnapped victim across a state line. The law contains an automatic presumption, twenty-four hours after the victim is abducted, of interstate transportation. This presumption remains in effect until interstate transportation is disproved. The Federal Bureau of Investigation automatically enters the investigation at the expiration of the twenty-four-hour period, and will withdraw when it is apparent that no state's line was crossed. The FBI may remain on the case, however, when the United States mails are used to deliver a ransom demand note. The use of the mails in this way, in turn, constitutes a violation of the Federal Extortion Act.

As in a number of other federal violations, the FBI enters the kidnapping because of the interstate transportation angle. As a side issue, we should note that the federal government has no general power to investigate or prosecute crime in the individual states. The United States Constitution gives Congress power to regulate commerce between the states, however. Thus, the federal courts have said that this carries with it the federal right to regulate crime involving interstate commerce.

Perhaps the main objective of the Federal Kidnapping Law is to curtail kidnapping for ransom, but the federal enactment is very broad in its language, prohibiting kidnapping "for ransom or reward or otherwise." This has been interpreted to mean a kidnapping for any sort of ulterior motive that the kidnapper may have—to settle a grudge, for sexual gratification, to beat up the victim, or for any other purpose. Money need not be involved.[17]

No violation under the federal law has occurred when a parent kidnaps his or her own child, regardless of who has been awarded custody by the courts. The federal statute is set out in the footnote below.[18]

[17] United States v. Healy, 376 U.S. 75, 84 S. Ct. 553.
[18] UNITED STATES CODE, title 18, sec. 1201, reads:

    (a)   Whoever knowingly transports in interstate or foreign commerce, any person who has been unlawfully seized, confined, inveigled, decoyed, kidnapped, abducted, or carried away and held for ransom or reward or otherwise, except, in the case of a

ABDUCTION

In early England abduction was taking away a man's wife, child, or ward by persuasion, fraud, or open violence. Some features of it were identical with modern kidnapping and false imprisonment violations. In fact, some aspects of common law abduction have been incorporated into present-day kidnapping and false imprisonment statutes. Under the common law, no force of threat of force was necessary since the victim could have gone on a free-will basis.

Almost all of our states provide some sort of abduction laws, but they differ widely. Yet, these in one form or another prohibit:

1. Enticing or taking a female to introduce her into a house of prostitution.
2. Detaining, taking, or alluring a female under a specified age, without the consent of her parent or guardian.
3. Taking or detaining a female against her will, with intent to cause her to be married or to engage in sexual relations.

Note, from the above, that some of these statutes require force to be used against a woman; in others, she may go of her own free will. Prosecuting attorneys sometimes use statutes of this kind to convict a male who has lured a young female away from her home but has not yet gone fo far as to commit rape or other serious offenses.

RAPE

modern day — penetration, force + the lack of consent

When the term "rape" is used, we generally mean forcible rape. The common law felony involved "unlawful carnal knowledge, by a man of a woman, forcibly and against her will." In the language of a modern case, "Rape is an act of sexual intercourse with a female, other than the wife of

---

(Footnote continued from page 184)

> minor, by a parent thereof, shall be punished (1) by death if the kidnapped person has not been liberated unharmed, and if the verdict of the jury shall so recommend, or (2) by imprisonment for any term of years or for life if the death penalty is not imposed.
>
> (b) The failure to release the victim within twenty-four hours after he shall have been unlawfully seized, confined, inveigled, decoyed, kidnapped, abducted, or carried away shall create a rebuttable presumption that such person has been transported in interstate or foreign commerce.
>
> (c) If two or more persons conspire to violate this section and one or more of such persons do any overt act to effect the object of the conspiracy, each shall be punished as provided in subsection (a).

the defendant, in which the female resists and her resistance is overcome by force."[19]

Either under the common law or by modern statutes, rape is a felony thoughout America. Every rape not only originates in, but itself includes, an assault; and when sexual penetration is accomplished, this is rape. When penetration is not accomplished, it is assault with intent to rape.

Rape is distinguished from seduction in that this crime is committed by force, without the consent of the female or on a female regarded by the law as incapable of giving consent. In seduction, the female is induced, not forced, to consent. In addition, a married woman may be raped, while usually seduction cannot be committed on her.

Generally, the courts do not attempt to regulate sexual relations between married couples. In most states a husband who forces his wife to have intercourse against her will has committed a criminal assault. In recent years, however, a few jurisdictions have passed statutes providing that the husband may be prosecuted for rape. Some courts treat parties living together as married, refusing to recognize the possibility of rape. A sexual assault on a former wife, without her consent and after the marriage has been dissolved by divorce, is rape.[20] A husband may, however, be convicted for rape against his wife when he assists another man in committing the crime, or when he forces her to submit to another at gunpoint.[21]

Rape cannot be committed upon a male, although a male may be the victim of a sexual assault or other criminal acts.

To be convicted for rape, the male must have sufficient mental capacity to entertain a criminal intent, and he must be physically capable of committing the act. Generally, when the defendant is under the age of fourteen, the prosecution must prove that he had the ability to commit the act.

Rape cannot be committed directly by a woman, although she may be convicted for aiding and abetting another or as a principal in physically using force to subdue the victim.

Lack of Consent

Sexual intercourse with the female's consent is not rape, provided she is above the age of consent and is capable, in the eyes of the law, of giving her consent. When a man holds a woman against her will and she eventually consents to intercourse prior to the initiation of the act, this activity does not constitute rape. When no force is used, although the female makes verbal protests and expresses refusal, the law regards her activity as willing.

[19] Smith v. Superior Court, 295 P.2d 982, 140 Cal. App. 2d 862.
[20] State v. Parsons, 285 S.W. 412.
[21] State v. Dowell, 11 S.E. 525, 106 N.C. 722.

Although resistance of the woman to the male's advances may be genuine at the outset, if the physical contact arouses her passion so much that she submits to the intercourse before the penetration is accomplished by force, she has not been raped.[22] The courts say that she eventually gave her consent.

When the female is mentally ill, is drugged, or is so drunk that she does not know what she is doing, the courts consistently say, as a matter of law, that she is incapable of consent. In these cases, no resistance is required. If this approach was not taken, a woman could be raped with impunity when she is anesthetized or becomes unconscious for any reason. Sexual assault on a woman who had fainted was held to be rape.[23]

In some cases, the female may continue to resist or cry out until after she has been penetrated by the male. Realizing that her struggle has been useless, she may discontinue resistance at this stage. The cases say that she need not continue to resist, since she did not give her consent.

The Amount of Force That Must Be Used

The cases consistently say that no specific amount of force on the part of the defendant is necessary to constitute rape. Some courts state that only enough force is needed to accomplish the rapist's purpose. Sufficient force to overcome the female's resistance is always required, unless, of course, threats to harm are also present. It is not essential that the force be so great that she reasonably believes she will be killed.

When the defense claims that no force was used, marks of violence on the body of the woman may be used as evidence to prove the use of force. Torn clothing, scratches and cuts, bruises, smashed personal articles, disarrangement of furniture, and similar evidence may also be introduced.

The Amount of Resistance by the Victim

Some earlier courts sometimes said that the woman must have resisted to the utmost.[24] Others said that she must fight off her attacker to the limit of her power and make an outcry, but few modern courts go this far; they say only that she must resist in good faith and that the amount of needed resistance is relative. In one case, a woman was kidnapped by six robust men; each had forcible intercourse with her. The victim offered considerable resistance to the first man, but did not put up the same fight against

---

[22] Wade v. State, 138 S.E. 921, 37 Ga. App. 121.
[23] Lancaster v. State, 148 S.E. 139.
[24] People v. Carey, 119 N.E. 83, 223 N.Y. 519.

the others; it was obvious to her that her struggles were futile. The court convicted all the males.[25]

Crying out in a loud voice is always regarded as evidence of refusal to consent. Yet, the law actually does not require an outcry by the victim when it is useless or when the female submits because of fear of great violence.[26] We should note, then, that rape can be committed through both threats and force combined or only by putting the victim in great fear.[27]

In general, modern cases say that the required resistance is a relative thing, depending on age, size, physical strength of the parties, and the physical location of the assault. It is not necessary that the rapist beat the victim into insensibility or kill her; the required force must be such that the objecting female is subjected to and put under the power of her attacker.

The Nature of the Sexual Act

Merely rubbing the sexual organs together is not sufficient to constitute rape. The male organ must actually penetrate the female sex organ. The amount of penetration is sufficient.[28] An emission of sperm by the male is not necessary; he need not obtain sexual satisfaction from the act.

Problems with Proof

The courts sometimes say that rape "is an accusation easily to be made and hard to be proved, and harder to be defended by the party accused." They uniformly agree that the intention to commit rape may be shown by circumstantial evidence[29] and the victim must show some evidence of genuine resistance other than mere verbal disapproval.[30]

Judges also frequently instruct the jury that the testimony of a person alleged to have been raped should always be scrutinized with care.[31] Frequently, no witnesses are available except the accused and the victim, and an unscrupulous woman can make a false claim of rape without much risk of prosecution. On the other hand, the man may have a great deal to lose. For example, an unprincipled woman may claim "rape" to blackmail the man into marriage. She may be a married woman caught in an extracur-

[25] Salerno v. State, 75 N.W.2d 362, 162 Neb. 99.
[26] People v. Silva, 89 N.E.2d 800, 405 Ill. 158.
[27] Lomax v. State, 144 S.W.2d 555, 142 Tex. Crim. 231.
[28] Bromin v. State 87 P.2d 112, 53 Ariz. 174.
[29] State v. Tomblin 20 S.E.2d 122, 124 W. Va. 264.
[30] Culbert v. State, 129 So. 315, 23 Ala. App. 557.
[31] Oakes v. State, 39 S.E.2d 866, 201 Ga. 365.

ricular sex act, unable to otherwise explain her misconduct to her husband. In still another case, the woman may be a prostitute who simply feels she was not paid enough.

As a result, many defense attorneys have taken the approach that an acquittal may hinge on whether the jury can be convinced that the victim was of questionable morality. Evidence concerning prior unchastity of the prosecutrix does not compel an inference of consent, although it constitutes a circumstance which indicates some likelihood that she consented. Yet, even a prostitute can be raped if she does not consent.

The idea that the defense attorney often tries to create is that the victim apparently "slept around quite a bit. Why should the defendant be singled out for punishment?"

Also we find many differences in rape cases. One prosecution may arise out of a drunken brawl, in which the participants hardly know whether the woman consented or whether the parties actually engaged in a sex act. At the other extreme, a rape may be an unusually brutal assault on a completely innocent woman. In some instances it seems clear that the defense attorney "badgered" the victim until she was too emotionally distraught to testify. The prosecution's case then collapsed for lack of evidence. When this happens, it is the victim who is "prosecuted," rather than the rapist. This kind of injustice has been dramatically brought to the public's attention by women's rights movements in the 1970s.

To prevent these tactics by a defense attorney, several states have taken steps to curb the cross-examination of a rape victim during the trial. At the same time, the defense must be allowed a fair trial. California and some other states have solved this problem through statutory controls. For example, section 782 of the California Evidence Code (passed in 1974) requires the defendant to make a motion to the judge, offering to present evidence of the rape victim's lack of chastity. The judge then conducts a hearing, from which the jury is excluded, to determine whether there is any real merit to the defense claim. If the defense attorney can convince the judge on this issue, then the judge will allow the evidence to be heard before the jury, but will limit the nature of the questions permitted.

Rape by Fraud

In some states the courts have held that consent to sexual intercourse through the use of any form of fraud also constitutes rape. A number of other states have written laws that cover this situation.[32] Most of these may be classified into three types of situations:

[32] CALIFORNIA PENAL CODE, sec. 261.

1. Sexual intercourse by a medical doctor or pretended doctor, under the guise of medical treatment.
2. Sexual intercourse by one who impersonates or pretends to be the husband of a married woman who is asleep or is in darkness.
3. Sexual intercourse by an individual who goes through a mock wedding ceremony or otherwise induces a woman to believe that he is legally married to her.

The courts generally say that a doctor who takes advantage of a woman to initiate intercourse with her is guilty of rape.[33] They differ in those situations where a male slips into bed with an unsuspecting married woman. Some have said that this woman gives her consent and that no violation has occurred. Statutes in some states make the act a violation when she submits under the belief that the person committing the act is her husband. Other courts have held that this is rape, even in the absence of a state statute.[34]

We also find some difference of opinion as to whether sexual relations that take place after a mock wedding ceremony constitute rape. Statutes in several jurisdictions seem to include this type of activity under violations for either rape or carnal knowledge.

Statutory Rape   *16 yrs of age*

Carnal knowledge of a child was not classified as rape under the early common law, so long as the female consented. Recognizing that young females might not be able to make mature judgments, the English Parliament provided a felony for intercourse with a child under the age of ten years. Similar statutes have been made into law in all states in this country, generally raising the age of consent to sixteen or eighteen years. Some jurisdictions declare that intercourse with a female under the age of twelve years constitutes a special crime called "aggravated rape." In the state of Illinois, sexual relations with a consenting female adolescent are covered under a felony called "indecent liberty with a child" and a misdemeanor entitled "contributing to the delinquency of a child."

Most states describe carnal knowledge of a consenting female under the statutory age of consent as "statutory rape." Of course, no element of force is involved in this violation. The underage girl in these cases is often publicly referred to as "jail bait," or "San Quentin quail," indicating that a sexual connection with her may lead to difficulties with the law.

---

[33] Eberhart v. State, 34 N.E. 637, 134 Ind. 651; State v. Atkins, 292 S.W. 422.
[34] See Mooney v. State, 15 S.W. 724, 29 Tex. App. 257.

In summary, most courts hold that a man engages in sexual relations with a youthful female at his own peril and that he is responsible for knowing whether she is above the age of consent. This clearly is not consistent with the usual guilty-state-of-mind requirement for crime. As a matter of policy, however, the courts usually say that the law must protect youthful females from sexual exploitation.

CITED CASES

Bowers v. State, 7 S.W. 247, 24 Tex. App. 542.
Brown v. State, 45 S.W.2d 586, 119 Tex. Crim. 12.
Browning v. State, 87 P.2d 112, 53 Ariz. 174.
Cowan v. State, 347 S.W.2d 37, 208 Tenn. 512.
Culbert v. State, 129 So. 315, 23 Ala. App. 557.
Eberhart v. State, 34 N.E. 637, 134 Ind. 651.
Hadden v. People, 25 N.Y. 373.
Harris v. Commonwealth, 142 S.E. 354, 150 Va. 580.
High v. State, 10 S.W. 238, 26 Tex. App. 545.
Hiller v. State, 218 N.W. 386, 116 Neb. 582.
Key v. State, 161 S.W. 121, Tex. Crim. 642.
Lancaster v. State, 148 S.E. 139.
Lomax v. State, 144 S.W.2d 555, 142 Tex. Crim. 231.
Mooney v. State, 15 S.W. 724, 29 Tex. App. 257.
Oakes v. State, 39 S.E.2d 866, 201 Ga. 365.
People v. Carey, 119 N.E. 83, 223 N.Y. 519.
People v. Chessman, 238 P.2d 1001, 38 Cal. 2d 166.
People v. Florio, 92 N.E.2d 881, 301 N.Y. 46.
People v. Silva, 89 N.E.2d 800, 405 Ill. 158.
Pierce v. State, 41 N.E.2d 797, 220 Ind. 225.
Salerno v. State, 75 N.W.2d 362, 162 Neb. 99.
Smith v. Superior Court, 295 P.2d 982, 140 Cal. App. 2d 862.
State v. Atkins, 292 S.W. 422.
State v. Ayres, 426 P.2d 21, 198 Kan. 467.
State v. Dewey, 136 N.W. 533, 155 Iowa, 469.
State v. Dowell, 11 S.E. 525, 106 N.C. 722.
State v. Parsons, 285 S.W. 412.
State v. Tomblin, 20 S.E.2d 122, 124 W. Va. 264.
United States v. Healy, 376 U.S. 75, 84 S. Ct. 553.
Wade v. State, 138 S.E. 921, 37 Ga. App. 121.

CHAPTER 12

Assault and Battery, Self-Defense, False Imprisonment

Like homicide, mayhem, kidnapping, abduction, and rape—assault and battery and false imprisonment are crimes against the person. In many respects, they are actually more important to the police officer than the more serious ones. At least, they occur more frequently; and, along with matters of self-defense, often involve the officer in a more personal way.

Because of the close relationship between the separate crimes of assault and battery, the two terms frequently are lumped together in a great number of our legal expressions; but because of the *nature* of the relationship, it may be helpful to reverse the usual order of presentation, first examining *battery*, then following with an analysis of *assault*.

BATTERY *look @ (oa hand out know definitions*

Someone has said that battery is, in essence, a violation of the "the right to be let alone." The court in one New York case has explained this in greater detail:

> . . . certain rights pertaining to mankind . . . which have their origin independent of any express provision of law . . . are termed "natural

> rights." One of these is the right of personal liberty. This includes not only absolute freedom to everyone to go where and when he pleases, but the right to preserve his person inviolate from attack from any other person. This right to one's person may be said to be a right of complete person. This right to one's person may be said to be a right of complete immunity, to be let alone.[1]

Here is another way it has been expressed:

> . . . Every man is the sole custodian of his own physical person. No other has a right to touch it unlicensed, and another wrongs him who does to him any physical violence, however slight.[2]

When someone violates this right to bodily privacy by the unlawful application of force, the law says that this is a battery. In the language of the courts, a battery may involve "wantonly laying hands upon, or applying force to the body of another,"[3] or "any touching by one person of another in rudeness or in anger."[4]

The Amount of Force Is Immaterial

While battery is sometimes recognized as a forceful or brutal physical attack, even the slightest touching of another is a battery when the action is unlawful or without consent. From a legal standpoint, the force used may be so slight as to cause no pain or physical damage, leaving no scars or marks.[5]

The mere act of inflicting unauthorized, unlawful force on the body of another constitutes the battery, regardless of its degree. Thus, the contact need not be made by a sharp blow, since any forcible contact actually is enough. In addition, the body or even the clothing of the victim need not be touched. Grabbing or striking an object from the hand or touching anything that is connected with the body is sufficient. The objectionable force need never reach the victim's body. If, for example, a person's clothes should be cut away with a knife, this is a battery. The crime may be achieved through any object the accused sets in motion. In fact, spitting in the face of another has long been regarded as a battery.

Taking the slightest unwarranted liberty with a woman's person is another example of this crime.[6] It is immaterial whether this activity is

[1] People ex rel. Bingham, 107 N.Y.S. 1011.
[2] Lutterman v. Romey, 121, N.W. 1043, 143 Iowa 233.
[3] Cornelius v. Montegut, 8 La. App. 358.
[4] Wilson v. Orr, 97 So. 133, 210 Ala. 93.
[5] Wood v. Cummings, 83 N.E. 318, 197 Mass. 80.
[6] Commonwealth v. Jaynes, 10 A.2d 90, 137 Pa. Super. 511.

merely an intent to brush against her, to obtain a kiss against her will, or to lay hands on her body for any purpose.[7]

The courts have phrased it this way:

> The inviolability of the person is as much invaded by a compulsory stripping and exposure as by a blow. To compel anyone, especially a woman, to lay bare the body, or to submit it to the touch of a stranger, without lawful authority, is an indignity . . . [and a battery].[8]

On the other hand, no battery has occurred when a man kisses a woman friend and has every reason to believe that his act will be agreeable to her.[9]

How Force May Be Applied

> It is a general principle of [all] criminal law that one may be guilty of a crime, where the prohibited act is committed through the agency of mechanical or chemical means, as by instruments, poison or powder, or by an animal, a child or other innocent agent acting under the direction and compulsion of the accused.[10]

Clearly, we see no limit to the means by which force may be applied to the body of another. It may be done directly, as by hitting with a clenched fist, by shooting or cutting, or using any kind of weapon. Deliberately riding a bicycle against a pedestrian, without regard for the consequences, is a battery.[11] Similarly, a person who unlawfully strikes a glass door while hitting at an enemy, thus breaking the glass and driving a fragment into the eye of the victim, is equally guilty of a battery.[12] Throwing a rock, placing poison in the victim's drink, planting a spring gun inside an unoccupied house, throwing acid at someone, or deliberately communicating a disease to another, is a battery.

Noteworthy, too, is the fact that in almost every battery the victim may recover money damages in a civil lawsuit, in addition to the criminal prosecution.

The Mental Intent for Battery

A few modern courts in the United States have insisted that the unlawful act in a battery must have been done in a vengeful, rude, or angry manner.

[7] Moreland v. State, 188 S.W. 1, 125 Ark. 24.
[8] Commonwealth v. Jaynes, above; Union Pacific Ry. Co. v. Botsford, 141 U.S. 250, 11 S. Ct. 1000.
[9] Weaver v. State, 146 S.W. 927, 66 Tex. Crim. 366.
[10] Beausoliel v. United States, 107 F.2d 292.
[11] Mercer v. Corbin, 20 N.E. 132, 117 Ind. 450.
[12] Schmitt v. Kurrus, 85 N.E. 261, 234 Ill. 578.

These are definitely in the minority, however. Most tribunals say that only a general intent (mens rea) is required. This means that the necessary intent is satisfied when the touching is willfullly or voluntarily done.

Some states, by statute, say that mere criminal negligence in the operation of an auto, without any sort of willful intent, is a battery. The problem in this situation is to determine just what constitutes criminal negligence. Some courts seem to construe any negligence that results in an accident as sufficient for this purpose.

Consent by the Victim

No battery, either criminal or civil, has occurred when the victim consents to the activity that results in the injury.[13] For example, when two fighters enter the boxing ring for a friendly sparring match, the courts say that both have consented to whatever blows they may receive in the usual course of this activity. The same, of course, is true in a backyard football game.

A situation involving this kind of physical contact is completely different, however, when an individual who is walking down a public street punches another in the jaw without prior conversation. The difference is, no consent was given by the victim.

In this connection, the law clearly says that some individuals cannot legally give their consent. A woman who is mentally incompetent cannot consent to any battery against her person, even though she appears to be willing to have sexual contact. Likewise, a child cannot consent to the activities of a child-molester. The defendant has no defense even if it is proved that the child made no protest and took no steps to advise his or her parents or the legal authorities.[14] Exactly when a child is old enough to consent to sexual molestation has not always been clear, but numerous indications are that the age of consent corresponds with that set by the state law in statutory rape cases.

Similarly, the courts say that an individual who is under duress cannot consent to a battery. It is only common sense to reason that a victim who is held at gunpoint cannot consent to blows that otherwise are objectionable, regardless of what the victim may submit to at the time.

If the Act Is Lawful—No Battery

When the force applied by the accused is lawful, it does not matter that the amount of force was more than the victim anticipated. In the friendly

[13] Witzka v. Moudry, 85 N.W. 911, 83 Minn. 78.
[14] Beausoliel v. United States. 107 F.2d 292.

boxing match mentioned earlier, one of the men involved cannot complain that a blow was harder than he had expected; but if it is obvious (by word or action) that he wants to break off the match, a battery occurs when the other boxer deliberately ignores this request and continues to throw some punches.

In summary, the courts say that lawful use of force never constitutes a battery. For example, a parent has a legal right to use reasonable force in disciplining a child, so long as this discipline is not cruel. In one case, a father accidentally struck a passing individual while administering reasonable discipline. When the incident was prosecuted, the court held no battery with respect to either the passerby or the child. Clearly, the decision would have been otherwise had the force been excessive.[15]

A person who has the right of entrance into a building does not commit a battery by removing someone who obstructs the entry, provided, of course, excessive force is not used.[16]

ASSAULT *definition*

As for assault, two kinds existed under the common law.

1. One was simply an attempt to commit a battery, whether the attempt was a success or a failure.
2. The other involved action by the accused that threatened harm to the victim, placing the latter in fear or apprehension of an impending battery.

Because of the wording of modern statutes, the second type is not recognized as a crime in a number of states. These jurisdictions see only an attempted battery as an assault violation.

One Type of Assault Is Simply a Battery in the Making (an Attempt)

An attempt to commit a battery is an assault in all jurisdicitons. When the battery is not completed, it remains an assault for which the person responsible may be prosecuted; but when the attempt is completed, the crime becomes a battery. In this sense, then, an assault is simply "a battery in the making."

We noted earlier that an assault and a battery are distinct, individual

[15] Turner v. State, 33 S.W. 972, 35 Tex. Crim. 369.
[16] Williams v. Lubbering, 63 A. 90, 73 N.J.L. 317.

crimes; but frequently the two go hand-in-hand, the assault blending into the battery. The *attempt* merges into the *completed crime*. When this happens, the attempt loses its individual identity; and the law is, thereafter, concerned only with the completed crime.

However, through long custom, lawyers and courts use the words *assault and battery* together, when they intend only the words *battery*. So, a completed assault is prosecuted in most states as an assault and battery. In legal effect, this is simply a single prosecution for a battery.

In those cases where prosecution for assault is based on an attempted battery, the prosecutor must prove that the accused made a direct move toward the commission of the prohibited act. This, of course, is a requirement in any attempted crime.

Practically all courts hold that only a general intent must be proved on a battery charge. Accordingly, only a general mental intent is required for the kind of assault that is an attempted battery; but the courts usually agree that the prosecution must present proof that, at the time of the attempt, the accused had the ability to commit the intended battery.

This requirement of "actual present ability" often allows the accused to escape conviction on the defense of factual impossibility. A typical case of this kind is one in which the accused points an unloaded gun at the victim, threatening immediate use of it if orders are not followed. The courts say the accused did not have the present ability and that the facts, therefore, do not constitute an attempt.

Some states cured this defect when they passed laws prohibiting menacing another with a gun, whether or not the weapon is loaded.

When the assault is based on an attempted battery, the purpose of this law is to punish the wrongful act. In a situation of this kind, the victim may be unaware of the attempt. This lack of knowledge on the part of the victim is immaterial, since the law is seeking to punish the wrongful act, not to relieve the mind of the victim.

Assault by Placing One in Fear of an Impending Battery

In assault by placing in fear, the courts say:

> An assault is an unlawful offer of corporeal bodily injury to another by force, or force unlawfully directed toward the person of another, under such circumstances as to create a well-founded fear of immediate peril.[17]

[17] Jackson v. Commonwealth, 247 S.W.2d 52.

A gun need not actually be loaded under the law as stated above. The object of this law is to prevent the victim from being placed in fear. Therefore, the law of assault has been violated when the victim is merely placed in fear, since there is no way for the victim to know whether or not the gun is loaded.

Also, the accused who has the *apparent* ability to commit the battery, rather than an actual ability, may be convicted of this kind of assault. The reasoning of the courts here is that the victim is just as fearful of an apparent ability as of the actual ability. It is, then, a desirable objective of the criminal law to prevent an individual from scaring law-abiding persons half out of their wits. In situations of this kind, the courts use the standard of a reasonable person in deciding whether it appeared that the accused had the ability to follow through with a threat. When the victim possesses an overactive imagination, this does have its effect. The test is whether a reasonable, ordinary person might think that he or she is about to become the victim of a battery.

Are Words Alone Sufficient?

The courts frequently say that mere words alone are not sufficient to constitute an assault; but when some menacing act or threatening gesture is made, they generally hold that this is sufficient to constitute an assault.

Clearly, the act of driving down the street and gawking at a woman or looking her over intently is not an assault;[18] and the cases sometimes say that the mere solicitation of intercourse, by words alone, is also not an assault.[19] In examining the cases, however, it appears that a number of courts make an exception in this type of situation. The explanation sometimes given is that the force of the words was such that the woman could reasonably anticipate an immediate battery, and so this type of conduct on the part of the man should be punished.

Threatening acts, however, are never regarded as an assault if it is obvious from the accompanying conduct or words that the accused has no present intention to cause harm. A threat to be accomplished in the future is not considered sufficiently definite to be punishable. Suppose, for example, a big, muscular man snarls at a smaller one, "If you weren't such a little shrimp, I would beat the hell out of you!" This is not an assault

---

[18] State v. Ingram, 74 S.E.2d 532, 237 N.C. 197. The testimony by the victim showed that the accused drove down the "road real slow and kept watching me, and when he got straight across from where I was he had his head out of the window leering at me [with] a curious look."

[19] State v. Sanders, 75 S.E. 702, 92 S.C. 427.

unless the accused lays hands on the smaller man or applies physical force to him in some way.

When a conditional threat of violence occurs, however, this is an assault, even though the victim can escape harm by complying with the conditions. Suppose the accused draws a gun on the victim stating, "Sign this deed, give me the land I paid for, or I'll kill you!" In this situation, the victim may expect to escape harm by signing the paper, but an assault has occurred, nevertheless.

SPECIAL TYPES OF ASSAULTS OR BATTERIES

Assault and battery each were only misdemeanors at common law. Some crimes included in these categories are far more serious, however, and modern governments have recognized this by the passage of special statutes, imposing heavier penalties for such offenses as aggravated assault, aggravated battery, and assault with a deadly weapon.

Aggravated Assault

Assaults committed with intent to kill, to rape, to rob, or to do great bodily harm are far more outrageous and dangerous than the common assault and battery violations. Therefore, statutes in a number of states designate each of these assaults as a distinct, technical *aggravated assault* violation punishable as a felony[20]

Aggravated Battery

A few states, in turn, have given special treatment to a certain type of battery, designating this crime *aggravated battery.* [21]

Assault with a Deadly Weapon

Statutes in a number of states impose greater penalties when the assault is made with a so-called deadly weapon. Generally, two classes of weapons may be involved in this type of case. Some—such as guns, knives, and brass knuckles—are specifically designed for the destruction of life or for at least

[20] Minnix v. State, 282 P.2d 772.
[21] WISCONSIN STATUTES, sec. 840.22 (1958). See this statute or those in some other states for legal definitions of "aggravated battery."

inflicting great injury. When a weapon of this kind is used, the courts declare, as a matter of law, that the instrument is a deadly weapon and of the class required for conviction under these statutes.

Obviously, other weapons that may be used to cause death are not necessarily dangerous if used according to their usual purpose. A shoe, for example, is not ordinarily a dangerous instrument. In numerous cases, however, the assailant caused death by repeatedly kicking the victim in the head. Generally, the courts leave the question to the jury as to whether an object, nor ordinarily dangerous, was in fact used as a deadly weapon.

Assaults on Peace Officers

Special statutes have long protected federal law enforcement officers from assaults or killings. Those protected include FBI agents, U.S. Treasury agents, customs officials, and others engaged in dangerous law enforcement pursuits. Copied after the federal statute, many states now provide felony punishment for assaults on any peace officers. Some of these enactments also protect prison guards against convicts.[22] In addition, both peace officers and average citizens enjoy the right of self-defense.

THE RIGHT OF SELF-DEFENSE

Basically, self-defense involves the right of an individual to repel force with force in protecting his or her life or person, family members, habitation, and property. In some instances, a person may go so far as to kill the attacker in self-defense. Rights vary considerably, however, from one kind of situation to another. In the words of one court:

> One may harbor the most intense hatred toward another; he may court an opportunity to take his life; may rejoice while he is imbruing his hands in his heart's blood; and yet, if to save his own life, the facts showed he was fully justified in slaying his adversary, his malice should not be taken into account. This principle is too plain to need amplification.[23]

Under no circumstance, however, is the defender justified in pursuing and killing the attacker after all danger of death or serious bodily injury has passed.[24]

[22] See CALIFORNIA PENAL CODE, secs. 245, 4500.
[23] State v. Matthews, 49 S.W. 1085, 148 Mo. 185; Golden v. State, 25 Ga. 527.
[24] People v. Keys, 145 P.2d 589, 62 Cal. App. 2d 903.

The Use of Nondeadly Force

An individual who is without fault may repel an attack with nondeadly force when three requirements are met:

1. There is reasonable cause to believe that the attacker plans to commit a battery against him.
2. The amount of force used in repelling the attack is not unreasonable under the circumstances.
3. The loss of the individual's usual rights is unavoidable without the use of force.

Nondeadly force is force that is not calculated or likely to cause death. When the defender is legally entitled to use nondeadly force, the force used must be reasonable. For example, a defender cannot repeatedly hit someone in the jaw, time after time, when a blow or two or a simple shove might clearly prevent a staggering drunk from coming through the defendant's front door.

Occasionally, when nondeadly force is used, death may nevertheless result. Without intending to kill, the defender may shove an intruder out of the way, using only reasonable force. It the intruder slips and death results from a fall to the sidewalk, the death is classified as justifiable homicide, not a crime.

As a practical matter, any situation of this kind is usually presented to a grand jury, in order that it may decide whether the defender should be indicted and brought to trial. If the doer is indicted, the trial jury must decide whether the amount of force used was reasonable and whether a reasonable person would have believed that a battery was about to be committed.

The Use of Deadly Force

We have previously seen from our study of homicide that people who are without fault themselves may use deadly force to save their own lives, to prevent great bodily harm, or to prevent the perpetration of a felony by surprise or violence against their persons, homes, or properties.

Many of the cases that cause legal problems, however, arise in self-defense situations that do not involve an impending felony by surprise or violence. A defender has no right of self-defense to kill someone for a mere slap on the face. A defender who shot another because of a slap would be guilty of murder or manslaughter, depending on whether the provocation was of a sufficient kind to cause a killing in the heat of passion. Most courts, as we have previously seen, hold that a mere slap is not sufficient to reduce the crime from murder to manslaughter.

The Requirements for the Use of Deadly Force

Unless a felony by violence or surprise is involved, the courts have set up four requirements for the use of deadly force in self-defense:

1. The attacker must act in such a way that an individual in the defender's position is in immediate fear of death or great bodily harm.
2. While this danger need not be real, it must appear to be well grounded to any reasonable person in the defender's situation.
3. The defender must retreat as far as possible to do so without encountering more danger (some cases say the defender must retreat except when it is futile, foolhardy, or dangerous, but then may use deadly force in self-defense).
4. The person who uses deadly force must not be the aggressor and may not use excessive force under the circumstances. In other words, a defender cannot kill an aggressor who merely administered a slap with a bare hand.

The Apprehension of Death or Serious Injury

The mere fact that an individual has sworn to kill another on sight does not justify the latter in killing. The one who threatens must perform some affirmative act in furtherance of the threat before the right of self-defense arises. Also, knowledge that an enemy has a weapon, with no present intent to use the weapon, will not give rise to a right to kill in self-defense.

In a situation of this nature, the jury must always determine whether the aggressor took an action that would cause a reasonable person in the defender's position to be in apprehension of death or serious injury. Once this apprehension has been created by the attacker, the defender clarly has the right of self-defense.

The Defender May Act on Reasonable Appearances

The courts uniformly say that the defender's acts of self-defense may be based on reasonable appearances. The danger to the defender need not be actually proved when a reasonable appearance of danger exists.

In one case, a man openly threatened to kill another on sight and drew a pistol on him. The attacker's pistol was not loaded; he had merely intended to frighten his victim. Nevertheless, the court said that the defendant was justified in acting on appearances and in killing the aggressor to protect himself.[25]

[25] Patillo v. State, 3 S.W.766, 22 Tex. App. 586.

Along this same line of reasoning, Justice Oliver Wendell Holmes of the United States Supreme Court said:

> Detached reflection cannot be demanded in the presence of an up-lifted knife. Therefore in this court, at least, it is not a condition of immunity that one in that situation should pause to consider whether a reasonable man might not think it possible to fly with safety or to disable his assailant rather than to kill him.[26]

Retreat as an Alternative to the Use of Deadly Force

While not all courts require it, most of them insist that the defender must make an honest effort to retreat prior to using deadly force in self-defense. They usually say, however, that retreat is not required when it would place the defendant in a greater danger, when it would be futile, or when self-defense would thus become impossible. Further, the defender is not required to retreat when at home or, in a few states, at his or her place of business or employment.

The Defender Must Not Be the Aggressor

On the other hand, when the accused is the aggressor in a dispute that ends in death, the courts do not generally allow the right of self-defense.
In deciding who the aggressor is, the courts say that it does not matter who started the bitter words or who first applied nondeadly force. The rule usually is that the aggressor is that party in the dispute who first did something that might reasonably be expected to cause the death of the other. For example, the drawing of a knife or a gun immediately marks that party as the aggressor, conferring the right of self-defense on the other.

The courts differ on this, but most of them allow the aggressor to withdraw after clearly showing to the other party a wish to break off the fight completely. This intent to stop must be very clearly shown, however.

Defense of Habitation

As proved earlier, the law has always given special consideration to a person's home. It is clear that the owner or any person who lives there may use deadly force to prevent anyone fron entering to commit a felony or to inflict serous bodily harm on people living there. This does not mean, however, that an occupant may kill to prevent someone from merely trespassing or entering. As a matter of law, the occupant is entitled to act on

---

[26] Beard v. United States, 158 U.S. 550.

appearances, and when it would appear to a reasonable person in the situation that a felony was intended, the homicide is not criminal. This, of course, is always a question for the jury to decide; and most juries are inclined to find in favor of an occupant or homeowner who has reasonable cause to believe that the intruder intended bodily harm. When it is evident that the person seeking to enter is a harmless drunk, the occupant is not justified in killing the intruder.

A person who occupies a residence or apartment may lawfully eject an intruder or an unwelcome guest from the house, but is entitled to use only necessary force to accomplish this. The occupant has no right to kick or beat the intruder. In some cases, the outsider may have been invited to come into the home, thereafter becoming an unwanted guest. In instances of this kind, the outsider may be lawfully ejected; but the occupant is not entitled to kill this unwelcome guest.

When the property is not a dwelling, reasonable physical force may be used to protect it. Deadly force cannot be used, however, to protect property other than the home, except when necessary to prevent a felony that involves surprise or violence.

Defense of Others

Any citizen may, at times, have occasion to observe one individual in the act of assaulting another; and almost everyone has an inclination to come to the aid of the person who is old, weak, or apparently absorbing a merciless beating without reason. Appearances may sometimes be deceiving, however. The person who is receiving the worst of a fight may turn out to have originally been an aggressor who badly misjudged the victim's ability to fight. Most of the courts say that a person who intercedes is privileged to use force only when the person who receives the aid is entitled to use force. In other words, when a third party intercedes in behalf of the original aggressor, then this third party has committed a battery on the defender.

However, a substantial number of other courts take the approach that a third person is entitled to act on the appearances at the time of arrival on the scene. When it appears, at that time, that one party is the aggressor, the third party is allowed to use force to beat off the aggressor.

Conversely, when the third party uses deadly force, most courts say that the person defended must be without fault and must be a close family member such as a brother, father, wife, or child. If, however, the attack is a felony, committed by force or surprise, any person, whether a stranger or an acquaintance, may use deadly force in defense of the victim.

Clearly, the police officer's position in this and similar matters is influenced by the legal aspects of false arrest and false imprisonment.

FALSE IMPRISONMENT OR FALSE ARREST

All imprisonments or arrests are either legal or false. Imprisonment and arrest mean the same thing in the criminal law. At least, every arrest involves an imprisonment. Any imprisonment or arrest means the restraint of a person's personal liberty. This is brought about by the imposition of either actual or apparent physical barriers. Confinement need not actually be in a jail. Blackstone, the early English legal writer, has said that confinement may be "in the common prison, in a private house, in the stocks, or by forcibly detaining one in the public streets."[27]

> Any exercise of force, or express or implied threat of force, by which in fact the other person is deprived of his liberty or is compelled to remain where he does not wish to remain, or to go where he does not wish to go, is an imprisonment.[28]

Imprisonment is that restraint exercised upon a person to pervent free exercise of the power of locomotion.[29]

Some people think that, when a false arrest occurs, a police officer surely must have been involved. Some cases do involve police who misuse authority, but false arrest is a crime that may be committed by private citizens as well. For example, a man might unlawfully detain a woman in his automobile, threatening to harm her unless she remains there. In this situation, he might not go so far as to rape her. Yet, he might be guilty of a false arrest (false imprisonment) if he detains her by force or threats of force, causing her to remain.

Actual use of force is not necessary. If the victim submits, this is enough. When the victim runs away and refuses to be detained by the show of force, no false arrest has taken place. Facts of this kind may constitute an attempt, however.

Merely illegally blocking the path or turning a person aside is not false arrest, so long as the victim may freely continue by some other route. Cutting off an escape constitutes the violation. Words alone are sufficient if they actually place restraint upon the individual to whom they are directed. When a law enforcement officer, without justification, informs an individual that he or she is under arrest and must go to a certain place, this is a false arrest. The person involved need not be physically detained or touched. An arrest has been accomplished if the victim submits to the asserted authority.

[27] BLACKSTONE'S COMMENTARIES, 127.
[28] Watkins v. Oaklawn Jockey Club, 183 F.2d 440.
[29] State v. Shaw, 50 A. 863, 73 Vt. 149.

Forms of Detention

No particular form of detention is required, as noted previously. The victim may be restrained by merely being locked in a room, by being driven in an automobile at such a speed as to cause fearfulness about jumping out, or by being thrown into the hold of a ship. In a rather common type of case, the violation may consist of stopping an automobile and detaining the driver against his will, on the belief that he is the boyfriend of the accused's wife.

False Arrest by Police Officers

False arrest should be of considerable interest to any police officer. The officer who makes a false arrest may be not only prosecuted criminally but also sued for money damages in civil court. Either or both of these actions may be initiated as an outgrowth of a single false arrest.

As a general principle of both criminal and civil law, any officer is protected and justified in executing any kind of court paper (process) or warrant that appears fair on its face. In other words, "An officer has a right to assume that the court that issued a warrant acted within its authority."[30] The officer need not be troubled as to whether the person named in the warrant is innocent or guilty, and is responsible only for bringing this person before the court for a judicial determination. This is a public policy which protects judges, police officers, game wardens, sheriffs, or other authorized officials who handle the administrative processes of the courts, including the service of arrest warrants.[31]

Even when the accused person is eventually acquitted, the previous arrest is not necessarily unlawful if all forms of law have been observed.[32]

Arrest of the Wrong Person

A police officer who executes a warrant of arrest should make certain that the person taken into custody is the one actually named and intended by the warrant, and must also take care that the identity of the suspect is established at the time of arrest. In fact, the officer may be sued or prosecuted when a mistake in this matter is made.[33] Most courts say, however, that reasonable care and good faith of the arresting officer is the test that will determine. Due diligence and care must be exercised to make the identification certain.

[30] DeWitt v. Thompson, 7 So. 2d 529, 192 Miss. 615.
[31] Brinkman v. Drolesbaugh, 119 N.E. 451, 97 Ohio St. 171.
[32] Finney v. Zingale, 95 S.E. 1046, 82 W. Va. 422.
[33] Landrum v. Wells, 26 S.W. 1001, 7 Tex. Civ. App. 625.

An officer is not criminally liable for arresting the wrong person on a John Doe warrant if there is reasonable cause to believe that the person arrested is guilty of the offense charged.[34]

When, from the description available, a police officer has reason to think that the person arrested is the individual sought in the warrant, the officer is not responsible for false arrest in holding this person until a firm identity can be established.[35] However, the officer is liable for detaining the arrestee for an unreasonable length of time. Unreasonable detention varies with the circumstances. Prompt action should, therefore, be taken to establish identity through fingerprints or other methods when this action seems justified.

Detention of an Insane Person

Insane persons who seem to be dangerous to themselves or to others may be detained in most jurisdictions without a warrant. Some courts say that the right to arrest is dependent upon an eventual determination of insanity, however. If the person arrested is a quiet sort, who does not pose a physical threat, most courts see no right to arrest without a warrant or court process of some kind. The courts in a few states also relax the rules of arrest applicable to arrests by relatives of an insane or suspected insane person. Here, if the detention is made in good faith and for the intended good of the person taken into custody, the cases hold no conviction on a charge of false arrest.[36]

Arrest without a Warrant

An arrest for crime can never be justified by information developed through investigation conducted after the arrest. A police officer may make an arrest without a warrant, however, if there are reasonable grounds for believing that the suspect has committed or is committing a felony. It does not matter that investigation subsequently discloses that no felony has actually been committed. An officer may also arrest without warrant for a misdemeanor committed in his or her presence.

An arresting officer who holds a prisoner for an unreasonable length of time, without allowing access to a committing magistrate or opportunity to appear for a hearing on bail, has committed a false arrest.[38]

---

[34] Mildon v. Bybee, 13 Utah 2d 400.
[35] White v. Jansen, 142 P. 1142, 81 Wash. 435.
[36] Davis v. Merrill, 47 N.H. 208.
[37] Cunningham v. Baker, 16 So. 63, 104 Ala. 160.
[38] Teel v. May Dept. Store, 155 S.W.2d 74, 348 Mo. 696.

When the charge is drunkenness in a public place, the courts have held that the arrestee need not be given an opportunity to make bail until sober enough to prevent a second arrest for drunkenness.[39]

Resisting Lawful Arrest

Most courts in agreement that a police officer may use any amount of force reasonably necessary to apprehend, or prevent the escape of, any felon or a person who perpetrates a misdemeanor that amounts to a breach of the peace. Even deadly force may be used, if necessary.

Some courts, however, take the position that deadly force is not justified when the felony is not one involving violence or surprise. These same courts also hold that deadly force is never justified in apprehending or preventing the escape of anyone who has committed a misdemeanor. While these courts are definitely in the minority, some legal writers think that additional courts may follow these views in the future.

When a police officer has a valid warrant for the arrest of an individual, it is the obligation of that person to submit immediately and peaceably, and to surrender any weapons. To resist under these circumstances constitutes *resisting arrest* or *obstructing justice;* these charges may be far more serious than the original charges against the accused.

Use of Excessive Force in Arrest

All too often police officers are required to arrest individuals who dare the officers to perform their duties, cursing or subjecting them to insults of various sorts. It is important to both the officer and the police department, however, that the arrest be made without the use of excessive force. Police officers have no right to act oppressively or to cause needless injury to prisoners. Negligent, wrongful, or needless acts resulting in personal injury or death in the making of an arrest constitute an assault and battery on the part of the officer. In addition to a civil lawsuit, the police officer who acts wrongfully may be faced with a federal prosecution under the federal civil rights statutes or with a state prosecution for assault and battery.[40]

Self-Defense in Resisting Arrest

When a question arises as to whether a warrant of arrest is defective, the issue can only be settled by the courts. It is, therefore, pointless for the

[39] Sheffield v. Reece, 28 So. 2d 745, 201 Miss. 133.
[40] Downs v. Swann, 73 A. 653, 111 Md. 53.

accused or the police officer to engage in either a verbal or a physical dispute. Accordingly, a number of states have passed statutes requiring the accused to submit to any police officer, even when the warrant is unlawful or the arrest without warrant is unlawful.

The old common law said, however, that a police officer who made an unlawful arrest or served a defective warrant did not have the authority of the law. The early courts took the approach that a police officer in this position was neither discharging the duties of office nor attempting to do so. This approach seems somewhat absurd, since the officer seldom has any means to determine whether a warrant was unlawfully issued; but this idea has persisted in the law of many states up to and including the present.

In the absence of a special statute, the courts say that an illegal arrest is an assault and battery.[41] Any unlawful interference with a fundamental right of personal liberty may be resisted, against a police officer or anyone else. A person placed under an unlawful arrest has the same right of self-defense in repelling any other assault and battery.[42] The individual who is illegally arrested does not have the right to initiate the use of force; but when the officer attempts to use force, the accused may oppose force with force. When the force used by the officer is so great that the arrestee can only save his or her life or prevent great bodily harm by killing the officer, the killing of the officer is excusable homicide.[43] If it is not apparent that great bodily harm or death will result, the accused has no right to use a deadly weapon merely to prevent an unlawful arrest. When death comes to the police officer under these circumstances, the killing is regarded as manslaughter in most jurisdictions; it is classified as murder in some others.

CITED CASES

Beard v. United States, 158 U.S. 550.
Beausoliel v. United States, 107 F.2d 292.
Brinkman v. Drolesbaugh, 119 N.E. 451, 97 Ohio St. 171.
Commonwealth v. Jaynes, 10 A.2d 90, 137 Pa. Super. 511.
Cornelius v. Montegut, 8 La. App. 358.
Cunningham v. Baker, 16 So. 63, 104 Ala. 160.
Davis v. Merrill, 47 N.H. 208.
DeWitt v. Thompson, 7 So. 2d 529, 192 Miss. 615.
Downs v. Swann, 73 A. 653, 11 Md. 53.
Finney v. Zingale, 95 S.E. 1046, 82 W. Va. 422.

[41] State v. Rosseau, 241 P.2d 447, 40 Wash. 2d 92.
[42] State v. Robinson, 72 A.2d 260, 145 Maine 77.
[43] Miers v. State, 29 S.W. 1074, 34 Tex. Crim. 161.

Golden v. State, 25 Ga. 527.

Jackson v. Commonwealth, 247 S.W.2d 52.

Landrum v. Wells, 26 S.W. 1001, 7 Tex. Civ. App. 625.

Lutterman v. Romey, 121 N.W. 1043, 143 Iowa 233.

Mercer v. Corbin, 20 N.E. 132, 117 Ind. 450.

Miers v. State, 29 S.W. 1074, 34 Tex. Crim. 161.

Mildon v. Bybee, 13 Utah 2d 400.

Minnix v. State, 282 P.2d 772.

Moreland v. State, 188 S.W. 1, 125 Ark. 24.

Patillo v. State, 3 S.W. 766, 22 Tex. App. 586.

People ex rel. Bingham, 107 N.Y.S. 1011.

People v. Keys, 145 P.2d 589, 62 Cal. App. 2d 903.

Schmitt v. Kurrus, 85 N.E. 261, 234 Ill. 578.

Sheffield v. Reece, 28 So. 2d 745, 201 Miss. 133.

State v. Ingram, 74 S.E.2d 532, 237 N.C. 197.

State v. Matthews, 49 S.W. 1085, 148 Mo. 185.

State v. Robinson, 72 A.2d 260, 145 Maine 77.

State v. Rosseau, 241 P.2d 447, 40 Wash. 2d 92.

State v. Sanders, 75 S.E. 702, 92 S.C. 427.

State v. Shaw, 50 A. 863, 73 Vt. 149.

Teel v. May Dept. Store, 155 S.W.2d 74, 348 Mo. 696.

Turner v. State, 33 S.W. 972, 33 Tex. Crim. 369.

Union Pacific Ry. Co. v. Botsford, 141 U.S. 250, 11 S. Ct. 1000.

Watkins v. Oaklawn Jockey Club, 183 F. 2d 440.

Weaver v. State, 146 S.W. 927, 66 Tex. Crim. 366.

White v. Jansen, 142 P. 1142, 81 Wash. 435.

Williams v. Lubbering, 63 A. 90, 73 N.J.L. 317.

Wilson v. Orr, 97 So. 133, 210 Ala. 93.

Witzka v. Moudry, 85 N.W. 911, 83 Minn. 78.

Wood v. Cummings, 83 N.E. 318, 197 Mass. 80.

CHAPTER 13

Arson and Burglary

Under early common law concepts, arson and burglary were principal crimes against the dwelling place or home; but, after continuous and drastic change through modern statutes, these may well be defined as offenses against property.

ARSON   *1, 2, 3ʳᵈ degree   hand out*

Common law arson consisted of the willful or deliberate burning of another's dwelling or outbuildings within the curtilage of the dwelling. "Curtilage" meant the enclosed area of land and the outbuildings immediately surrounding the dwelling. Today, practically all jurisdictions in the United States provide specific statutes that define this type of offense as a serious felony. Some of the earliest English cases speak of the great danger, as well as the terror and fright, associated with arson. Even with modern fire departments, arson involves serious risk, because of the possibility not only of uncontrolled destruction of property but of the loss of human lives as well. No one knows how far or how fast the flames may spread. The sleeping, the aged, and the young are frequently trapped. Then too, neighbors and persons passing by may be injured when they dash into the flames to aid the occupants, or they may be killed by a collapsing structure. Since deliberate burning of a building is a dangerous felony, the crime may even become murder through the application of the felony-murder rule, when lives are lost.

Under the common law approach, designating arson as an offense was planned to provide some security for a habitation or dwelling place and was not designed to protect property in general. In fact, we may assume that the offense was a part of the old legal idea "A man's home is his castle"; it was entitled to more protection than a mere piece of property. We will see more of this concept in the protection extended to a dwelling place under the ideas of common law burglary and the special statues given to the home in that offense.

The burning, under common law arson, could take place by day or by night, while some modern statutes provide for a more serious crime when the burning occurs during hours of darkness. This, of course, is recognition of the increased danger when a person may be trapped during the hours when most people are asleep.

What Is Meant by Malicious and Voluntary or Willful, Burning?

Under the common law and a number of current statutes, "arson" is frequently described as a "malicious and willful burning"; but the original legal meaning of "malice" is now lost in antiquity. The law does not require ill will or hate. Modern courts uniformly say that the accused shall deliberately, and without justification, set out to burn a building. All that is required is a general type of mens rea, not a specific intent. Specifically, the accused's intent must be malicious only in the sense of having a plan of doing wrong.[1] Setting fire while committing another crime is arson.

Burning a house by negligence, accident, or mischance is not arson, under either the common law or modern statutes. The degree of carelessness or negligence in handling a fire is of no consequence. Arson requires a burning that is conscious, intentional, and according to purpose.[2]

A number of states have statutory crimes that fall into this area. *Reckless burning,* for example, is a violation of the penal code in some states.

Motive is, of course, frequently the force that induces or originates the criminal action. While purpose, or motive, involves a state of mind and the human will, it need not be proved in court. One of the most frequently encountered motives in arson involves the burning of property to collect on insurance policies. Revenge and malicious mischief are also rather common causes. When the motive can be shown, of course, it may help the prosecution's case; but willful burning is the essential act that must be proved.

Some rare cases have reached the opposite conclusion, but most decided cases have held that a prisoner committed arson by setting fire to the jail for the purpose of making a jailbreak. The courts have reasoned that there

[1] Love v. State, 144 So. 843, 107 Fla. 376.
[2] Jones v. State, 3 So. 2d 388, 147 Fla. 677.

was a willful burning in the jailbreak attempt, and that this was sufficient to constitute the crime of arson.[3]

The Burning

The courts generally say that "burn" and "set fire to" have the same legal meaning.[4] The law shows no real interest in how the fire started or was applied. When a direct method is not used, arson may be accomplished by setting a blaze in one building, so that it may spread to the structure that the arsonist is seeking to destroy. Fire also may be applied indirectly by a wick that will carry the flame to the building. The act of directing a blaze toward a house does not constitute arson when the fire is extinguished before any part of the building is burned. These facts may, however, in some jurisdictions constitute an attempt. In other states, the wording of particular statutes may bring this activity within the class prohibited by the arson statute.

Under statutes in a few states, an individual who maliciously or intentionally causes damage to property by use of an explosive is also guilty of arson, even when a fire did not result from the explosive charge.[5]

Before conviction in any jurisdiction, other than for an attempt, the prosecution must prove that the fire actually reached the building. Generally, the law does not require that the building shall have any known value or that it be completely destroyed. An actual outbreak of flames is not essential, but some part of the building must be charred or destroyed. It is not necessary for the burning to be complete. The test here is whether the building was actually charred. If the structure was only discolored or blackened by smoke, then the courts have found insufficient burning to complete the crime. The courts also say that where the fire "made very little headway," the crime of arson was completed.[6]

What Kind of Building Must Be Involved?

Common law arson did not apply to stores, shops, or business buildings; the offense dealt exclusively with protection of the dwelling place or with a situation where an owner actually lived within a business establishment.

In early England the typical dwelling was a farmhouse, with outbuildings generally enclosed in a fenced yard behind the living quarters. Usually a smokehouse, barn, storage cribs, and an outhouse were included, and pos-

[3] Willis v. State, 25 S.W. 123.
[4] State v. Quatro, 105 A.2d 913, 31 N.J. Super. 51.
[5] Fannin v. State, 80 S.W.2d 992, 128 Tex. Crim. 185.
[6] State v. Shaw, 196 P. 1100; also see 128 S.W. 953.

sibly servants' quarters as well. Common law arson extended to all these outbuildings. The law set no rule as to how many buildings must be included; it was not necessary that the curtilage or yard be actually inside a wall or fence. Early courts said that all buildings conveniently and habitually used for family purposes and domestic pursuits were subject to destruction by arson. Infrequently the farmer's barn was not included because it was set off some distance from the house, not in the compound or enclosure around the dwelling. After a time, however, the courts saw no need for a fence or wall enclosing the compound in order legally to bring the building within the curtilage.

Statutes throughout the United States characteristically have extended arson to practically all business or residential buildings (occupied or unoccupied), to public buildings, to sailing vessels and ships, to railroad bridges, and to similar structures. The burning of automobiles and personal property is widely prohibited by other modern arson statutes.

The United States Code, applicable to federal government lands and buildings as well as ships on the high seas (federal territorial jurisdiction), is very broad:

> 81. Arson within special maritime and territorial jurisdiction.
>
> Whoever, within the special maritime and territorial jurisdiction of the United States, willfully and maliciously sets fire to or burns, or attempts to set fire to or burn any building, structure or vessel, any machinery or building materials or supplies, military or naval stores, munitions of war, or any structural aids or appliances for navigation or shipping, shall be fined not more than $1,000 or imprisoned not more than five years, or both.
>
> If the building be a dwelling or if the life of any person be placed in jeopardy, he shall be fined not more than $5,000 or imprisoned not more than twenty years, or both.[6]

Coverage of Other Buildings

By "house," present-day arson statutes mean a building enclosed with walls and covered with some sort of roof. An uncompleted structure, not yet ready for occupancy or use, is not a house or building, according to the courts.[7]

A house trailer is not a house within the meaning of arson statutes in some states, but is included when the statute prohibits burning of an automobile or motor vehicle.[8]

[6] UNITED STATES CODE, title 18, sec. 81.
[7] McGary v. People, 45 N.Y. 153.
[8] Simmons v. State, 129 N.E.2d 121, 234 Ind. 489.

Barns are covered under current arson statutes in practically all jurisdictions, whether or not the structure contains hay or grain or regardless of where it is located.[9] Under most modern statues and court decisions, an enginehouse or a millhouse has been defined as a building, although they differ in opinion as to a sawmill. A railroad freight car was held to be a building under one arson statute, inasmuch as the wheels had been removed and it had been converted into a storehouse.

Special Arson Statutes

We have seen that the old common law idea made arson a crime against a possession, rather than one against the property itself. Under this line of reasoning, an owner who lived in a house might burn it to defraud an insurance company and avoid arson prosecution.

In order to close this loophole, statutes have been widely established providing punishment for burning to defraud insurers. Frequently these laws are so worded that the owner may be prosecuted as a principal for counseling, aiding, abetting, or procuring someone to set the actual blaze, even though the owner may be out of town at the time.[10]

Degrees of Arson

In some states statutes divide arson into degrees, based on whether an individual was in the building at the time of the burning and whether the fire occurred at night. Some other enactments vary the penalty with the value of the burned property.

Extending the crime of arson to include the burning of personal property, some states cover practically any burning of the property of another if its value is above a specified amount, whether it is real estate, automobiles, furniture, stocks and bonds, or any other kind of personal property.[11]

BURGLARY

Common law burglary consisted of breaking and entering the home of another at nighttime, with intent to commit a felony therein, whether the intent was executed or not.

[9] Carlton v. People, 37 N.E. 244, 150 Ill. 181.

[10] Commonwealth ex rel. Guiffrida v. Ashe, 10 A.2d 112, 137 Pa. Super. 528; Mai v. People, 79 N.E. 633, 224 Ill. 414.

[11] See GEORGIA CODE ANNOTATED, sec. 26-2210, and ARKANSAS STATUTES ANNOTATED, SEC. 41-501.

Like arson, the crime was one against the security of a person's habitation or dwelling place, not a violation that came into being to protect property. Few banks existed in early England, and most of the money and valuables were hidden inside the family home. With no telephone to obtain assistance and few police officers, average citizens were forced to rely on their own resources in defending their dwellings. The possibility for serious harm in incidents of this kind was always present. Early English legal writers commented on nighttime terror and the possibility of loss of life.

Perhaps one of the most widely held misconceptions in the law of burglary is the idea that the offense consists of breaking into a home or building to commit larceny inside. The fact is that the law has always required that the person making the illegal entry shall intend to commit a felony in the building; it is immaterial whether the planned felony is larceny. It might just as well be murder, robbery, arson, rape, or any other felony. Neither the common law definition of burglary nor the modern statutory ones make specific mention of larceny or theft. A felonious purpose need not be successful. The intruder may be beaten off or frightened away, or may have a change of heart. In any event, the burglary is complete at the time of the entry, not when the felony is attempted after getting inside. For example, when the illegal entry is made to commit murder and the accused finds no victim, a burglary conviction is proper. As a practical matter, of course, we know that the great majority of burglaries are committed to establish an opportunity for larceny, but burglary has always consisted of a break-in for the purpose of committing *any* felony.

Modern statutory changes in burglary have been widely adopted, setting out new definitions or adding to the common law one. In many instances these present-day laws cannot be understood or enforced by practitioners unless they first understand the elements of common law burglary.

Elements of Common Law Burglary

The elements of common law burglary may be listed as follows:

1. A breach or breaking into the dwelling house of another person, during the nighttime, including constructive breaking.
2. An entry of the dwelling house of another or a building within the curtilage of the dwelling by the burglar (entry by use of an instrument satisfies this requirement).
3. An intent to make the breaking and entry, as well as the intent to commit a felony inside.

As we shall see from the following discussion, some of these common law requirements definitely have been modified.

The Breach or Breaking

With rare exceptions, such as entry through a chimney, a real breach or break-in must take place. This does not mean that the accused must actually batter a hole in a brick wall of the building, although this is one way to make the breach. The old common law ideas and the decisions of the modern courts are all in agreement that entry through an open window or door is not a breach or breaking. When the place of entry has a screen, it is a breaking to open that screen, even though it is not fastened or latched in any way. The test here is that the use of any effort or force, however slight, is sufficient to make the activity a *breach or breaking*. Where the door is standing open or the window is without a screen, the accused may step inside without committing a burglary. This does not mean, however, that the accused cannot be prosecuted for a larceny or for any other crime thereafter committed.

The use of even a slight amount of force will satisfy the requirements. In a Tennessee case, the court held that raising a window sash enough to allow admission was a breaking, in spite of the fact that the window was partly open.[12]

In addition, most courts are in agreement that when the accused gets into the building without force, the eventual use of force to gain further entry is a breach or breaking, with respect to that part of the building. Under this approach, the opening of a bedroom door or a closet satisfies the breaking requirement.

Breaking through a fence or a wall attached to a house, regardless of the amount of force, is not sufficient. The use of force must be against the house itself. Entering without force and, thereafter, battering open a locked chest or trunk is not burglary; the force used in this "breaking" is not directed against the house itself.

We should emphasize here that the word "breaking" in burglary cases is not used in the common meaning of the word. The slightest force will suffice. Pushing open a door transom, held only by its own weight, or turning the knob of a door is enough force.[13]

Under the common law the breaking had to be for the purpose of getting into the building. Therefore, a person who got in without the use of force but later used force to break out of the building did not burglarize. The result has been that a number of states have passed statutes that make a forcible exit sufficient to satisfy the breaking requirement.

All the courts agree that a breaking does not occur in the absence of the actual use of force, for example when the entry is made by fraud, trick,

[12] Claiborne v. State, 83 S.W. 352, 113 Tenn. 261.
[13] State v. Chappell, 193 S.E. 924, 185 S.C. 111; State v. Edell, 183 A. 630, 7 W.W. Harr. Del. 404.

threats, or duress; this is called a "constructive breaking." The courts hold that practically any kind of fraud or trick is sufficient. For example, a burglar who pretends to be selling cosmetics in order to gain entry has committed this kind of breaking. This also covers the situation where a burglar hides in a building until a store or warehouse is locked for the night (a "hide-in" burglary).

In one line of cases, a servant or employee may deliberately open or fail to lock a door, thus providing entry for a confederate for the purpose of committing a felony. Both parties to this kind of action are guilty of burglary.[14]

The Entry

In burglary, both a breaking and an entry into the premises must occur. The courts have consistently upheld the ruling in an early English case in which the *entry* was made although only the defendant's fingertips actually entered the building. Therefore, the courts say the slightest entry is sufficient.[15]

An instrument of any kind may also be used to make an entry while the culprit actually remains outside. A long stick equipped with a hook or a common garden rake may be used by the burglar. Somewhat similarly, a trained dog may be sent into a residence to pick up and carry a purse. Breaking a window and shoving a gun through it, with intent to commit a felony inside, satisfies the breaking and entering requirements of burglary, even though a shot is not fired at an occupant.

Entering the floor or wall of a grain storage building by the use of a grain auger or bore, with intent to steal grain, is sufficient for both breaking and entry.[16]

Some modern statutes have completely eliminated the old breaking requirement. The language of a typical statute states, "Every person who enters . . . is guilty of burglary."[17]

What Buildings Are Subject to Burglary?

As pointed out previously, common law burglary strictly was an offense against habitations. Therefore, the violation was committed by breaking

[14] State v. Rowe, 4 S.E. 506, 98 N.C. 629.
[15] Franco v. State, 42 Tex. 276.
[16] State v. Crawford, 80 N.W. 193, 8 N.D. 539.
[17] CALIFORNIA PENAL CODE, sec. 459. The effect of this statute is to eliminate the need for a breaking, where there is an entry. See also State v. Hall, 150 N.W. 97, 168 Iowa 221; Nicholls v. State, 32 N.W. 543, 68 Wis. 416; Pinson v. State, 121 S.W. 751, 91 Ark. 434.

and entering into a dwelling house or the outbuildings within the curtilage. Breaking into the curtilage itself, even though it was surrounded by a high fence or wall, was not a burglary. The essence of the crime was breaking and entering into the home or the buildings within the curtilage. Stores, shops, places of business, and public buildings were not covered. The text traditionally used by the early courts was whether the structure was regularly used as a place to sleep. If so, the building was protected by the burglary law.

Under some state laws burglary continues as a crime against the habitation, but present-day legislation has included under the legal coverage a great number of additional types of buildings, quarters, and structures. Churches have always been included, even under the common law. Practically all modern statutes include public buildings, schools, business houses, stores, shops, warehouses, and dwellings. Some of these statutes give broad coverage to all types of buildings, while others specifically name types of structures that usually are subject to doubt.[18] For example, in some of the Western states, where mining is common, statutes sometimes extend coverage to mine shafts and mine buildings.

Where the common law is followed, a dwelling has always been covered; and homes, of course, are covered by statutes where the common law is not followed. The courts have seldom had a great problem in defining a dwelling. A cave, equipped with a door, qualifies so long as it is regularly used as a place of abode. It makes no difference that the place of habitation is a hovel or a shanty, made from packing boxes or orange crates, so long as the victim has a right to maintain it at that location. We doubt that a court would recognize a lean-to occupied by a hobo or tramp in a railroad jungle as a dwelling; but in one case a regular living place was ruled a dwelling although it consisted of nothing more than a sheet stretched over poles, secured to planks, nailed to wooden posts for sides, with an old wooden door for entry. The courts have also held that a canvas-covered "sheep wagon" was a dwelling since it was occupied continously by the sheepherder. A regularly occupied house trailer also was a house, although it was not placed on a foundation or parked in any particular locality. If used only as a recreational residence or vehicle, not as the usual residence of the owner, the trailer was not covered, some courts have said, in the absence of a specific statute.

The common law definition of burglary specified that the structure must be the "dwelling of another." This meant that people could not burglarize their own homes. An owner could be prosecuted, however, for burglarizing

18 ILLINOIS CRIMINAL CODE, 1961 (ILLINOIS REVISED STATUTES, 1965, c. 38, sec. 19-1), specifically included coverage of house trailers and aircraft.

a house that had been rented to another person. In one old case, a husband did not want his wife to know his drinking habits. When she was away, he broke in and "stole" his own property, pawning it to obtain money for whiskey. The court refused prosecution for burglary since the house was not the "dwelling of another."

In the eyes of the law, each living unit in a residential building is recognized as a separate dwelling. Accordingly, the occupant of one apartment who breaks into the quarters of another in the same building may be guilty of burglary.

When two people occupy a room or an apartment jointly, each has the legal right to be there. One cannot commit burglary against the other by entering the premises with the intent to commit a felony therein.

The Time of the Breaking and Entering

The common law rule was that both the breaking and the entry must occur at nighttime. The exception was, however, that "a breaking could occur on one night and an entry on another." English courts defined nighttime as lack of enough daylight to recognize facial features. The common law judges refused, however, to allow light from the moon, street lights, and lights of buildings aided by the reflection of newly fallen snow to influence their definition. This approach has been followed in the United States where common law or nightime burglary is a distinct crime.[19]

Nighttime, under modern burglary statutes, is usually from sunset to sunrise, or from one hour after sunset to one hour before sunrise. A number of states have completely abolished the nighttime requirement,[20] while some jurisdictions have statutes covering both "nighttime" and "ordinary burglary."

Some state laws divide burglary into degrees, imposing more serious penalties for those perpetrated by use of explosives or by persons armed with a deadly weapon.

The Mental Requirement in Burglary

A very specific type of mental intent (mens rea) is required for burglary. The accused must have the specific intent to break and enter, as well as the intent to commit a specific felony after the entry is made. When a breaking and entry has been committed, the courts examine the intention of the accused at the exact time of the actual breaking and entering.

As a general proposition, judges hold that the intent to perpetrate a

[19] State v. Morris, 47 Conn. 179; State v. McKnight, 16 S.E. 319, 111 N.C. 690.
[20] People v. Glickman, 36 N.E.2d 720, 377 Ill. 360.

felony at the time of the breach and entry may be concluded as a matter of law, when a felony is actually committed after the illegal entry. An inference may also be made from the course of conduct of the accused that a felony after gaining admittance was not intended.

Shoplifting actually is often burglary under present-day statutes, at least when state law defines burglary in terms of entry into a commercial building with the intent to commit a felony. As a matter of fact, very few prosecutions are brought on the burglary theory in this situation, since it is extremely difficult to prove that the defendant had the felonious intent when entering the store.

When an intruder is apprehended after breaking into a building or home containg valuables, the courts say an intent to steal may be inferred unless the burglar can prove some other motive for being there.[21]

In one case, where an intruder broke into the home of a woman in the middle of the night and laid his hand on her, the court held that an intent to commit rape might be inferred in this burglary prosecution.[22] The burglary had been completed before the accused heard the victim's screams and fled in fear.

In another case in which the intended felony was never accomplished, the accused broke in and entered to ambush an enemy by gunfire from an upstairs window. The court held sufficient intent to constitute burglary.

Every larceny was a felony at common law; therefore, any breaking and entering for larceny was a felony. Some modern statutes say that a breaking and entering for the purpose of committing petit larceny (generally under $50) is also sufficient for burglary.

When the value of money or property taken is not enough for grand theft (generally $50 or more), this fact is not a defense for burglary when the accused fails to realize this fact. This is consistent with legal reasoning behind the crime of burglary; it never is essential that the intended felony be completed.[23]

We have not yet studied larceny, but it is basic that a person cannot steal his or her own property, whether legal papers or personal items. In any case, when a person breaks and enters to take such items, no burglary has occurred, since the accused has no felonious intent.[24] However, this does not mean that the intruder may not be prosecuted for a criminal trespass or other possible violations. Although we find some decisions to

[21] Steadman v. State, 8 S.E. 420, 81 Ga. 736.
[22] State v. Boon, 35 N.C. 244.
[23] Harvick v. State, 6 S.W. 19, 49 Ark. 514.
[24] People v. Wilson, 131 N.E. 609, 298 Ill. 257. But see also People v. Spencer, 201 P. 130, 54 Cal. App. 54.

the contrary, most courts emphasize the fact that a felony must have been intended.

CITED CASES

Carlton v. People, 37 N.E. 244, 150 Ill. 181.
Claiborne v. State, 83 S.W. 352, 113 Tenn. 261.
Commonwealth *ex rel.* Guiffrida v. Ashe, 10 A.2d 112, 137 Pa. Super. 528.
Fannin v. State, 80 S.W.2d 992, 128 Tex. Crim. 185.
Franco v. State, 42 Tex. 276.
Harvick v. State, 6 S.W. 19, 49 Ark. 514.
Jones v. State, 3 So. 2d 388, 147 Fla. 677.
Love v. State, 144 So. 843, 107 Fla. 376.
McGary v. People, 45 N.Y. 153.
Mai v. People, 79 N.E. 633, 224 Ill. 414.
Nicholls v. State, 32 N.W. 543, 68 Wis. 416.
People v. Glickman, 36 N.E.2d 720, 377 Ill. 360.
People v. Spencer, 201 P. 130, 54 Cal. App. 54.
People v. Wilson, 131 N.E. 609, 298 Ill. 257.
Pinson v. State, 121 S.W. 751, 91 Ark. 434.
Simmons v. State, 129 N.E.2d 121, 234 Ind. 489.
State v. Boon, 35 N.C. 244.
State v. Chappell, 193 S.E. 924, 185 S.C. 111.
State v. Crawford, 80 N.W. 193, 8 N.D. 539.
State v. Edell, 183 A. 630, 7 W.W. Harr. Del. 404.
State v. Hall, 150 N.W. 97, 168 Iowa 221.
State v. McKnight, 16 S.E. 319, 111 N.C. 690.
State v. Morris, 47 Conn. 179.
State v. Quatro, 105 A.2d 913, 21 N.J. Super. 51.
State v. Rowe, 4 S.E. 506, 98 N.C. 629.
State v. Shaw, 196 P. 1100.
Steadman v. State, 8 S.E. 420, 81 Ga. 736.
Willis v. State, 25 S.W. 123.

CHAPTER 14

Larceny, Embezzlement, and False Pretenses

The average person usually has little knowledge of the differences between theft, larceny, stealing, embezzlement, swindling, obtaining property by false pretenses, and a confidence game. All of these represent slightly variable circumstances under which a wrongdoer seeks to obtain advantages from the property or money of another, but the legal distinctions between these somewhat similar situations are of even greater importance. This stems from the fact that, as the criminal law developed, gaps or crevices separated particular crimes of this general class, so that people with all the indications of guilt sometimes escaped through the breaches.[1]

Today, in many or even most jurisdictions, the following three related criminal violations may be committed in the wrongful taking or use of property:

1. *Larceny.* Most people think this crime is identical with theft or stealing. In essence, the offense is the taking of property from an individual in lawful possession, without right and with the intention to keep it,

---

[1] Morissette v. United States, 342 U.S. 246, 72 S. Ct. 240.

wrongfully. The taking may be from the owner or from one to whom the property is entrusted.

2. *Embezzlement.* This involves a wrongful appropriation of property by one who is in lawful possession of it at the time of the wrongful appropriation.

3. *False Pretenses.* Obtaining property by false pretenses, as it is sometimes called, involves inducing another to give up money or property (goods) through misrepresentation of existing facts or conditions.

The Model Penal Code combines all these violations into a single statute,[2] greatly simplifying the technical problems of the prosecuting attorney in making certain that the accusation fits the available proof. In many jurisdictions—where the three separate crimes remain in the criminal code—the judge, prosecutor, and jury each must make technical distinctions between these types of stealing.

LARCENY *— a crime against possessions*

Larceny at common law was the taking and carrying away of money or personal belongings of another, with the intent to use it or deprive the owner of it. The taking was from any place, and no specific value was placed on the goods. The value of the property did, however, make some difference in the assessed penalty. When the stolen property was worth more than twelve pence, the penalty was death.[3] Under modern standards this was obviously an extremely severe penalty; and long before this was reduced, common law judges seemed to be searching for technicalities on which acquittals might be based. Some of these were incorporated into the law and remain there today.

On the other hand, the courts apparently handed down decisions that closed some loopholes in the law; but written records of these earlier decisions do not exist. We have some reason to believe that the earliest version of larceny was only the wrongful taking of property from the owner. Apparently, it turned out in one of these trials that the accused did not deny taking the property in question; but he was quick to point out that he had not stolen from the owner, but from someone who had been given posses-

---

[2] Sec. 223.1. The MODEL PENAL CODE is a suggested draft of penal statutes, some of which have been adopted into law in a few states. The code was drawn up by an organization of judges, law professors, prosecutors, and practicing attorneys to eliminate some of the difficult technicalities and inequities caused by prior court decisions.

[3] This meant that, when the value of the stolen article was more than one-twentieth of an English pound, the court had no choice but to impose the death penalty. Petit larceny involved the theft of twelve pence or less, while a theft of greater value constituted grand larceny under the common law.

sion by the owner. The property may well have been in the custody of an agent of the owner, or of some business associate. Yet, the early English courts were very technical in their procedural requirements; and when the prosecutor alleged that the theft was from the owner, the case was thrown out since the article had been taken from another.

In any event, we know from some of the earliest recorded common law cases that larceny came to be wrongful taking from whoever was in rightful possession; and this concept has persisted to the present day. Therefore, we can understand larceny only when we recognize that the crime is one against possession.

Since larceny is stealing not merely from the owner, but from any person who is in lawful possession, it is possible that an owner might steal his or her own property. For example, if a man pawns his watch, the pawnbroker has the right to retain it until the debt is paid. When he steals the timepiece without repaying the owed money, he is guilty of larceny.

Similarly, when a woman leaves her automobile to be repaired, the garage has a mechanic's lien against the property. That is, the mechanic has a legal right to hold the vehicle until the debt is paid. If the owner returns in the night and drives away without paying her bill, she too has committed a larceny.

To the contrary, business in early England was a simple, uncomplicated matter. The merchant and apprentices manufactured whatever was sold in the shop. Goods were seldom shipped for great distances, and the purchaser had little need for credit transactions. Furthermore, with few wholesalers, the goods were usually delivered directly to the consumer. As business became more complicated, some apparent and damaging loopholes developed. Since larceny was recognized as an offense against possession, no common law crime occurred when the wrongful taking was by a business associate to whom the goods had previously been entrusted. This was, then, the essence of a relatively modern crime: embezzlement, the wrongful appropriation by one to whom the owner had already granted possession. Modern embezzlement statutes closed this gap.

In larceny, the owner has no intention to part with the property, although perhaps intending to part with its possession. In embezzlement, the owner does intend to part with ownership of the property, but is deprived of it by fraud or misrepresentation. So, obtaining property by false pretenses is another relatively modern crime, created to plug the remaining loopholes, in spite of existing larceny and embezzlement violations.

What Kind of Things Are Subject to Larceny?

As previously noted, some of the common law judges were reluctant to enforce the death penalty for grand theft. Therefore, they reasoned that no larceny violation had occurred unless the thing taken had been reduced to ownership; someone had to have an actual property right in it. Most of the time it was difficult for working people to wrest a living from their small plots of land and their inadequate livestock. When times were unusually bad, they often poached deer or other game on forest preserves. Noblemen who owned these large estates wanted them protected; besides, they considered hunting an exclusive privilege of the nobility.

Wild Animals. On the other hand, the common law judges said that animals, fish, and birds were subject to larceny only when they were possessed. Wild animals belonged to everyone; they become property only when confined to a pen or cage and were usable for food. These animals, even in a fenced field, were not sufficiently contained to be subject to larceny, unless completely confined. The mere fact that a wild deer frequented a farm did not mean that the farmer owned the animal. The common law courts said that the deer belonged to the taker; the taking was not larceny. Larceny occurred only when a second individual stole the deer from someone who had already reduced it to possession.

In an attempt to avoid enforcing the death penalty for grand theft, the common law judges indulged in some other technicalities that now seem quite contradictory. For example, they held that a man might leave his dogs to his heirs through a will, but that he did not have sufficient property right in these dogs to make them subject to larceny.

Under modern law, at least in some states, wildlife is owned by the state, but can be acquired by a hunter who captures or kills the specimen in question. A hunter acquires legal title, however, only when the acquisition is legal; in other words, when hunting and game laws have been complied with. This, of course, raises some outside legal questions beyond the scope of this book. It is also worth noting that, under all modern laws, tame animals are the subject of larceny; but specific statutes are necessary to reach this result in some states.

Unclaimed or Abandoned Property. In the absence of special statutes, the courts also have said that goods and merchandise from a shipwreck or treasure trove (money or coin, gold, silver, plate, or bullion found under the sea or buried in the earth) are not subject to larceny. The finder of trove does not commit larceny in taking the treasure, but is entitled to keep loot taken from the sea. Usually, statutes specify whether the finder, the landowner, or both are entitled to recover treasure when it is taken from the land. This taking is not larceny, in the absence of special statutes.[4] Seaweed, between the high and low tide marks, drifted and ungathered, also is not subject to larceny.

[4] Groover v. Tippins, 179 S.E. 634, 51 Ga. App. 47.

All courts consistently hold that property right to abandoned goods does not exist; it is not subject to theft. Therefore, an individual who goes through a trash can and removes something of value has not stolen it, since the owner abandoned it. Placing the article in the trash container, from which the owner does not expect to retrieve it, is evidence of abandonment.

Lost or misplaced property, however, is subject to theft, since the owner does not intend to give up the property right in it. If, for example, a passenger inadvertently leaves a sweater on a commercial airplane, it is larceny when an airline employee takes the article, failing to place it in a lost and found department.

Real Estate and Crops.   Under the common law real estate was not subject to larceny. In fact, the courts have almost always recognized the fact that anything permanently affixed to the land is also a part of the land. Through this line of reasoning, common law courts held that crops growing on the land were not subject to theft, that is, if they were severed and taken away in one continuous action. This was apparently because the common law judges looked for some excuses to find accused thieves not guilty, especially when the stealing was to satisfy pangs of hunger.

Modern statutes have changed this situation in practically all jurisdictions. Today it is theft to steal crops, trees, or fruit, or to take any part of the land. If changes of this kind had not been made, a thief might take thousands of board feet of marketable timber without penalty. These statutes also protect the owners of gold ore (miners called this "high grading").[5]

In looking for technicalities to excuse theft, the common law courts also said that stealing a valid contract or written agreement was not larceny. The reasoning was that the document in question represented value only in the sense that it was evidence of the right to sue in court. Since only the right itself was valuable, the paper was merely a scrap—without value, not subject to theft. This obviously is illogical reasoning in the minds of modern lawyers and courts, but it probably saved some individuals who might otherwise have been hanged on the gallows.

Continuing this line of reasoning, the common law courts held that when the contract or legal document written on the paper was void or unenforceable in the courts, then the document itself represented only the value of the paper. Since the scrap of paper had little value, any conviction that resulted was for petty theft only; this did not require the death penalty.

[5] State v. Berryman, 8 Nev. 262.

Under modern statutes, and in most jurisdictions, the person who steals any document or legal paper that has significance or value to anyone has committed larceny. Documents or instruments brought within the scope of the offense by typical statutes include checks, shares of stocks, certificates of deposit, promissory notes, warehouse receipts, and receipted vouchers. The result of these statutes has been that these documents are now put on the same footing as the money they represent.

Some states hold that personal rights never reduced to possession (these are called by lawyers "choses in action"), such as lottery tickets, cannot be the object of theft. Since these are illegal in most jurisdictions, the right represented by them does not exist and the tickets are regarded as mere scraps of paper, not subject to theft.

Early courts also selected a number of intangibles that could not be picked up and carried away, and that were therefore not the subject of theft. On the other hand, modern statutes provided criminal punishment for withdrawing electrical current from a line without paying the utility company.[6] This seems somewhat out of line with the old common law idea that theft was solely taking possession of something that belonged to another and carrying it away. The result, however, seems to be good. Under present-day law the courts also provide criminal punishment for stealing a railroad ticket, using a hotel room without paying for it, or sneaking into a movie theater. This does not mean that the law of theft has changed radically, only that statutes have been passed to furnish needed protection to existing businesses.

Even under present-day law the courts generally say that the thief must take actual or constructive possession of the property and carry it away.

Larceny Requires a Special Mens Rea—
To Deprive the Owner Permanently of Property

A general intent is not sufficient for larceny. The law requires a specific mens rea; the intent must be permanently to deprive the owner of property. Yet, the courts realize that a thief may take property and abandon it when it is no longer useful. The old cases held that, when a thief took the horse of another and abandoned it at another location, the taker had permanently deprived the owner of the horse.

Later, when the automobile came into common use, the vehicle offered a great attraction to boys and young men; they commonly took vehicles for trial spins. Many of these wrongdoers did not become involved in other types of crime and often returned the vehicles to the exact spots from which they had been taken. Under circumstances of this kind, the courts

[6] People v. Menagas, 11 N.E.2d 403, 367 Ill. 330.

said that the taker was a joyrider, not a thief with intent permanently to deprive the owner as required in the law of larceny. On the other hand, these youthful culprints often wrecked or damaged the automobiles and killed or injured pedestrians. To bring this social evil under control, most state legislatures have passed statutes designating joyriding as a type of larceny, minus the specific intent characteristic of the usual theft.

Taking Property in the Belief That It Is One's Own

In some situations individuals may take property, believing that it is their own. This cannot be larceny, since the taker does not intend to deprive the owner of the property. The taker, therefore, does not have the necessary mental intent.

It is of no consequence that the person who carries the article away may be completely mistaken as to its ownership. So long as the taker has a genuine belief that the property is his or her own, no theft has been committed. At the trial this may be referred to a jury. If the jury finds that the taker's belief was bona fide, it will not convict.

Trespass as a Necessary Part of Larceny

The courts consistently say that larceny must include a trespassory taking. This usually means that the taking must be without the permission of the owner. When the owner actually gives permission to the taking, no larceny occurs, unless the consent is obtained by duress or fraud.

Taking Possession and Carrying the Property Away

The thief need not personally take possession of the property. For example, a woman may hire a man with a truck to remove a racehorse from a field, on the false representation that the animal is her property and has been pastured there. On the other hand, either the thief or a representative of the thief must take possession of the property in question. In the well-known situation, a con artist "sells" the Brooklyn Bridge to a naive buyer; there has been no larceny, unless the buyer physically takes possession of the bridge. The con artist is however, guilty of obtaining property (money) by false pretenses.

Also, in a situation where a thief attempts to grab a money bag from a store messenger and the money falls through a grating into a sewer, without actually coming into the thief's possession, no larceny violation has occurred, since the property never went into the possession of the wrongdoer. Of course, the wrongdoer may be convicted for attempted theft under these facts.

Court decisions differ as to whether possession by the thief may come about through enticement. In a situation of this kind, a poultry dealer might illegally obtain chickens by dropping grain along the road to entice the birds into a truck.

The old cases uniformly held that stolen property must actually be carried away by the thief. If the thief dropped the loot in flight, that too was sufficient.

Some of the early English courts held it no larceny when the victim detected a pickpocket but managed to retain the money. The reasoning was that the thief had not taken possession of the victim's money. American courts in recent years have usually held that this does constitute larceny, when the pickpocket takes possession of the loot and moves if far enough to alert the victim to what is happening. Perhaps these early English cases represented efforts on the part of the common law judges to find technicalities that would save criminals from hangings, but even when this activity was not sufficient to constitute larceny, it was enough to prosecute for attempt.

Another difficult type of case is one in which a criminal has killed a beef animal, intending to haul it away for sale or food. When the wrongdoer is apprehended before actually loading the meat, some courts say that the "carrying away" aspect of larceny has not been satisfied. In other cases, when the butcher has actually skinned the animal, the courts have held that the crime is complete. To protect the interests of farmers and ranchers, specific statutes cover situations of this kind in most of the Western states.

Previously Stolen Property

A new larceny occurs when a thief steals property that has previously been stolen. The courts clearly are in agreement on this. For example, in an old bank robbery case handled by the Los Angeles police and the FBI, a gang of criminals observed a lone bank robber make his getaway from the scene of the holdup. Members of the gang then stole some of the bank loot from the robber. They were found guilty of state larceny and of the federal crime of receiving loot from a bank robbery.

The fact that the stolen property is contraband or otherwise illegal is immaterial. When one gang of thieves steals a packet of heroin from another, a larceny has occurred in addition to some narcotics violations.

Jointly Owned Property

Under the old common law, a partner could not steal property from the partnership. The theory was that the partner was only doing "what by law he might do"; it treated partnership property as belonging to both or either. Specific statutory provisions have changed this, at least in some jurisdictions.

Also under ancient rules of law, a wife could not own separate property. All her possessions became the property of the husband, upon marriage. Thus, a man could not steal from his wife; but, as women obtained political and property rights, this idea changed in most states. While some exceptions exist, most courts in the United States now hold that a person may be guilty of larceny of the separate property of his or her spouse.[7] All courts consistently say that a child who wrongfully takes property from his or her parents is guilty of larceny.

Delivering Property to a Bailee

As pointed out earlier, before England became highly industrialized, almost all merchandise offered for sale in the shops was manufactured on the premises by apprentices or servants of the shop owner. When goods were shipped to another area for sale, they were generally turned over to an agent or bailee, with the maker retaining ownership of the property. Legally, this was called bailment. In the words of the courts, *bailment* was the delivery of merchandise by one party to another, to be held according to the purpose of the delivery and returned or paid for when that purpose was accomplished.[8]

In the usual course of business, a shop owner who manufactured more merchandise than he could sell allowed his bailee to take goods to another area for sale. Civil courts provided some good remedies whereby the manufacturer could force his agent to return the proceeds or the unsold goods. When this was not successful, the manufacturer obtained money judgment against the bailee in the civil courts. Since the manufacturer had good civil remedies against the agent, the criminal courts did not feel unusually pressured to make a crime out of the bailee's bad management. This situation illustrates the fact that the criminal law sometimes follows the needs of the business community in protecting property. At any rate, the law became so settled that when a bailee took property in good faith, he was not guilty of larceny when he later appropriated some or all of this to his own use. If he kept the property too long or spent some of the proceeds of sale, no common law crime was committed. The rule applied, however, only in those situations where the bailee had no intent to steal at the time he took the property. When he entered into the transaction with the intent at the outset to appropriate the owner's goods to his own use, the bailee was

---

[7] Beasley v. State, 38 N.E. 35, 138 Ind. 552; People v. Morton, 123 N.E.2d 790, 308 N.Y.96.
[8] Hardin v. Grant, 54 S.W.2d 189.

guilty of larceny. This was the basic common law test in the bailment situation; it still is, except when changed by state statutes.

One important exception to the general rule (a bailment entered in good faith is no larceny) developed about A.D. 1600. Pilferage from commercial shipments began to occur with considerable frequency. The carriers did not steal entire shipments; only quantities were taken out of the container, and the bulk of the merchandise was delivered as if it had been undisturbed. Eventually this problem became so troublesome that common law judges extended the law of larceny to cover the situation; this was *breaking bulk.*

Recognizing breaking bulk as a crime served a social need at the time, but it produced a very strange result. A man who entered into a good faith bailment could be convicted of larceny by taking a part of the shipment; he was free to steal the whole lot. Modern statutes have, of course, eliminated this absurdity in the law of larceny. Most of these enactments do away with the distinctions between stealing part of a shipment and stealing all of it. Then too, as business and manufacturing expanded, the need for additional protection against thieves became apparent. The inability of the courts to hold a bailee responsible for taking the merchandise of another led to the development of modern embezzlement. Present-day statutes in a number of jurisdictions make theft by bailee a criminal act and combine larceny and embezzlement in a single larceny statute.

Delivering Property to a Servant

Under the apprentice system early English merchants retained considerable control over their servants and apprentices. The courts reasoned that the employer needed to exercise this close supervision and control over the servant's work. Hence, common law judges said that the employer had *constructive possession* over the property; the servant who took property for his or her own use was guilty of larceny. This *ordinary servant rule* is still followed in common law jurisdictions, unless changed by statute. If the owner gave the merchandise to a trusted employee, no larceny occurred when the latter appropriated the goods. The questions are, who was an ordinary servant and who was a trusted employee? Generally, an ordinary servant was one who remained entirely under the control and direction of the employer. The servant who had had authority to exercise judgment was a trusted employee. Today, management employees, executive secretaries, and bank messengers offer excellent examples.

Deliveries in common law, discussed earlier, involved those by an employer to the servants. When the delivery was by a third person to the servant and the servant placed the property in a place where it was his or her duty as servant to put it, the courts took the approach that the property was in the employer's *constructive care* from that time forward; and, it was larceny for the servant, thereafter, to appropriate it. When the servant appropriated the property before it was deposited in a place of safekeeping for the employer, no taking from the constructive possession occurred, thus no larceny.

The courts today recognize a difference in giving possession and in giving *bare custody*, although this distinction is a very fine one. What the courts are saying is that bare physical presence of property does not necessarily constitute possession. The registered guest of a hotel, for example, may have bare custody of the TV set, towels, and bed linen; but to carry these items away and convert them to the guest's use is larceny. Similarly, when a merchant hands a valuable ring to a customer for inspection and the customer appropriates it, a larceny has occurred. When a jeweler gives a ring to an agent for sale and the agent, thereafter, appropriates it, the crime is embezzlement—not larceny.

Distinguishing between Grand and Petty Larceny under Modern Statutes

While theft is theft, regardless of the amount taken, society has shown leniency to those who restrict their activities to objects of small value. As early as A.D. 1275 an English law classified larceny as either grand or petit larceny (now petty larceny), in terms of the value of the property taken.

This breakdown has continued in almost all modern jurisdictions. Statutes in force in the United States usually set the value at $50 for a grand larceny conviction; others may set the figure as high as $200. In some states the theft of certain items automatically constitutes grand larceny, regardless of value. Livestock and automobiles generally are included in this category.

Generally, the laws of the individual states classify grand larceny as a felony; petty larceny is a misdemeanor.

EMBEZZLEMENT

We have seen from the study of common law larceny that the agent or bailee who obtained lawful custody of goods and, thereafter, developed a criminal intent and appropriated the merchandise, had not committed any crime. However, this type of obvious wrong became so common that it became *embezzlement* by statute in England in 1529 (embezzlement is, therefore, not a common law crime).

In defining embezzlement, we can say that it is the unlawful appropriation of the personal property of another by an individual who has gained rightful possession because of employment by or a trust relationship with the owner.

In the words of one judge, embezzlement is "the fraudulent appropriation of property by a person to whom it has been entrusted, or to whose hands it has lawfully come."[9]

Embezzlement, then, is a trespass against ownership; larceny is a trespass against possession. As in larceny, embezzlement involves a fraudulent intent to deprive the owner of his property. However, intent in embezzlement must be formed after the property or money of the owner is entrusted to the accused. Intent in larceny may exist before the entrustment. Generally, any kind of property that can be taken by larceny is also subject to embezzlement. In some jurisdictions this also has been expanded to include interests in real property, such as a deed to land.

The defendant who shows that something embezzled from a corporation was acquired without legal authority on the part of the firm, or that the corporation has no right to do business under the laws of the state, has no defense.[10] Embezzlement exists when the property taken is owned by anyone other than the accused. Therefore, the embezzlement of funds by a madam of a house of prostitution is punishable, even though she appropriates money earned through illegal acts. Similarly, bribe money, intended to pay off a public official for illegal activity, is subject to embezzlement.[11]

As noted, the essential difference between larceny and embezzlement is that in the latter the original taking of the property is lawful. The person who holds the property later decides to become dishonest about it. In embezzlement it is obvious, then, that a trust relationship exists at the outset; embezzlement is a breach of this trust. In most cases this relationship arises through employment or through a business agent of the property owner.

One frequent problem here is that the person who appropriates the money originally and honestly intends to return it after a short time. In other words, the taker borrows the money and has no real intent to deprive the owner permanently of it. The courts in many jurisdictions construe this temporary borrowing without authority as a clear appropriation under the embezzlement statutes.Conversely, when the accused does not have an intent permanently to deprive the owner of property, the courts of some states hold that the necessary mens rea for the crime does not exist. This allegation is easy for the defendant to make; however, a jury of reasonable people is completely justified in refusing to believe it, unless the accused

[9] American Life Insurance Co. v. U.S. Fidelity and Guaranty Co., 246 N.W. 71, 261 Mich. 221.
[10] People v. Hawkins, 64 N.W. 736, 106 Mich. 479.
[11] State v. Shadd, 80 Mo. 358; Commonwealth v. Cooper, 130 Mass. 285.

offers some proof of efforts to return the money before appropriation was discovered by the owner. While statutes differ, perhaps the laws of most states specify that an appropriation is a criminal embezzlement, even though the accused intends to borrow the money or property for only a short time.

FALSE PRETENSES

The modern crime of false pretenses, or obtaining property by false pretenses, did not exist under the common law. It first became law by English statute in 1757. Adopted by the early colonists in the United States, this crime is of such early origin that it is clearly treated by the courts as a part of the common law.[12] Present-day statutes provide penalties for this offense in practically all jurisdictions.

The crime is obtaining money or property of another through a scheme utilizing untrue claims of fact with intent to defraud the owner.

In the language of the courts, "In false pretenses the owner intends to part with his property, money or chattel, but it is obtained from him by fraud."[13] "Only a very narrow distinction exists between 'larceny' and 'false pretense'; the character of the crime depends on the intention of the parties."[14]

To distinguish between larceny and false pretenses, the courts point out: "In larceny the owner has no intention to part with title to and possession of the property taken, while in false pretenses he does so intend, but it is obtained from him by fraud."[15]

As seen from these statements of the courts, one of the distinguishing features of false pretenses is that ownership of the property passes to the criminal, while in larceny ownership never passes.

To take an actual situation, a confidence man convinced his victim, who had considerable property, that he had an inside source that could furnish advance information on "fixed" horse races. Relying on this false representation, the confidence man persuaded his victim to furnish some stock certificates destined to be taken to a bank as security for a loan to obtain funds to bet on the fixed races. After obtaining the stocks, the confidence man sold them and kept the proceeds, taking the next plane for an undisclosed destination. The victim did not intend to turn ownership of the stocks over to the confidence man; he planned to give possession only, so

[12] Durland v. United States, 161 U.S. 306, 16 S. Ct. 508.
[13] People v. Santora, 125 P.2d 606, 51 Cal. App. 707.
[14] Riley v. State, 78 P.2d 712, 64 Okla. Crim. 183.
[15] Simmons v. State, 167 A. 60, 165 Md. 155.

that the securities might be used as collateral for a loan. Since the confidence man intended to defraud the victim at the time he obtained possession, the facts constituted larceny by the bailee (the confidence man). This is sometimes called "larceny by trick."

In a similar, but different, situation the victim furnished shares of stock to the confidence man to be sold to obtain cash to bet on the fixed horse races. In this case the victim intended to turn over ownership in the stocks; the facts, therefore, constituted false pretenses.

Under false pretenses, the intent is the same as in larceny or embezzlement: to deprive the owner of money or property. In addition, the false representations must actually be false statements of facts. A mere false opinion is not sufficient. The untrue facts must be calculated to deceive the victim; mere silence of failure to disclose facts is seldom sufficient. Predictions, promises, and statements of intention are generally not included in the statutes against false pretenses. Also, obtaining money from someone on a promise to marry that person is not a false pretense violation, although another specific statute may make this conduct a violation.[16]

Some states provide laws requiring some corroboration of the false representations as a standard for conviction for false pretenses. Therefore, in these jurisdictions some additional evidence must be developed to augment the unsupported testimony of the victim.[17]

Passing a worthless check to obtain money usually is classified as false pretenses. Some courts, however, regard this as larceny by trick, on the theory that the person who accepts the check does not intend to relinquish title to the money or merchandise if the check is not honored by the bank. This, however, seems to be the minority view.

STATUTORY THEFT

Recognizing the unclear distinctions between larceny, embezzlement, and false pretenses, many jurisdictions fortunately provide statutes merging these three crimes into a single statutory classification; they call it "theft."[18]

Legislation of this kind is of great value to the prosecutor and to the police officer, especially to the prosecutor. Under procedures in effect before the passage of these laws, cases were often dismissed when the facts indicated that the crime was embezzlement or false pretenses and the accused actually was charged with larceny. The same result occurred when an error was made in charging the accused with embezzlement or false

[16] See People v. Miller, 116 N.E. 131, 278 Ill. 490.
[17] CALIFORNIA PENAL CODE, sec. 1110.
[18] *Id.*, sec. 484.

pretenses. Adopting and using this statute eliminated most of the technical differences in all varieties of fraud and theft; the job of prosecution has been greatly simplified.

CITED CASES

American Life Insurance Co. v. U.S. Fidelity and Guaranty Co., 246 N.W. 71, 261 Mich. 221.
Beasley v. State, 38 N.E. 35, 138 Ind. 552.
Commonwealth v. Cooper, 130 Mass. 285.
Durland v. United States, 161 U.S. 306, 16 S. Ct. 508.
Groover v. Tippins, 179 S.E. 634, 51 Ga. App. 47.
Hardin v. Grant, 54 S.W.2d 180.
Morissette v. United States, 342 U.S. 246, 72 S. Ct. 240.
People v. Hawkins, 64 N.W. 736, 106 Mich. 479.
People v. Menagas, 11 N.E.2d 403, 367 Ill. 330.
People v. Miller, 116 N.E. 131, 278 Ill. 490.
People v. Morton, 123 N.E.2d 790, 308 N.Y. 96.
People v. Santora, 125 P.2d 606, 51 Cal. App. 707.
Riley v. State, 78 P.2d 712, 64 Okla. Crim. 183.
Simmons v. State, 167 A. 60, 165 Md. 155.
State v. Berryman, 8 Nev. 262.
State v. Shadd, 80 Mo. 358.

CHAPTER 15

Robbery, Extortion, Receiving Stolen Goods, Malicious Mischief, and Forgery

Robbery, extortion, receiving stolen goods, malicious mischief, and forgery have at least one characteristic in common: each is an offense against property.

 **ROBBERY**

Robbery is the felonious taking of personal property in the possession of another, from that individual's person or immediate presence and against the victim's will, accomplished by means of force or fear.[1]

[1] BLACK's LAW DICTIONARY, 4th ed.

This crime is sometimes described as compound larceny, or larceny from the person, through the use of force or threats of force. Robbery often is a combination of assault and larceny.

A common law felony from very early times in England, the offense is still a felony in almost all American jurisdictions. Highway robbery, which was simply any robbery on or near a public highway, was the earliest variation of this crime. Highway robbery has now acquired a broader meaning, being absorbed into robbery in general.

Effective administration of justice requires a strong social interest in the crime of robbery, since it is always a threat to property. Of perhaps even greater importance, the lives and safety of citizens and police officers are constantly at stake when this violation occurs. Truly, robbery may be described as "death looking for a place to happen."

An analysis of robbery reveals all the elements of larceny, plus two additional requirements:

1. The object taken must be personal property, capable of being stolen.
2. It must be taken and carried away.
3. The taking must be with the intent to steal—to fraudulently deprive the owner of property.

The above elements are necessary to both larceny and robbery. Robbery requires two additional ones:

1. The object taken must be from the individual's person or immediate presence.
2. It must be taken against the individual's will, either by violence or by threats that the victim thinks it unwise to resist.

The Thing Taken Must Be Capable of Being Stolen

As in larceny, the object taken in the robbery must be property that logically can be the subject of theft. If a man should force a woman into sexual intercourse at gunpoint, this is not robbery. While we might argue that the gunman took something of value, it was not personal property, capable of being stolen.

Somewhat similarly, if an organized gang should hold a victim's companions at gunpoint while others beat him up, the crime is not robbery, since nothing of value was taken. Undoubtedly, charges of assault and battery or assault with intent to commit murder might be filed, depending on the state laws.

Under common law larceny, the English courts said that certain legal documents, e.g., contracts, had no value in themselves but merely represented a legal right to sue or take other action. In terms of this logic, they held that the theft or taking of a document in a robbery was not a crime. In most jurisdictions in the United States, these documents have been made the subject of larceny by statute; they have, in turn, also become the subject of robbery.[2]

At common law, an individual who found that a thief had recently stolen his or her money and who immediately retook the money at gunpoint was not guilty of robbery. The point is that the victim still owned the money. The victim had not taken the property of another and could not be charged with robbery.

Taking and Carrying the Loot Away

The cases have always insisted that the loot in any robbery must be "taken from the person of another." This does not mean that the victim must be actually clutching the money at the time it is snatched away. The law has never required that the property taken be in actual physical contact with the victim. When it is taken from the presence of the person who is robbed, this is sufficient. In fact, the courts have never laid down definite guidelines; apparently, all that is required is that the victim be near enough to resist.

Determining by force and intimidation where a woman hid her valuables, the accused in one case left her bound in one room while he obtained her money and property in another room in the same residence. The court held that his act was a "taking from the presence of another" and that the facts were sufficient to constitute robbery.[3]

In another case, the occupant of property remained in his smokehouse, after intimidation and threats, while the defendant looted his home. The smokehouse was located about fifteen steps from the house. A robbery conviction was upheld on the ground that property was "taken from his presence."[4]

The Use of Force or Physical Violence

The taking in a robbery may be accomplished in either of two ways: (1) by force or violence, or (2) by causing the victim to be afraid to resist.

A pickpocket may be convicted for larceny, but obviously doesn't usually use the kind of force needed to constitute robbery. Ordinarily, all that the pickpocket does is to remove the loot from the victim's pocket. If any

---

[2] State v. Gorham, 55 N.H. 152; Turner v. State, 1 Ohio St. 422.
[3] State v. Calhoun, 34 N.W. 194, 72 Iowa 432.
[4] The courts sometimes say that an accused cannot avoid conviction for this crime by removing the victim to another place before taking the property that may be nearby.

additional force is used, a robbery has been committed. For example, the crime is only larceny when a thief removes a watch from the pocket of a victim; but if the timepiece is attached to clothing in such manner that it is necessary to break a watch chain or tear the owner's clothing, the taking is robbery.

The difference between larceny and robbery is illustrated by the taking of diamond earrings from a woman sitting on a park bench. If the culprit sneaks up behind her and removes the earrings by stealth, the crime is larceny. When he rips the jewelry from the owner's ear, tearing an earlobe in the process, the offense is robbery.

Clearly, whatever force is used must also be applied at the time of the taking. For example, a pickpocket was successful in obtaining the money of a tourist, leaving the scene before the victim realized that anything had disappeared. Somewhat later, after the tourist realized what had happened, he chanced to observe the pickpocket and made an issue of the theft. The thief then used force to retain the stolen money and fled. The crime is larceny since the use of force did not coincide with the unlawful taking.

In another situation that occurs rather frequently, the accused uses force to take property from another, but does this in the belief that the property is his or her own. So long as this belief is honest and so long as the claim is a bona fide one, no robbery occurs.

Although, in the typical robbery, the force used is overpowering, as in the case of the frail victim who is smashed to the ground and robbed by a young ruffian, a great amount of force need not be used. Some pushing or shoving of the victim is usually held sufficient by the courts, as where one pickpocket jostles or shoves the victim while another obtains the victim's wallet during the distraction. It is not even necessary that the victim be aware of the robbery. The courts recognize the fact that surprise may be used to aid the application of force; but when any force is used, the offense is robbery.

Robbery by Placing the Victim in Fear

When actual force is not used, a robbery may be completed by placing the victim in fear. The fact that the victim appears to remain cool and collected throughout the incident does not nullify the fact that a robbery actually occurred. Note, however, that the placing in fear must be immediately before or during the time of the taking from the presence of the victim. When threats are used to retain property taken by a thief, the crime is larceny—not robbery. The victim is not put in fear at the time the property is unlawfully taken.

On the other hand, not every threat is regarded as sufficient to constitute robbery, even though the victim may be intimidated by it. All the cases seem to agree that, when the robber threatens death or *great bodily harm*, this is sufficient. Just what amounts to great harm varies from case to case, depending on the place where the threat was made, the physical sizes and ages of the parties involved, the number of attackers, whether weapons of some kind were exhibited, and other factors.

A majority of courts also hold that a threat to harm property is also sufficient, provided it is a substantial threat, such as to burn the victim's house.

In some states threats to harm a person's reputation may even be sufficient, when that person allows property to be taken as a result of these threats. Generally, however, the courts hold that a threat of this kind is not sufficient, with one exception. The situation involves the giving up of property on the threat of another to accuse the victim of sodomy. This accusation is so feared that the law makes an exception of it; and the crime is robbery, whether the accusation is true or false.

On the other hand, let us note that a threat to file suit against the victim or a threat to prosecute for a usual crime supposedly committed by the victim is not sufficient.

In any robbery when force is not used, the facts must show that the victim gave up property because of fear induced by the robber. When no violence is used and no threats to induce fear are made, no robbery exists.

A victim who is simply overpowered and loses property by force need not be afraid. A person may say, "I was not afraid, but I saw nothing I could do about it"; the crime is still robbery. Actually, in some cases, the victim may be struck and rendered unconscious before realizing fear. This, of course, is also robbery when property is taken. In this connection, let us note that the courts sometimes describe robbery as a crime in which property is taken "against the will of the owner." The courts say an owner who is knocked unconscious has no will and cannot consent.

Statutory Changes in Robbery

Characteristically, modern statutes define robbery and classify it by degrees. Some of these enactments declare robbery a more serious crime when committed on a public highway or in a private dwelling. In other jurisdictions the crime may be placed in a more serious classification when a deadly weapon is used or when the robbery is accomplished by torture.[5]

[5] See California Penal Code, sec. 211(a).

EXTORTION

In legal terminology, to extort "is to obtain money or other valuable things either by compulsion, by actual force, or by the force of motives applied to the will and often more overpowering and irresistible than physical force."[6]

Modern legal understanding of extortion grew out of two ideas: (1) the old common law crime called "extortion" and (2) the more modern unlawful practice termed "blackmail."

Common law extortion was a crime possible of commission only by officials of the government. This violation involved corruptly demanding and receiving an unlawful fee by the officer under the pretense of being entitled to it. It made use of the exceptional power and authority given to government officials in early England.

In one of its original meanings, blackmail was the payment of tribute by English dwellers along the Scottish border to influential chieftains of Scotland as protection against marauders and border thieves.[7]

Extortion is now punished by statute in practically all jurisdictions. Fortunately, we find considerable uniformity in these statutes that define the modern version of the crime as "obtaining property from another, with his consent, induced by the wrongful use of force or fear."[8]

Modern extortion statutes cover two basic situations:

1. The forced payment of money or valuables by means of a threat of a lesser nature than that required for robbery by fear.
2. A communication of some type designed to force payment of money or valuables, based on a threat.

You will recall that we earlier defined robbery as a demand for money or valuables based on a threat to kill or do great bodily harm, to destroy a person's home, or to make an accusation of sodomy. All other threats to expose misconduct or to harm a person's reputation are the kind that make this activity bribery. *Extortion, then, involves threats less serious than those included in robbery.*

Most of the modern statutes punish as extortion the sending of any threatening communication, even though the threat may be the kind that amounts to robbery when it is made by the accused in person.

The old common law idea of extortion exists today in most locations, so

---

[6] BLACK'S LAW DICTIONARY, quoting Commonwealth v. O'Brien, 12 Cush. Mass. 90.
[7] From BLACK'S LAW DICTIONARY and from the AMERICAN COLLEGE DICTIONARY (1948).
[8] CALIFORNIA PENAL CODE, sec, 518, seems typical.

that government officials who demand fees knowing they are not entitled to have them committed the violation.[9]

In some states the courts hold that a threat to institute criminal prosecution against an individual is not extortion if this threatened person is, in fact, guilty of the crime and the threat is made in a genuine attempt to collect civil damages as an outgrowth of the offense. Opinions by the courts differ in this situation, however.

As a general rule, the courts provide no extortion violation unless the money or valuables are turned over to the accused because of fear. In fact, most courts insist that the fear must be the motivating or controlling inducement.

RECEIVING OR CONCEALING STOLEN PROPERTY

If wrongdoers never stole property except what they wanted for their own use, the number of criminal violations might be greatly reduced. Judges and criminologists sometimes express concern about the social harm that may result from certain types of criminal activity. For example. the "fence," or semiunderworld character who deals in stolen property, frequently contributes to thefts and burglaries that might not otherwise be committed. The truth is that the receiver of stolen goods tends to put this kind of crime on an organized business basis. The fence oftentimes influences juveniles to steal and, on occasions, even teaches them some of the tricks of the trade. From the standpoint of social harm, fences may do more damage to the community than the burglars and thieves they encourage.

Receiving or concealing stolen property was a misdemeanor at common law—not as a separate kind of crime but as misprision of larceny or a compounded felony. Today the crime is a distinct one, defined by statute as a felony in practically all jurisdictions.[10]

As a specific violation, receiving or concealing stolen property continues as a comparatively frequent offense because of our characteristically impersonal and complex society. The ease with which goods may be transported long distances is also a factor in reducing the chances for detection and prosecution.

Basically, the prosecution needs to prove four elements in a receiving case.

[9] Martin v. United States, 278 F. 913.
[10] Larceny and receiving stolen goods are separate and distinct crimes. Milanovich v. United States, 81 S. Ct. 728.

1. The property in question must be stolen property. This means that it must have been taken illegally as a result of some other type of criminal activity, whether by theft, robbery, embezzlement, or false pretenses.

2. The property must have been received or concealed.

3. It must have been accepted with the knowledge that it was stolen or obtained by criminal means.

4. The illegally obtained property must be received with a fraudulent or criminal intent.

Since the essence of this crime is receiving *stolen* property, some courts declare to violation when the property can no longer be characterized as stolen. In a case in which authorities apprehend a criminal in possession of stolen merchandise, when the thief is advised to go ahead and make delivery to the fence who has previously agreed to dispose of it, some courts say that the receiver cannot be convicted, even for an attempt violation. Others, however, have allowed an attempt conviction to stand under these circumstances.[11]

Entrapment is not an issue here, since the original idea for the crime began in the minds of the thief and the receiver, rather than with the police. Yet, a most interesting question arises in situations when the fence has not received the goods in question. However, courts are in general agreement that no receiving or concealment takes place when only an agreement to accept the "hot" goods has been reached.

Interestingly enough, the receiver need not be acquainted with, nor even have an inkling as to the identity of, the thief. At one time some of the courts decided that the receiver must personally take the property from the thief, with no intervening people; but, under contemporary statutes, they have abandoned this requirement. In some cases, a person who has no knowledge of the criminal nature of the transaction may be used as a transfer agent.[12]

While receiving is essential, the receiver need not actually touch the stolen goods. Nor is it essential that the receiver, in fact, see the accepted material. For example, a guilty fence has stolen items delivered to a wooded area behind her barn and found herself arrested before she actually got around to inspecting the merchandise. Court opinions say that such possession is constructive. The test generally used by the judge is whether the receiver had control of the stolen goods. In other words, was the hot merchandise placed in a position where the receiver had the option of disposing of it or allowing it to remain there?

[11] People v. Rojas, 55 Cal. 2d 252.
[12] Commonwealth v. White, 123 Mass. 430.

Additionally, it is worth noting that the receiving is complete when an employee or servant accepts the property on instructions of the fence, whether or not the latter has any knowledge as to the stolen character of the goods. The law does not require an elaborate scheme to conceal the stolen property. It may be left completely in the open or be offered for sale in a public place. The general attitude of the courts is that any act which tends to prevent recovery by the rightful owner is sufficient.

When the receiver makes the claim of having accepted the stolen property for the sole purpose of returning it to the rightful owner, this is a defense. A claim of this kind, however, is a question for the jury, under all circumstances. Seldom will a jury believe this defense, unless the receiver has taken some affirmative steps to locate the owner or to notify police authorities. The fact that the receiver has held the property for some time or has offered it for sale at a fraction of its true worth weighs against a receiver who claims the above defense.

The thief need not be paid for the stolen materials by the receiver. The holding may be as a mere convenience to the thief, with no agreement for compensation.

Often in these cases a real question is, "Just what is stolen property?" The majority of the courts take the approach that receiving and concealing statutes apply so long as the property in question was taken by any criminal means. Therefore, anything taken by robbery, larceny, embezzlement, or false pretenses is included in the kind of material that subjects the receiver to prosecution.

In some localities the courts hold that a conviction for receiving stolen property cannot be supported when the property is obtained by embezzlement or false pretenses. Truthfully, receiving and concealing is a statutory crime; and the wording of a statute may not be general enough to include property taken through embezzlement or false pretenses. Some states have cured this evil in the receiving laws through an additional statute which specifies that any money or property feloniously taken is covered under the receiving enactments. The key phrase is "feloniously taken"; the courts have extended this to mean any kind of felony.

Specific words of the statutes in some states prohibit receiving money or goods obtained by embezzlement, false pretenses, robbery, burglary or through other crimes against property, knowing them to have been so obtained.[13]

Sometimes the prosecuting attorney is quite reluctant to press charges, since it is difficult to prove that the receiver knew the stolen nature of the merchandise. When the thief can be persuaded to testify as to the agreement with the fence, this problem may be eliminated. If the thief is unwill-

[13] Commonwealth v. Leonard, 4 N.E. 96, 140 Mass. 473.

ing to take the witness stand or refuses to make admissions, the receiver's knowledge can often be proved only be circumstantial evidence. The general rule is that the receiver must have known or have had good reason to know that the property was stolen when it was received. The receiver who has no knowledge until later is not guilty at the time of acceptance of the property. If the receiver subsequently learns that the property was stolen and continues to hold it, some legal authorities contend that the receiver is guilty from that time forward. This does not appear to be a settled principle, however.

In deciding whether the accused should have had knowledge of the stolen character of property, the courts sometimes assert that the question is not what a prudent, cautious person would have believed or known under the circumstances, but what the accused actually knew or believed. In other words, and accused person who is too naive to realize wrong cannot be held accountable.

Other cases, however, take the approach that, when the circumstances surrounding the receiving of the goods gave the receiver reason to think that the merchandise was stolen, this substitutes for actual knowledge. If a reasonable person of ordinary observation would have realized that the merchandise was questionable, then a jury should decide that the receiver had guilty knowledge. As it was said in one leading case, "Guilty knowledge, or its equivalent—guilty belief—is of the gist of this offense . . . this has been declared in many decisions. . . ."[14]

The court in another decision said, "Guilty knowledge is sufficiently shown if the circumstances proven are such as must have made or caused the recipient of stolen goods to believe they were stolen."[15]

Just what circumstances may put the accused on notice as to the stolen nature of the merchandise varies from case to case. Great variance between the actual worth of the merchandise and the selling price may be an obvious indication. Another factor is whether the seller comes openly, with nothing to hide, or comes to the receiver's back door, under the cover of darkness. Concealing the merchandise or mislabeling it in shipping are other circumstances that put the buyer on notice that the merchandise is questionable.[16]

The courts also agree that the receiver must accept the stolen property with a fraudulent intent. This is identical with the intent required for larceny: the intent to deprive the owner of the goods. It does not mean that the prosecution must allege and prove some unusual state of mind of the receiver. When the facts show that the receiver intended to aid the thief or acted because of a desire for personal gain, this is sufficient.

[14] Meath v. State, 182 N.W. 334, 174 Wis. 80.
[15] Reaves v. Commonwealth, 65 S.E.2d 559, 192 Va. 443.
[16] People v. Ferris, 52 N.E.2d 171, 385 Ill. 186.

MALICIOUS MISCHIEF

Malicious mischief is the malicious destruction of, or injury to, the property of another. A misdemeanor at common law, the crime is now almost wholly statutory.

Some early courts held that the accused must act out of malice, spite, or ill will toward the person whose property was damaged; but today the tribunals require only a showing that the wrongdoer acted willfully and intentionally, or in wanton disregard of damage that might obviously result to property, with no legal excuse or justification.

On the other hand, the courts hold that the intent must be to cause the very injury that ultimately resulted, or at least some injury of the same general nature. To illustrate, the accused aimed a blow at a man, but missed him and made a large dent in the intended victim's automobile. The crime was an assault and battery, rather than a malicious mischief violation, because the intent was not to damage the property.

As to the property involved, this may be any kind, provided it is the property of another. That is, the damaged property may be either real estate or personal property. A hot-tempered woman may kick her own stereo set to bits because of frustration at the set's failure to perform. This is not a malicious mischief violation; the destruction did not involve the property of another.

Of course, additional statutes in a number of jurisdictions are designed to prevent the destruction of one's own property to defraud insurance companies. However, these are special laws not regarded as part of the law of malicious mischief.

Conversely, destruction of public buildings or public property is included in malicious mischief statutes, since the courts regard public property, park equipment, trees, etc., as the property of another. Clearly, the only property excluded is that owned by the accused.

Then too, the law requires some actual damage to the property. Mutilating road signs, poisoning a well, or knocking out the windows of a neighbor's house are examples of actual damage. In the absence of special statutes, dumping rubbish or garbage on the land of another is not malicious mischief. This property owner is only inconvenienced; the property is not destroyed or seriously damaged.[17]

In one case, a stack of firewood was intentionally knocked down; the wood was not harmed. This was held no violation.[18] The result might have

[17] Dumping rubbish is a special statutory offense in some states. See MASSACHUSETTS ANNOTATED LAWS, C. 270, sec. 16.
[18] Pollet v. State, 41 S.E. 606, 115 Ga. 234.

been different had the falling sticks of wood broken a window of a building or otherwise injured the property.

Deliberately spitting tobacco on an expensive oriental rug owned by another is a malicious mischief violation; the same action done on a bare cement floor is not.

When the accused commits the damage under a genuine claim of right, no malicious mischief violation occurs. For example, a landlord might place a padlock on the door of a warehouse previously rented to another person. If the tenant should break the lock to gain access to property which she believes she has paid for, she is not subject to a civil damage suit if she is mistaken. The landlord also is liable to no criminal action, whether right or wrong, so long as the person causing the property damage has a genuine claim of right.[19] The necessary intent for the criminal violation is lacking under these circumstances.

In addition, an individual may destroy or disable an animal, the property of another, in order to protect a person or property from that animal. For example, an attacking dog may be killed without criminal penalty.[20]

FORGERY

Forgery is "false making or material altering, with intent to defraud, of any writing which, if genuine, might apparently be of legal efficacy or the foundation of a legal liability."[21] In more simple terms, forgery involves the fraudulent preparation of false writing, typing, or printing which may be used to establish legal rights, or that may have legal significance.

Our society must make certain that documents circulating in business or trade are genuine. When large numbers of fraudulent documents are in existence, the general public is reluctant to deal in written instruments or negotiable papers, and commerce and industry are hampered considerably. Then too, when forgery is commonplace, people who are not directly involved in business are inclined to ignore the preparation of wills, trusts, and contracts, or not to buy negotiable stocks and bonds. In fact, the whole economic fabric of society may become involved.

Legally, the entire document need not be a forgery. The amount on a check may be raised, a signature or date on a will may be false, or only a part of a contract may be forged. Nevertheless, one fact must be understood: *this falsity must relate to the validity or authenticity of the document itself, rather than to the contents of the paper in question.* The

[19] Woodward v. State, 28 S.W. 204, 33 Tex. Crim. 554.
[20] Wright v. State, 30 Ga. 325.
[21] People v. Routson, 188 N.E. 883, 354 Ill. 573.

falsity must cause the document to seem to be something other than what is really is.

When Jennifer Smith fraudulently signs a contract as Sarah King, this is a forgery, even though nothing improper exists in the body of the document. Through her action Smith has not forged when she signs her own name; she has forged when she enters a false statement of fact in the contract, representing that she has authority which she does not have.

What Matters Are Subject to Forgery?

Let us also recognize the difference between the common understanding of the word "forgery" and its legal meaning. In everyday conversation "forgery" may be used to designate anything that is imitated, counterfeited, or duplicated. The courts say that a document is the subject of a criminal forgery only when it is a writing of apparent legal efficacy. In other words, it must be a document on which legal rights may be based.

A clever writer has not forged when she imitates the penmanship of Washington's Farewell Address, intending to sell it to a rare document collector. We find nothing in the Farewell Address that has any legal significance or legal efficacy. While the first President's notable speech has great historical significance, it is not the foundation of some legal right or liability. A deed to a farm, however, is used to pass ownership of this piece of land to another; therefore, it is of legal significance. In a similar vein, a mortgage, will, bill of lading, or contract is a document that has a legal purpose other than for its own existence.

Documents other than the usual legal papers—mortgages, deeds, securities, or checks—may also be a basis for forgery. For example, a United States passport confers certain legal rights on the holder. A state driver's license is similar, and a college diploma may assist in proving qualifications for a high-level position. Any of these may, therefore, be the subject of legal forgery.

This does not mean that it is not criminal to sell a counterfeit copy of Washington's Farewell Address, claiming that it is genuine. Conduct of this type constitutes the crime of false pretenses. In like manner, it is not forgery when a talented artist duplicates one of the old masters, selling his copy as an original. It is, however, interesting to note that newspaper accounts of an incident of this kind often refer to it as forgery, when it is legally, in fact, false pretenses.

The Required Specific Intent to Defraud

A conviction for forgery demands a specific intent to defraud, but we find no requirement that the forger must intend to swindle any particular individual at the time of preparing the forgery or altering the document in question. In fact, the courts do not insist that actual injury be proved. It is the actual preparation or alteration of the document, not the passing of it, that is the forgery. To pass or make use of a forged instrument is uttering a forged document. This, of course, is closely related to forgery, but clearly a companion crime. Since the crime (forgery) is completed when the forgery or alteration is made, an accused may be convicted of forging a document found on his or her person upon arrest for another crime.

Uttering

Uttering is putting or sending a forged document into circulation, knowing it is forged, with the intent to defraud.

To publish, or utter, a false instrument is to declare or assert, by words or action, that it is valid. The act is a representation that the document is good, with an intention or offer to pass it. Mere presentment is enough for the violation. This must, however, be coupled with an intent to defraud. Exhibiting a forged check or document to impress friends, rather than to defraud anyone, does not constitute uttering.

On the other hand, most states require that the uttering of a worthless check be accompanied with the intent to defraud. Several states have statutes which cause the uttering of a check with insufficient funds to be a prima facie case; and, without more, the defendant can be convicted. There is however, the option to argue, even without testifying, that no intent was shown, basing this upon other facts and circumstances of the case.

Bad Checks

Checks have been used in banking for many years, but they were not common until recently. Obviously, the common law did not recognize passing a bad check as a crime; this was a false pretense violation. Note that when the writer of a fraudulent check today signs the name of another person as maker of the check, the crime is forgery. A bad check is an insufficient funds check—one in which the maker uses his or her own name, but does not have enough money in the bank to cover the check.

Because of the current prevalence of the bad check practice, most jurisdictions now provide statutes prohibiting the making or issueance of a check or other negotiable document when the maker has insufficient funds in the account. Frequently, this crime is a felony, although this is not always true.

Some of these statutes do not require knowledge on the part of the maker that the check is bad. Therefore, in these jurisdictions, makers pass checks at their own peril.

CITED CASES

Commonwealth v. Leonard, 4 N.E. 96, 140 Mass. 473.
Commonwealth v. O'Brien, 12 Cush. Mass. 90.
Commonwealth v. White, 123 Mass. 430.
Martin v. United States, 278 F. 913.
Meath v. State, 182 N.W. 334, 174 Wis. 80.
Milanovich v. United States, 81 S. Ct. 728.
People v. Ferris, 52 N.E.2d 171, 385 Ill. 186.
People v. Rojas, 55 Cal. 2d 252.
People v. Routson, 188 N.E. 883, 354 Ill. 573.
Pollet v. State, 41 S.E. 606, 115 Ga. 234.
Reaves v. Commonwealth, 65 S.E.2d 559, 192 Va. 443.
State v. Calhoun, 34 N.W. 194, 72 Iowa 432.
State v. Gorham, 55 N.H. 152.
Turner v. State, 1 Ohio St. 422.
Woodward v. State, 28 S.W. 204, 33 Tex. Crim. 554.
Wright v. State, 30 Ga. 325.

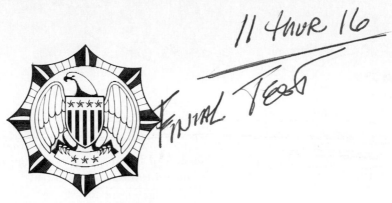

11 thru 16

Final Test

CHAPTER 16

Offenses against Public Health, Safety, and Morality

All persons are entitled to their rights as individuals, but anarchy results unless our governments control those activities that are contrary to the comfort, safety, health, and welfare of the general public. Individuals frequently do not take into account the harm they cause others, either through misuse of property or through personal misconduct. Often the responsible person has not committed a crime in the true sense of the word since there was no mens rea, or guilty intent.

Sometimes these situations can be corrected by civil lawsuits for damages; but frequently this is not practical. As a result, both civil and criminal courts have combined to work out the doctrine of *strict criminal liability*. They say that the accused may not have really intended a crime, but inconvenienced the general public or subjected others to risks that they should not be required to tolerate. The way to cure this is to impose a criminal penalty, thus substantially reducing the repetition of these incidents. State statutes prohibiting criminal nuisances, adultery, fornication, bigamy, incest, sodomy, seduction, prostitution, obscenity, indecency, and illegal abortion, along with an array of other health, safety, and morality laws represent governmental effort to do this.

civil court   *public + private nuisances*

NUISANCES

Legally, a nuisance is any serious disturbance, annoyance, or discomfort to one's neighbors or to the public at large while they are exercising their property rights. In the words of the courts, the offense is "that which annoys and disturbs one in possession of his property, rendering its ordinary use or occupation physically uncomfortable."[1]

In the language of one statute:

> Anything which is injurious to health, or is indecent or offensive to the senses, or an obstruction to the free use of property, so as to interfere with the comfortable enjoyment of life or property, or which unlawfully obstructs the free passage or use . . . of any navigable lake, river, bay, stream, canal, or basin, or any public park, square, street, or highway, is a nuisance.[2]

In defining a nuisance, the problem is whether the activity in question

> . . . will or does produce such a condition of things as, in the judgment of reasonable men, is naturally productive of actual physical discomfort to persons of ordinary sensibility and ordinary tastes and habits.[3]

Nuisances are of two kinds: public, or common, and private. Public nuisances are those that harm the public at large—for example, a factory discharges poisonous chemical fumes over a wide area, subjecting large numbers of people to the possibility of lung problems. Similarly, an obstruction placed in the middle of a highway causes inconvenience to many. Bottling adulterated milk and offering this for sale in public stores is a public nuisance.

Private nuisances are those that affect only a few people. When an individual builds a residence in such a manner that the roof of this structure overhangs the property of a neighbor, discharging large quantities of water onto the patio of the adjoining residence, this is a private nuisance.

Generally, making and selling explosives or fireworks in an unlicensed or undesignated place, operating a house of prostitution or gambling establishment, keeping pigs inside the city limits, or operating injurious and offensive trades or manufacturing plants are all public nuisances.

An individual who has been personally harmed by a nuisance may collect damages in a lawsuit. The civil courts also allow injured parties to take the law into their own hands—removing, destroying, or abating the nuisance. Yet, this can seldom be done without trespassing on the property of the

[1] Yaffe v. City of Ft. Smith, 10 S.W.2d 886, 178 Ark. 406.
[2] CIVIL CODE OF CALIFORNIA, sec. 3479.
[3] Meeks v. Wood, 118 N.E. 591, 66 Ind. App. 594.

offending party; and the courts allow this action only when no damage is caused beyond that required to abate the nuisance. As a practical matter, this type of activity frequently leads to assaults, counterclaims, and lawsuits, and is seldom advisable. In addition and under some circumstances, the injured party can obtain a court injunction, requiring the offender to control or discontinue the nuisance.

These remedies are, however, those provided by the civil courts. In addition, public nuisances may be punished under state statutes, and city ordinances often contain elaborate provisions on nuisances. Because of the great number and variety of these, a working police officer will be well advised to take up the involved legal questions with a city attorney or state prosecutor.

ADULTERY AND FORNICATION

A sex crime, such as a forcible rape, is usually classified by legal writers as a crime against the person. Other sex violations, including adultery and fornication, are not violations on the above basis. This is because no transgression of another is involved; nor is force used. Instead, these clearly are violations against public decency and morality.

Those who oppose these laws frequently argue that all sexual relationships between two consenting adults should be legal. They also argue that legal prohibitions of this kind are only a part of an outmoded moral code that has been forced on society by the religious standards of the past; but regardless of this argument and those made for complete sexual freedom, the laws of almost all states punish for a variety of sexual activities on the ground that they are in conflict with the moral standards of the community. While still on the books, some laws of this type are seldom prosecuted.

These laws are defended on the theory that unpunished moral violations create confusion among younger people and cause them not to understand those standards expected of them. As a result, the entire fabric of society, including the family unit, is seriously damaged. Of course, we find exceptions; but mankind has learned through the experience of hundreds of generations that an infant can best be cared for, emotionally developed, and educated for a useful life in the family unit.

Unquestionably, children may be loved, nourished, and furnished all the advantages of life when the parents are not married. In the majority of cases, however, the father of an illegitimate child may be less inclined to accept parental responsibility. In addition, we find legal difficulties in compelling financial support for a child born out of wedlock; and all parties involved may live under constant emotional handicaps. Consequently, the community as a whole benefits when the law reduces the occurrence of such relationships.

In early England unmarried couples who engaged in voluntary sexual activity were guilty of no crime, but the church, through ecclesiastical law, prohibited it. In those times the church owned much of the land and maintained separate courts. At an early date, however, the ecclesiastical courts lost their authority to those of the king (common law courts). By the year 1650 adultery was a crime by statute, but neither adultery nor fornication was ever recognized as a common law crime.

Definitely, "adultery" and "fornication" carry different meanings. The definitions under church law did not correspond with those established by the English courts, and today state laws define the offenses differently. However, these differences are of no great concern to us, since modern American statutes spell out that activity required for each violation.

Generally, our courts say that adultery is voluntary sexual intercourse between a married person and one who is not that individual's spouse. Fornication is voluntary sexual intercourse between unmarried people. When one party is married and the other is not, the courts usually find adultery on the part of the married individual and fornication on the part of the unmarried one. In some jurisdictions both persons commit adultery when the woman is married, whether the man is married or not.[4]

Adultery is a statutory crime in most, but not all, states; it may be a misdemeanor or a felony, punishable by fine or even a prison term. Fornication, likewise, is prohibited by statute in most jurisdictions, but the offense is usually punishable as a misdemeanor, with a wide range of penalties.

Illicit cohabitation means living together in either adultery or fornication, and a number of states make this type of activity a criminal violation. Some of these enactments require that the sexual relationship shall be in "open and notorious" cohabitation[5] or that the participants must "lewdly and notoriously" associate together.[6] In most of these jurisdictions, the courts have held that a single act of illegal sexual intercourse is not sufficient to satisfy the statutes. Although the wording of these laws varies considerably, generally they require that the parties shall live together so openly that their conduct is considered "scandalous" or "notorious."

In California simple adultery or fornication alone is not a crime—neither is fornication, even coupled with cohabitation. A statute in that juris-

---

[4] Banks v. State, 11 So. 404, 96 Ala. 76.
[5] ARIZONA REVISED STATUTES, sec. 13-222. The Alabama Code, title 14, sec. 16, however, only requires the "man and woman shall live together in adultery or fornication."
[6] IDAHO CODE, sec. 18-6604.

diction, however, provides a misdemeanor for living "in a state of cohabitation and adultery."[7]

PIMPING OR PROCURING

A pimp, procurer, or panderer is one who solicits trade for a prostitute or lewd woman.[8] Most jurisdictions define pimping or procuring as:

1. Receiving financial support from the earnings of a woman, with knowledge that she is a prostitute.
2. Soliciting business for her.

must have both

In general, society disapproves of the activities of pimps. They often entice females into a life of prostitution, keeping them in the racket by force, persuasion, and narcotics. The pimp seldom works; he lives from the immorality of the women in his "stable." Statutes against his activity are designed to eliminate this parasite who lives off the earnings of others. In turn, they help to make prostitution more manageable from a law enforcement standpoint.

Some people argue negatively that a certain amount of prostitution will always exist and that regulating this activity has little beneficial effect on the community as a whole.

Positive arguments made in this connection are that regulation of a minimum number of prostitutes reduces the spread of venereal disease, cuts down the frequency of forcible rape, and eliminates much of the possibility that the prostitute's customer will be robbed by the pimp while the customer is engaged in the illegal sex act. The argument is also made that pimps contribute to our social problems by keeping prostitutes in the business and supplying these women with narcotics. The validity of all these arguments is questionable; but even when a limited amount of prostitution is tolerated it seems desirable at least to eliminate the activity of pimps and procurers.

THE DISORDERLY HOUSE AS A PUBLIC NUISANCE

Brothels, disorderly houses, bawdy houses, houses of ill repute, and whorehouses are all, by law, houses of prostitution or houses of assignation. Generally, these places legally may be closed by the prosecuting attorney on the ground that they constitute public nuisances. This law stems from a

[7] *In re* Lane, 372 P.2d 897, 58 Cal. 2d 99. Sec. 269a, CALIFORNIA PENAL CODE.
[8] United States v. Richmond, 17 F.2d 28.

strong social interest in maintaining standards of decency and morality throughout the entire community. The continued activity of one lone prostitute may be adequate to constitute sufficient cause for prosecution.

INCEST

Incest is sexual intercourse or cohabitation between a man and a woman who are related by blood—people who are related by descent from a common ancestor.[9]

The exact blood relationship between the parties to incest is variously prescribed by a number of state statutes. The crime may be completed either by marriage or by a single act of sexual intercourse. Incest was not a common law crime, but was punished by the church courts in early England. It is wholly statutory in the United States and usually classed as a felony.

Persons who are related by affinity generally cannot be guilty of incest. That is, the prohibited type of kinship does not exist in a relation which one spouse has because of marriage to blood relatives of the other.[10] Usually, incest may be committed only when a person is "of the blood" of another, or of the blood derived from a common ancestor. The crime may be committed by those who have a "half blood" relationship, that is, those who have the same father or same mother, but not both parents in common.[11]

Children by adoption or stepchildren are also often forbidden from entering into marriage or sexual relations with a parent.[12]

While incest is recognized as a criminal act in all states, jurisdictions vary considerably in the degree of relationship specified in the statutes. For example, approximately one-third of the states prohibit marriage or sexual relationships between first cousins. Some jurisdictions, Texas, for example, forbid relations between a father-in-law and daughter-in-law, mother-in-law and son-in-law, and stepbrother and stepsister. Illinois prohibits only three relationships: (1) brother-sister, (2) father-daughter, and (3) mother-son. Oklahoma extends the prohibition to include even second cousins.[13]

The courts generally hold that an individual may be prosecuted for both rape and incest, as a consequence of a single sexual act; and some state statutes specifically provide that a party who had no knowledge of the

[9] Swasey v. Jacques, 10 N.E. 758, 144 Mass. 135.
[10] Norman v. Ellis, 28 S.W.2d 363, 325 Mo. 154.
[11] People v. Jenness, 5 Mich. 305.
[12] Lee v. State, 17 So. 2d 277, 196 Miss. 311.
[13] OKLAHOMA STATUTES ANNOTATED, sec. 2; and ILLINOIS CRIMINAL CODE, secs. 11-10 and 11-11.

kinship with the other person involved in the prohibited relationship may not be convicted.

SEDUCTION

Seduction is that activity of a man in enticing a woman to have unlawful sexual intercourse with him through persuasion, solicitation, promises, bribes, or other means, without the use of force.[14]

At common law, seduction gave rise only to a civil lawsuit for damages, but seduction is still a criminal act in some jurisdictions in the United States. Because of the wide differences in the wording of statutes, we find very little uniformity in the state laws.

The reason for prosecution is to give protection to the inexperienced, perhaps somewhat trusting, woman who may surrender her virginity in the belief that the accused made a good-faith offer to marry her. The general interest of society is served when restrictions are imposed on men who take advantage of well-intentioned females without assuming the obligations of marriage. These ideas may conflict with the modern concept of liberated women, but the laws still exist.

Most, but not all, of the statutes punish a man who persuades an unmarried woman of chaste character to have sexual intercourse on a promise of marriage. Generally, the prosecution must show that the woman submitted in response to this promise, rather than to a mere sexual stimulation.

Some courts have indicated that they cannot always lay down hard-and-fast rules as to what is needed to satisfy the requirements of the law.

> That kind of seductive art that is necessary to establish the offense, cannot be defined. Every case must depend upon its own peculiar circumstances, together with the condition in life, advantages, age, and intelligence of the parties.[15]

Most courts hold that the woman must actually be a virgin at the time of the seduction and that she can be seduced only once,[16] but a number of holdings are to the effect that a widow or divorcee may be seduced, provided she has restricted her sexual activities to those done in a lawful marriage.

While the law fails to require that the man be single, the majority of the courts take the attitude that a woman cannot expect a lawful marriage

---

[14] BLACK'S LAW DICTIONARY, citing Van De Velde v. Colle, 152 A. 645, 8 N.J. Misc. 782.
[15] State v. Higdon, 32 Iowa 262; State v. Hughes, 76 N.W. 520, 106 Iowa 125.
[16] State v. Newcomer, 54 P. 685, 59 Kan. 668.

from a man who is already married. Therefore, when she knows his marital status, he is not guilty of seduction.

Most of the seduction laws seemingly are designated to protect women from the loss of their virginity without the benefit of marriage. Therefore, when the man decides to marry the seduced woman, he cannot be convicted. Some statutes do not contain a provision of this type, however; and in Kansas, for example, the seducer may be convicted even after marrying the victim. This seems to carry a rather strange result, since the object of the law is to provide the woman the protection of the marriage relationship.

BIGAMY

Know the 2 Types   *7 year wait for missing spouse before remarry*

Bigamy is generally defined as having more than one wife or husband at the same time. Some definitions say that the second marriage must be entered into willfully and knowingly by the guilty party.[17]

Sometimes the condition of having more than one wife is called *polygamy*; *polyandry* is the practice of having two or more husbands. Either situation is punishable as bigamy—a felony in practically all states. While it was not a common law offense, an early English statute made this offense a felony.

One particular feature of the early English law has been widely copied in the statutes of the states. This is an exception excusing the accused from criminal guilt when the missing husband or wife has been absent and not seen or heard from for a period of seven years. Under these circumstances, the missing spouse is recognized as *legally dead*.[18]

Under some circumstances, legal problems arise as to the validity of a divorce or marriage entered into while one of the parties is in a foreign country or in another state. In fact, a number of these situations may involve such detailed legal research that they do not merit consideration here. As a general proposition, however, most states recognize the validity of either a marriage or a divorce that is in agreement with the laws of the jurisdiction where the last marriage relationship took place.

The courts also consistently hold that bigamy cannot occur without a valid prior marriage ceremony. Generally, the fact that a man and a woman lived together is not sufficient for purposes of a bigamy prosecution, although the parties may be able to claim a *common law marriage* that affects property rights and other legal relationships between them.

---

[17] Scoggins v. State, 32 Ark. 213; People v. Manfredonio, 191 N.Y.S. 748, 39 N.Y. Crim. 41.
[18] Some state statutes require an absence of only two years for the missing mate to be presumed to be legally dead; others continue the old English requirement of seven years. The statutes in a number of states set this requirement at an absence of five years.

One of the most troublesome problems in bigamy prosecutions involves a second marriage by one who honestly believes that the other party to the first marriage is dead or divorced. Most of the state bigamy statutes do not require any criminal intent. Thus, in interpreting these statutes, the courts have usually held that no criminal intent is required; the burden is on the accused to know he or she is no longer married. This clearly is contrary to the usual legal rule that a reasonable mistake of fact is a defense to a criminal charge. Accordingly, a number of courts have held, in recent years, that an honest belief that a person is no longer married is a valid defense.[19]

ILLEGAL ABORTION

28 weeks time frame for illegal abortion

"Abortion" is the expulsion of an unborn child so early in pregnancy that the unborn has not acquired the power of sustaining independent life. Willfully and deliberately bringing about the miscarriage of a woman without legal justification constitutes "illegal abortion." Illegal abortion can be said to be "a criminal miscarriage."[20]

For most legal purposes, a woman is pregnant for the entire period that she carries an infant. Under the common law idea of abortion, however, the embryo or fetus was not recognized as existing until the "woman quickened with child"—until movement occurred within the mother. Therefore, when a miscarriage happened prior to this time, no abortion was possible under the common law. Any operation or use of drugs to induce a miscarriage that resulted in a stillborn infant after the child had quickened in the mother was a misdemeanor at common law. When the child was born alive and died as a result of the criminal miscarriage, the crime was murder. Regardless of the fact that the mother consented, the person who induced the miscarriage was criminally responsible. On the other hand, the common law provided for legal abortion when a competent physician believed the operation was necessary to save the life of the mother.

All the discussion in this section is concerned with abortions not performed by medical personnel. The U.S. Supreme Court has held that a state cannot declare an abortion as such illegal. The federal law appears to be that the state can regulate abortions in a reasonable way, by specifying the qualifications of practitioners, the type of hospital facilities that must be available, and other standards. The states may still forbid abortion by nonmedical people and specify that such an act is a criminal offense.

[19] See Keedy, *Ignorance and Mistake in the Criminal Law*, 22 HARVARD LAW REVIEW, 75–96.
[20] Commonwealth v. Sierakowski, 35 A.2d 790, 154 Pa. Super. 321.

There is considerable lack of uniformity in laws concerning nonmedical abortion. In some states it is no longer a crime, while other states make such abortion a felony by statute.

In any event, abortion always involves an element of risk to the life of the mother. When death does result to the woman as a consequence of a criminal abortion, this death is either murder or manslaughter under the prevailing law of homicide in the jurisdiction. Most frequently the crime is manslaughter.[21]

PROSTITUTION, INDECENCY, OBSCENITY

Prostitution is the activity of a woman in permitting a man to pay her price to have sexual intercourse with her. It is a criminal misdemeanor in almost all jurisdictions. A few states define the offense as indiscriminate sexual conduct with a number of men, whether or not the woman is paid.

Pandering, or "pimping" as it is often termed, usually carries heavier criminal penalties than prostitution because of the degrading influence that such activity has on the community in general.

Obscenity is that which is offensive to modesty or decency. The term "indecency" may be used in the same sense, but it also may be extended to mean that which is unfit to be seen or heard, that which is vulgar or grossly disgusting. In general, anything that was obscene or indecent was a misdemeanor at common law. State and federal statutes widely prohibit the mailing, sale, publication, or display of obscene books, writings, or other materials. The courts also quite uniformly recognize that the display of materials of this kind constitutes a public nuisance and may be suppressed.

The U.S. Supreme Court has said that "a distaste, however strong, for commercial vendors of alleged pornography is no justification for denying petitioners [their constitutional rights]."[22] But the Supreme Court also noted that obscene material is not protected under the First Amendment right to free speech. In *Roth v. United States*,[23] the court simply held that not all forms of writing, speech, or printing are protected by the constitution and that obscenity laws may properly be used to protect the morality of a community.

The problem since the *Roth* case has been in deciding which pornographic materials are obscene. Beginning in 1959, the courts looked at the social worth of the material in deciding the question of obscenity. If a

---

[21] Provision is made under the Colorado Code for this kind of death to be recognized as murder (COLORADO REVISED STATUTES, 40-2-23).

[22] Eaton v. Tulsa, 418 U.S. 152.

[23] Roth v. United States, 354 U.S. 476; Alberts v. California, 354 U.S. 476.

book of photographs, a movie film, or other materials had some offsetting or redeeming social worth, it would not be regarded as obscene. The courts were to determine whether the material in question had some redeeming social value. This test failed to set clear standards, and considerable confusion resulted.

In 1973 a new test for obscenity was laid down by the U.S. Supreme Court in *Miller v. California*, 413 U.S. 15. In that case, the court said the material should be judged as a whole, and that it will be considered legally obscene if it appeals to the prurient interest in sex and portrays sexual conduct in a patently offensive way—without having serious artistic, literary, or scientific value. Stated in other terms, obscene materials would be those that appeal to lewdness or purely sexual cravings, in a blatant way. The court rejected the old test as to whether the material had "redeeming social values."

In the *Miller* case and a later case, *Hamling v. United States*,[24] the Supreme Court said that obscenity was to be judged by the jury, not by the individual juror's ideas as to what was obscene, but according to the prevailing standards in that particular community at that particular time. The court pointed out that material regarded as obscene in a small town probably would not be regarded as objectionable in New York City or Las Vegas, Nevada. In this series of cases the court left individual standards of obscenity to individual communities, at the same time giving the jury a definite set of standards for arriving at a decision as to obscenity.

The Supreme Court of the United States has upheld the authority of an individual state to prohibit the sale of obscene materials to juveniles on the ground that it may be harmful to them, even though this same material may not be obscene when applied to adults.[25]

The use of profane or obscene language in a public place is a public nuisance. Most states provide laws prohibiting this language, while others additionally require that the profanity must be in the presence of women or children or that the objectionable words must be uttered in a loud voice.

Also, indecent exposure is generally prohibited by statute.[26] The courts differ in opinion as to whether an accidental exposure is criminal, but some of them hold that an accused person who is only negligent in self-exposure can be successfully prosecuted.

---

[24] Hamling v. United States, 418 U.S. 87; also see Jenkins v. Georgia, 418 U.S. 153.

[25] Ginsberg v. New York, 390 U.S. 629, 88 S. Ct. 1274. Law enforcement officers should be warned that this pornography area is extremely complex. As a general rule, arrests cannot be made without warrants; prosecutors or legal advisors should be consulted before legal action is taken.

[26] FLORIDA CRIMINAL CODE, sec. 800.03: "It is unlawful for any person to expose or exhibit his sexual organs in any public place, or on the private premises of another, or so near thereto as to be seen from such private premises, in a vulgar and indecent manner.. . ."

SODOMY

Both Blackstone and the common law courts spoke of the "crime not fit to be named," "the infamous crime against nature," or "the unnatural crime." Today this offense is rather universally defined as sodomy; but even in our time some courts and some statutes continue to refer to the offense as "the abominable and detestable crime against nature."[27]

Since the early judges and writers refused to name this crime, one wonders little that modern American courts have difficulty in providing accurate interpretation of it. Variations from state to state add to the confusion.

Coming from the name of a sinful city described in the Bible (one destroyed by fire and brimstone), the word "sodomy" is apparently quite ancient. The following modern definitions may serve to clarify some of the terms associated with it:

know these

1. *Bestiality* is a sexual connection between a human being and an animal, or beast, of the opposite sex.[28]
2. *Penetration per os* means sexual penetration of the mouth of another individual of either sex.
3. *Fellatio* is defined as stimulation of the male sex organ by oral manipulation or copulation (sexual connection) by mouth.
4. *Cunnilingus* means the oral stimulation of the female sex organ, performed by either man or woman.

While the story of this crime is not completely clear, most legal authorities are in agreement that sodomy included only bestiality and anal sexual connection in early English law; and sodomy was originally and solely an ecclesiastical or church crime. In the development of the common law, however, a statute was passed so early in England that the colonists believed that the crime was a part of the common law, putting it into effect here.

The early English statute did not include sex acts committed in or by the mouth as a type of sodomy. For many years, however, almost all our states have punished fellatio as a crime, some reaching this result by statute and some by interpretation of the courts.[29] Interestingly enough, most of the statutes that regulate sexual behavior do not refer to homosexuality as such. Some describe the various types of forbidden activity as "sodomy," "the infamous crime against nature," "fellatio," "cunnilingus," or simply

[27] Phillips v. State, 222 N.E.2d 891.
[28] State v. Poole, 122 P.2d 415, 59 Ariz. 44.
[29] The ILLINOIS CRIMINAL CODE of 1961 stated that it was lawful in that jurisdiction for willing adults to engage in homosexual relations, voluntarily and in private.

"copulation with the mouth";[30] but, to generalize, most jurisdictions today regard bestiality, fellatio, or cunnilingus as criminal behavior, usually punishable as a felony.

MISTREATMENT OF DEAD BODIES

The common law provided criminal punishment for mistreating the body of any dead person, exposing a corpse without proper burial, or disturbing, digging up, selling, or dissecting one who had been buried. The only allowed exceptions were those granted by the authorities for reburial, medical examinations, or other legal reasons.

Most modern jurisdictions prohibit mistreatment of dead bodies. Any death must be reported to legal authorities, and the body must be protected until burial, cremation, or other legal disposition.[31] Cemeteries, grave sites, and interred bodies are also commonly protected from intrusion or mistreatment.

In addition and prior to burial or disposition, relatives, undertakers, or other persons who come into contact with the body are not allowed to mutilate it. Removal of gold crowns from the deceased's teeth, in such a way that this action does not change the appearance of the face, is not mutilation or disfigurement of a dead body,[32] but removal without authority may result in a larceny charge.

DRUNKENNESS AND OFFENSES
RELATING TO INTOXICATING LIQUORS

Drunkenness in private has apparently never been a crime; and public drunkenness, in itself, was not a crime at common law unless attended by other facts that caused the creation of a public nuisance. As stated in an Alabama case, the mere fact of intoxication alone is not sufficient misconduct to warrant punishment. The court further pointed out that whether the accused's conduct "is violative of proper conduct from a social sense is not the question at issue, but rather whether the evidence offered by the state" constitutes a public nuisance.[33] In the words of another court:

> . . . a man while intoxicated can be on the public streets or highways, or within the curtilage of private residences, without violating the law,

[30] CALIFORNIA PENAL CODE, sec. 288a.
[31] At least some jurisdictions allow disposition by quick freeze processes, if continuing care of the corpse is provided.
[32] People v. Bullington, 80 P.2d 1030, 27 Cal. App. 2d 396.
[33] Thompson v. State, 42 So. 2d 640.

provided he does not then and there make manifest his drunken condition by some disorderly conduct. . . .[34]

The required elements of public drunkenness as set out in *Thompson v. State* are:

1. That the person accused, at the time complained of, was intoxicated or drunk.
2. That, while so intoxicated or drunk, the person appeared at a public place where one or more persons were present.
3. That the person manifested a drunken condition by boisterous or indecent conduct or loud and profane discourse.[35]

Some courts have decided, however, that mere intoxication—nothing more—is sufficient to constitute the common law crime of public drunkenness.[36] Most other jurisdictions now provide public drunkenness by statute, some requiring nothing except proof of intoxication in a public place.

Several modern statutes present no specific requirement as to where the drunken accused may be arrested. Ordinarily, the offense must be committed in a public place, in a named public location, or at or within the curtilage of a private dwelling, not his own residence.

Additionally, some statutes provide that the accused may not enter private property in an intoxicated condition "to the annoyance of another." The test used by the courts is that the annoyance must be sufficient to disturb any reasonable person.[37]

Under the statutes prohibiting people from being drunk in a public place, the courts say that this includes any location where the public has a right to go and to be. Public taverns, sidewalks, highways, streets, and roads are included in the prohibited areas, along with areas in which public businesses are located. This does not mean that any place where a large number of people may come together is a public place. A large party in a private home, for example, is not a public place within the meaning of these statutes.[38]

Generally, in order to be found guilty of drunkenness, the accused must be under the influence of alcohol to such an extent as to have lost control over mental and bodily activities. In turn, this does not mean passing out or even becoming boisterous. The accused may sit quietly in the corner and still be intoxicated. Loss of normal control seems to be the test usually accepted by the courts.[39]

---

[34] Coleman v. State, 59 S.E. 829, 3 Ga. App. 298.
[35] Thompson v. State, above; Tatum v. State, 22 So. 2d 350, 32 Ala. App. 128.
[36] State v. Kelly, 195 S.W. 1126, 138 Tenn. 84.
[37] People v. Beifuss, 67 P.2d 411, 22 Cal. App. 2d Supp. 755.
[38] Pugh v. State, 117 S.W. 817, 55 Tex. Crim. 462.
[39] Simmons v. State, 232 S.W. 597, 149 Ark. 348.

Most large police departments arrest more people daily for public drunkenness than for any other criminal offense. In recent years a number of writers have pointed out that a substantial number of these offenders are chronic alcoholics and that this condition must be treated as a disease rather than a crime. Their argument is that society benefits when these people are given treatment and rehabilitation, provided they are merely helpless and have committed no additional crimes. Until relatively recent times the courts continued to sentence all these chronic offenders to jail.

Conversely, in *Driver v. Hinnant,* a federal court said:

> Alcoholism is a chronic illness that manifests itself as a disorder of behavior . . . and appearances in public, unwilled and ungovernable by the victim of chronic alcoholism, cannot be the basis for a judgment of criminal conviction. . . .[40]

In a similar case, the court found that the accused, DeWitt Easter, was a chronic alcoholic who had lost all control of himself. Thus, the decision of the court was that chronic alcoholism is an adequate defense to a charge of public intoxication, therefore not criminal. It further pointed out, however, that the accused may be legally committed for treatment when facilities are available.

In the Easter case the court noted also that:

> . . . voluntary drunkenness is no excuse for crime. The chronic alcoholic has not drunk voluntarily, although undoubtedly he did so originally. His excess now derives from disease. However, our excusal of the chronic alcoholic from criminal prosecution is confined exclusively to those acts on his part which are compulsive as symptomatic of the disease. With respect to other behavior—not characteristic of confirmed chronic alcoholism—he would be judged as would any person not so afflicted.[41]

No one can predict, with certainty, the direction that future court decisions will take. The Supreme Court of the United States has not yet been faced with the question as to whether drunkenness is a physical condition that cannot be controlled and therefore, standing alone, not criminal. Appellate court decisions have pointed in that direction, as indicated by *Driver v. Hinnant* and the *Easter* case.

On the other hand, the courts have always said that drunkenness cannot be used to excuse crime. "Unconsciousness produced by voluntary intoxication does not render a defendant incapable of committing a crime."[42] "An act committed by a person while unconscious, in a state of voluntary intoxication, is none the less criminal by reason of his having been in such a condition."[43]

[40] Driver v. Hinnant, 356 F.2d 761.
[41] Easter v. District of Columbia, 361 F.2d 50.
[42] People v. Cox, 153 P.2d 362, 67 Cal. App. 2d 166.
[43] People v. Anderson, 197 P.2d 839, 87 Cal. App. 2d 857.

When an accused drinks to build up courage to commit a crime already intended, the conviction is for the crime previously decided upon, even though the person is later too drunk to retain the intent for the crime.[44]

The situation is different, however, when the accused becomes so drunk as to commit a violation which was not thought of when sober. When the crime in question is one that requires a specific mental intent, that particular requirement of the crime may be absent if the accused is so drunk as to be unable to perform that mental process. For example, in a Montana case, the accused killed a man without justification while so drunk that he was incapable of harboring malice aforethought. The court held that his drunkenness was not an excuse, but that it had wiped out the specific mental requirement of malice aforethought; the killing was, therefore, manslaughter—not murder.[45]

Regulating the Making and Sale of Alcohol

The federal government and all state jurisdictions have laws designed to control the making, sale, and serving of alcoholic beverages of all kinds. The theory behind these laws is that controls must be exercised to protect the immature from those problems that result from uncontrolled use of alcohol, and to protect the general public from adulterated intoxicants that can cause blindness, severe internal injury, or even death.

Laws vary from state to state, but all jurisdictions require licensing and inspection for those who intend to manufacture alcoholic products. Generally too, the states or individual cities regulate the hours and conditions under which intoxicants may be served. Differences in these laws must be studied on a local basis.

Driving While under the Influence of Alcohol

Driving a vehicle while intoxicated is a criminal violation in practically all jurisdictions. Under some statutes of this kind we find no violation unless the vehicle is operated on a public street or highway.

The most troublesome problem with laws of this type is in the differences of opinion as to what constitutes intoxication, and how this can be proved. Most court decisions hold that an individual who is drunk and only sits in the car should not be charged with driving while intoxicated. The drunk may even start the engine; without some observable motion of the vehicle, the person is not liable for driving while intoxicated, in the absence of a special statute to the contrary.

[44] State v. Butner, 206 P.2d 253, 66 Nev. 127.
[45] State v. Brooks, 436 P.2d 91.

CITED CASES

Alberts v. California 354 U.S. 476.

Banks v. State, 11 So. 404, 96 Ala. 76.

Book v. Attorney General of Massachusetts, 383 U.S. 413, 86 S. Ct. 975.

Coleman v. State, 59 S.E. 829, 3 Ga. App. 298.

Commonwealth v. Sierakowski, 35 A.2d 790, 154 Pa. Super. 321.

Driver v. Hinnant, 356 F.2d 761.

Easter v. District of Columbia, 361 F.2d 50.

Eaton v. Tulsa, 418 U.S. 152.

Ginsberg v. New York, 390 U.S. 629.

Hamling v. United States, 418 U.S. 87.

Jenkins v. Georgia, 418 U.S. 153.

In re Lane, 372 P.2d 897, 58 Cal. 2d 99.

Lee v. State, 17 So. 2d 277, 196 Miss. 311.

Meeks v. Wood, 118 N.E. 591, 66 Ind. App. 594.

Miller v. California, 413 U.S. 15.

Norman v. Ellis, 28 S.W.2d 363, 325 Mo. 154.

People v. Anderson, 197 P.2d 893, 87 Cal. App. 2d 857.

People v. Beifuss, 67 P.2d 411, 22 Cal. App. 2d Supp. 755.

People v. Bullington, 80 P.2d 1030, 27 Cal. App. 2d 396.

People v. Cox, 153 P.2d 362, 67 Cal. App. 2d 166.

People v. Jenness, 5 Mich. 305.

People v. Manfredonio, 191 N.Y.S. 748, 39. N.Y. Crim. 41.

Phillips v. State, 222 N.E.2d 891.

Pugh v. State, 117 S.W. 817, 55 Tex. Crim. 462.

Redrup v. New York, 386 U.S. 767, 87 S. Ct. 1414.

Roth v. United States, 354 U.S. 476.

Scoggins v. State, 32 Ark. 213.

Simmons v. State, 232 S.W. 597, 149 Ark. 348.

State v. Brooks, 436 P.2d 91.

State v. Butner, 206 P.2d 253, 66 Nev. 127.

State v. Higdon, 32 Iowa 262.

State v. Hughes, 76 N.W. 520, 106 Iowa 125.

State v. Kelly, 195 S.W. 1126, 138 Tenn. 84.

State v. Newcomer, 54 P. 685, 59 Kan. 668.

State v. Poole, 122 P.2d 415, 59 Ariz. 44.

Swasey v. Jacques, 10 N.E. 758, 144 Mass. 135.

Tatum v. State, 22 So. 2d 350, 32 Ala. App. 128.

Thompson v. State, 42 So. 2d 640.

United States v. Richmond, 17 F.2d 28.

Van De Velde v. Colle, 152 A. 645, 8 N.J. Misc. 782.

Yaffe v. City of Ft. Smith, 10 S.W.2d 886, 178 Ark. 406.

CHAPTER 17

Special Problems of Drug Offenses: The Juvenile Offender

DRUG VIOLATIONS

Narcotics have a strong effect on the human central nervous system, and can cause insensibility to pain, stupor, or coma. Continued usage, of course, may lead to addiction with serious harm to both body and mind. Aside from protecting people from the damaging effects of these substances, the criminal law is concerned with the fact that addicts feel so compelled to get drugs that they often are uninhibited from committing any crime; and while under the influence, users may commit violations that they would ordinarily never consider.

For the above reasons and others, society, in order to protect itself, has long opposed the use of narcotics for nonmedical purposes. As early as 1907 President Theodore Roosevelt was seeking ways to regulate the drug traffic. Some laws, at both the state and federal level, have been in force for many years. The original federal law, known as the Harrison Act, provided regulations and penalties for persons who illegally imported, manufactured, compounded, produced, sold, or dispensed narcotic drugs. In upholding this law, the federal courts went on the legal theory that the Harrison Act was a tax measure, designed to regulate importation and provide control.

While no provision in the U.S. Constitution specifies federal power to regulate drug and narcotic traffic and use, the U.S. Supreme Court has consistently implied that this control was proper, both under the commerce clause and as a tax measure. The Supreme Court has also held that the individual states, under the police powers, may regulate the possession, sale, use, or prescription of narcotic drugs.[1]

This problem appears to be of great concern, both to the federal government and to the states. Interstate and foreign angles are both frequently involved in a single drug investigation. Narcotic drugs have been in the past and are still, to a large extent, extracted from plants: the opium poppy, the coca shrub, and the cannabis. The first two of these plants grow in only limited geographical areas, coming from the so-called "producing countries," Turkey, India, Iran, the U.S.S.R., Yugoslavia, and China. Obviously, the volume of this traffic cannot be known, but cooperation between federal and state officers is often needed.

The basic state law, passed with variations in forty-nine states, was made into law in some states in 1932, under the title Uniform Narcotics Drug Act. Amendments were added in some states in 1942 and 1958.

In 1970 the federal government also enacted the Comprehensive Drug Abuse Prevention and Control Act (often known as the Controlled Substances Act). This act was passed so that state laws could be made more uniform. For many years prior to 1970 we had experienced conflicts and differences between state and federal laws. In 1972, the U.S. Commission on Uniform Laws also drew up a model Uniform Controlled Substances Act for state use. This model law has been adopted by more than two-thirds of the states, and additional adoptions are expected to obtain rather complete uniformity.

As drafted, the Uniform Act set out prohibited activities in detail, but left actual penalties and sentencing to the individual states. The act classifies all kinds of narcotics, dangerous drugs, and marijuana into five different categories. This classification system allows the proper officials to add to the list new drugs or substances found to be dangerous, or to remove them if circumstances should justify removal at a later time.

As under previous laws, the Uniform Act specifies who may lawfully possess or otherwise deal in controlled or restricted substances. It is unlaw-

[1] Reyes v. United States, 258 F.2d 774; Nigro v. United States, 276 U.S. 332.

ful to knowingly or intentionally possess restricted drugs that have not been received through legal channels.

As to the cases upholding the Uniform Act and prior laws, it is immaterial how long the illegal possession exists, if there is adequate proof of actual possession or control.[2]

As to what is possession or control, some courts have held that the possession may be shared by several individuals, yet it may be applied to convict any one of them.[3] Most tribunals require that the accused person must understand the illegal nature of the drug and must have deliberately and consciously retained possession of it.[4]

In reference to the amount of forbidden drug that must be possessed to support a conviction, some courts have held that the quantity is immaterial, so long as the substance can be definitely identified. Others have declared that the quantity found in the accused's possession must be sufficient for the use commonly made of the drug.[5]

Control of the drug seems to be the test that the courts usually look to in the matter of determining whether the accused actually had possession. In a Texas case, the defendant was arrested while watering marijuana plants growing in cultivated patches owned by the county government. Since he had authority to be at this location and had access to the land where the cultivation occurred, the court held that possession meant "care, management, and control of the narcotics in his charge"; a conviction was upheld.[6]

A medical doctor, a dentist, or a veterinarian legally may prescribe, dispense, or administer narcotics, or may allow them to be administered under supervision, according to the Uniform Act; but, if a professional person does not act in good faith, he is in violation of the law. Usually the jury must decide whether the physician actually believed that the drugs were needed for treatment.[7]

According to the Uniform Act, specific records must be retained, in detail, for all narcotics sold, shipped, administered, or transferred. Generally, these reports must be made available to all federal and local officers who have authority to investigate drug violations; however, the records are maintained in confidence against unauthorized disclosure.

[2] State v. Reed, 170 A.2d 419, 34 N.J. 554.
[3] Mickens v. People, 365 P.2d 679, 148 Colo. 237; Gallegos v. People, 337 P.2d 961, 139 Colo. 166.
[4] Carrol v. State, 368 P.2d 649, 90 Ariz. 411.
[5] Blaylock v. State, 352 S.W.2d 727, 171 Tex. Crim. 665; Pelham v. State, 298 S.W.2d 171, 164 Tex. Crim. 226.
[6] Massiate v. State, 365 S.W.2d 802.
[7] Commonwealth v. Noble, 119 N.E. 510, 230 Mass. 83.

Although druggists are not responsible for inquiring into the legality of a narcotics prescription, it may be a federal violation for a druggist to fill a prescription knowing or having reason to believe that it was issued to evade the law.[8] Both the doctor and the druggist may be guilty when they do not act in good faith in issuing and filling prescriptions for narcotics.[9]

Drug Addiction as a Condition

In *Robinson v. California*,[10] the U.S. Supreme Court struck down the conviction of an individual convicted under a vague California statute which said that being a drug addict was a crime. The court reasoned that the California statute spelled out a criminal offense from a mere physical condition and implied that the law would have been upheld if the statute had required some voluntary act or drug use on the part of the addict that resulted in the prohibited condition. The court further pointed out that the addict could have gotten into that physical state through innocent overdosage by a doctor treating a medical condition, without having any wrongful intent.

Marijuana as a Separate Problem

For a number of years, some segments of the public have agitated repeatedly for reduced penalties for the possession of small quantities of marijuana. This has resulted in special legislation in some jurisdictions, permitting the legal possession of small amounts of the drug or drastically reducing the penalty.

Those police authorities who express their opinions are generally opposed to laws that permit possession of limited quantities of prohibited drugs of any kind. Whether laws of this kind will remain popular cannot be predicted with certainty.

Other Legal Problems of Serious Concern

In any event and in recent years, a high percentage of criminal cases reviewed by the appellate courts have been concerned with narcotics cases. We should point out, however, that most of these decisions do not involve unsettled matters in the substantive criminal law. Because of the ways in which illegal drugs are frequently concealed, many of these cases involve

[8] Doremus v. United States, 262 U.S. 849.
[9] Webb v. United States, 249 U.S. 96.
[10] Robinson v. California, 377 U.S. 660 (1962).

problems in evidence law—search and seizure situations, rather than substantive criminal law questions.

Since many narcotics cases are made by means of a "buy" by a police informant, the earlier section of this book on the law of entrapment may prove helpful.

JUVENILE OFFENDERS

juvenile custody + adoption cases are heard by juvenile courts

In Chapter 8 we examined the capacity of certain individuals to commit a crime. We pointed out that, according to the English common law, a child under the age of seven years was regarded as not having the judgment or capacity to commit an offense. From age seven to fourteen, the common law said that children were not yet old enough to be tried for crime, but that this was a rebuttable presumption if the youth had the maturity and mental capacity to understand the nature and consequences of the criminal act.

When common law ideas were brought to the United States, many lawmakers believed that individuals over fourteen should not be held to the same standards as mature adults until they reached the age of twenty-one. This thinking led to the creation of the first juvenile court system in the United States in Cook County, Illinois, in 1899. From this beginning, the movement spread; all states now have juvenile court systems.

We find, however, no uniformity in juvenile court procedures. In the first place, people differ in opinion as to who is a juvenile. This is an arbitrary chronological standard set by legislatures, varying from those below fifteen years of age to those under nineteen years of age at the time the crime was committed. In this connection, we should note that the age specified by law for juveniles may be different from the legal age for a minor. Generally, a minor is an individual who is under twenty-one years of age. Some states have laws creating a special youth aid authority or youth aid administration, permitting juvenile courts to handle young offenders who have not yet reached the age of twenty-five.

Jurisdiction of Juvenile Courts

Juvenile courts cannot handle young offenders until the tests of jurisdiction have been met, both as to geographical jurisdiction (territorial jurisdiction) and as to the age of the offender (jurisdiction over the person).

Under state laws, juvenile courts retain jurisdiction of the youth, provided the offender was actually a juvenile at the time the violation was committed.

State juvenile courts handle two basic types of cases:

1. Violations of law committed by juveniles (delinquency situations).
2. Child custody, neglect, dependency, and adoption cases where the court assumes the role of a legal protector (status situations).

Basic Philosophy of Juvenile Court Systems

The basic philosophy of the juvenile courts is important and should be considered here. Founders of the system believed that nothing would be gained by sending youthful offenders to prison with murderers, thieves, and hardened criminals. Every effort should, therefore, be directed toward solving the child's problem before coming into court. As a consequence of this thinking, the juvenile courts are not to be regarded as courts at all, but rather as places where youth problems are treated and dealt with. The idea is to give helpful advice, guidance, and direction, while placing the juvenile under the court's guardianship. Regardless of the seriousness of the offense committed by the youth, juvenile court proceedings are regarded as civil in nature, rather than as criminal prosecutions. This is true, even though the judge may send the offender to a reformatory or juvenile institution. The approach is sometimes described by courts and lawyers as the legal doctrine of *parens patriae*, meaning the juvenile court must act as a substitute parent, provided by the government.

The principles on which the juvenile courts were founded include much that is commendable. Nevertheless, many modern critics of the juvenile justice system point out that numerous juveniles are simply beyond rehabilitation and that the system merely shelters these offenders and excludes them from accountability for their criminal acts. Most states now have procedural arrangements whereby juveniles can be brought into adult court, particularly in very serious cases.

Delinquency Hearings

For many years, juvenile court hearings throughout the several states were conducted on the idea that the proceedings were civil in nature—not a prosecution at all. Following this idea, the juvenile had no right to a lawyer or to other civil rights specified in federal and state constitutions and statutes.

In the case of *in re Gault* (1967),[11] the Supreme Court of the United States held that an offending juvenile was entitled to the following basic information prior to the hearing:

---

[11] *In re* Gault, 387 U.S. 1; see also Kent v. United States, 383 U.S. 541.

1. Notice to the juvenile and parents or guardian of contemplated juvenile court action, to allow time for the preparation of a defense.
2. Notice of the nature of the accusation, and details of the particulars.
3. Notice of the right to an attorney, and that a lawyer may be provided if the young person or the family is unable to provide one.
4. Notice of the right to confront witnesses, and that the accused is not required to testify at the hearing.

   In handing down the opinion in the *Gault* case, the court said, in effect, that juvenile delinquency hearings are actually criminal, rather than civil in nature. The Supreme Court did not, however, curtail juvenile court hearings by requiring a jury trial, or by insisting on the adversary process that is so characteristic of a criminal trial.

   Clearly, the *Gault* case did away with some of the basic philosophy of the founders of the juvenile court system, and until additional cases are decided we may be rather confused as to whether some aspects of juvenile delinquency hearings may continue to be administrative or may become criminal in nature.

CITED CASES

Blaylock v. State, 352 S.W.2d 727.
Carrol v. State, 368 P.2d 679.
Commonwealth v. Noble, 119 N.E. 510.
Doremus v. United States, 262 U.S. 849.
Gallegos v. People, 337 P.2d 961.
In re Gault, 387 U.S. 1.
Kent v. United States, 383 U.S. 541.
Massiate v. State, 365 S.W.2d 802.
Mickens v. People, 365 P.2d 679.
Nigro v. United States, 276 U.S. 332.
Pelham v. State, 298 S.W.2d 171.
Reyes v. United States, 258 F.2d 774.
Robinson v. California, 377 U.S. 660.
State v. Reed, 170 A.2d 419, 34 N.J. 554.
Webb v. United States, 249 U.S. 96.

CHAPTER 18

Crimes against the Public Peace

Among the common and statutory crimes against the public peace, unlawful assembly, rout, riot, disturbance of lawful assemblies, lynching, breach of the peace, carrying or concealing dangerous weapons, affray, and criminal libel should be of greatest concern to the police officer.

UNLAWFUL ASSEMBLY

Of these, unlawful assembly is most interesting since it often involves careful consideration of the right of the public to assemble, along with facts which indicate abuse of this right.

The Right of Public Assembly

On the one hand, civilized communities have always been disturbed by turbulent bodies of men seeking to disrupt organized society or to force their wills on others. The earliest beginnings of criminal justice in the British Isles involved efforts by the king and his followers to develop and maintain public order. As later quoted by an American court:

> The common law hath ever had a special care and regard for the conservation of the peace; for peace is the very end and foundation of

civil society . . . public order and sense of security . . . is one of the first objects of the common law.[1]

Courts in the United States have consistently recognized the fact that "unquestionably the purpose of the law today remains, as anciently, to preserve the peace and prevent breaches of it."[2]

It is almost always easier for the police to maintain order by curbing the peaceful meetings of the unpopular minority than to move against those threatening the violence; but, if police were never to have the right to order a group to disperse, public order is at the mercy of those who may resort to street demonstrations just to create public tensions and provoke street battles.[3]

As further pointed out by Justice Roberts of the Supreme Court of the United States:

Municipal authorities, as trustees for the public, have the duty to keep their communities' streets open and available for movement of people and property, the primary purpose to which the streets are dedicated. . . . It may lawfully regulate the conduct of those using the streets. For example, a person could not exercise this liberty by taking his stand in the middle of a crowded street, contrary to traffic regulations, and maintain his position to the stoppage of all traffic; a group of distributors could not insist upon a constitutional right to form a cordon across the street and to allow no pedestrian to pass who did not accept a tendered leaflet. . . .[4]

On the other hand, serious problems often complicate the enforcement of regulations for crowd control; at times the rights of the people and the duties of police authorities appear to be in direct conflict.

Although a municipality may enact regulations in the interest of the public safety, health, welfare, or convenience, these may not abridge the individual liberties secured by the constitution. . . .[5]

"The Fourteenth Amendment to the Constitution of the United States does not permit a state to make criminal the peaceful expression of unpopular views,"[6] while the First Amendment assures "the right of the people peaceably to assemble. . . ."

All individuals have the constitutional right to meet at any public or private place in an orderly way, for any lawful purpose, regardless of illegal threats made by others in an attempt to prevent the assembly; and this

[1] State v. Huntley, 25 N.C. 418.
[2] Kolenda, Luz. Leg. Reg. 45.
[3] EDWARD S. CORWIN and J. W. PELTASON, UNDERSTANDING THE CONSTITUTION, 4th ed., Holt, Rinehart and Winston, New York, 1967, p. 113.
[4] Schneider v. State, 308 U.S. 147, 60 S. Ct. 146.
[5] Id.
[6] Edwards v. South Carolina, 372 U.S. 229.

meeting does not become an unlawful assembly because of the fact that the individuals joined there have reason to believe that they will be attacked or that they are attacked.[7]

In addition, the Supreme Court of the United States does not allow public officials or police officers to determine, at their own discretion, which groups will be permitted to hold public meetings or to specify where these meetings must be held.[8] In summary, *people have the right to assemble, but the assembly must be a peaceful one.* No group has the right to assemble for an unlawful purpose or with the intent to create a breach of the peace.

Unlawful Assembly Defined

An unlawful assembly, then, is a meeting (usually of three or more persons)

with an intent to commit violence upon persons or property, to resist the execution of the laws, to disturb public order, or for the perpetration of acts inspiring public terror or alarm.[9]

Stated another way, an unlawful assembly is:

. . . common intent of persons assembled to attain a purpose, whether lawful or unlawful, by commission of acts of intimidation and disorder likely to produce danger to the peace of neighborhood, and actually tending to inspire courageous persons with well-grounded fear of serious breaches of public peace.[10]

An unlawful assembly, in the words of another judge, is "any meeting assembled under such circumstances as, according to the opinion of rational and firm men, [are] likely to produce danger to the tranquility and peace of the neighborhood."[11]

Under some modern statutes a meeting of only two persons may be an unlawful assembly;[12] the common law required a minimum of three persons; these were required to come together at the same time. A few states continue to follow this common law principle.

Some courts say the group need not intend an unlawful purpose at the outset. However, if the eventual outcome is to disturb the peace or commit some other violation of law, the assembly is an unlawful one.[13] Still, in

[7] Beatty v. Gillbanks, 15 Cox C. C. 138.
[8] Cox v. Louisiana, 379 U.S. 536.
[9] People v. Judson, 11 Daly 1.
[10] State v. Butterworth, 142 A. 57, 104 N.J.L. 579.
[11] Regina v. Vincent, 173 Eng. Rep. 754.
[12] CALIFORNIA PENAL CODE, sec. 407, "Whenever two or more persons assemble together to do an unlawful act, or do a lawful act in a violent, boisterous, or tumultuous manner, such assembly is an unlawful assembly."
[13] Koss v. State, 258 N.W. 860, 217 Wis. 325.

some jurisdictions the original purpose of the meeting must have been unlawful, otherwise the courts will regard the meeting as a lawful one.

Remaining at an unlawful assembly after being warned to disperse is generally a misdemeanor, except as to police officers or persons assisting them.[14] Obviously, a meeting of this kind poses such a threat to the overall interests of society that the peace of the community is threatened by the very meeting itself.

THE CRIME OF ROUT   *no Crime today Common Law*

From a legal point of view, unlawful assembly, rout, and riot usually occur in consecutive order. Under the common law any move or advance toward the execution of the illegal plan by those in an unlawful assembly constituted a rout. Thus, rout was the movement toward the completion of a planned riot—the advancement of those unlawfully assembled from the meeting place to the scene of trouble. A rout may exist even though a riot has not actually started or no movement has been made in a violent manner.

A Texas court has said a rout has occurred

> whenever two or more persons, assembled and acting together, make any attempt or advance toward the commission of an act, which would be a riot if actually committed.[15]

The legal interplay between unlawful assembly, rout, and riot is well illustrated in the following statement:

> The difference between a riot and an unlawful assembly is this: If the parties assemble in a tumultuous manner, and actually execute their purpose with violence, it is a riot; but if they merely meet upon a purpose, which, if executed, would make them rioters, and having done nothing, they separate without carrying their purpose into effect, it is an unlawful assembly.[16]

THE CRIME OF RIOT

A riot is essentially a crime by a group of people against the public peace and order. As defined by a Minnesota court:

---

[14] CALIFORNIA PENAL CODE, sec. 409.
[15] Follis v. State, 40 S.W. 277, 37 Tex. Crim. 535. The definition in the CALIFORNIA PENAL CODE, sec. 406, reads: "Whenever two or more persons, assembling and acting together, make any attempt or advance toward the commission of an act which would be a riot if actually committed, such assembly is a rout."
[16] Rex v. Birt, 172 Eng. Rep. 919.

Whenever three or more persons, having assembled for any purpose, shall disturb the public peace by using force or violence against any other person or property, or shall threaten or attempt to commit such disturbance, or to do an unlawful act by force or violence, accompanied with power of immediate execution of such threat or attempt, they shall be guilty of a riot.[17]

As with unlawful assembly, the courts differ from state to state as to whether two or three persons are required to constitute the riot. Most modern statutes fix the number at two. The decisions unanimously hold that all who encourage, incite, promote, or take part to any extent are guilty as principals to the riot. A rioter need not be actively engaged, if present and giving support. Mere presence alone, however, is not enough to make an individual a rioter.[18]

Some riots, of course, arise out of student confrontations. Sometimes people decide to take the law into their own hands or go too far in injuring persons or property in incidents that started as practical jokes. Still other riots arise out of labor differences or inability of crowds at sporting events or public gatherings to refrain from physical violence. In any event, the law will not excuse a breach of peace through a riot started by a group of individuals who are trying to enforce a private right. The courts were created for the enforcement of private rights; breaking the law is not tolerated, regardless of the justice of the cause.[19]

Rout has been omitted from some modern state statutes, but most states punish unlawful assembly, rout, and riot. Unlawful assembly and rout are generally misdemeanors, while riot is a misdemeanor in some states and a felony in others.

Remaining at the Place of the Riot

Spectators to a riot are not guilty of anything.[20] Frequently, however, statutes punish for remaining at the place of the riot, after an order to disperse has been given, as a misdemeanor. The crime does not exist until after the command to disperse has been given.

Riot Suppression by Citizens

Almost all legal authorities also are in agreement that private citizens, acting on their own initiative, may obtain arms and lawfully suppress a riot.

---

[17] State v. Winkels, 283 N.W. 763, 204 Minn. 466.
[18] People v. Bundte, 197 P.2d 823, 337 U.S. 915.
[19] People v. Spear, 89 P.2d 445, 308 U.S. 555.
[20] People v. Sklar, 292 P. 1068, 111 Cal. App. Supp. 776.

As a practical matter, a great amount of violence may occur when this happens. Thus, it is usually far better for any citizens' group to operate under the control and supervision of the duly constituted law enforcement agencies in that area.

Incitement to Riot

Incitement to riot is frequently an offense separate from riot itself. It does not apply to, or in any way affect, forbid, or interfere with, lawful activities of labor unions or their members.

DISTURBANCE OF A LAWFUL ASSEMBLY

Most states also provide misdemeanor statutes prohibiting willful disturbance or breaking up of any kind of lawful meeting or assembly.

LYNCHING   *Ga. does not have a lynching statute*

The taking, by means of a riot, of any person from the lawful custody of a peace officer is lynching. It is not necessary that the abducted prisoner be either harmed or freed. In most states this crime is a felony.

RIOTS OR BREACHES OF THE PEACE ON COLLEGE CAMPUSES

Riots on college and university campuses have caused recent passage of special statutes in some states. For example, the California statute reads as follows:

> 415.5 Disturbance of peace of state college or university; punishment
> (a) Every person who maliciously and willfully disturbs the peace or quiet of any junior college, state college, or state university by loud or unusual noise, or by tumultuous or offensive conduct, or threatening, traducing, quarreling, challenging to fight, or fighting, or by using any vulgar, profane, or indecent language within the presence or hearing of women or children, in a loud and boisterous manner, is guilty of a misdemeanor and shall be punished as follows:
> (1) Upon a first conviction by a fine not exceeding two hundred dollars ($200) or by imprisonment in the county jail for a period of not more than 90 days, or by both such fine and imprisonment.
> (2) If the defendant has been previously convicted once of a violation of this section or of any offense defined in Chapter 1 (com-

mencing with Section 626) of Title 15 of Part 1, by imprisonment in the county jail for a period of not less than 10 days or more than six months, or by both such imprisonment and a fine of not exceeding five hundred dollars ($500), and he shall not be released on probation, parole, or any other basis until he has served not less than 10 days.

(3) If the defendant has been previously convicted two or more times of a violation of this section or of any offense defined in Chapter 1 (commencing with Section 626) of Title 15 of Part 1, by imprisonment in the county jail for a period of not less than 90 days or more than six months, or by both such imprisonment and a fine of not exceeding five hundred dollars ($500), he shall not be released on probation, parole, or any other basis until he has served not less than 90 days.

(b) For the purpose of determining the penalty to be imposed pursuant to this section, the court may consider a written report from the Bureau of Criminal Identification and Investigation containing information from its records showing prior convictions, if the defendant admits them, regardless of whether or not the complaint commencing the proceedings has alleged prior convictions.

(c) As used in this section "state university," "state college," and "junior college," have the same meaning as these terms are given in Section 626.

BREACH OF THE PEACE

Police officers are duty-bound to maintain the tranquility of the community against any breach of the peace. Thus, breach of the peace includes a great variety of conduct that destroys or menaces public order and tranquility. It includes not only violent acts, but acts and words likely to produce violence in others.[21] It is deliberate conduct that may cause unreasonable disruption, "a violation or disturbance of the public tranquility and order."[22]

Breach of the peace does not come into existence without actual or threatened violence or behavior which is likely to create a disturbance. A nonviolent act is not a violation of this branch of the criminal law, unless, of course, the act incites or threatens others to violence.[23]

As pointed out earlier, we find an almost limitless number of situations that may constitute a breach of the peace. In one case, members of the Jehovah's Witnesses religious sect entered the halls of a hotel over the manager's objection and persisted in knocking loudly on all doors. The

[21] Cantwell v. Connecticut, 310 U.S. 296, 60 S. Ct. 900.
[22] BLACK'S LAW DICTIONARY.
[23] *In re* Bushman, 463 P.2d 727, 83 Cal. Rptr. 375.

purpose of this was to get the guests to accept printed matter and to discuss the religious beliefs and tenets of this group. Brought to trial, members of the sect maintained that the constitutional guarantee of freedom of speech made their activity proper. A conviction for breach of the peace was upheld.[24]

Deliberately disrupting a school classroom has been held a breach of the peace. Willfully blocking automobile traffic in the street, illegally ripping down political advertising, making off with the mascot in a school parade, or throwing rotten fruit at a public speaker are all forms of disturbing the peace. (Incidentally, we should point out that "breach of the peace" and "disturbing the peace" have an identical meaning in the criminal law.)

When we can reasonably anticipate that specific conduct will cause others to disturb the peace, willfully and maliciously engaging in this behavior constitutes a disturbance of the peace.

City and county ordinances frequently prohibit the use of abusive, profane, or obscene language on the streets or over a telephone. These ordinances are generally upheld by the courts. Other offensive or dangerous conduct such as racing in the streets, fighting, and firing guns is frequently forbidden by statute. Section 415 of the California Penal Code is typical:

> **415. Disturbing the peace; noise; use of public streets of unincorporated town for offensive conduct, horse racing, or shooting; indecent language; punishment**
>
> Every person who maliciously and willfully disturbs the peace or quiet of any neighborhood or person, by loud or unusual noise, or by tumultuous or offensive conduct, or threatening, traducing, quarreling, challenging to fight, or fighting, or who, on the public streets of any unincorporated town or upon the public highways in such unincorporated town, runs any horse race, either for a wager or for amusement, or fires any gun or pistol in such unincorporated town, or uses any vulgar, profane, or indecent language within the presence or hearing of women or children, in a loud and boisterous manner, is guilty of a misdemeanor, and upon conviction by any Court of competent jurisdiction shall be punished by fine not exceeding two hundred dollars or by imprisonment in the County Jail for not more than ninety days, or by both fine and imprisonment, or either, at the discretion of the Court.

CARRYING OR CONCEALING DANGEROUS WEAPONS

The constitutions of a number of the states guarantee the right to bear arms. In addition, the U.S. Constitution provides that this right may not

[24] People v. Vaughan, 150 P.2d 964, 65 Cal. App. Supp. 844.

be removed by Congress; but these guarantees are generally intended to give the citizen a means of self-defense, not to guarantee the right of any person to use arms in private feuds or brawls. The courts have consistently said that the possession or sale of deadly weapons may be regulated by the legislatures under the so-called police powers reserved to the states. Practically all jurisdictions have, therefore, provided legislation restricting the sale, use, transportation, and possession of guns or other deadly weapons, carried concealed or openly.[25] Since the days of the early English kings, we have recognized the fact that armed individuals cause terror among peaceful people.

The foreseen danger on the part of the early English courts was in the open display of arms in a way designated to cause consternation to the general public. Yet, many of our modern American laws only prohibit the transportation of *concealed arms.* This difference may lie in the old frontier idea that a man did not fear those enemies who came out in the open; he wanted to eliminate only those who utilized concealment or attack from ambush.

A number of current state statutes and city ordinances, however, prohibit the possession or transportation of any handgun or pistol, concealed or otherwise. This stems from the belief that many individuals are far more inclined to crime when a gun is readily available.

Deadly or Dangerous Weapons Defined

Many of the state statutes and local ordinances also prohibit the use, possession, or transportation of a *deadly or dangerous weapon.* The courts uniformly define as deadly any weapon which, when used in the usual and ordinary manner, is contemplated by its construction or design to cause great bodily injury or death. Any gun is clearly within this requirement; a "zip gun" or a tear gas gun is generally regarded as a dangerous weapon if constructed so that a missile or bullet may be discharged from it. The question is often raised as to whether a particular knife is a dangerous weapon, depending on its size and the purpose for which it was manufactured. According to some decisions, a dirk, "butcher knife," bowie knife, "hunting knife," straight razor, brass or metallic knuckles, or a sword is a dangerous weapon. The decision of many courts is that even a gun is not a dangerous weapon when it is carried unloaded and is not used as a club or bludgeon. So much variation exists in the wording of individual ordinances and statutes that a student of the subject must carefully read and analyze each individual enactment.

[25] Biffer v. Chicago, 116 N.E. 182, 278 Ill. 562.

What Is Concealing a Weapon?

Carrying a concealed weapon is generally interpreted broadly by the courts. Any method of carrying is generally within the prohibition of the laws when the weapon is so carried that it is readily accessible and available for use.[26] The courts generally hold that transportation of the weapon in one's luggage is not sufficient to constitute carrying, unless the luggage is near at hand and relatively easy of access. Difference of opinion usually occurs on concealment in an automobile or other vehicle. The courts generally define *carrying* as having the weapon readily available for use.

Complete invisibility is not absolutely essential to concealment, within the meaning of ordinances or statutes prohibiting the carrying of concealed weapons. If the weapon is concealed from ordinary observation, this is generally sufficient. In one case, an individual who carried the parts of a gun distributed about his body was found guilty of concealment when the parts could be quickly assembled and used as a dangerous weapon.[27]

The courts in some jurisdictions say that carrying a concealed weapon is not an exception to the general rule that requires criminal intent; these courts look to the intent with which the forbidden article was carried. So in these jurisdictions, when the gun is merely carried as a piece of merchandise, the courts see no violation of law. Similarly, when the gun is taken from the owner's home to a repair shop or is taken to his or her home after purchase, no violation occurs. Of course, the owner of the weapon is not allowed to deviate from the route between the two locations. Other courts, however, hold that the intent of the accused is immaterial since any and all transportation is forbidden by law.

Carrying a Weapon for Self-Defense

A number of states have statutes allowing an individual who has good reason to expect a serious assault and battery to carry a weapon. When such laws do exist, the courts generally demand a reasonable basis for belief that a serious attack will occur. In a situation of this kind, the jury must be convinced that, at the time of the alleged offense, the accused believed the danger of serious harm was imminent, and further, that the accused was in possession of the weapon for self-defense only. Testimony that the accused is a peaceable citizen of good repute in the community is allowed.[28]

[26] Clark v. Jackson, 124 So. 807, 155 Miss. 668.
[27] Hutchinson v. State, 62 Ala. 3.
[28] State v. Workman, 14 S.E. 9, 35 W. Va. 367.

Peace Officers, Soldiers, etc., Are Usually Allowed to Carry Weapons at Any Time

Some state laws also make specific exceptions as to when peace officers and other officials may carry arms. A few courts allow the officer to carry a gun only in his or her own jurisdiction; others hold that the officer may do so regardless of the place of jurisdiction.[29] Generally, the courts allow this right to a peace officer, whether on private or official duty, since the officer may be called upon for self-defense against the criminal element at any time.

A member of the armed forces has the right to carry weapons only in terms of military regulations.

Statutes Prohibiting Drawing or Exhibiting Firearms

Some states attempt to control the use of firearms and other deadly weapons by prohibiting the drawing, exhibiting, or using of such a weapon.[30]

FIGHTING: AN AFFRAY

- misdemeanor
2 or more persons
- disturbing the public -
has to be in a public place
common + modern law

When the word "fighting" is used to mean a friendly contest in the nature of a sporting event, this act may not be a violation of law. Yet, many states and municipalities do strictly regulate boxing matches and wrestling contests. When mutual fighting occurs in a public place, under circumstances likely to cause public alarm, then the facts do constitute a breach of the peace. Also, when the fight is a one-sided affair and one of the parties is merely defending against attack, the defender is innocent and the aggressor is guilty of an assault and battery.

Fighting under the common law was not a violation; but when two or more individuals voluntarily fought in a public place, to the consternation or terror of onlookers, this was called an *affray*. This was a misdemeanor under the common law and is still so regarded in some jurisdictions. At the same time, affray may be a breach of the peace. Legal authorities sometimes say that an affray differs from a riot in that the former is not premeditated, but is a sudden mutual combat.[31] Most courts consider this type of fighting to be a violation only when it is observable by the public.

[29] Shirley v. State, 57 So. 221, 1000 Miss. 799.
[30] CALIFORNIA PENAL CODE, sec. 417, reads: "Every person who, except in self-defense, in the presence of any other person, draws or exhibits any firearm, whether loaded or unloaded, or any other deadly weapon whatsoever, in a rude, angry or threatening manner, or who in any manner, unlawfully uses the same in any fight or quarrel is guilty of a misdemeanor."
[31] State v. Maney, 138 S.E. 441, 194 N.C. 34.

Dueling

Dueling is forbidden by statutes in a number of jurisdictions. Violations are comparatively rare in this modern world. Dueling differs legally from an affray in that the latter occurs on a sudden quarrel, while dueling is by previous arrangement.[32]

CRIMINAL LIBEL

Criminal libel, a crime against public peace, is publicly printing, writing, or drawing a statement of facts that subject any individual to ridicule, contempt, hatred, or scorn. This was a misdemeanor at common law and is usually the same under present-day statutes, although it is a felony in a few states.[33] Under the common law, the objectionable material had to be printed; however, modern statutes usually cover verbal expression (slander) as well.[34]

Let us not forget, however, that the victim of the libel may sue for damages in civil court or ask for a prosecution under the criminal laws.

Criminal statutes usually say that the publication must be intentional or malicious. The courts generally interpret this to mean that the accused did make a detrimental publication and intended to do it. In other words, a general mens rea will satisfy the intent; no malice is required.

In some states truth of the information published is a complete defense to a charge of criminal libel.[35] In others the courts have said that truth will not excuse.

Regardless of this, the law does exhibit a definite interest in protecting freedom of speech. When the victim of the libel is a public officeholder, a candidate for office, or someone involved in serving the public interest, no violation of the criminal libel laws exists unless the accused understood that the publication was false and put out the false information with malice in deliberate disregard for the truth.[36]

In addition, Article I of the U.S. Constitution allows members of the Senate or the House to be excused for any libel in speech or debate on the floors of Congress.

[32] BLACK'S LAW DICTIONARY.
[33] See ARIZONA REVISED STATUTES, secs. 13-103, 13-351.
[34] CALIFORNIA PENAL CODE, sec. 258.
[35] State v. Kerekes, 357 P.2d 413, 225 Ore. 352.
[36] Garrison v. Louisiana, 379 U.S. 64, 85 S. Ct. 209.

CITED CASES

Beatty v. Gillbanks, 15 Cox C. C. 138.
Biffer v. Chicago, 116 N.E. 182, 278 Ill. 562.
In re Bushman, 463 P.2d 727, 83 Cal. Rptr. 375.
Cantwell v. Connecticut, 310 U.S. 296, 60 S. Ct. 900.
Clark v. Jackson, 124 So. 807, 155 Miss. 668.
Cox v. Louisiana, 379 U.S. 536.
Edwards v. South Carolina, 372 U.S. 229.
Follis v. State, 40 S.W. 277, 37 Tex. Crim. 535.
Garrison v. Louisiana, 379 U.S. 64, 85 S. Ct. 209.
Hutchinson v. State, 62 Ala. 3.
Koss v. State, 258 N.W. 860, 217 Wis. 325.
People v. Bundte, 197 P.2d 823, 337 U.S. 915.
People v. Judson, 11 Daly 1.
People v. Sklar, 292 P. 1068, 111 Cal. App. Supp. 776.
People v. Spear, 89 P.2d 445, 308 U.S. 555.
People v. Vaughan, 150 P.2d 964, 65 Cal. App. Supp. 844.
Regina v. Vincent, 173 Eng. Rep. 754.
Rex v. Birt, 172 Eng. Rep. 919.
Schneider v. State, 308 U.S. 147, 60 S. Ct. 146.
Shirley v. State, 57 So. 221, 100 Miss. 799.
State v. Butterworth, 142 A. 57, 104 N.J.L. 579.
State v. Huntley, 25 N.C. 418.
State v. Kerekes, 357 P.2d 413, 225 Ore. 352.
State v. Maney, 138 S.E. 441, 194 N.C. 34
State v. Winkels, 283 N.W. 763, 204 Minn. 466.
State v. Workman, 14 S.E. 9, 35 W. Va. 367.

CHAPTER 19

Offenses Affecting the Administration of Justice

Early in our history we recognized that any act that hindered or blocked the workings of our courts or their legal processes must be resisted or punished by the courts themselves. As a matter of public policy, our courts could not long continue to maintain respect and demand obedience unless they controlled conduct that tended to obstruct or corrupt the administration of justice.

Bribery of court officials, the giving of false evidence (perjury), and influencing or tampering with jurors (embracery) were recognized as threats upon the common law courts and became established as individual common law crimes; but, as time passed, people discovered any number of other ways by which the courts could be hindered. Many of these have been lumped together under a single crime—obstruction of justice.

OBSTRUCTION OF JUSTICE  *Know definition*

The offense applies to interference with those who perform a variety of duties in the administration of justice: probation officers, court bailiffs, and others who serve papers for the courts. It has been defined as:

> The act by which one or more persons attempt to prevent, or do prevent, the execution of lawful process. The term applies also to obstructing the administration of justice in any way—as by hindering witnesses from appearing.[1]

In addition, most states have provided general statutes that prohibit any obstruction of executive officers and peace officers. Some legislatures have passed separate statutes providing more serious penalties for resisting these officers by use of force, threats, or violence.[2]

A typical violation of this kind involved a police officer engaged in quieting a public disturbance and in arresting those who had disturbed the peace. The accused physically attacked the officer, preventing him from making these arrests. The court held that the accused had obstructed a public officer in the performance of his duty.[3] Resisting arrest is another closely related offense.

Resisting Arrest

An arrest is made by actual restraint of a person or by the individual's submission to the custody of an officer. The person taken into custody may be subjected to as much restraint as is reasonable for arrest and detention. The courts have always said that, when the police officer has the full authority of the law, no one has any authority to interfere in any way. Some states, however, still follow the old common law idea that force may be used to prevent an unlawful arrest. The problem, of course, is that the accused seldom knows for certain whether the arrest is lawful or unlawful. Clearly, then, this is a problem that is best settled by the courts. So, stat-

[1] Melton v. Commonwealth, 170 S.W. 37, 160 Ky. 642.

[2] The CALIFORNIA PENAL CODE, secs. 69 and 148, reads as follows:

69. Obstructing or resisting executive officers in performance of their duties; attempts; threats; violence; punishment. Every person who attempts, by means of any threat or violence, to deter or prevent an executive officer from performing any duty imposed upon such officer by law, or who knowingly resists, by the use of force or violence, such officer, in the performance of his duty, is punishable for a fine not exceeding five years or in a county jail not exceeding one year, or by both such fine and imprisonment.

148. Resisting, delaying, or obstructing officer; punishment. Every person who willfully resists, delays, or obstructs any public officer, in the discharge or attempt to discharge any duty of his office, when no other punishment is prescribed, is punishable by a fine not exceeding one thousand dollars, or by imprisonment in a county jail not exceeding one year, or by both such fine and imprisonment.

[3] People v. Powell, 221 P.2d 117, 99 Cal. App. 2d 178.

utes in a number of states specify that no one has the right to use force in resisting a peace officer who is making an arrest.[4]

Generally, the courts demand a forcible resistance of some kind, but some of them have recently said that merely going limp is sufficient to constitute resistance. In addition, the statutes frequently say that the accused must knowingly resist. Therefore, an accused who does not know that the person making the arrest is a peace officer cannot be convicted under these statutes. Of course, the identity of an officer in uniform is obvious.

On the other hand, obstruction of justice is not limited to the arrest situation. Even the butcher shop owner who carries a fraudulent scale out the back door to prevent a weight inspector from testing its accuracy is obstructing justice, provided the inspector has the authority to make this kind of test in the first place.

One federal statute, often copied in state enactments, provides punishment for obstructing, resisting, opposing, assaulting, beating, or wounding a person who serves a legal or judicial writ or process for the federal courts.[5] Another provides criminal prosecution for bribery, intimidation, force, or threats to obstruct or prevent the communication of information about a federal criminal violation to a criminal investigator.[6] Still another declares as criminal the use of threats or force to obstruct, impede, or interfere with an order of a federal court.[7]

Refusing to Aid an Officer

no requirement Today to aid an officer

Under the criminal law a police officer is entitled to the help of each private person in efforts to maintain peace, to apprehend criminals, or to pursue fleeing felons. This idea originated under the common law authority of the sheriff to summon the entire population (above the age of fifteen) of his county to aid him in keeping the peace and in pursuing and in arresting felons.[8] In the days when few peace officers worked along the frontier in the American West, it was not unusual for the sheriff to orga-

---

[4] This has been accomplished, at least in part, by states that follow the MODEL PENAL CODE. A California statute, which is typical, states: "If a person has knowledge, or by the exercise of reasonable care should have knowledge, that he is being arrested by a peace officer, it is the duty of such person to refrain from using force or any weapon to resist such arrest." CALIFORNIA PENAL CODE, sec. 834a.

[5] UNITED STATES CODE, title 18, sec. 1501.

[6] UNITED STATES CODE, title 18, sec. 1510.

[7] UNITED STATES CODE, title 18, sec. 1509.

[8] Some common law writers have indicated that the sheriff had this power in the event of invasion, rebellion, riot, breach of the peace, or forcible resistance to the service of process, and that only male residents could be called upon.

nize a posse, especially when a band of outlaws threatened the peace of his community.

Eventually, this practice came to be fully recognized by the courts. Any peace officer had the right to call on any private person to assist in effecting an arrest and in preventing crime. Thus, almost all modern criminal codes now impose penalties for refusing to give aid to any officer who requests it. When this help is demanded, the citizen is not allowed to delay or inquire into the facts. To be effective, the response must be immediate; this is what the law demands.

As a practical matter, many people are surprised when this legal responsibility is called to their attention; but the general public must be aware of the obligation. Many occasions arise when a single officer may need help before other police units arrive at the scene.

Hiding, Suppressing, or Destroying Evidence

Relatives or friends of an accused may often be present at the scene of a crime. When these people are not principals or accessories, often they may be guilty of destroying or suppressing evidence. The courts also recognize this as a form of obstruction of justice, either under common law concepts or under modern statutes.

For example, when someone at the crime scene deliberately obliterates the tire tracks of a getaway vehicle, to the extent that a comparison cannot be made with the suspected vehicle, the courts regard the act as obstructing justice. Note that this requires a positive act. The courts reach the same conclusion, however, when the accused merely stands on a small piece of evidence, intending to hide it from the view of an investigating officer. The courts generally hold that destroying business records sought in connection with a criminal prosecution or a court hearing is obstructing justice. Even if records are not deliberately destroyed, shipping them out of state so that they cannot be brought into court on a state subpoena[9] is also an obstruction of justice. The cases indicate that this is removing evidence from the reach of the court as effectively as if it were deliberately burned.

Wrongfully Influencing Jurors, Tampering with Witnesses

In early common law, *embracery* was an attempt corruptly to influence a jury (in one way or another) through promises, persuasions, entreaties, entertainment, and the like.[10] In practically all our states, this kind of activity is today a criminal violation, although the old name of the crime

[9] Commonwealth v. Russo, 111 A.2d 359, 177 Pa. Super. 470; Commonwealth v. Southern Express Co., 169 S.W. 517, 160 Ky. 1.
[10] Commonwealth v. Fahey, 173 A. 854, 113 Pa. Super. 598.

has often been dropped. Generally, the prosecution must only prove that an attempt was made illegally to influence a juror, whether or not the juror actually changed his or her mind.

Still another form of obstruction of justice is the act of making a witness or witnesses unavailable. This may be done in many ways: by actually kidnapping and holding them until the trial is over, by beating them, or by scaring them with threats of serious violence. When tampering with witnesses causes them to be absent at the time of trial, the courts say that it is immaterial whether their testimony would have been unimportant or irrelevant. Obviously, the real worth of their information is not known. Witnesses must have been tampered with to such an extent that they deliberately absent themselves. An absent witness need not have been served with a subpoena. When the prosecution can demonstrate that the missing person was expected as a witness, the courts are generally satisfied.[11]

PERJURY

At common law, *perjury* was deliberately and knowingly testifying falsely in a court proceeding when the false testimony was a material matter being decided before the court.[12]

In perjury, an oath must have been administered by one authorized to do so, and the false statement must have been given under oath; but modern statutes very generally extend both the definition and the punishment for this offense to willful false swearing in many kinds of affidavits and depositions such as those required on tax returns, customs house declarations, pension applications, before legislative investigating committees, and in numerous other administrative proceedings. This clearly is in contrast to the common law, where the false oath was punished only in judicial (court) procedures.

Under the statutes in some states, we find degrees of perjury, with varying penalties; some of these offenses are called *false swearing*.[13] The elements of perjury are interesting and often difficult to prove.

The False Information Must Be Given under Oath

An individual who furnishes false information to a police officer during an interview is not guilty of perjury; but under some circumstances this may

---

[11] Smith v. United States, 274 F. 351.
[12] People v. Glenn, 128 N.E. 532, 294 Ill. 333.
[13] Michigan statutes specify two degrees of the crime (MICHIGAN CODE, secs. 750.422 and 750.423), while the New York State statutes spell out three levels (NEW YORK PENAL LAW, secs. 210.05–210.16). The federal law lumps all kinds of criminal false swearing into one offense. (UNITED STATES CODE, title 18, sec. 1621.)

constitute furnishing a *false report*, at least in jurisdictions where providing false information is prohibited by state law or city ordinance. Generally, however, convictions under false report enactments are upheld by the courts only after the accused furnishes false information on his or her own initiative and this information misleads the police or causes them to conduct a useless investigation. When a witness or suspect furnishes false information during the course of inquiries made by a peace officer, however, the officer may eventually be able to testify regarding this conversation if the individual testifies falsely under oath. The term "oath" includes every affirmation or declaration that people are allowed to make instead of a formal oath. This substitution is sometimes included in state codes relating to perjury.[14]

The case decisions also reflect the fact that it is immaterial whether a swearing-in took place, if the witness signs written testimony and makes a statement swearing to it.[15]

The False Testimony Must Be Given with Wrongful Intent

A witness who gives untrue testimony through mistake or carelessness is not guilty of perjury. The law looks to the witness's real intent in the matter.[16]

The False Testimony Must Be Material to the Case at Hand

For example, in one case the accused attacked a woman who was walking her dog on a darkened street. When a witness falsely testified that he (the accused) did not attack the victim, this was material testimony. If, for some perverse reason, however, the witness had falsely testified that the woman's dog was black, when it was in fact solid white, that testimony in itself would not have been perjury. Whether the dog was black or white makes no real difference.

Let us suppose further that the accused testified in his own defense that he did not attack the woman, because she was walking a large, vicious dog, and that the animal had actually attacked him. The color of the dog is still immaterial. A witness's testimony as to the size of the dog and its vicious qualities is material, and false testimony by a witness constitutes perjury. Testimony that is clearly opinion, however, cannot be considered as sufficient for a perjury prosecution.

When the witness testifies to a material fact and later retracts the testimony, this does not erase the fact that a perjury was committed if the first

[14] Georgia Penal Code, sec. 259, 1910.
[15] State v. Woolridge, 78 P. 333, 45 Ore. 389.
[16] Commonwealth v. Douglas, 46 Mass. 241. People v. Frost, 120 N.Y.S.2d 911.

testimony was knowingly false. It is true, however, that the courts are generally lenient in this regard and leave to the jury the question as to whether the witness merely discovered a mistake in the first testimony or was telling a lie. The cases state that the mere fact that a witness has given contradictory testimony does not, in itself, prove perjury. They recognize that the witness may have believed that the testimony was true in each instance, and that the person's recollection may have changed in the interim. From a study of all the circumstances, however, a jury might possibly be justified in finding that the witness committed perjury in a situation of this kind.

Two Independent Witnesses Are Necessary to Perjury, or at Least One Witness Coupled with Circumstantial Evidence

The courts have always refused to convict for perjury on circumstantial evidence alone, or on the singular testimony of one individual against another. These proof requirements are followed by all courts.[17]

SUBORNATION OF PERJURY   *fine or imprisonment (felony) if it is*

Subornation of perjury is procuring another to furnish false evidence in court—the soliciting of untrue testimony.

Generally, one who arranges the commission of a criminal act by another is guilty of the same crime. Under the old common law idea, the person who requested perjured evidence was guilty of an even more serious crime than the person who falsely testified. Therefore, the common law regarded subornation of perjury as a criminal offense distinct from perjury. This separation has generally continued under modern American statutory law. We should note, however, that current penalties for perjury and subornation of perjury are usually identical.

The courts say that subornation of perjury has not been committed until the false testimony has actually been given to a court or judicial body, and for subornation the false testimony must be by someone other than the accused.

As in perjury, proof is one of the primary problems in a prosecution for the crime. Because of the possibility for error or "framing" of the accused, the courts have always refused to convict on the testimony of only one witness in opposition to the accused. Accordingly, the courts require the same number of witnesses as in perjury: (1) either two independent witnesses against the accused, or (2) one independent witness and separate

---

[17] Hammer v. United States, 46 S.Ct. 603, 271 U.S. 620.

circumstantial evidence that supports (corroborates) the story of the witness.

As a practical matter, a police officer who investigates a case that involves conflicting testimony may want to reduce the evidence to signed statements from each of the witnesses. After a written version has been signed, the witness is far less likely to stray later from the truth or to forget the whole matter.

To establish the corpus delicti of subornation of perjury, the prosecution must prove that:

1. An illegal arrangement to testify falsely was established.
2. The testimony was actually false, as given to the court.
3. This false statement was vital or material to the case being tried—not something of little consequence.
4. Both the procurer and the false witness knew that the testimony was false, and the procurer knew the false witness was aware of the falsity.

If a witness is approached and asked to testify falsely, no subornation of perjury occurs when the witness insists on testifying to the truth. The procurer is guilty of an attempt, however, and may be convicted on this charge.

MISPRISION OF FELONY

As previously discussed under the common law, every citizen had some responsibility to assist law enforcement. Each individual who observed the commission of a felony was expected to "raise a hue and cry of alarm" and to try to detain the criminal. Failing in this, he was guilty of a misdemeanor, *misprision of a felony.*

We can say, then, that misprision is concealing or failing to report a felony in which the accused is not involved. Of course, a person who observes the felony aids or assists the felon, or helps in any way, is also guilty as a principal or as an accessory before or after the fact, depending upon the circumstances; but under most modern criminal codes, no violation is involved when a person merely watches another commit a crime.

With few exceptions under most present-day criminal codes, misprision is not a crime of any kind. One federal statute sets criminal penalties for misprision of a federal felony and misprision of treason.[18] The federal courts have consistently held, however, that mere failure to report a federal crime, or failure to "raise a hue and cry" is not sufficient to constitute a federal violation of the misprision statutes. The federal laws require some

[18] UNITED STATES CODE, title 18, secs. 4, 2382.

active concealment of the crime, or at least some active concealment of evidence from authorities. Mere knowledge of the violation is not enough.[19]

COMPOUNDING A CRIME   *Rave general idea*

Under common law, compounding a felony occurred when someone who had been injured or harmed as a result of a felony accepted something of value in return for withholding prosecution. The principal difference between this offense and misprision of a felony was that, in compounding a crime, the victim was rewarded for silence. One court has said:

> Compounding a felony is the offense of taking a reward for forbearing to prosecute a felony; as where a party robbed takes his goods, or other pay, upon an agreement not to prosecute.[20]

Public policy has always favored prosecuting all violations. Truly, the victim is the one individual who suffers harm as a result of crime; but in a larger sense, society itself has been victimized. Under this theory, no single individual has the right to overlook that harm done to society as a whole. Even though it seems certain that the trial judge will later grant probation, it is better for the courts to make the ultimate decision. Because of this basic policy, some courts have disapproved of acts that discourage or hamper prosecution; others have allowed restitution but object to settlement in excess of the value of property taken or the damage done.

The essence of compounding a felony is the making of the unlawful agreement. The victim who does not accept and goes ahead with prosecution has committed no wrong. The victim who agrees to withhold prosecution, however, may be prosecuted as an accessory after the fact.

In a situation of this kind, one who accepts offered money while police officers observe the transaction from some hiding place is not involved in an entrapment. Of course, in this case, the victim may not keep the money but must turn it over to the court after it has been properly identified by police witnesses. To do this properly, police authorities should, in the victim's presence, make a written record of the serial numbers and series year of each bank note or bill received by the victim.

If a police officer requests the victim of a felony to make an approach to the accused for the purpose of requesting money, this does not constitute entrapment; but even when the victim declines to withhold prosecution, the accused who makes an offer to buy off the victim is guilty of an attempt to compound a crime.

[19] Miller v. United States, 230 F.2d 486.
[20] Rieman v. Morrison, 106 N.E. 215, 264 Ill. 279.

Present-day statutes in almost all jurisdictions provide that compounding a crime is a felony. This is actually more severe than the common law where compounding was only a misdemeanor. Let us note, however, that the courts have applied these statutes only to true crimes. Misdemeanors, offenses less than misdemeanors, violations under the police powers or under public welfare laws are regarded by the courts as exempt from compounding. For example, should a dairy sell improperly bottled milk, the victim of this violation may be paid off to drop prosecution without suffering prosecution for compounding.

ESCAPE, RESCUE, BREAKING JAIL, AND BREAKING PRISON

Escape, rescue, breaking jail, and breaking prison are the so-called custodial crimes.

Escape

Escape is departure or deliverance out of custody of a person who is lawfully imprisoned, before that person is entitled to liberty by due process of law. Not only may a jailer or police officer who permits an escape be guilty of this offense, but the prisoner also commits the crime in escaping. This was the view under the common law that has been continued under modern state and federal statutes. The place of the prisoner's escape is of no consequence—whether along the street en route to jail or out of the most secure prison. Even when a trusty is allowed to work outside the walls, the courts recognize *constructive escape* when the prisoner walks away.[21]

Generally, two types of escapes are punished by the statutes. One of these covers negligently allowing an escape, for example under the mistaken impression that the prisoner was admitted as a visitor. The second, usually carrying a more severe penalty, is voluntarily allowing the prisoner to depart.

Before conviction for either type of escape, however, the prosecution must first prove that the person charged with the crime was actually under arrest. In the event an arrest was not completed, because of resistance, the charge will not hold in court.

Rescue

Rescue consists of forcibly and knowingly freeing another from arrest or imprisonment without any effort on the part of the prisoner to seek free-

[21] People v. Vanderburg, 227 P. 621, 67 Cal. App. 217.

dom.[22] Under the common law a person who effected the escape of another was prosecuted for the same offense for which the prisoner was held. The modern crime is now spelled out by statutes in most jurisdictions; it is a felony, with punishment specified in the statutes.

Breaking Jail or Prison

Prison breaking or jailbreaking is actually and forcibly breaking out of a prison or jail with intent to escape.[23] Under the requirements laid down by the courts, the breakout must be by force rather than by some kind of trickery. To merely walk away when the prison door is unlocked does not satisfy the requirements for *breach of prison* but is sufficient for an *escape.*[24]

CONTEMPT

> Any act . . . calculated to embarrass, hinder, or obstruct a court in the administration of justice, or which is calculated to lessen its authority or its dignity is contempt of court.[25]

Under the law in England the courts declared that the power to make decisions carried with it the right to regulate the operation of the courts. Therefore, judicial authorities reasoned that the courts had an inherent, or built-in, power to punish for contempt.

Civil Contempt

Today civil courts sometimes order individuals to take certain specific actions. For example, one person may enter a contract for the sale of a piece of property to another. If the seller decides not to go through with the deal, the buyer may go into civil court and ask either for money damages or for *specific performance* of the contract. Under specific performance the court may order the seller to prepare a deed and deliver it to the buyer. If this is not done, the court may declare contempt and may order the seller to jail until the order of the court is complied with. The seller may then be released from jail after signing the deed ("purging oneself of contempt" is the legal language).

In civil contempt the harm is to one of the parties in a civil dispute. The power of a court to imprison an unwilling party in a civil lawsuit is not in

[22] Merrill v. State, 26 P.2d 110, 42 Ariz. 341.
[23] BLACK'S LAW DICTIONARY.
[24] State v. King, 87 N.W. 282, 114 Iowa 413.
[25] BLACK'S LAW DICTIONARY, quoting *Ex parte* Hobrook, 177 A. 418, 133 Me. 276.

execution of the criminal laws of the land, but it does exist to force obedience to the rights to which the court has adjudged people are entitled.[26]

Criminal Contempt   *now definition &* ✓

*fine or —
go to jail*

On the other hand, criminal contempt, resulting from the ability of the court to punish, is designed to protect the public interest through effective functioning of the judicial system.[27]

To give actual examples, continued disobedience on the part of an attorney to the instructions of the judge or deliberate harassment of other attorneys or witnesses constitutes criminal contempt. Willfully interrupting procedures or shouting out in open court, talking to jurors in disobedience to instructions of the judge, and assaulting an official of the court, have each been defined as criminal contempt.

Many examples of the crime occur in the immediate presence of the judge, who can, therefore, observe them directly. Those not seen or heard by the judge may, nevertheless, be the subject of inquiry. A most usual procedure is one in which the court issues an attachment under which a claimed offender is taken into custody, brought before the court, called upon to answer the charge previously made, or held in contempt for failure to appear.

The U.S. Supreme Court has held that "contempt is a crime in the ordinary sense . . . punishable by fine or imprisonment or both."[28]

For many years the courts have allowed the same judge who presided at the trial to decide whether the accused was in contempt. In *Mayberry v. Pennsylvania*[29] the U.S. Supreme Court held (in 1971) that on demand "another judge, not bearing the sting of those slanderous remarks and having the impersonal authority of the law, [sit] in judgment on the conduct of petitioner [the alleged contemnor]."

In addition, until 1968 the courts held that no one had the right (under the U.S. Constitution) to a jury trial in a criminal contempt case. In *Bloom v. Illinois*,[30] the court said that federal judges would be allowed to impose contempt sentences up to six months, without a jury trial. In *Codispoti v. Pennsylvania*,[31] the U.S. Supreme Court added that state courts could not sentence to more than six months in the absence of a jury trial.

In 1975, the U.S. Supreme Court laid down some additional rules re-

[26] State *ex rel.* Pulitzer Publishing Co. v. Coleman, 152 S.W.2d 640, 347 Mo. 1238.
[27] Juneau Spruce Corp. v. International L. & W. Union, 131 F. Supp. 866.
[28] Bloom v. Illinois, 391 U.S. 194, 88 S. Ct. 1477.
[29] Mayberry v. Pennsylvania, 400 U.S. 455.
[30] Bloom v. Illinois, 391 U.S. 194.
[31] Codispoti v. Pennsylvania, 418 U.S. 506; Taylor v. Hayes, 418 U.S. 488.

garding criminal contempt. The accused in *United States v. Wilson*[32] had refused to testify in a court trial after being granted immunity to prosecution. Wilson was immediately taken before another judge and sentenced for criminal contempt after being given another opportunity to go into court and testify. Wilson appealed on the basis that he should have been given a formal hearing, with an attorney representing him, along with some time to prepare a defense. When the appeal reached the Supreme Court, it held that this is the type of situation that can be immediately punished without a formal hearing.

The Supreme Court pointed out that in the *Wilson* case the contemnor (Wilson) was interrupting an ongoing trial, and that "trial courts . . . cannot be expected to dart from case to case on their calendars any time a witness who has been granted immunity decides not to answer questions. In a trial, the court, the parties, witnesses, and jurors are assembled in the expectation that it will proceed as scheduled."

In the *Wilson* decision, however, the Supreme Court pointed out that, had the refusal to testify not held up trial proceedings, the accused would have been entitled to a formal hearing, with an attorney, prior to being sentenced for contempt.[33]

Criticizing a Court

Another related question that sometimes arises is whether a newspaper, TV commentator, or other observer may openly criticize a court or hold a judge up to public ridicule. It is clear that all courts have the authority to punish persons who misbehave inside the courtroom or interfere with the operation of court procedures, but what is the answer to these out-of-court situations?

The attitude taken by the English courts has always been that any type of disrespectful remark or caustic comment should be punished, even those made outside the court after a completed trial. In the United States the approach has been different. Freedom of speech and the right to criticize are basic and necessary to the survival of our democracy. As further stated by the Supreme Court of the United States in *Craig v. Harney:*

> Regulations concerning contempt were not made for the protection of judges who may be sensitive to the winds of public opinion. Judges are supposed to be men of fortitude, able to thrive in a hardy climate.[34]

[32] United States v. Wilson, 421 U. S. 309.
[33] Harris v. United States, 382 U.S. 162, was a case in point that was distinguished from United States v. Wilson.
[34] Craig v. Harney, 331 U.S. 367, 67 S. Ct. 1249.

In passing, let us recognize the fact that a majority of the courts in the United States follow the rule that courts may be criticized without fear of punishment so long as this does not involve activities inside the courtroom or is not contrary to a lawful order of a court.

Since 1831 federal legislation has allowed federal courts to hold individuals in contempt only in specified situations:

> A court of the United States shall have power to punish by fine or imprisonment, at its discretion, such contempt of its authority, and none other, as—
> 1. Misbehavior of any person in its presence or so near thereto as to obstruct the administration of justice;
> 2. Misbehavior of any of its officers in their official transactions;
> 3. Disobedience or resistance to its lawful writ, process, order, rule, decree or command.[35]

In its interpretations of this federal statute, the Supreme Court of the United States has held that limitations on the power to punish for "outside" contempt applies to state courts as well as federal.[36] In *Pennekamp v. Florida*[37] the court held that newspaper or any other published criticism of a court is not punishable by any court, state or federal, unless the contemptuous act goes so far as to create "a clear and present danger" to the administration of justice. The practical effect of this holding is to do away with contempt violations involving the press and TV agencies.

Legislative Contempt

Although it is less extensive than contempt of court, legislative bodies in the United States do possess and exercise the authority to cite for legislative contempt.

The early English kings considered themselves to be rulers by divine right. No power anywhere, so they believed, could question this authority. Therefore, any insult to the king brought quick punishment. To criticize the governmental acts of the king's ministers was almost as serious as criticism of the ruler himself. Over the years English lords were able to wrest part of this power from the king and place some governmental authority in the two houses of Parliament; but the king continued to recognize Parliament as an extension of his government, and allowed both houses of Parliament to punish for contempt.

When the English law came to the United States, legislative bodies in this country took the position that they, like Parliament, had the authority

---

[35] UNITED STATES CODE, title 18, sec. 401 (formerly 4 Stat. 487).
[36] Bridges v. California, 314 U.S. 252, 62 S. Ct. 190.
[37] Pennekamp v. Florida, 328 U.S. 331, 66 S. Ct. 1029.

to cite for contempt. American courts have generally supported this position but have placed some restrictions on it. In summary:

> . . . any legislative body, in order to carry out the objects of its existence, must have the means of informing itself about subjects with which it may be called upon to deal . . . and has, as an attribute of its legislative function, the power to summon witnesses and to compel them to attend and make disclosures of pertinent facts and documents.[38]

As a necessary part of this authority to inquire into legislative matters, the courts hold that any legislative body has the authority to punish those who willfully fail to testify or produce evidence in their possession. They also generally hold that this authority extends to the committees of each legislative body. Clearly, this legislative authority extends to state legislatures, as well as to the U.S. Senate and the House of Representatives. Federal legislative contempt is a misdemeanor by statute.[39]

Basic, however, is the fact that action of the legislative body must not be a mere exploratory inquiry into the private lives of its citizens. The scope of the investigation must be restricted to matters under consideration for control or prohibition through the passage of new statutes. Since any legislative body has wide authority to pass new laws or repeal old ones, the courts have experienced difficulty in restricting the subject matter of legislative investigations.

A witness called before a legislative body may refuse to testify when he or she believes that the testimony will be self-incriminating. The courts frequently have recognized this procedure under the Fifth Amendment of the U.S. Constitution: no individual "shall be compelled in any criminal case to be a witness against himself."

CITED CASES

Bloom v. Illinois, 391 U.S. 194, 88 S. Ct. 1477.
Bridges v. California, 314 U.S. 252, 62 S. Ct. 190.
Codispoti v. Pennsylvania, 418 U.S. 506.
Commonwealth v. Douglas, 46 Mass. 241.
Commonwealth v. Fahey, 173 A. 854, 113 Pa. Super. 598.
Commonwealth v. Russo, 111 A.2d 359, 117 Pa. Super. 470.
Commonwealth v. Southern Express Co., 169 S.W. 517, 160 Ky. 1.
Craig v. Harney, 331 U.S. 367, 67 S. Ct. 1249.

[38] See "Opinions of the Justices," Supreme Judicial Court of Massachusetts (11/14/1951), 102 N.E.2d 79, 328 Mass. 655.
[39] UNITED STATES CODE, title 2, sec. 192.

Hammer v. United States, 46 S. Ct. 603, 271 U.S. 620.

Harris v. United States, 382 U.S. 162.

Ex parte Hobrook, 177 A. 418, 133 Me. 276.

Juneau Spruce Corp. v. International L. & W. Union, 131 F. Supp. 866.

Mayberry v. Pennsylvania, 400 U.S. 455.

Melton v. Commonwealth, 170 S.W. 37, 160 Ky. 642.

Merrill v. State, 26 P.2d 110, 42 Ariz. 341.

Miller v. United States, 230 F.2d 486.

Pennekamp v. Florida, 328 U.S. 331, 66 S. Ct. 1029.

People v. Frost, 120 N.Y.S.2d 911.

People v. Glenn, 128 N.E. 532, 294 Ill. 333.

People v. Powell, 221 P.2d 117, 99 Cal. App. 2d 178.

People v. Vanderburg, 227 P. 621, 67 Cal. App. 217.

Rieman v. Morrison, 106 N.E. 215, 264 Ill. 279.

Smith v. United States, 274 F. 351.

State *ex rel.* Pulitzer Publishing Co. v. Coleman, 152 S.W.2d 640, 347 Mo. 1238.

State v. King, 87 N.W. 282, 114 Iowa 413.

State v. Woolridge, 78 P. 333, 45 Ore. 389.

Taylor v. Hayes, 418 U.S. 488.

United States v. Wilson, 421 U.S. 309.

CHAPTER 20

Offenses against the Existence of Government

Unlike the offenses affecting the administration of justice, some crimes, for example bribery, affect the entire machinery of government or the processes by which it operates. Certain others—such as treason, sedition, and espionage—are directed toward the destruction of the government itself. Obviously, no government can function properly unless violations of this kind are controlled or eliminated.

BRIBERY *felony if you go to jail*

When a person is elevated "to a public office, he owes the duty to the public not to betray the trust, and one of the most despicable crimes that can be suggested is that a public officer misuses the trust that has been imposed on him by using his office for private gain."[1]

The offense suggested and characterized above is *bribery*. It may be defined as ". . . receiving or offering any undue reward by or to any person concerned in the administration of public justice or a public officer to

[1] Fromm v. State, 173 N.E. 201, 36 Ohio App. 346.

influence his behavior in office."[2] In different words, bribery is "the offering, giving, receiving, or soliciting of any thing of value to influence action as an official or in the discharge of a legal or public duty."[3]

The gist of the crime is the wrong done to the general public through corruption of the public service.[4] When bribery exists, matters that should be decided in an objective way are handled in the private interest of the bribegiver or the bribetaker, thus perverting justice.

The common law idea of bribery was very narrow in that it was limited to corruption of judges and other court officials involved in the administration of justice. This basic concept has been expanded considerably; practically all states now define bribery by statute. Although we find no general uniformity in these laws, most statutes now include corruptly influencing any kind of public officer or official, election judges, and even private citizens who owe some legal responsibilities to the government.

Clearly, bribery is not a joint offense on the part of the person offering and the person receiving the thing of value. Therefore, failure to convict one party to the offense is not a defense in the prosecution of the other.

> The giver of a bribe is punishable . . . and his offense is complete when he corruptly offers a bribe, although the other may refuse it . . . take it innocently or . . . deliver the giver to justice.[5]

Failure to accept the offer of the bribe is no defense to the person who offers it. The intent of the accused is what matters; the motive or intent of the other party is immaterial.[6]

Our courts consistently say that a corrupt intent must exist, but that this intent need not be in the minds of both parties to the solicitation or offer of money. The crime is complete when the intent is in the mind of either, the one having the corrupt intent being guilty.[7]

No real problem is posed as to what constitutes sufficient value to meet the requirements of a bribe. Clearly, the involved value need not be in the form of money. It can even be a sexual favor[8] or anything that has enough worth in the mind of the person bribed to sway his or her honest judgment. In one case, the thing of value was a diamond ring.[9]

From a legal standpoint, the purpose for which a bribe is offered can be

[2] Walsh v. People, 65 Ill. 65.
[3] Allen v. State, 72 P.2d 516, 63 Okla. Crim. 16.
[4] People v. Lafaro, 165 N.E. 518, 250 N.Y. 336.
[5] People v. Frye, 227 N.W. 748, 248 Mich. 678.
[6] People v. Johnston, 43 N.W.2d 334, 328 Mich. 213.
[7] Sims v. State, 198 S.W. 883, 131 Ark. 185.
[8] Scott v. State, 141 N.E. 19, 107 Ohio St. 475.
[9] State v. Cooney, 161 P.2d 442, 23 Wash. 2d 539. (The ring was valued at about $300.)

to cause the government official to take a specified course of action or to withhold action that might otherwise be taken. For example, the thing of value might be made available to obtain a zoning permit, to allow the operation of an illegal gambling game, to withhold prosecution for a criminal violation, or for countless other reasons. In any event, the official's judgment must be corrupted by the offer.

No personal contact is necessary between the giver and receiver of the bribe. A third party may handle all the necessary negotiations or contacts.[10]

Although most statutes establish no distinction between an attempt to bribe and the completed act, some jurisdictions set out separate statutes covering these two activities. Usually, however, the laws say that an attempt to bribe also is punishable as bribery. In fact, solicitation of a bribe was a violation at common law and today is generally regarded as a type of bribery.

Generally, the kind of position the public official holds is immaterial. An official who owes a duty or responsibility to the government is eligible as the subject of a bribery violation. For example, the civilian members of a federal draft board are not legally employees of the United States government, but they make decisions as to which persons registered with the board are subject to the draft. An attempt to pay off one of these draft board members is, therefore, a violation of bribery statutes, even when no specific provision in the Selective Service statutes makes this a federal violation.

The federal statute on bribery is quite broad, prohibiting the promising, offering, or giving of anything of value to any officer or employee of the United States government, or to any person acting for or on the behalf of the United States or any of its departments or agencies.[11]

Additionally, along with the increase of public interest in sporting events, a number of states have passed laws prohibiting the promising, offering, or giving of anything of value to a player, sports official, or referee in a sporting contest. These statutes are designed to penalize a participant who "throws" a game or contest or deliberately changes the margin of victory.

One federal statute provides criminal punishment for utilizing interstate telephone messages, telegraph lines, or radio in perpetrating any swindle or fraudulent scheme.[12] Others prohibit the interstate transportation of wagering information. These, along with the state statutes, at least tend to discourage sports bribery and betting.

[10] State v. Whetstone, 191 P.2d 818, 30 Wash. 2d 301.
[11] UNITED STATES CODE, title 18, sec. 201.
[12] UNITED STATES CODE, title 18, sec. 1343.

MISCONDUCT IN OFFICE   *felony*

Misconduct in office was a misdemeanor at common law, punishable by fine or imprisonment as well as removal and future disqualification from office.

The offense may be defined as "any unlawful behavior by a public officer in relation to the duties of his office, willful in character."[13] Literally thousands of situations, therefore, may be classified as misconduct in office.

When a public officer commits a crime, the offense stands on its own merits. A single violation, standing alone, is not enough to constitute misconduct in office. First, the offense must be one performed in the exercise of the duties or responsibilities of the position, or "under color of the office." Second, it must be something done because the accused is the officeholder or because of the opportunity afforded by the position.

Obviously, no crime occurs when an officeholder or official makes an honest mistake in the performance of the job. An official who acts in good faith is not a criminal, although civil suit may be brought. The courts insist upon proof of some corrupt or evil intent.

Let us also note that the official may commit this violation through *misfeasance*—that is, failure to perform a duty connected with the official office or position. To illustrate, if a police officer refuses to arrest an old acquaintance, knowing that a felony warrant is outstanding against this friend, the officer is guilty of misconduct in office; but, when the officer fails to make the arrest because of an honest mistake in identity, the omission does not constitute misconduct in office.

Also, if an officer disclaims the official position while engaging in misconduct that arose as a result of the official position, the misconduct is not excused. In other words, a deputy sheriff cannot set aside his badge and gun and proceed to beat up an inmate of the county jail. Likewise, a county official cannot accept a valuable present for illegally awarding a government contract on the claim that she was on vacation from her job when she received the gift.

In summary, the common law demanded illegal conduct or failure to act, coupled with a corrupt intent on the part of government officials. This basic understanding of misconduct in office has been incorporated into modern statutes in most of the states.

The United States statutes go further: they say that mere negligent failure of an officer to perform the lawful duty of the office is all that is necessary; outright corruption is not required.

Other statutes have specified that intoxication while in the performance of official duties is punishable as a separate crime.[14]

[12] UNITED STATES CODE, title 18, sec. 1343.
[14] MISSOURI STATUTES, sec. 105.250.

There must be 2 witnesses

TREASON

Federal Treason is only crime defined by the US Constitution

As defined by Webster, "Treason is the offense of attempting by overt acts to overthrow the government to which the offender owes allegiance, or of betraying the state into the hands of a foreign power."

2 witness

death penalty given in gen

prison (15 yrs)

Life

In the earliest form of treason of which we find a record, the individual who aided the enemies of his own tribe was executed.[15] Somewhat later, in early English law, high treason consisted of attempting to kill the king, queen, or prince, engaging in war against the king, or helping his enemies. Since the king was the government (in a sense), any attempt against his person was regarded as an attack against the government itself.

By the time the government of the United States was established, treason was regarded as activity that threatened the very existence of the nation itself. Treason is the only crime defined in the Constitution of the United States:

> Treason against the United States, shall consist only in levying war against them, or in adhering to their enemies, giving them aid and comfort.[16]

Clearly, the essential functions of civilization cannot be carried on unless government is protected. Society uses the law to safeguard those conditions necessary to its very existence. Therefore, the government must be protected, at all costs, against violent overthrow. This is why the Supreme Court of the United States has said, "No crime is greater than treason."[17]

Under constitutional definition we find two ways to commit treason:

1. To actually wage war against the United States
2. To give physical assistance to the enemy, while having a disloyal state of mind[18]

Treason against the United States, however, is only possible for an individual who owes allegiance to the United States. A German citizen, fighting in the army of Nazi Germany, who had never been in the United States, could not have been guilty of this crime. Yet, an American citizen owes this duty of allegiance to the United States wherever he or she may reside.[19] Furthermore, the Supreme Court of the United States has said

[15] POLLOCK and MAITLAND, HISTORY OF ENGLISH LAW, 2d ed., 1899, p. 503.
[16] Art. III, par. 3.
[17] Hanauer v. Doan, 79 U.S. 342, 347 (1870).
[18] Cramer v. United States, 325 U.S. 1, 29, 65 S. Ct. 918, 932 (1945).
[19] D'Aquino v. United States, 192 F.2d 338 (1951); Kawakita v. United States, 343 U.S. 717, 72 S. Ct. 950 (1952).

that, under some certain circumstances, an alien living within the United States owes a temporary allegiance to this country.[20]

Levying War

Actually fighting against the United States, while a member of the armed forces of an enemy nation, is treason. Signing up in the armed services of the enemy in time of war has also been interpreted as treason. An actual declaration of war is not necessary; the war may be of a civil nature or against a foreign country.[21]

Armed resistance against the draft has been held by the U.S. Supreme Court as levying war—therefore, treason.[22]

"Adhering to Their Enemies, Giving Them Aid and Comfort"

This aspect of treason has two parts: a state of mind that favors that enemy over the United States, coupled with some assistance to the enemy cause.

The necessary assistance to the enemy may be given in many ways: for instance, manufacturing gunpowder for enemy troops[23] or making radio broadcasts to harm troop morale and to destroy confidence; both have been held to be the giving of that aid and comfort required to constitute treason.[24]

Two Witnesses to Treason Required under the United States Constitution

Our U.S. Constitution further provides:

> No person shall be convicted of treason unless on the testimony of two witnesses to the same overt act, or on confession in open court.[25]

The required overt act under this provision must be a physical one—not merely a disloyal thought or statement; but only one act is required if two witnesses testify to that act. In *Haupt v. United States*, the defendant helped a German agent purchase a car, hid him for a period of six days, and helped the German agent obtain employment as a cover for sabotage activities. The testimony of two witnesses regarding this activity was held sufficient for conviction.[26]

[20] Carlisle v. United States, 83 U.S. 147 (1872).
[21] See the so-called Prize Cases, 67 U.S. 635 (1862).
[22] Drucker v. Salomon, 21 Wis. 621 (1867).
[23] Carlisle v. United States, above.
[24] D'Aquino v. United States, above.
[25] Art. III, par. 3.
[26] Haupt v. United States, 330 U.S. 631, 67 S. Ct. 874 (1947).

TREASON AS A STATE VIOLATION

Some states have constitutional provisions for the punishment of treason against the state government, modeled somewhat after the federal Constitution. Several others provide statutory laws that serve the same purpose. It is, therefore, possible for one specific act to constitute treason against both the federal and a state government. The courts have held, however, that if the treason were directed against the United States government only, "the state courts would not have the jurisdiction of the crime."[27]

MISPRISION OF TREASON   *federal*

Misprision of treason is the knowledge and concealment of an act of treason or of a treasonable plot on the part of others. This is a federal crime by statute,[28] and also a statutory crime in some of the states, although very few test cases have been heard regarding misprision of treason in the courts, either state or federal.

With regard to the federal crime, however, "Mere silence after knowledge of the commission of the crime of treason is not sufficient." Apparently, the defendant must also perform some affirmative act of concealment.[29] *can't be convicted by only having knowledge*

SEDITION

In the days of the early English law, the ruler was an absolute monarch who was supposed to be above criticism. Therefore, the early English were guilty of sedition when they said or published any words that expressed hatred, dissatisfaction, or contempt of the monarch or the government.

When American colonists came to the new world, they insisted on freedom of speech, as well as the right to criticize activities of the government with which they disagreed. This right was incorporated into the U.S. Constitution, and the U.S. Supreme Court has continuously and jealously upheld this principle, even when some have maintained that it conflicted with other rights guaranteed under the document.

Nevertheless, the right to free speech does not extend to verbal urgings to overthrow the government or to change the government by other than lawful means. Sedition, under modern American law, is in simple terms, "stirring up rebellion" against the government. As defined by the courts:

[27] State v. Conti, 216 N.Y.S. 442 (1926).
[28] UNITED STATES CODE, title 18, 2382.
[29] United States v. Farrar, 38 F.2d 515, affirmed in 281 U.S. 624.

> Sedition is an insurrectionary movement, tending toward treason, but wanting an overt act; attempts made by meetings or speeches, or by publications, to disturb the tranquility of the state.[30]

Sedition, then, is the urging of anarchy or revolution. An insurrection may be the result of sedition, since it is an uprising against the government. It is a physical attempt to force a change. An act of treason or a revolt goes beyond both sedition and insurrection; it is an attempt to actually overthrow the entire machinery of government.

The United States Criminal Code prohibits two types of sedition: one is sedition committed during peacetime; the other is sedition during time of war. The penalty for the latter, obviously, is more severe.[31]

Practically all the court decisions on sedition are in agreement that the accused must do more than speak strongly against the government of the United States. In *Schenck v. United States*,[32] the Supreme Court demanded a "clear and present danger" to the United States. In other words, the person advocating destruction of the government must be urging concrete and immediate action for its forcible overthrow. An isolated crackpot standing on the corner and shouting slogans or mere doctrines cannot be held as a criminal. The evidence must clearly demonstrate that the accused advocated violent action, not mere ideas. To convict, the prosecution must present some proof of intent to accomplish the proposed objectives; some real danger must appear to stem from the speech in question.

CRIMINAL SYNDICALISM

Criminal syndicalism is characteristically similar to both treason and sedition. Originating from trade union movements in France, the offense aims at the control of society and government by workers, seeking to realize their purposes by general strikes, widespread terrorism, sabotage, violence, and other criminal means.

Some states provide statutes that define criminal syndicalism as any doctrine or precept advocating, teaching, or aiding and abetting the commission of crime, sabotage, unlawful acts of force and violence, or terrorism as a means of accomplishing a change in the ownership of industry or in effecting political change.[33]

[30] Arizona Publishing Co. v. Harris, P. 373, 20 Ariz. 446.
[31] UNITED STATES CODE, title 18, secs. 2385 (peacetime), 2388 (wartime).
[32] Schenck v. United States, 249 U.S. 47, 39 S. Ct. 247.
[33] See People v. Leese, 199 P. 46, 52 Cal. App. 280; State v. Dingman, 219 P. 760, 37 Idaho 253.

ESPIONAGE

Espionage is the act or practice of spying on the secrets of another nation. As defined in the federal statutes, it involves gathering or transmitting information relating to the national defense of the United States, with intent or reason to believe that the information will be used to the harm of the United States or to the advantage of any foreign nation.[34]

Federal criminal laws also forbid harboring or concealing spies, photographing or preparing sketches of defense installations, and using aircraft in photographing these installations.[35]

Violations of the espionage laws are under the investigative jurisdiction of the FBI, or under military jurisdiction when the offender is a member of the armed forces.

ABUSE OF ELECTION FRANCHISE

In order to assure fair and lawful elections, the federal government and all the states have legislated against a number of election abuses.

The federal Hatch Act of 1939, subsequently upheld by the Supreme Court of the United States, provides for a criminal violation when a federal employee takes any active part in political management or political campaigns or uses his or her position in any way to influence the election or nomination of any candidate for a federal office. The act was amended in 1940 to prohibit any state employee from actively participating in any federal election.

To prohibit wealthy people from buying elections, some states have set up laws that establish a limit on campaign and election expenses. These laws usually require the filing of itemized, sworn statements as to paid expenses along with criminal penalties for misstatement.

Other statutes regulate the conduct of election officials, setting forth duties and penalties for misconduct.[36] Still others regulate the conduct of voters. It is uniformly criminal to tamper with voting machines or ballots, to intimidate or treat any voter, to offer a bribe, or to control the vote of employees.[37] Detailed statutes to provide fair elections are in force throughout all jurisdictions in the United States.

[34] UNITED STATES CODE, title 18, secs. 793, 794.
[35] UNITED STATES CODE, title 18, secs. 792, 795, 796.
[36] WISCONSIN LAWS, sec. 348.241.
[37] See Maine's Corrupt Practices Act (ELECTION LAWS, chap. 8, sec. 1); PENNSYLVANIA ELECTION CODE, art. XVIII; OREGON LAWS, 24-133.

CITED CASES

Allen v. State, 72 P.2d 516, 63 Okla. Crim. 16.
Arizona Publishing Co. v. Harris, 181 P. 373, 20 Ariz. 446.
Carlisle v. United States, 83 U.S. 147.
Cramer v. United States, 325 U.S. 1, 29, 65 S. Ct. 918, 932.
D'Aquino v. United States, 192 F.2d 338.
Drucker v. Salomon, 21 Wis. 621.
Fromm v. State, 173 N.E. 201, 36 Ohio App. 346.
Hanauer v. Doan, 79 U.S. 342, 347.
Haupt v. United States, 330 U.S. 631, 67 S. Ct. 874.
Kawakita v. United States, 343 U.S. 717, 72 S. Ct. 950.
People v. Frye, 227 N.W. 748, 248 Mich. 678.
People v. Johnston, 43 N.W.2d 334, 328 Mich. 213.
People v. Lafaro, 165 N.E. 518, 250 N.Y. 336.
People v. Leese, 199 P. 46, 52 Cal. App. 280.
Prize Cases, 67 U.S. 635.
Schenck v. United States, 249 U.S. 47, 39 S. Ct. 247.
Scott v. State, 141 N.E. 19, 107 Ohio St. 475.
Sims v. State, 198 S.W. 883, 131 Ark. 185.
State v. Conti, 216 N.Y.S. 442.
State v. Cooney, 161 P.2d 442, 23 Wash. 2d 539.
State v. Dingman, 219 P. 760, 37 Idaho 253.
State v. Whetstone, 191 P.2d 818, 30 Wash. 2d 301.
United States v. Farrar, 38 F.2d 515.
Walsh v. People, 65 Ill. 65.
Wysong v. Walden, 196 S.E. 573, 120 W.Va. 122.

CHAPTER 21

Some Common Federal Criminal Law Violations

Since most encountered offenses are violations of local ordinances or state statutes, a study of federal criminal laws is not usually included in the training provided for state and local police officers. Yet, in many jurisdictions the oath administered to these officers requires them to uphold the laws of the nation, as well as those of the city and state.

After some time on the job, many peace officers acquire fair knowledge of federal violations, received principally from regular contacts with federal officers; but other, less fortunate ones, having assignments that do not bring them into frequent contact with federal officers, continue to perform with little knowledge of the federal statutes. This final chapter, containing a brief discussion of some of the more common of these violations, is included largely for their benefit.

DUAL JURISDICTION

In many criminal violations, both local and federal officers possess the authority to investigate, arrest, search, and seize. All these officials are expected to testify and cooperate in any criminal prosecution. A bank robbery, for example, may be a state felony under a statute prohibiting armed robbery or robbery from the person; in turn, it usually is a federal felony under the Bank Robbery and Related Crimes Statute. Similarly, a kidnapping may be a violation of both state and federal laws. Depending on the facts in the case, either the U.S. Attorney (federal prosecutor) or the state prosecutor justifiably may charge the violator with a crime.

In some unusual cases charges actually may be filed against the accused in both state and federal courts; and, under some circumstances, this may be double jeopardy, particularly since several federal statutes specifically state that double jeopardy precludes conviction in both courts. Yet, this rule does not apply to most criminal situations. When the penalty in one court seems inadequate or the public is outraged by a particular crime, prosecution often may be pressed in both federal and state jurisdictions without double jeopardy. Usually, however, either the state or federal prosecutor will decline prosecution in favor of handling by the other prosecutive authority.

While local policies vary from area to area, certain kinds of violators traditionally have been turned over to federal authorities for prosecution. For example, it is usually cheaper and easier to prosecute in federal court for the interstate transportation of a stolen vehicle than to extradite the accused to a distant state on an auto theft violation.

Also, prosecutions for bank robbery traditionally are handled by federal authorities. This policy originated in the 1930s and 1940s, when practically all people found guilty of the crime were sentenced to Alcatraz, a feared maximum security federal prison. In those days bankers usually refused to surrender their deposits without a fight; practically all these offenders were vicious, hardened members of organized gangs; and both state and federal authorities saw advantages in housing all of them in a single maximum security location.

On the other hand, both time and social conditions often have caused changes in the mental attitude and method of operation of the individuals accused of this crime. Still highly dangerous, the modern bank robber may be a professional criminal, armed and ready to shoot. Mingled with the hardened criminals, however, may be those with no prior arrest record, armed with only a toy pistol or a threatening note requesting the teller's money. Regardless of the changes in the mental makeup of the bank robber, authorities still offer good reason for most of these cases to be turned over to the Federal Bureau of Investigation for investigation and to the federal courts for prosecution. The modern criminal is very mobile. A person responsible for a bank robbery in Sweet Home, Oregon, may subsequently have committed similar offenses in Rutland, Vermont, and Palestine, Texas. Obviously, cases of this kind can best be coordinated by an agency that is able to tie details together in all these states.

Then too, it is usually most practical to have even the local counterfeiter handled in federal court by the U.S. Secret Service. The average Secret Service agent invariably has more expert knowledge than anyone in the local agency regarding detailed aspects of engraving and printing of bogus money and the modus operandi of the professional counterfeiter.

While both state and federal officers may have jurisdiction to investigate some crimes, we need not assume that both have jurisdiction under all circumstances. Federal jurisdiction is sometimes quite limited. For example, local police agencies usually have jurisdiction over all kidnappings. On the other hand, the federal statute eliminates "family" abductions, even though custody of a child has been awarded by a court to only one of the parents.

Clearly, in kidnapping for ransom the FBI has jurisdiction only when the act includes transportation from one state to another, or to a foreign country. As pointed out in earlier discussion, the federal kidnapping statute also gives the FBI a presumption of jurisdiction, allowing that agency to enter the case within twenty-four hours. This enables the Bureau to stay abreast of developments as they occur, but this presumption of jurisdiction disappears when facts are uncovered providing that the victim was not carried across a state line.

The Interstate Angle in Many Federal Crimes

The facts above remind us again that the Constitution of the United States left most authority over crime to the individual states.[1] Congress does, however, have the power to regulate commerce among the several states.[2] It is on this commerce clause that many of the federal criminal laws are based. The federal courts have consistently held that the regulation of trade carries with it that authority necessary to control all criminal activity that might develop as an aspect of interstate commerce. Therefore, federal crimes such as interstate transportation of a stolen motor vehicle, interstate flight to avoid prosecution or giving testimony, interstate transportation of stolen property, wrecking a train (in interstate commerce), white slavery, interstate transportation of stolen cattle, and many others are based on this interstate commerce angle.

[1] Amendment X provides: "The powers not delegated to the United States by the Constitution, nor prohibited by it to the States, are reserved to the States respectively, or to the people."

[2] UNITED STATES CONSTITUTION, Art. I, sec. 8.

Federal Crimes Based on Ownership or Control of Federal Institutions or Property

In addition, federal courts and officers often have jurisdiction over other criminal matters related to federal ownership and control of property or federal institutions. Federal bank robbery, for example, is actually an outgrowth of the power of federal authorities to organize and regulate certain types of banks. Crimes on a government reservation and theft of government property are other violations of this same type.

Authority of Federal Enforcement Agencies to Investigate

A majority of federal criminal violations are investigated by the FBI. The Secret Service handles counterfeiting, and protection of and threats against the President. Other federal agencies handle violations of the laws that created those agencies. In case of doubt, a federal agency or the Office of the United States Attorney advises as to which agency has jurisdiction. Detailed delimitation agreements specify under what circumstances an investigation will be conducted on a military reservation by United States military investigative agencies or by civilian officers.

FLIGHT TO AVOID PROSECUTION OR THE GIVING OF TESTIMONY

The Federal Flight to Avoid Prosecution or the Giving of Testimony Statute[3] is more commonly called the Unlawful Flight to Avoid Prosecution (UFAP) Law, or simply the Unlawful Flight statute. Handled by the FBI, this law is one of the most useful tools available to any local or state police agency in locating persons who hide from authorities.

This statute provides federal criminal punishment for fleeing from one state to another, or to a foreign country, to avoid prosecution for a state felony.[4] Including those persons who flee from one state to avoid custody or confinement, this statute is applied to individuals who seek concealment in another state after a jail break or prison escape. It also applies to a person who is charged with an attempt to commit any state felony.

From a practical standpoint, police agencies in a given state often experience difficulty in interesting distant state and local officers in searching for a fugitive. Then, too, extradition of a wanted person is sometimes an expensive legal procedure, requiring time and the expenditure of consider-

---

[3] UNITED STATES CODE, title 18, sec. 1073.
[4] A specific exception in the statute was made for New Jersey, providing that the crime must be one "punishable by death or which is a felony under the laws of the place from which the fugitive flees, or which, in the case of New Jersey, is a high misdemeanor under the laws of said state. . . ."

able effort on the part of officers in the state from which the person fled. In the past, governors of a few distant states have refused to give up wanted people.

In the application of this law, a felony warrant (high misdemeanor warrant in New Jersey) necessarily must be obtained. Then, after sufficient investigation has been conducted to prove that the wanted felon actually has left the state, the assistance of the federal law may be requested. As a matter of fact, the requesting agency need not prove interstate flight by a great mass of evidence. The U.S. Attorney General usually allows the appropriate local U.S. Attorney to authorize a federal warrant on almost any reasonable showing that the wanted person has fled to another state. On some occasions the fact that felons could not be found in the state where they were wanted has been accepted as sufficient proof that they must have fled to another state.

After some showing of flight, the U.S. Attorney authorizes the local FBI office to file a federal warrant, charging flight to another state to avoid prosecution or confinement. With the filing of this warrant, the wanted individual becomes a federal fugitive; and FBI agents may then cover leads over the entire United States, searching for the accused. Until the federal warrant is obtained, the FBI has no authority to conduct the search.

When wanted persons are arrested on the federal warrant, they are taken before the United States commissioner (the federal committing magistrate). Realizing that they can be removed by the federal government to the place where the original crime was allegedly committed, most fugitives who find themselves in this position will agree to waive state extradition or federal removal and return to face state prosecution, if federal charges are dismissed. When the accused decides to fight the federal charge, local officers usually proceed to the place of arrest and initiate extradition. In practically all cases, the federal warrant is dismissed at this stage of the investigation.

In effect, then, an unlawful flight warrant is nothing more than a tool or device to enable the FBI to locate persons who are wanted for serious state crimes. The federal law also covers those who flee to avoid testifying in court; in this way it may be used to locate or return frightened or reluctant witnesses.

INTERSTATE TRANSPORTATION OF STOLEN VEHICLES

The transportation in interstate or foreign commerce of a motor vehicle or aircraft, with knowledge that it is stolen, is one of the most common federal criminal violations.[5] Known as the Dyer Act, the law is often used

---

[5] UNITED STATES CODE, title 18, sec. 2312.

to break up interstate car theft rings. Most federal violations, however, are committed by relatively young, unencumbered men and teenage boys.

In essence, the Dyer Act is directed against the transporter rather than the thief. Of course, the thief usually is the same person who drives the vehicle in interstate commerce. In any event, the same individual may be convicted of car theft in state court and the knowing transportation of a stolen car in federal court. No double jeopardy is involved, since the acts involved in the state and federal crimes are not the same act.

In a case of this type, it is not unusual for a youth to steal a car and to be joined by several others in transporting the vehicle into a number of states. Gasoline and expense money may be obtained by picking up hitchhikers or by selling spare tires and accessories. Interestingly enough, all the transporters are guilty under the federal statute when they have knowledge of the stolen nature of the vehicle. Yet proof of this knowledge is sometimes difficult.

This statute clearly applies to airplanes, motorbikes, or any vehicle propelled by an engine; it does not cover sailplanes or gliders.

Another section of this same federal statute is directed primarily at car theft rings—prohibiting the receiving, concealing, or disposing of a stolen motor vehicle moving in interstate or foreign commerce.[6] All prohibited activities under these federal laws are felonies handled by the FBI under its investigative authority.

INTERSTATE TRANSPORTATION OF STOLEN PROPERTY OR SECURITIES

The federal statute prohibiting interstate transportation of stolen property or securities also is handled by the FBI.[7] Three of the more significant sections of this statute are summarized as follows: Section 1 provides a federal felony for transporting any kind of property or money in interstate or foreign commerce, with the knowledge that it is stolen, if the value of the transported articles is $5000 or more.

The section above applies whether the criminal merely received the stolen property from an actual thief or obtained it by committing a burglary or robbery. A federal felony has been committed when the culprit takes or sends the property into another state. This section, then is aimed at the transporter, whether a receiver or a thief. Just be sure, however, that the property is worth at least $5000; the retail market value is allowed by the courts in proving this requirement. If the property in question is worth

[6] UNITED STATES CODE, title 18, sec. 2313.
[7] UNITED STATES CODE, title 18, sec. 2314.

$5000, yet broken down into a series of small shipments, the cases have held that the federal law is violated when shipments are in a continuous pattern or when the property is reassembled in another state.

Section 2 states that a federal offense has been committed when anyone travels in interstate or foreign commerce in any kind of confidence game or swindle involving $5000 or more. This section covers most situations in which professional con artists induce a victim to enter another state in order to obtain the victim's savings.

Section 3 provides federal punishment for transporting a falsely made or counterfeit security in interstate or foreign commerce. Clearly, the first section of the above statute allows federal officers to pursue a criminal who transports stolen stocks or bonds in interstate commerce if the value is $5000 or more. On the other hand, section 3 does not specify a value, since the security (stock certificate, bond, check, etc.) is counterfeit, forged, or altered. This part of the law covers the transportation of forged shares of stock, bogus bonds, or negotiable paper that simulate or falsely represent securities of value.

Presently, under the meaning of this law, certain forged checks are regarded as falsely made securities. On the other hand, the federal courts have said that a *true name check* is not the kind of false document intended. By this they refer to the kind of situation where a person opens a bank account in his or her own name, proceeds to overdraw the account, and continues to write checks on this account. These securities have not been falsely made.

If, however, a person takes a fictitious name, writes checks, and claims to be identical with that fictitious name, we do have a falsely made security. Add interstate transportation, and we have a violation of the federal statute. Note that when a bank sends the check to another bank in interstate commerce, attempting collection, the act performed is sufficient to satisfy the interstate transportation requirement.

Therefore, when a check is drawn on an out-of-state bank by a maker who uses an alias or a fictitious name, a federal violation has occurred. This, of course, is a difficult situation for a local forgery squad to control effectively. If the check is of the true name variety, the identity of the maker is known, and the investigation merely becomes a question of locating a known individual; but the check-passer who assumes a false name, presents false identity, and passes a check on an out-of-state bank, obviously is very difficult to locate. Usually the check-passer is far away by the time the fraudulent check is returned as "maker unknown."

Actually, the apprehension of the professional check-passer is most frequently made by a local police officer, alerted by some merchants in time to question the suspects and determine whether their identities are false. If the matter is then referred to the FBI, the local police department may follow through on the local prosecution, while the FBI files may reveal that the check-passer has cashed hundreds of checks over a wide geographical area. Strangely enough, we find no set pattern as to who investigates and who prosecutes in these cases; the local police department investigates some and the FBI handles others.

THE WHITE SLAVE TRAFFIC ACT

The White Slave Traffic Act, sometimes called the Mann Act, prohibits the transportation of a woman or girl in interstate or foreign commerce for prostitution or debauchery.[8] The cases have not always been clear as to what the law means by the term "debauchery," but the statute has usually been interpreted to prohibit transportation for prostitution or any other sexually immoral practices. Handled by the FBI, this statute is particularly designed to prevent the spread of commercialized prostitution. In a typical case, a pimp or panderer induces a girl to engage in prostitution through seductive techniques, expensive presents, beatings, and threats—possibly coupled with the use of narcotic drugs or alcohol. After the girl has been hooked, she may be transported to another state and left in the care of a madam, the operator of a local house of prostitution. A single pimp may "own" several women, rotating from one to another, visiting and collecting his earnings from each of them.

The courts have held that this sort of commercialism is not necessary, however, and that the prohibition applies to isolated, single acts of immorality when the transportation is for that purpose. Also, the included sexual activity need not be for pay.[9] Construing polygamy as involving illegal sexual activity, the federal courts have upheld the conviction of an individual who transported plural wives from an old home to a new dwelling place across a state line.[10] On the other hand, transportation for the purpose of taking pornograhic photographs has been rejected as a violation under the White Slave Traffic Law.[11]

THE BANK ROBBERY AND INCIDENTAL CRIMES STATUTE

The Federal Bank Robbery and Incidental Crimes Statute[12] is based on the authority of Congress to regulate all financial institutions organized under federal law.

---

[8] UNITED STATES CODE, title 18, sec. 2421.
[9] Gebardi v. United States, 287 U.S. 112, 53 S. Ct. 35; Langford v. United States, 178 F.2d 48.
[10] Cleveland v. United States, 329 U.S. 14, 67 S. Ct. 13.
[11] United States v. Mathison, 239 F.2d 358.
[12] UNITED STATES CODE, title 18, sec. 2113.

Of the many sections of this statute, one provides a felony for the taking of money or property by force or violence from the possession, custody, or control of the variously organized federal banks, federally insured banks (FDIC), or federal savings and loan associations (FSLIC).[13] Under this section of the law, the FBI assumed jurisdiction in the celebrated Brink's case; some of the money transported by armored car was in transit from one bank to another, thus under the custody and control of one of the federally controlled banks.

Another section of the law provides for federal felony conviction when a person enters or attempts to enter any bank or savings and loan association covered by the statute, for the purpose of committing a felony. In short, this means that an individual who enters the building to commit a burglary, a holdup, or a larceny of more than $100 has committed a federal violation.

Still another section provides a penalty of twenty-five years imprisonment when a dangerous weapon is used in the commission of this crime, or is used in assaulting any person or placing human life in jeopardy during a bank robbery.

A special file of prints of individual fingers of all known or suspected bank robbers throughout the United States constitutes one of the most valuable tools maintained by the FBI in solving these cases. This single fingerprint file allows the search for a single fingerprint that may be left at the crime scene. A comprehensive album of photos of known criminals also aids in these kinds of investigations.

THE FEDERAL TRAIN WRECK STATUTE

Prohibiting the derailment, disabling, or wrecking of a train or railroad car moving in interstate commerce, the Federal Train Wreck Statute imposes a penalty of twenty years' imprisonment for this activity.[14] However, prosecution on the merits under a state charge acts as a bar to federal prosecution (double jeopardy). This offense also is handled under the investigative authority of the FBI.

COUNTERFEITING

Counterfeiting is the making of federal false money or securities, intended to be passed as genuine. Handled by the Secret Service, the offense is

---

[13] These are institutions insured by the Federal Deposit Insurance Corporation (FDIC) or Federal Savings and Loan Insurance Corporation (FSLIC).

[14] UNITED STATES CODE, title 18, sec. 1992.

forbidden by the United States Code.[15] While most commonly applied to the criminal imitation of money, the alteration, counterfeiting, forging, or criminal imitation of any obligation or security of the United States government is a federal violation.

EXTORTION *felony*

To compel payment of money or goods by means of threats or injury to the person, the property, or the reputation of any individual is the essence of federal extortion.[16] Several distinct violations are possible under federal extortion laws.

One involves the transmission in interstate commerce of any communication containing a demand for ransom in a kidnapping.[17] This section, handled by the FBI under its investigative authority, frequently gives that organization federal jurisdiction in kidnapping situations, even when no federal violations are involved in the kidnappings themselves.

A second part of the same section provides felony punishment for the sending of a communication in the mails containing a threat to injure or kidnap any person. This also is handled by the FBI.

Enforcement of a third part of this section, however, is handled by the U.S. Secret Service. The violation involves the sending of a communication in the mails that threatens to injure the property or reputation of the addressee, or one that threatens to falsely accuse anyone of crime.

A subsequent section of the federal extortion statutes provides felony punishment for mailing a communication containing threats against the President of the United States or a successor to the President.[18] This too is a violation within the jurisdiction of the U.S. Secret Service.

FEDERAL CIVIL RIGHTS STATUTES

Although a number of federal civil rights statutes exist, those of greatest concern to local and state police officers are: (1) Conspiracy against the Rights of Citizens,[19] and (2) Deprivation of Rights under Color of Law.[20]

[15] UNITED STATES CODE, title 18, secs. 485, 486, 490.
[16] State v. Richards, 167 P. 47, 97 Wash. 587.
[17] UNITED STATES CODE, title 18, sec. 875.
[18] UNITED STATES CODE, title 18, sec. 871.
[19] UNITED STATES CODE, title 18, sec. 241.
[20] UNITED STATES CODE, title 18, sec. 242.

Conspiracy against the Rights of Citizens *only citizens*

The first statute (United States Code, title 18, section 241) provides for federal prosecution when two or more persons conspire to injure, oppress, threaten, or intimidate any citizen in the free exercise or enjoyment of any right guaranteed by the Constitution or laws of the United States.

Clearly, the victim of this crime must be a citizen of the United States. This law does not protect the citizen of another country.[21] We should also note that this statute affords protection as to those rights granted to all citizens by the U.S. Constitution, but these are relatively few in number. This fact, of course, is contrary to the belief of many people who think that a great number of rights are guaranteed by the document. For example, we find nothing in the U.S. Constitution that guarantees an individual the right to a free public education. Therefore, a conspiracy to prevent someone from receiving such an education is not a violation of this statute.

Deprivation of Rights under Color of Law *applies to everyone not only citizens*

Title 18, section 242, applies to any inhabitant of a state, territory, or district of the United States, whether or not this individual is a citizen. It prohibits acts *under color of law* that deprive any person of his or her rights under the U.S. Constitution. No conspiracy is required, but the accused must be acting under color of law or with pretended or supposed authority. The courts have held that sheriffs or police officers who mistreat prisoners under their control or authority are acting under color of law. Beating or kicking prisoners to cause them to confess is a civil rights violation based upon the assumption that accused persons have a constitutional right to remain silent and that people shall not be forced to give evidence against themselves. Any cruel or unusual treatment applied to a prisoner designed to force confession is, in turn, a violation of this section. For example, deputy sheriffs who caused a police dog to bite a suspect in order to coerce him to admit to a local crime were convicted for this federal violation.[22]

When a sheriff "strapped" a prisoner after his escape and capture, rather than file a criminal escape charge, the sheriff himself was found guilty of a federal civil rights violation.[23]

Let us not assume, however, that the federal law outlaws all forms of prisoner discipline or punishment. The mere fact that a prison or jail administration punishes a prisoner is not necessarily criminal. If the institu-

[21] Baldwin v. Franks, 120 U.S. 678, 7 S. Ct. 656.
[22] Miller v. United States, 404 F.2d 611.
[23] United States v. Ragsdale, 403 U.S. 919, 91 S. Ct. 2231.

tion has rules regulating the conduct of prisoners and these are publicized in advance, the courts have indicated no violation of the prisoner's rights, unless the applied punishment is inhuman or unusual.

ASSAULTING A FEDERAL OFFICER

It has long been a crime to assault or kill a federal officer, under the terms of the United States Code, section 111. In *United States v. Feola*[24] the U.S. Supreme Court held that it was not necessary for the accused to know that the person being assaulted was a federal officer. The court said that it was enough for the accused to intend the assault, without knowing the real identity of the victim. Pointing out that undercover agents would not be protected by a contrary decision, the court upheld the conviction of Feola.

ORGANIZED CRIME CONTROL ACT OF 1970

Passed into law in 1970, the Organized Crime Control Act (Public Law 91-452 and Statutes at Large, p. 922, title 18, United States Code) is a series of lengthy, complicated federal enactments, designed to open up new ways for the prosecution of organized gangs and racketeers in the federal courts.

For the implementation of the act, the U.S. Department of Justice has set up a series of specialized "Strike Forces" in large metropolitan areas, coordinated by a special prosecutor from Washington, D.C., who functions at the local level.

The investigative attention of the Strike Force may be directed against criminal activity in syndicated gambling; loan sharking; the theft and fencing of stolen property; the sale and distribution of narcotics and dangerous drugs; the importation, manufacture, and distribution of explosives; the prostitution racket; and other businesses and schemes operated by "organized crime."

Under the provisions of the Act, a special federal grand jury may be impaneled, with power to look into alleged violations and call witnesses. The federal prosecutor, in conjunction with the grand jury, has authority to offer immunity to reluctant witnesses, to compel testimony, and to provide protection and special housing facilities for key witnesses. The Act also has special provisions that declare a federal violation when two or more persons conspire to obstruct state or local criminal laws under special circumstances involving the operation of gambling establishments. In some

[24] United States v. Feola, 420 U.S. 671.

cases, criminals convicted under the Act may be given increased sentences upon a showing that the persons convicted are dangerous special offenders.

The attorney in charge of the Strike Force works closely with specialized intelligence units of police departments and other agencies, coordinating information from all sources. He or she utilizes Special Agents from the FBI, the Internal Revenue Services, and other investigative agencies to pursue leads and compile information. Additionally, the attorney assumes responsibility for supervising the prosecution in the federal courts. The Strike Force also compiles evidence which can be used for prosecutions at the state and local levels.

CITED CASES

Baldwin v. Franks, 120 U.S. 678.
Cleveland v. United States, 329 U.S. 14.
Gebardi v. United States, 287 U.S. 112.
Miller v. United States, 404 F.2d 611.
United States v. Feola, 420 U.S. 671.
United States *ex rel.* Pope v. Hendricks, 326 F. Supp. 699.
United States *ex rel.* Verde v. Case, 326 F. Supp. 701.
United States v. Mathison, 239 F.2d 358.
United States v. Ragsdale, 403 U.S. 919.

Index